RECONSIDERING FEMINIST RESEARCH IN EDUCATIONAL LEADERSHIP

SUNY series in Women in Education
Margaret Grogan, editor

RECONSIDERING FEMINIST RESEARCH IN EDUCATIONAL LEADERSHIP

EDITED BY

MICHELLE D. YOUNG

LINDA SKRLA

STATE UNIVERSITY OF NEW YORK PRESS

Published by
State University of New York Press, Albany

© 2003 State University of New York

All rights reserved

Printed in the United States of America
No part of this book may be used or reproduced in any manner
whatsoever without written permission. No part of this book may be
stored in a retrieval system or transmitted in any form or by any means
including electronic, electrostatic, magnetic tape, mechanical,
photocopying, recording, or otherwise without the prior permission in
writing of the publisher.

For information, address State University of New York Press,
90 State Street, Suite 700, Albany, NY 12207

Production by Kelli Williams
Marketing by Anne M. Valentine

Library of Congress Cataloging-in-Publication Data

Reconsidering feminist research in educational leadership / edited by
Michelle D. Young, Linda Skrla.
     p. cm. — (SUNY series in women in education)
   Includes bibliographical references (p.) and index.
   ISBN 0-7914-5771-0 (alk. paper) — ISBN 0-7914-5772-0 (pbk. : alk
paper)
   1. Women school superintendents—Research—United States.
   2. Women school administrators—Research—United States.
   3. Educational leadership—Research—United Staes. I. Young,
Michelle D. II. Skrla, Linda, 1957– III. Series.

LB2831.72 .R43 2003
371.2'011'082—dc21

2002042645

10 9 8 7 6 5 4 3 2 1

Contents

Acknowledgments	vii
1 Introduction: Reconsidering Feminist Research in Educational Leadership *Linda Skrla and Michelle D. Young*	1
Part I Troubling Feminist Research Methods in Educational Leadership	7
2 Laying the Groundwork for a Reconception of the Superintendency from Feminist Postmodern Perspectives *Margaret Grogan*	9
3 Considering (Irreconcilable?) Contradictions in Cross-Group Feminist Research *Michelle D. Young*	35
4 The Linguistic Production of Genderlessness in the Superintendency *Jennifer Scott*	81
5 Mourning Silence: Women Superintendents (and a Researcher) Rethink Speaking Up and Speaking Out *Linda Skrla*	103

Contents

Part II Reconsidering Feminist Epistemologies in Educational Leadership — 129

6 The Substance of Things Hoped for, the Evidence of Things Not Seen: Examining an Endarkened Feminist Epistemology in Educational Research and Leadership — 131
Cynthia B. Dillard

7 Chicana Feminism and Educational Leadership — 161
Sylvia Méndez-Morse

8 A Loving Epistemology: What I Hold Critical in My Life, Faith, and Profession — 179
Julie C. Laible

9 Life Lessons and a Loving Epistemology: A Response to Julie Laible's Loving Epistemology — 193
Colleen A. Capper

10 Research on Women and Administration: A Response to Julie Laible's Loving Epistemology — 201
Michelle D. Young and Linda Skrla

11 The Emperor and Research on Women in School Leadership: A Response to Julie Laible's Loving Epistemology — 211
Catherine Marshall

Part III Reconceptualizing Applications of Feminist Research in Educational Leadership — 221

12 In Our Mother's Voice: A Native Woman's Knowing of Leadership — 223
Maenette K. P. AhNee-Benham

13 Normalized Femininity: Reconsidering Research on Women in the Superintendency — 247
Linda Skrla

14 Troubling Policy Discourse: Gender, Constructions, and the Leadership Crisis — 265
Michelle D. Young

Author Biographies — 299

Index — 303

Acknowledgments

Preparing, writing, and editing a book on reconsidering feminist research in educational administration has been a stimulating and rewarding task. We engaged in numerous energizing conversations as the work before us challenged and stretched us as scholars. We owe debts of gratitude to many people without whose assistance this project would never have been possible. First, love and thanks go to our families, Derek, Ethan, and Aden Young, and Steve Jr., Steve III, Scott, and Eric Skrla, for serving as major sources of encouragement and support for our scholarship.

Our deepest appreciation also goes to the individuals who opened their lives in research interviews to the scholars who wrote chapters for this book. They are impressive and generous leaders and individuals from whom, we believe, we can all learn.

A number of our colleagues contributed to the development of this manuscript and to its individual chapters. Jim Scheurich provided the initial opportunity and encouragement to publish a special journal issue on this topic. Thanks also go to Jim for his mentoring and support of both of us as new scholars. Our colleague Julie Laible was instrumental in identifying and inviting scholars to participate in that initial publication. More significantly, her work and her life inspired many of the contributors to this book as well as several chapters of the book. Our gratitude goes, as well, to Julie's family for their permission to reprint her last piece of scholarly writing in this book.

Marilyn Fehn and Ellen Fairchild, graduate students at the University of Iowa, also provided valuable editorial assistance in the earliest stages of development of this manuscript. We are also indebted to Margaret Grogan, series editor for the State University of New York's (SUNY) Women in Education series, and Priscilla Ross, SUNY Director, for their patient and supportive help with this project. We also wish to thank the

viii   *Acknowledgments*

anonymous reviewers and the SUNY editorial board who provided invaluable feedback and suggestions.

In addition, we are deeply indebted to a group of pioneer female researchers in educational leadership, both in the United States and in the international community, on whose work the scholarship in this volume builds. These women (the work of whom we have cited often in the chapters that follow) laid the groundwork for an exciting and expanding field of epistemological and methodological work, often at great personal and professional cost. We deeply appreciate their courage, their intellectual virtuosity, and their sacrifices. Because they were willing to risk doing work that they were told "no one will care about," persist through endless rejections by mainstream educational administration journals, suffer through denial of tenure, and endure derision and outright rejection by their male and traditionally female colleagues, the type of scholarly thought that is collected in the chapters of this book became possible. Thus, our heartfelt thanks go to Colleen Bell, Susan Chase, Barbara Jackson, Catherine Marshall, Flora Ida Ortiz, Patricia Schmuck, Charol Shakeshaft, and Marilyn Tallerico, among many other wonderful women scholars who did the early work in this field.

We owe a tremendous debt of gratitude to our colleagues who contributed substantive, interesting, and cutting-edge work to this volume. Many thanks to: Maenette Benham, Colleen Capper, Cynthia Dillard, Margaret Grogan, Julie Laible, Catherine Marshall, Sylvia Méndez-Morse, and Jennifer Scott.

We wish to express our appreciation to the University Council for Educational Administration (www.ucea.org) for permission to reprint the following chapter that previously appeared in volume 36, issue 1 (Feb. 2000) of *Educational Administration Quarterly*: chapter 2, "Laying the Groundwork for a Reconception of the Superintendency from Feminist Postmodern Perspectives" by Margaret Grogan.

We also wish to express our appreciation to Taylor and Francis (www.tandf.co.uk) for permission to reprint the following chapters that previously appeared in volume 13, number 6 (Nov.–Dec. 2000) of the *International Journal of Qualitative Studies in Education*:

> Chapter 3, "Considering (Irreconcilable?) Contradictions in Cross-Group Feminist Research" by Michelle D. Young;
>
> Chapter 5, "Mourning Silence: Women Superintendents (and a Researcher) Rethink Speaking Up and Speaking Out" by Linda Skrla;
>
> Chapter 6, "The Substance of Things Hoped for, the Evidence of Things Not Seen: Examining an Endarkened Feminist

Acknowledgments

Epistemology in Educational Research and Leadership" by Cynthia B. Dillard;

Chapter 8, "A Loving Epistemology: What I Hold Critical in My Life, Faith, and Profession" by Julie C. Laible;

Chapter 9, "Life Lessons and a Loving Epistemology: A Response to Julie Laible's Loving Epistemology" by Colleen A. Capper; and

Chapter 11, "The Emperor and Research on Women in School Leadership: A Response to Julie Laible's Loving Epistemology" by Catherine Marshall.

Chapter 1

Introduction:
Reconsidering Feminist Research in
Educational Leadership

Linda Skrla and Michelle D. Young

Research on women in U.S. educational leadership changed substantially during the second half of the twentieth century.[1] Numerous scholars have chronicled and categorized these changes and have described periods or phases through which research on female educational leaders has passed (e.g., Banks, 1995; Blount, 1998; Marshall, this volume; Shakeshaft, 1987, 1999). From its virtual nonexistence prior to the early 1960s, through a largely positivistic and functionalist period in the late 1960s and 1970s, to a span of increasingly sophisticated work in the 1980s and 1990s, the field has both expanded and evolved. Especially within the past two decades, feminist epistemology and advocacy have played important roles in shaping the changes in the field.

Through feminist research in educational leadership we have learned much about how gender inequalities were created and structured within our systems of school administration and how they are maintained and perpetuated (Bell, 1988; Estler, 1975). Feminist research on school leadership has documented, among other things, the persistent underrepresentation of women in high-paying and prestigious leadership positions (Blount, 1998; Glass, 1992). It has revealed the ceiling that keeps women out of upper management positions and has shown us that this ceiling is glass if one is White, but concrete if one is a woman of color (Alston, 1999; Banks, 1995; Jackson, 1999; Ortiz, 1999).

Researchers of gender and educational leadership also have centered women in their work and have explored the characteristics of women leaders and the institutional and professional cultures within which they work

(Lynch, 1990; Tallerico, Burstyn, & Poole, 1993). These researchers and others have examined traditional theories of leadership and have found them to be based on traditional male experiences and understandings (Brunner, 1997). Research on women in educational leadership has also explored how these traditional theories and understandings have been normalized, while women's experiences, understandings, and values have been ignored (Bell & Chase, 1993). In addition, feminist study of gender and educational leadership has concerned itself with gender socialization, with myths about gender and leadership, and with the operation of power and language in producing inequity (Chase, 1995; Grogan, 1996). Such feminist research has also theorized about how and why these phenomena persist and even thrive in U.S. educational administration despite sweeping social changes and women's progress in other societal spheres (Blackmore, 1999; Shakeshaft, 1987, 1999).

In spite of these impressive accomplishments, however, feminist research in educational leadership has not always followed a uniform or smooth path of steady advancement. There have been periods of rapid growth in interest in the field and periods of significant maturation of theory (Shakeshaft, 1999). There have also been stretches of time during which interest has stagnated or declined and during which progress in the field has seemed to slow as promising lines of inquiry become more fully excavated and new paradigmatic, philosophical, and epistemological boundaries are reached (Blackmore, 2000). In much the same way that Denzin and Lincoln (2000) characterized the field of qualitative research as being "at the edge of the seventh moment," when deep reflection and reexamination would be required to move forward, feminist research in educational leadership has reached an edge point. After an intense period of rising interest and increasing sophistication in the middle 1990s that saw, among other things, the introduction of feminist poststructural frameworks into research in educational leadership, the field in the early years of the twenty-first century needs reexamination to consider its past and to contemplate its future.

Additionally, there is mounting evidence of a backlash and retrenchment of dominant, androcentric discourses (Blackmore, 1999, 2000), as well-recognized individuals and powerful groups within the educational leadership community have begun to comment with increasing frequency that "too much has been made of the gender thing" and that "we already know everything there is to know about women in educational leadership." One of the key lessons that past feminist research in the field has taught us is that oppression is not monolithic or static. As gains are made by feminists on some fronts, the dominant discourses and structures of oppression shift and adapt to continue (Blackmore, 1999). Thus, this is a crit-

Introduction 3

ical time for feminist researchers in educational leadership to reconsider our field of work and to carefully contemplate where our own shifts and adaptations may be occurring and where they may be needed. The collection of work in this book is intended to prompt, support, and contribute to such a reexamination in two important ways.

First, the book is a work of critical reflection on the field of feminist research in educational leadership as a whole. The writings collected here emerge from and build on critical feminist traditions. These chapters focus on and ask critical questions about the theories, methods, and epistemologies researchers use when conducting feminist research in educational leadership. They analyze the impact of feminist research on participants. They assess the ethical and political implications of researching across groups. They examine the types of strategies feminist researchers have developed to address the problems of the field. They propose alternative epistemologies that the authors hope will provide for more sensitive research methods and more complex research results. They probe for research possibilities that "might, perhaps, not be so cruel to so many people" (St. Pierre & Pillow, 2000, p. 1). And they offer examples of applications of these reconceptualized, alternate methodologies and epistemologies to research.

Second, this book serves as a sourcebook for feminist researchers in education leadership (and in other fields) who are engaged, perhaps unknowingly or unwillingly, in their own individual reexamination projects. Several of the chapters in this book were originally written as articles for a special issue of the *International Journal of Qualitative Studies in Education (QSE)*. In planning the special journal issue, the guest editors, Michelle Young and Julie Laible, were looking to create a resource for educational researchers that explored some of the issues and questions with which the editors frequently found themselves preoccupied, troubling over, and discussing. They wanted to create a space in which such dilemmas could be confronted, examined, and discussed. Likewise, the current book is intended to fill a similar need in more depth than was possible in a single journal issue.

The book is organized into fourteen chapters, one introductory chapter followed by three main parts. In part I, "Troubling Feminist Research Methods in Educational Leadership," the authors of the four chapters explore a number of feminist methodological dilemmas in educational leadership research such as power imbalances, ill-fitting theories, unanticipated impacts, and disputable representations. Although researchers who do not consider themselves feminists may also trouble over the dilemmas discussed in this part, these dilemmas are particularly problematic for feminists because they contradict and unsettle the foundational beliefs of many feminist researchers. The contributors to part I draw on the research literature in educational administration and other, related fields, and on their own fieldwork experiences to explore and problematize how we do research, with whom we conduct research, why we do it, how we represent participants, and how we present our findings.

Part II, "Reconsidering Feminist Epistemologies in Educational Leadership" contains six chapters that explore alternate, expanded epistemologies for research in educational leadership. These chapters critique traditional ways of knowing in the educational leadership field that have been grounded almost exclusively in white, male, and heterosexist epistemologies and propose new epistemologies that are more responsive to complexity and diversity. Two of this part's chapters explore the epistemological intersections of gender, race, ethnicity, and language. The remaining four chapters in this part comprise a dialog among several researchers about the concept of a "loving" epistemology.

Part III, "Reconceptualizing Applications of Feminist Research in Educational Leadership" offers three examples of reconsidered methods and epistemologies outlined in the first two parts of the book. The chapters in part III demonstrate the type of knowledge about school leadership that can be generated by researchers who are guided by reexamined feminist epistemologies and who use reconceptualized feminist methods. The chapter authors apply reconsidered epistemologies and methods to explore the topics of a native/indigenous model for educational leadership, the normalization of femininity in research styled as critical or poststructural, and the social construction of a leadership crisis.

The questions raised and tensions addressed by the contributors to all three parts of this book reflect to some degree concerns expressed by researchers in other areas of study. This is a propitious time for researchers in many areas, but particularly for feminist researchers in educational leadership. The issues raised in this book provide an opportunity for feminist and other educational researchers to review, critique, and rethink our research practices and theoretical understandings. The complexity of tensions such as these can paralyze. However, in analyzing and addressing these issues, the contributors to this volume use the tensions they have identified practically, responsibly, and creatively to reflect on ways to improve both thought and practice. Each author seeks to make clear that feminist research is entangled in problematic ethical and political dilemmas and also seeks to provide different ideas and insights about how one might proceed with feminist research within such problematics. By no means do these chapters cover the entire terrain of feminist research dilemmas in educational leadership. Rather, these texts represent a glimpse of both the questioning of formerly accepted practices and theoretical notions, and the generation of new ideas that emerge as the twenty-first century begins.

NOTE

1. Portions of the text in this chapter have been adapted from the introduction to a special issue of the *International Journal of Qualitative Studies in Education* (volume 13, number 6) on "Re-examining Feminist Research in Educational Leadership."

REFERENCES

Alston, J. A. (1999). Climbing hills and mountains: Black females making it to the superintendency. In C. C. Brunner (Ed.), *Sacred dreams: Women and the superintendency* (pp. 79–90). Albany: State University of New York Press.

Banks, C. A. M. (1995). Gender and race as factors in educational leadership and administration. In J. A. Banks & C. A. M. Banks (Eds.), *Handbook of research on multicultural education* (pp. 65–80). New York: Macmillan.

Bell, C. S. (1988). Organizational influences on women's experience in the superintendency. *Peabody Journal of Education, 65*(4), 31–59.

Bell, C. S., & Chase, S. (1993). The underrepresentation of women in school leadership. In C. Marshall (Ed.), *The new politics of race and gender* (pp. 141–154). Washington, DC: Falmer Press.

Blackmore, J. (1999). *Troubling women: Feminism, leadership, and educational change.* Buckingham, UK: Open University Press.

Blackmore, J. (2000). Warning signals or dangerous opportunities? Globalization, gender, and educational policy shifts. *Educational Theory, 50*(4), 467–486.

Blount, J. M. (1998). *Destined to rule the schools: Women and the superintendency 1873–1995.* Albany: State University of New York Press.

Brunner, C. C. (1997). Working through the "riddle of the heart": Perspectives of women superintendents. *Journal of School Leadership, 7*(3), 139–162.

Chase, S. (1995). *Ambiguous empowerment: The work narratives of women school superintendents.* Amherst: University of Massachusetts Press.

Denzin, N. K., & Lincoln, Y. S. (2000). Introduction: The discipline and practice of qualitative research. In N.K. Denzin & Y.S. Lincoln (Eds.), *Handbook of qualitative research* (2nd ed., pp. 1–29). Thousand Oaks, CA: Sage.

Estler, S. (1975). Women as leaders in public education. *Signs: Journal of Women in Culture and Society, 1,* 363–386.

Glass, T. E. (1992). *The 1992 study of the American school superintendency.* Arlington, VA: American Association of School Administrators.

Grogan, M. (1996). *Voices of women aspiring to the superintendency.* Albany: State University of New York Press.

Jackson, B. L. (1999). Getting inside history—against all odds: African-American women school superintendents. In C. C. Brunner (Ed.), *Sacred dreams: Women and the superintendency* (pp. 141–160). Albany: State University of New York Press.

Lynch, K. K. (1990). Women in school administration: Overcoming barriers to advancement. *Women's educational equity act publishing center digest.* Washington, DC: U.S. Department of Education.

Ortiz, F. I. (1999). Seeking and selecting Hispanic female superintendents. In C. C. Brunner (Ed.), *Sacred dreams: Women and the superintendency* (pp. 91–102). Albany: State University of New York Press.

Shakeshaft, C. (1987). *Women in educational administration.* Newbury Park, CA: Sage.

Shakeshaft, C. (1999). The struggle to create a more gender inclusive profession. In J. Murphy & C. S. Lewis (Eds.), *Handbook of research on educational administration* (2nd ed., pp. 99–118). San Francisco: Jossey-Bass.

St. Pierre, E. A., & Pillow, W. (2000). *Working the ruins: Feminist poststructural theory and methods in education.* New York: Routledge.

Tallerico, M., Burstyn, J. N., & Poole, W. (1993). *Gender and politics at work: Why women exit the superintendency.* Fairfax, VA: National Policy Board for Educational Administration. (ERIC Document Reproduction Service No. ED 361 911)

Part I

Troubling Feminist Research Methods in Educational Leadership

Any reexamination project such as that represented by this book must consider the contributions of past research and the accumulations of current understandings. The first two chapters in this part do this using different approaches. Chapter 2 by Margaret Grogan, "Laying the Groundwork for a Reconception of the Superintendency from Feminist Postmodern Perspectives," reviews the literature on the superintendency from the past 50 years to promote understanding of what has been written about the position. By juxtaposing traditional thought about issues such as working and forming relationships with members of a highly pluralistic society, a challenging leadership activity that she describes as "high politics," with ideas from feminist and postmodern literature, Margaret offers possibilities for reconceptualization of the superintendency grounded in acknowledgment of postmodern paradoxes that emerge using this approach. Recognizing such paradoxes allows for questioning of current constructions of the superintendency. This leads to suggested leadership strategies that differ from the traditional in hopes of developing a more socially committed superintendency in the future.

Chapter 3 by Michelle Young considers both the history and the future of a particular type of feminist research dilemma frequently encountered in educational leadership research—researching across differences. Michelle argues that while all research involves crossing (i.e., researching across difference) and all crossings involve problems of understanding, interpretation, and representation, some crossings will be, for different researchers, more difficult than others. She then delineates what she sees as

8 *Troubling Feminist Research Methods in Educational Leadership*

the most difficult problems involved in cross-group feminist research and examines the concerns other researchers have raised with regard to contradictions inherent in this type of research. Subsequently, Michelle explores how feminist and other scholars have worked with or around the problematic issues and contradictions involved in cross-group research.

Chapters 4 and 5, by Jennifer Scott and Linda Skrla, trouble the use of feminist frameworks in research with women school leaders. In Jennifer's piece, "The Linguistic Production of Genderlessness in the Superintendency," she uses her ethnographic research with two highly successful female superintendents to explore the ways in which these women were constructed by their environments into congruence with universal and masculine norms that are conflated with genderlessness. Jennifer shows how this genderlessness is linguistically produced through the use of conversational forms that *index* (depend for their meaning on reference to other concepts) the masculine and feminine genders in particular contexts. The author further demonstrates how the production of genderlessness in the superintendency "resides in the unconscious and remains unknown to the women" that she studied.

Linda Skrla also explores the terrain inhabited by women superintendents, but uses a feminist poststructural framework to navigate it. She uses Derrida's concept of philosophical mourning to probe the aftermath of her research participants' broken silence regarding sexism. This silence was shattered during a series of research interviews with three female former public school superintendents who articulated their differential treatment as women working in a male-dominated profession. Linda's chapter, which highlights the silences that surround women's unequal positions in society as well as in prestigious male-dominated occupations like the public school superintendency, focuses primarily on the mourning work done by herself and her research participants in reconstructing their thinking following the breaking of their silence.

Chapter 2

Laying the Groundwork for a Reconception of the Superintendency from Feminist Postmodern Perspectives

Margaret Grogan

The contemporary superintendent of public schools has few maps to guide his or her negotiation of an increasingly unpredictable environment. Ambiguous messages from a variety of publics force the superintendent to be both a politically astute entrepreneur and an expert educator. Public outcries are often translated into pressures to change. This means that few school districts are free of reform efforts of one kind or another. But the various publics present very different perspectives and demand very different solutions to educational problems as each group defines them. Reflective of what has been called a postmodern era (Anderson, 1990; Cherryholmes, 1988; Hargreaves, 1994; Harvey, 1989; Lyotard, 1984; Nicholson, 1990), this lack of coherence and direction poses many challenges for current superintendents.

To illustrate the point, I think of two examples. The first is an example of information management. Unlike the superintendents of the past, the men and women who lead school districts into the twenty-first century need increased knowledge and skills to help them make sense of the vast amounts of information that reach them on a daily basis: not only data, but information that defines the context within which they must operate— standardized test scores, for instance, and statistics on school violence or the increasing incidence of school dropouts, teacher testing programs, rapidly changing state and federal laws and so on. Once the significance of the information has been grasped, it must be disseminated in ways that increase public confidence in the superintendent and school district. But different groups look for different kinds of reassurance from the superintendent. Superintendents must choose which information they present carefully and sensitively. They hope for good timing, but they must also show clearly that their districts are responding to a variety of pressures such as media criticism, employee union demands, state accreditation requirements, and the increasing need to provide expanded special education services, to name a few.

The second is an example of the heightened need for finely tuned human relations skills, ones that allow superintendents to understand the diverse and often divisive groups they serve. Increasingly, superintendents are being asked to meet personally with interest groups and stakeholders. They are expected to have in-depth knowledge of the groups, know what their issues are and who the major figures are. And as issues and personages change, superintendents must work to keep abreast of the situation. Superintendents must devote a great deal of time and energy to build coalitions among their constituents and forge ties between schools and local communities. Again, because no two groups may want the school district to go in the same direction, superintendents must work constantly to negotiate and renegotiate trust. They must be especially attentive to the needs of the different groups, but they must do so in a way that allows common goals to be identified and reached whenever possible.

Although these skills are not new, they require more care and attention than they did in the past. Until recently, for instance, the testing of students or teachers has not been a burning issue in the local press. Now test scores and other district-specific data are disseminated not only locally, but statewide and are often interpreted in the media in a comparative mode that takes in not just the state but also the nation. Therefore, superintendents have little control over how they and their districts are represented in the media. While a sense of control has always been difficult to achieve, today, if reporters need a story on schooling, they have access to many more sources of information than in the past and might well ignore the superintendent altogether.

In the past, human relations skills were more often than not defined in terms of political skills. There have always been external political dimensions to the superintendency, but politics were often limited to high politics played out sometimes in partisan fashion and mostly in the arena of local and state government. Superintendents have always found it wise to know important community leaders. However, the range of individuals and groups with whom superintendents must now meet has been extended, and the necessity to collaborate with community members has become imperative. Although the superintendent today is still drawing on his or her political skills to deal with high politics, the arenas of conflict have widened to include everyday issues. The challenge of forming relationships with members of a highly pluralistic society in which we now live is more difficult to meet today. Furthermore, it is understood that these demands must be met on top of all the other fundamental ones that are required to manage the fiscal and human resources of a school district.

As I study the superintendency, I find that I am considering it from various angles. Schooled in administrator preparation programs, I am aware of the traditional literature that has been written about the position in various textbooks. Since I have also done an extensive review of the literature from the 1950s to the present, I have come to understand its development over the past half century. Because of the rapidly changing context of school leadership, however, I have found it most helpful to consider the contemporary superintendency in the light of some thoughts that come out of feminist literature and postmodern literature.

By feminist literature, I mean work from the 1970s onwards grounded in such disciplines as philosophy, sociology, psychology, and history that explores the significance of gender relations (Belenky, Clinchy, Goldberger, & Tarule, 1986; Card, 1991, 1995; Chodorow, 1989; Collins, 1991, 1995; Gilligan, 1993; Harding, 1991; Hartsock, 1985; Held, 1993; Noddings, 1984; Ruddick, 1989; Scott, 1986). Feminist theories arising from this body of literature differ from each other. What links them in a loose fashion is their attention to what have been described as "the distinctively feminist issues [which are] the situation of women and the analysis of male domination" (Flax, 1990, p. 40).

By postmodern literature, I refer in the first instance to the work of French writers, Foucault (1980) and Lyotard (1984), and then to the work of scholars who have identified postmodernism as an intellectual movement influencing most of the academic disciplines (Anderson, 1990; Cherryholmes, 1988; Craib, 1992; Giroux, 1993; Harvey, 1989; Huyssen, 1990; Sarup, 1988). Some of the works that have influenced my thinking combine both feminist and postmodern perspectives (Benhabib, 1990, 1992; Capper, 1992, 1993; Davies, 1994; Flax, 1990; Haraway, 1990; Lather, 1991, 1992; Nicholson, 1990; Probyn, 1990; Weedon, 1997).

This chapter, first, looks at what the literature has to say about the superintendency in the latter half of this century, then considers some relevant constructs from feminist/postmodern thought. Combining these perspectives allows me to problematize the current conception of the superintendency. In the next section, I put forward some suggestions for an individual reconception of the superintendency that are derived from a synthesis of the literature on the superintendency and feminist/postmodern thought. A final section widens the lens briefly to comment on the context within which the superintendent operates.

THE MODERN SUPERINTENDENT

Not a particularly well researched leadership position in educational administration, the superintendency has attracted some attention from scholars and practitioners over the past forty years. To understand the context of the position, a few scholars have provided historical overviews (Blount, 1998; Crowson, 1987; Kennedy 1984; Joseph Murphy, 1991; Thomas & Moran, 1992; Tyack & Hansot, 1982). We learn from these and from the early works on the subject (Boyd, 1974; Callahan, 1962; Carlson 1972; Clabaugh, 1966; Cuban, 1976; Spalding, 1954; Wilson, 1960) that the superintendency was conceived of in distinctly male terms. In the postwar literature, superintendents are often referred to as larger-than-life symbols of the community. In the 1950s and 1960s, for instance, the modern superintendent was likened to the new executive in peacetime America. The superintendent borrowed principles of action from business, government and the military. Spalding (1954) describes the superintendent as one whose "main responsibility is to impart [democratic] qualities to a school system and to preserve them for it" (p. 53). Highlighting a superintendent's moral duties, Wilson (1960) views the community educational leader as second only to the minister in representing and upholding the community's values. Most writers saw the superintendent as wielding important symbolic power in this period. Images of warrior and priest recur. Clabaugh (1966) put it succinctly: "The American school superintendent accepts the fact that his school system is . . . the lengthened shadow of himself" (p. 1).

In a rapidly changing economy, though, the position was being transformed from a scholar–educator to a businessman (Callahan, 1962). By the end of the 1960s, influenced strongly by scientific management theory, the superintendent is seen atop a hierarchical administration. There is also much attention paid to the stewardship expected of the superintendent in managing the public resources efficiently. As parents and citizens demanded more specialized services and curricular offerings in the public schools, superintendents were expected to manage their growing districts cost-effectively. According to a 1968 pamphlet, *Selecting a School Superintendent*, published by The American Association of School Administrators (AASA) and the National School Boards Association, the expanded nature of the position was clearly defined. Superintendents were to be responsible for such functions as planning and evaluation; organization; management of personnel, business, buildings, and auxiliary services; provision of information and advice to the community; and coordination of the entire school system (p. 6).

As we move into the 1970s, the most conspicuous feature of the position, as it is reported, is its politically conflictual nature (Boyd, 1974;

Cuban, 1976) defying earlier efforts to keep public education removed from politics. Lutz and Iannacone's (1978) dissatisfaction theory of democracy explains the particular vulnerability of a superintendent when the school board that appointed him or her is replaced over time by different members of the community who do not share the same values as the original board members. More often than not, the superintendent is removed as the new board evolves. Combined with the continuing emphasis on efficiency then, by the 1980s, the position had become associated more with corporate leadership skills infused with political maneuvering than with fundamental educational knowledge and expertise. While educational aspects of the position had not been neglected entirely, they were either taken for granted or were plainly not matters that were going to get many superintendents into trouble.

In a work that received much attention, Blumberg (1985), echoing Boyd (1974) and Cuban (1976) further developed the notion of superintendent as "educational statesman" or "political strategist," or a combination of both. He also reinforced the image of the superintendent engaged in high politics and added a morally disturbing element. He drew on Burlingame (1981) who argued that the best tactics that a superintendent should use to retain power include deliberate mystification, cover-up, and tactical rules. Blumberg admitted that, at times, a superintendent's ethics are subordinated to the "higher goal of keeping the system in balance and peaceful" (p. 68).

Against the background of school reform efforts begun in the eighties, an interest in the superintendent's role in reform began to emerge (Burnham, 1989; Crowson & Morris, 1987; Cuban, 1984; Murphy & Hallinger, 1986; Paulu, 1989). What is most striking about this, though, is that up until that time there had not been any research done on the relationship between the superintendent and the improvement of learning. Indeed, changing priorities in curriculum, which had been ranked as an issue or challenge of significant importance to superintendents in the 1971 AASA report, dropped out of sight in the 1982 AASA report (Cunningham & Hentges 1982, p. 38–39). This reinforces the sense of a superintendent's disengagement from instructional activities. He was no longer seen as educational statesman. Whether for better or worse, the superintendent became detached or appeared to become detached from these areas. This does not mean that superintendents were unaware of or unconcerned about issues of accountability for educational outcomes. Since the beginning of the 1970s, with an increase of federal involvement in public education, superintendents have been immersed in what Marland (1970) called a "new era of educational appraisal" (p. 369). There simply is not much attention paid to the superintendent's influence on outcomes.

A significant section of the scant literature during this period is focused on the precarious relationship between the school board and the superintendent (Beni, Cooper, & Muth, 1988; Kennedy, 1984; Plucker & Krueger, 1987; Wilson, 1980). Pictured as whimsical and fragmented, school boards then, as now, provided the superintendent with many of the greatest challenges to his or her leadership.

Related to general board issues, there is also interest in women accessing the position, which had remained firmly in the hands of White males (Blount, 1998; Dopp & Sloan, 1986; Maienza, 1986; Marshall, 1986; Ortiz & Marshall, 1988). Or as Wilson (1980) blandly asserts, "The most successful superintendent is male, Anglo-Saxon, middle-aged, Republican, intelligent, and a good student but not 'gifted'" (p. 20). It became increasingly clear during this time that despite predictions to the contrary, women superintendents still comprised only 5.25 percent of the national total in 1990, up from 3.38 percent in 1970 (Blount, 1998). By comparison, the reported two percent gain in 1993, resulting in women's holding 7.1 percent of superintendencies nationwide (Montenegro, 1993), suggests dramatic improvement. Nevertheless, despite the increase, the modern superintendent is not a position associated with women. The most influential work to address the issue in broad terms was Charol Shakeshaft's (1989) *Women in Educational Administration.* Although not focused specifically on the superintendency, her research helped identify the androcentric contexts within which all women administrators work.

The late 1980s and early 1990s saw much more attention on the superintendent's part in reform and restructuring, focusing particularly on decentralizing efforts (Doyle & Tetzloff, 1992; McWalters, 1992; Jerome Murphy, 1989; Tewel, 1994), on the superintendent as change agent, (Johnson, 1993, 1996; Joseph Murphy, 1991, 1993, 1994) and on various definitions of superintendent effectiveness (Burnham, 1989; Crowson & Morris, 1987; Holdaway & Genge, 1995; Leithwood, 1995; Myers, 1992; Wills & Peterson, 1992, 1995). Along with these aspects of the superintendency, there was renewed interest in the superintendent as instructional leader (Bjork, 1993; Glass, 1992, 1993a, 1993b, 1993c; Hord, 1993; Murphy & Hallinger, 1986; Myers 1992; Paulu, 1989). Tying in the previous emphasis on the political aspect of the position, Cuban (1988) claimed that in the past the superintendent's instructional role had been eclipsed by his managerial one, but that a crucial intersection between the two occurs when the superintendent uses political skills to achieve educational goals. This attitude characterizes an understated theme in much of the recent literature: that a superintendent must be closely involved (or at least be influential) in the instructional proceedings of the district but must at the same time view these proceedings with a political eye. In other words, where the superintendent differs from principals in this regard is in his or her knowledge of not only the "big picture" but also of how to utilize community resources effectively to address the most outspoken critics.

Relationships between superintendent and school boards remain one of the most frequently cited critical challenges to a superintendent's effective leadership (Grady & Bryant, 1991; Henkin, 1993; Lindle, Miller, & Lagana, 1992; McCloud & McKenzie, 1994; Ornstein, 1991; Tallerico, 1991, 1994; Zlotkin, 1993). Often accused of micromanaging a school district, school boards hold the ultimate power over a superintendent and contribute to the perception that superintendents must be a peripatetic group, smart enough for their own good to see a separation coming before it puts them out of a job.

In the last two decades of the twentieth century, gender issues surrounding the superintendency also emerge as a particular focus of research and writing. There is general interest in access to the superintendency, in understanding what school boards and consultants are looking for in women candidates, and in what it is like to aspire to the superintendency (Bell & Chase, 1994; Chion-Kenney, 1994; Grogan, 1996; Grogan & Henry, 1995; Maienza, 1986; Marietti & Stout, 1994; Rees, 1991; Scherr, 1995). Another related focus of research is on what life is like as a woman superintendent, including women's leadership styles and concepts of power (Bell & Chase, 1995; Brunner, 1995, 1998, 1999, 2000; Chase, 1995; Lindle et al., 1992; Rist, 1992a, 1992b; Wesson & Grady, 1995). Although many and various themes emerge from this literature, it is no surprise that much of the research draws attention to the relational aspects of women's approaches to leading schools, to their capacity for leading through others, their focus on the community and for empowering decision-making throughout the organization. At the same time, Shakeshaft's (1989) insights into the field of educational administration itself are reinforced by many of the studies that show that women are still being viewed as women first and administrators second (Grogan, 1996). Terms like "glass ceiling" remain in the literature and there is a fuller understanding of the power and influence of the "old boys" networks that appear to remain in place.

Another specific context shaping the superintendency that has received attention in the last twenty years is the urban one (Cuban, 1976; Hess, 1999; Jackson, 1995; Lunenberg, 1992; McCloud & McKenzie, 1994; Ornstein, 1991; Tallerico, 1994; Yee & Cuban, 1996). Highlighting political, social and economic factors that impact the urban superintendency to a greater extent than they do other superintendencies, this research offers strategies and intervention models designed to alleviate pressing needs in some of America's poorest districts. Urban districts are especially vulnerable to reform efforts that may or may not be effective. Hess (1999) argues that urban superintendents must be involved in change activity if they hope to survive. Indeed, it is apparently the activity itself rather than the result that determines success for the superintendent. One initiative advocating a proactive stance under less than desirable conditions is Harvard University's Urban Superintendents Program designed to "build a better school leader—someone with the thick skin and determination to take on a job that, more and more, appears impossible to do" (Richardson, 1995, p. 20).

Finally, a recent interest in ethics and leadership is finding its way into literature on the superintendency (Beck, 1996; Fenstermaker, 1996; Goens, 1996; Grogan & Smith, 1996; Leithwood, Steinbach, & Raun, 1993; Mijares, 1996; K. Walker, 1995; Walker & Shakotko, 1996). The revised professional standards for the superintendency published by AASA in 1993 also reflect this awareness in standard 8: Values and Ethics of Leadership (p. 11). Among the many other skills and competencies expected of a superintendent is the ability to act morally and wisely. It is argued that this is perhaps the most fundamental orientation of all, although there is no one definition of what morally appropriate action is. Indeed the very discussion provokes intense and lively debate. I interpret this trend, however, as one that takes the opposite position of the earlier, essentially amoral, perspective suggested in Blumberg (1985) and Burlingame (1981). It is an encouraging return to the notion of the superintendency as a position with moral responsibility. An especially promising outcome of the focus is apparent in the call for the inclusion of the dimensions of ethical leadership in superintendent preparation programs (Johnson, 1996).

In sum, in the literature of the past half-century, we get a multilayered and contradictory picture of the superintendency. According to the research, to survive today as superintendent long enough to see reforms through is considered quite a feat in many urban and suburban districts. Nevertheless, the superintendent must be a reformer. With the public outcry for accountability gaining momentum, the superintendent is a good, removable target for community dissatisfaction. Superintendents are hired to accomplish agendas of one school board and fired when new agendas and new boards form (Lutz & Iannacone, 1978). In the last years of the twentieth century, a superintendent must be far more knowledgeable of curriculum and instructional issues than was required in the postwar years. The superintendent must be an astute politician but the focus of his or her efforts in the public arena should be on forming coalitions and garnering resources to accomplish district goals and objectives. The superintendent should be an ethical and considerate problem-solver, one who has the interest of the children uppermost in his or her mind at all times. But he or she is not encouraged to put his or her own family needs first. For this reason among others, women are still largely absent from the position. And the kinds of men and women often described as successful in the position have to act in ways that are sometimes at odds with their earlier roles as relational, nurturing teachers.

Many variables and factors render the position unknowable in the modernist sense of knowledge as certainty. To be superintendent in a rural district may not prepare one to be superintendent in an urban district for instance. The two positions may be more dissimilar than they are similar. One community's needs and composition may be so different from another's that a superintendent who moves to a new district might not be able to draw on past experiences to inform him or her to the same degree that he or she might have been able to in the past. Although there is no doubt that some skills remain constant, such as the ability to manage the fiscal resources of the district efficiently, other skills and aptitudes emerge as the social, political and economic dramas of a community unfold. And they often unfold in ways that might not have been predicted even five years earlier. Changing school board members and the changing political contexts, federal, local—and most influential, state—require superintendents to live very much in the present.

FEMINIST/POSTMODERN PERSPECTIVES

How might one consider the modern superintendency from feminist/postmodern perspectives? One way is to use feminist and postmodern ideas as points of departure from the way the superintendency has been studied in the past. Using such concepts, I believe we can see the position in a new light. We see dimensions to the superintendency that we have not considered before. Most important, we can use feminist/postmodern constructs to lay the groundwork for a reconception of the position of superintendent in the future.

In general, feminist theories contribute to the discussion of the superintendency by introducing the dimension of gender. Feminist theory is founded on the recognition of gender as a legitimate category of analysis (Scott, 1986). Flax (1990) argues that feminist theory aims "to analyze gender relations: how gender relations are constituted and experienced and how we think or, equally important, do not think about them" (p. 40). I have thus found it to be very useful to examine the research on educational administration and on the superintendency, in particular, from the point of view that it represents necessarily gendered perspectives: the majority of both practitioners and researchers in the field have been men. This is not to judge such perspectives as good or bad, right or wrong. It is to acknowledge that they are, for the most part, male ones.

The second aspect of the feminist project that has influenced my thinking follows from the first. If we accept gender as a useful category of

18   *Margaret Grogan*

analysis to help us understand the superintendency better, then we need to draw on the experiences of women in the position. We need to take particular notice of how women define the superintendency. Biklen and Shakeshaft (1985) call for scholarship on women that focuses on how women perceive their own worlds. The belief is that this scholarship will contribute to a fuller comprehension of human behavior and society "since an inadequate conception of the female experience distorts our perspectives on the human experience as a whole" (p. 47). In other words, the traditional literature on the superintendency might provide only a partial understanding of what it is all about.

Third, perhaps the most significant contribution of feminist theory to the way we can consider the superintendency is to adopt its paradigm of social criticism. Feminist scholarship advocates action that results in a more equitable distribution of resources and opportunities for those who have been marginalized. We might look more closely at how the superintendency does or does not concern itself with such issues. We might question whether a focus on equity and care could prompt different approaches to the superintendency for instance. Encouraged by feminist moral theorists, we might urge the superintendent to become immersed in the particular lives and histories of his or her district. As M. U. Walker (1995) states, "If the others I need to understand really are others in a particular case at hand, and not repeatable instances or replaceable occupants of a general status, they will require of me an understanding of their/our story and its concrete detail" (p. 142).

Similar to feminism, postmodernism provides us with concepts that enable us to understand the superintendency in terms different from those that have been used in the past. Such concepts include discourse, subjectivity, power and knowledge, and resistance.

Discourse

We have become conscious of language games and of the transparency of language. Foucault (1980) uses the term "discourse" to help us understand how we are positioned as subjects in different relationships with others. Our understanding of the ways we should behave and what we should think in the various discourses within which we are positioned are dependent on our relative power in each discourse. "There are rules within a discourse concerning who can make statements and in what context, and these rules exclude some and include others" (Craib, 1992, p. 186). In the discourse of educational administration, for example, those with the power to define good practice are the male administrators whose experiences form the basis of most texts and much of the early research on the profession. Moreover, it is likely that people experience particular conflict and fragmentation if the discourses within which they are immersed are not aligned with each other. For instance, a woman superintendent may experience tension and stress as she tries to reconcile the discourse of educational administration with that of mothering because the two make very different demands on her (see Grogan, 1996 for a fuller discussion of this.)

Subjectivity

A key to understanding the concept of subjectivity is that discourses "systematically form the objects of which they speak" (Sarup, 1988, p. 70). Therefore, a man or woman who becomes superintendent is shaped by the discourse of the superintendency. The discourses in which we participate teach us what to do and how to do things approved by the discourse and how to avoid what is proscribed. We are molded by or subjectified by a discourse in the sense that we learn to make meaning of our experiences according to the dominant values and beliefs expressed within the discourse. "'Subjectivity' is used to refer to the conscious and unconscious thoughts and emotions of the individual, her sense of herself and her ways of understanding her relation to the world" (Weedon, 1997, p. 32).

The notion that one is subjectified by a discourse contradicts the enlightenment belief in a fixed identity. This is because discourses are often antithetical and not all are accorded the same weight. Within education, for instance, the discourse of administration is sometimes in direct contrast to that of teaching. Teaching encourages relationship building, administration recommends keeping distance. Therefore, teachers who become administrators often have to adopt a different subject position from the one they held previously. The tensions are even more apparent when one is concurrently immersed in conflicting discourses like administration and mothering or female partnering. Because discourses offer a range of gendered subject positions, the responsibilities of some women who are also partners or wives, for instance, clash with superintendent responsibilities such as attending frequent public meetings or work-related traveling. Some women superintendents are able to negotiate subject positions that do not conflict with their positions as partners but others are less successful. Subject positions in any discourse are negotiated according to social relations ". . . which are always relations of power and powerlessness between different subject positions" (Weedon, 1997, p. 91). The extent to which positions are accessible is dependent on factors such as race, class, gender, age and cultural background. If an individual is denied

20 *Margaret Grogan*

access by virtue of one or the other factors, she or he must fight to transform existing power relations.

Knowledge and Power

Another idea that has come to be synonymous with postmodernism is Lyotard's (1984) skepticism of the "grand narrative." A postmodern approach to knowledge is one that rejects the comfort of universalizing philosophies that seek truth. It is an approach that invites us to focus on the local and not to seek understanding of social reality necessarily within theories that purport to explain all of human history. This approach respects knowledge and understanding that comes from local stories for instance, that comes from a critical awareness of the particular historical situatedness of the set of conditions that contribute to the local context. Instead of seeing a local context as merely representative of wider social, political and economic trends and forces, it allows us to pay attention to the distinctive features of a local context and to hear the local players in their particular places and times. Superintendents are encouraged to ask who is being best served by policies and practices that are in place.

This approach is also informed by Foucault's (1980) insights into the interdependence of power and knowledge. The awareness that knowledge is contested and that what counts as knowledge depends on the relative power of those who claim it urges a critical analysis of the power relations that contribute to a local context. We are encouraged to notice who is best served by knowledge claims and to recognize that conflict itself is essential to the exercise of power. Foucault (1980) draws on two hypotheses of power: that the basis of the relationship of power is in hostilities and that the mechanisms of power are those of repression (p. 91). These insights first of all warn us to expect conflict, and, second, allow us to question taken-for-granted assumptions, particularly about the implications of local policies and practices. Superintendents would be forced to remain focused on what is happening in the immediate rather than to look beyond and explain away actions as justifiable in some larger context. Hargreaves (1994) talks of how social reality can thus be questioned. If superintendents "give voice to other versions [of reality] which are normally neglected or suppressed" (p. 39), their decisions will likely be better informed.

Resistance

A postmodern perspective also implies a sense of resistance. If the definition of knowledge is expanded to include others' voices as previ-

Laying the Groundwork for a Reconception   21

ously suggested, then it is to be expected that such new knowledge will include a resistance to the formerly accepted knowledge claims. The kind of inquiry and questioning suggested by postmodernism, as it is used here, will lead to a productive lack of certainty. In other words, the doubt that knowledge is fixed and independent of the knower will produce a constructive appreciation of multiple perspectives. However, contrary to some criticisms of a postmodern perspective, this appreciation need not render superintendents helpless. Implicit in this criticism is the relativist notion that once multiple perspectives have been understood, they are all equal and indistinguishable. As Huyssen (1990) argues, postmodernism itself suggests a resistance to "that easy postmodernism of the 'anything goes' variety" (p. 271). The usefulness of the postmodern approach to knowledge is in its questioning and its insistence on understanding the relationship between knowledge and power. Once these ideas have been grasped, a more comprehensive understanding of the local context is made possible. How that is translated into action depends on who the actor is and what power is at his or her disposal. A superintendent, for instance, wields a great deal of power over people's lives, albeit power that is limited by law, school board policies and state and federal regulations.

PROBLEMATIZING THE SUPERINTENDENCY

In applying these feminist and postmodern concepts to the superintendency as we know it now, we are able to consider our knowledge of the position partial and limited by gender. We know little about how the superintendency has been linked to issues of social justice. Has the position been thought of as one from which equitable policies must emerge? We learn that superintendents have been encouraged to think and behave in ways that have been dictated by a white, male-dominated discourse shaped by a different age. Most important for the possibility of future change, we become aware that superintendents retain a great deal of power despite the intrusions of local, state and federal politics.

At the same time, one immediately notices the paradoxical nature of the post. When I reflect on what the literature expects of the successful contemporary superintendent, I conclude that he or she is to be child-centered, relational, community-sensitive, instructionally expert, politically savvy, ethically oriented and efficient, and deeply involved in reform. Some of those expectations contradict each other. Reform, for instance, often involves hard-nosed decisions affecting loyal personnel and their carefully crafted programs. Child-centeredness sometimes collides with the need for efficiency.

In thinking this way, I have identified a number of particular paradoxes. These appear to be the result of the opposing forces at work, each making different demands on the superintendency. Acknowledging these paradoxes and expecting that others may exist or arise allows us to move forward in our attempt to understand the position. If, instead, we ignore them or try to smooth them over as reconcilable in one way or another, we miss an opportunity to view the superintendency differently. The most compelling reason for us to try to imagine a different superintendency is that we are moving into an era that is quite unlike the one in which the traditional models were developed. Is the current model of the superintendency robust enough to take us into the twenty-first century? My contention is that it is not, particularly in light of the predicted demographic changes that suggest there will be even more children who are not served well by our traditional leadership practices (Reyes, Wagstaff, & Fusarelli, 1999).

A RECONCEPTION OF THE SUPERINTENDENCY

Recognizing these paradoxes (see Table 2.1) creates the circumstances for us to examine critically what superintendents do. We become aware that current practice is fraught with contradiction. This reflects the different social, political and economic forces that are at work in the larger society. Identifying the paradoxes provides us with a foundation for questioning what superintendents might do differently in the future—thus laying the groundwork for the reconception of the superintendency. I argue new theories of leadership must emerge. These theories must stress different approaches to leadership such as the following ones. Although traditional educational leadership theories did not necessarily prevent superintendents from adopting these approaches in the past, the theories did not advocate them as I define them. I have tried to capture the essence of each of these ideas in a brief phrase which I then elaborate on. Simply put, to survive in office long enough to effect change that promises better outcomes for all students in the future, superintendents need to:

- be comfortable with contradiction;
- work through others;
- appreciate dissent;
- develop a critical awareness of how children are being served; and
- adopt an ethic of care.

Laying the Groundwork for a Reconception

TABLE 2.1
Paradoxes of Superintendency

The Paradox of Vision. To be hired, a superintendent often has to articulate a vision of where the district should be in five years before he or she even begins to understand the community. Sometimes the superintendent does not last the five years. Sometimes it is a different community in five years. Much of the literature reflects the turbulence and turmoil that increasingly characterize superintendencies.

Successful Reformers Need Not Reform. Superintendents must be seen as engaging in reform. However, those who are highly visible and proactive in their efforts are often recruited elsewhere before the results of reform become apparent. Therefore, the superintendency is associated with the reform activity not with measuring the outcomes of such efforts.

Public Schools Adopt Private Sector Values. The private sector is being called upon to rescue public education. Just as the movement towards charter schools and vouchers across the country introduces an element of competition into public schools, the threat of privatization of management hangs over the heads of certain districts as unwieldy and expensive central offices share the blame for poor student performance. A few large systems are also currently led by superintendents from the private sector: lawyers, military men, and fiscal experts, none of whom were hired for their educational expertise.

Decentralized Authority and Increased Accountability. It is ironic that as superintendents become more accountable for student outcomes, they are pressed to decentralize authority and empower others. At the same time, pluralistic communities create agendas for improvement that are often irreconcilable with each other. Yet another tension is created as superintendents are forced to spend much time with community members at the expense of meeting with their own teaching faculties. Teachers increasingly have difficulty gaining access to the superintendent.

Comfort with Contradiction

Districts need superintendents who are experienced at dealing with fragmentation and contradiction. In a reconceived superintendency, superintendents must be comfortable with contradiction. This capacity requires more than a tolerance for ambiguity that was advocated in the past. It suggests a more fundamental ease with being pulled in opposite directions. Although it is human to try to find coherence, a feminist postmodern skeptic does not try too hard (Weedon, 1997). Instead he or she puts the energy into achieving goals in a very local and piecemeal fashion. Alert to the existence of multiple perspectives and sensitive to the particular community context, a reconceived superintendency empowers others. Leadership becomes the capacity to involve others honestly by respecting and legitimizing different perspectives. Leadership resides in the kinds of relationships the superintendent forms and maintains. It is predicated on caring about those he or she serves.

Working through Others

Caring allows school leaders to remain focused on local conditions, seeing them for what they are. Remaining aloof tends to dull our senses by making us confident of what we know. A feminist postmodern perspective shakes this confidence by forcing us to question why things are the way they are, and by making us aware of who is best served by things the way they are. If superintendents are to be the agents of change as much of the literature asserts, then they must reflect deeply on who will benefit from the changes to be made. An added advantage of this approach is the openness to learning it fosters. Johnson (1996) found that effective superintendents "were as eager to learn as they were to instruct" (p. 275) and that they "modeled the kind of leadership that they hoped to inspire in others—listening attentively, asking good questions, and explaining their commitment to important principles" (p. 276).

Appreciating Dissent

These principles are rooted in caring about improving the learning opportunities for all children. Superintendents who are focused primarily on the local and who analyze the local power mechanisms will be better informed about how to provide those opportunities. Such superintendents will not squelch dissent in the name of consensus. Following Foucault's (1980) line of thought, these superintendents take into account how differing voices contribute to a better understanding of pluralistic contexts. This does not mean that the superintendent is to be paralyzed by the resulting conflict or swayed by the loudest noise. Guided by a focus on children and cautioned by a critical awareness of how children are being served, the superintendent will find direction in resisting easy solutions.

A Critical Awareness of How Children are being Served

A feminist postmodern reconception of the superintendency, as I see it, implies a commitment on the part of the superintendent to ask tough questions, to consider issues from multiple perspectives and to put himself or herself on the line. In sum, it means taking a stand on issues of social justice (and communicating that stand to others) that reinforces an active inquiry into what is happening in a district. It means being prepared to change practices and policies that continue to disadvantage children in poverty, children of color, and other children who are outside the mainstream.

An Ethic of Care

In studying the way some women have defined the superintendency, the importance of adopting an ethic of care is revealed (Grogan & Smith, 1996). An ethic of care allows us to deal with particular individuals as individuals with whom we have relationships, not as representatives of social groups. Caring encourages understanding of a variety of lived experiences. For instance, I refer to the experiences of individuals who have been marginalized by poverty, disability, ethnicity, gender, and sexual orientation, to mention some of the possible marginalizing conditions. Feminist postmodern thought cautions me against regarding such individuals as defined by their conditions in any universal manner. No lived experience can ever be exactly the same as another. In recognizing this, leaders who adopt an ethic of care are more likely to see themselves in relationship with others. Care prompts positive working relationships that emphasize high educational standards and a commitment to equity (Noddings, 1992).

THE CONTEXT OF THE SUPERINTENDENCY

In this chapter I lay the groundwork for the reconceptualization of the superintendency from the perspective of the potential superintendent. I recognize, however, that the collective mind or context within which superintendents work can be an inhibiting factor. Local school boards, county boards of supervisors, city councils, union leaders and other interested parties may not appreciate or identify the same priorities as a superintendent acting in the ways previously suggested. This is likely to increase the level of conflict between a superintendent and his or her stakeholders. It is important to understand the power of contexts in determining the behavior of superintendents in the position. There is no easy way to reach the collective mind. A second level of reconceptualization is necessary for superintendents to be most successful. We must work to engage communities in the same struggle. As a society, we must acknowledge the failure of our education system to provide equitably for all. This is not a simple task. It requires the concerted effort of scholars, educators, policymakers, and governing bodies to change the way we do business. By themselves, superintendents will have little impact if they are constantly fighting an uphill battle. I have suggested that superintendents must change their worldview, but at the same time, so must communities.

CONCLUSION

The context of the superintendency cannot be ignored. The notion of the superintendency is larger than the individual superintendent. The discourse of educational leadership that informs school boards and consultants of what to look for in a potential superintendent is a force more powerful than the hopes or wishes of a superintendent. A community's expectations for what superintendents must accomplish and how they should accomplish it exert a tremendous influence over the school leader. However, if individual superintendents do not resist the mind-numbing pressures to perform business as usual, no change can occur at all. Little by little, the approaches argued in this chapter promise to enable superintendents to serve all stakeholders better—if the measure is unqualified student growth and development.

Today, superintendents need these approaches to leadership to enable them to deal with the fragmented and contradictory environment outlined in the beginning of this chapter—particularly because communities that are served by public schools are unlikely to become more homogenous in the near future. Class, wealth, race, ethnicity, religion and competing values divide most communities now, and unless there are significant gains made in the educational outcomes for children of poverty, these conditions will only worsen. Good educators have always sought ways to lessen the gap between the haves and the have-nots through better schooling. But the traditional strategies that they have employed have had little sustained success. More than ever, superintendents must hone their critical awareness of how well children in their care are being served. The most effective means of doing that are learned by connecting with the communities, by hearing the voices of dissent, and by working through others.

Abandoning the desire for certainty is an important first step. Good research is very helpful, past practice is informative but there are no silver bullets to aid superintendents in their endeavors. Living with the kind of paradoxes identified in this chapter and recognizing others helps one to accept the inherent tensions in managing pluralistic school districts. Accepting as background the fact that local, state and federal directions do change and that demanding publics are always unsatisfied allows superintendents to keep their eyes on the children. Ignoring these conditions would be fatal, learning how to mine them for necessary resources will present the superintendent with opportunities.

Such a reconception of the superintendency might make it a more effective position. Kids might benefit. The superintendent who adopts the approach suggested previously will have to remain very much in touch with the students and wider community. Ways to address the needs of the communities can best emerge with this approach. There is no one reform mechanism that works everywhere. A superintendent will only be able to discover what works by paying close attention and being in relationship with those she or he serves.

It is also possible that a reconception of the superintendency as I have suggested will make it more attractive to nontraditional aspirants, the majority of whom are the women who make up the teaching force and who are entering assistant superintendencies in ever increasing numbers.[1] The emerging research on women in leadership suggests that some women lead in the ways already described. Moreover, Pounder (1994) argued that several trends may come together to enhance the likelihood of more women gaining administrative positions. She envisions trends such as decentralized decision making and changing student demographics and student needs will have implications for changing administrator role conceptions. However, no research indicates that the leadership approaches advocated in this chapter are gender specific. Men and women are equally capable of adopting such approaches. The point is that if the superintendency were associated more with these leadership approaches and less with the top-down, removed-from-students approaches that are endorsed in the traditional literature, more women and men who lead differently might aspire to the position. There are numerous candidates for the superintendency who do not wish to lead the way many superintendents before them have led. It is true that the candidate pools for the superintendency are not yet dominated by nontraditional candidates. Nevertheless, I believe that a reconception of the superintendency offers the kinds of challenges that are gratifying to educators who lead in ways encouraged above. Also true is the fact that candidate pools for the superintendency are not perceived to be as deep as they once were. Is the position becoming less attractive to the typical White, male candidate who sought it in the past? Superintendents are retiring, resigning or being fired in increasing numbers. The highly politicized, conflictual nature of the position deters many committed educators. A reconception of the superintendency is one line of thought that might rekindle educators' interest and enthusiasm for this pivotal position.

28 *Margaret Grogan*

NOTES

The author would like to thank Pam Tucker, Brian Pusser, Lars Björk and three anonymous reviewers for their suggestions and comments on various drafts of this chapter.
1. In 1989–90 women held 20.6 percent of assistant superintendencies nationwide (Restine, 1993). In 1998 women held 33 percent of assistant, associate, deputy or area superintendencies nationwide (Hodgkinson & Montenegro, 1999).

REFERENCES

Anderson, W. (1990). *Reality isn't what it used to be.* San Francisco: Harper & Row.

Beck, L. (1996). Why ethics? Why now? Thoughts on the moral challenges facing educational leaders. *The School Administrator, 54*(9), 8–11.

Belenky, M., Clinchy, B., Goldberger, N., & Tarule, J. (1986). *Women's ways of knowing: The development of self, voice and mind.* New York: Basic Books Inc.

Bell, C., & Chase, S. (1994). How search consultants talk about female superintendents. *School Administrator, 51,* 36–38.

Bell, C., & Chase, S. (1995). Gender in theory and practice of educational leadership. *Journal for a Just and Caring Education, 1*(2), 200–222.

Benhabib, S. (1990). Epistemologies of postmodernism: A rejoinder to Jean-Francois Lyotard. In L. Nicholson (Ed.), *Feminism/postmodernism* (pp. 107–132). New York: Routledge.

Benhabib, S. (1992). *Situating the self: Gender, community, and postmodernism in contemporary ethics.* New York: Routledge.

Beni, V., Cooper, B., & Muth, R. (1988). Schooling loses when either the board or the superintendent always wins. *The American School Board Journal, 175*(8), 24–25.

Biklen, S., & Shakeshaft, C. (1985). The new scholarship on women. In S. Klein (Ed.), *Handbook for achieving sex equity through education* (pp. 44–52). Baltimore: Johns Hopkins University Press.

Björk, L. (1993). Effective schools—effective superintendents: The emerging instructional leadership role. *Journal of School Leadership, 3*(3), 246–259.

Blount, J. (1998). *Destined to rule the schools: Women and the superintendency, 1873–1995.* Albany: State University of New York Press.

Blumberg, A. (1985). *The school superintendent: Living with conflict.* New York: Teachers College Press.

Boyd, W. (1974). The school superintendent: Educational statesman or political strategist? *Administrator's Notebook, 22*(9), 1–4.

Brunner, C. C. (1995). By power defined: Women in the superintendency. *Educational Considerations, 22*(20), 21–26.

Brunner, C. C. (1998). Women superintendents: Strategies for success. *Journal of Educational Administration, 36*(2), 160–182.

Brunner, C. C. (1999). *Sacred dreams: Women and the superintendency.* Albany: State University of New York Press.

Brunner, C. C. (2000). *Principles of power: Women superintendents and the riddle of the heart.* Albany: State University of New York Press.

Burlingame, M. (1981). Superintendent power retention. In S. Bacharach (Ed.), *Organizational behavior in schools and school districts* (pp. 429–464). New York: Praeger.

Burnham, J. (1989). Superintendents on the fast track. *The School Administrator, 46(9)*, 18–19.

Callahan, R. (1962). *Education and the cult of efficiency.* Chicago: University of Chicago Press.

Capper, C. (1992). A feminist poststructural analysis of nontraditional approaches in educational administration. *Educational Administration Quarterly, 28,* 103–124.

Capper, C. (1993). Educational administration in a pluralistic society: A multiparadigm approach. In C. Capper (Ed.), *Educational administration in a pluralistic society* (pp. 7–35). Albany: State University of New York Press.

Card, C. (1991). The feistiness of feminism. In C. Card (Ed.). *Feminist ethics* (pp. 3–31). Lawrence: University Press of Kansas

Card, C. (1995). Gender and moral luck. In V. Held (Ed.), *Justice and care* (pp. 79–100). New York: Teachers College Press.

Carlson, R. (1972). *School superintendents: Careers and performance.* Columbus, OH: Charles E. Merrill.

Chase, S. (1995). *Ambiguous empowerment.* Amherst: University of Massachusetts Press.

Cherryholmes, C. (1988). *Power and criticism: Poststructural investigations in education.* New York: Teachers College Press.

Chion-Kenney, L. (1994). Search consultants: Boon or bane to non-traditional candidates for the superintendency? *The School Administrator, 51(2)*, 8–9.

Chodorow, N. (1989). *Feminism and psychoanalytic theory.* New Haven, CT: Yale University Press.

Clabaugh, R. (1966). *School superintendent's guide: Principles and practices for effective administration.* West Nyack, NY: Parker.

Collins, P. (1991). *Black feminist thought.* New York: Routledge.

Collins, P. (1995). Black women and motherhood. In V. Held (Ed.), *Justice and care* (pp. 117–135). New York: Teachers College Press.

Craib, I. (1992). *Modern social theory.* New York: St. Martin's Press.

Crowson, R. (1987). The local school district superintendency: A puzzling administrative role. *Educational Administration Quarterly, 23(3)*, 49–69.

Crowson, R., & Morris, V.C. (1987). The superintendency and school reform: An exploratory study. *Metropolitan Education, 5,* 24–39.

Cuban, L. (1976). *Urban school chiefs under fire.* Chicago: University of Chicago Press.

Cuban, L. (1984). Transforming the frog into a prince: Effective school research, policy and practice at the district level. *Harvard Educational Review, 54(2)*, 129–151.

Cuban, L. (1988) Superintending: Images and roles. In L. Cuban (Ed.), *The managerial imperative and the practice of leadership in schools.* (pp. 111–147). Albany: State University of New York Press.

Cunningham, L., & Hentges, J. (1982). *The American school superintendency 1982: A summary report.* Arlington, VA: American Association of School Administrators.

Davies, B. (1994). *Poststructuralist theory and classroom practice.* Geelong, Victoria: Deakin University.

Dopp, B., & Sloan, C. (1986). Career development and succession of women to the superintendency. *The Clearing House, 60*(3), 120–126.

Doyle, R., & Tetzloff, P. (1992). Waivers provide relief, allow improvements. *The School Administrator, 49*(1), 9–10.

Fenstermaker, W. (1996). The ethical dimension of superintendent decision-making. *The School Administrator, 54*(9), 16–25.

Flax, J. (1990). Postmodernism and gender relations in feminist theory. In L. Nicholson (Ed.), *Feminism/postmodernism* (pp. 39–62). New York: Routledge.

Foucault, M. (1980). Two lectures. In C. Gordon (Ed.), *Power/Knowledge: Selected interviews and other writings 1972–1977* (pp. 78–108). New York: Pantheon.

Gilligan, C. (1993). *In a different voice* (new ed.) Cambridge, MA: Harvard University Press.

Giroux, H. (1993). *Living dangerously.* New York: Peter Lang.

Glass, T. (1992). *The 1992 study of the American school superintendency.* Arlington, VA: American Association of School Administrators.

Glass, T. (1993a). Exemplary superintendents: Do they fit the model? In D. Carter, T. Glass, & S. Hord (Eds.), *Selecting, preparing and developing the school district superintendent* (pp. 57–70). Washington, DC: Falmer Press.

Glass, T. (1993b). Point and counterpoint: What is in the context of what might be? In D. Carter, T. Glass, & S. Hord (Eds.), *Selecting, preparing and developing the school district superintendent* (pp. 37–56). Washington, DC: Falmer Press.

Glass, T. (1993c). Through the looking glass. In D. Carter, T. Glass, & S. Hord (Eds.), *Selecting, preparing and developing the school district superintendent* (pp. 20–36). Washington, DC: Falmer Press.

Goens, G. (1996). Shared decisions, empowerment, and ethics: A mission impossible for district leaders? *The School Administrator, 54*(9), 12–15.

Grady, M., & Bryant, M. (1991). School board turmoil and superintendent turnover: What pushes them to the brink? *The School Administrator, 48*(2), 19–26.

Grogan, M. (1996). *Voices of women aspiring to the superintendency.* Albany: State University of New York Press.

Grogan, M., & Henry, M. (1995). Women candidates for the superintendency: Board perspectives. In B. Irby & G. Brown (Eds.), *Women as school executives: Voices and visions.* (pp. 164–175). Huntsville, TX: Texas Council of Women School Executives.

Grogan, M., & Smith, F. (1996, April). *Exploring the perceptions of superintendents: Moral choices or procedural alternatives.* Paper presented at the annual meeting of the American Educational Research Association, New York.

Haraway, D. (1990). A manifesto for Cyborgs: Science, technology, and socialist feminism in the 1980s. In L. Nicholson (Ed.), *Feminism/postmodernism* (pp. 190–233). New York: Routledge.

Harding, S. (1991). *Whose science? Whose knowledge?* Ithaca, NY: Cornell University Press.

Hargreaves, A. (1994). *Changing teachers, changing times.* New York: Teachers College Press.

Hartsock, N. (1985). *Money sex, and power.* Boston: Northeastern University Press.

Harvey, D. (1989). *The conditions of postmodernity.* Cambridge: Polity Press.

Held, V. (1993). *Feminist morality: Transforming culture, society and politics.* Chicago: University of Chicago Press.

Henkin, A. (1993). Social skills of superintendents: A leadership requisite in restructured schools. *Educational Research Quarterly, 16*(4), 15–30.

Hess, F. (1999). *Spinning wheels: The politics of school reform.* Washington, DC: Brookings University Press.

Hodgkinson, H., & Montenegro, X. (1999). *The U.S. school superintendent: The invisible CEO.* Washington, DC: Institute for Educational Leadership.

Holdaway, E., & Genge, A. (1995). How effective superintendents understand their own work. In K. Leithwood (Ed.), *Effective school district leadership* (pp. 13–32). Albany: State University of New York Press.

Hord, S. (1993). Smoke, mirrors or reality: Another instructional leader. In D. Carter, T. Glass, & S. Hord (Eds.), *Selecting, preparing and developing the school district superintendent* (pp. 1–19). Washington, DC: Falmer Press.

Huyssen, A. (1990). Mapping the postmodern. In L. Nicholson (Ed.), *Feminism/postmodernism* (pp. 234–280). New York: Routledge.

Jackson, B. (1995). *Balancing act: The political role of the urban school superintendent.* Washington, DC: Joint Center for Political and Economic Studies.

Johnson, S. M. (1993). Vision in the superintendency. *The School Administrator, 50*(1), 22–29.

Johnson, S. M. (1996). *Leading to change: The challenge of the new superintendency.* San Francisco: Jossey-Bass.

Kennedy, J. (1984). When collective bargaining first came to education: A superintendent's viewpoint. *Government Union Review, 5*(1), 14–26.

Lather, P. (1991). *Getting Smart: Feminist research and pedagogy with/in the postmodern.* New York: Routledge.

Lather, P. (1992) Critical frames in educational research: Feminist and post-structural perspectives. *Theory into Practice, 31*(2), 87–99.

Leithwood, K. (1995). Toward a more comprehensive appreciation of effective school district leadership. In K. Leithwood (Ed.), *Effective school district leadership* (pp. 315–340). Albany: State University of New York Press.

Leithwood, K., Steinbach, R., & Raun, R. (1993). Superintendents' group problem-solving processes. *Educational Administration Quarterly, 29*(3), 364–391.

Lindle, J., Miller, L., & Lagana, J. (1992). Coping in the superintendency: Gender-related perspectives. In F. Wendel (Ed.), *Issues of professional preparation and practice* (pp. 33–53). University Park, PA: UCEA.

Lunenberg, F. (1992). The urban superintendent's role in school reform. *Education and Urban Society, 25*(1), 30–44.

Lutz, F., & Iannacone, L. (1978). *Public participation in local schools: The dissatisfaction theory of American democracy.* Lexington, MA: Lexington Books.

Lyotard, J. (1984). *The postmodern condition: A report on knowledge.* (G. Bennington & B. Massumi, Trans.). Minneapolis: University of Minnesota Press. (Original work published in 1979)

Maienza, J. (1986). The superintendency: Characteristics of access for men and women. *Educational Administration Quarterly, 22*(4), 59–79.

Marietti, M., & Stout, R. (1994). School boards that hire women superintendents. *Urban Education, 28*(4), 373–385.

Marland, S. (1970). The changing nature of the school superintendency. *Public Administration Review, 30*(4), 365–371.

Marshall, S. (1986). Women reach for the top spot. *The School Administrator, 43*(10), 10–13.

McCloud, B., & McKenzie, F. (1994). School boards and superintendents in urban districts. *Phi Delta Kappan, 75*(5), 384–385.

McWalters, P. (1992). Handing accountability and authority to schools. *The School Administrator, 49*(1), 9–10.

Mijares, A. (1996). Escaping the malaise: First-hand guidance for ethical behavior. *The School Administrator, 54*(9), 26–29.

Montenegro, X. (1993). *Women and racial minority representation in school administration.* Arlington, VA: American Association of School Administrators.

Murphy, J., & Hallinger, P. (1986). The superintendent as instructional leader: Findings from effective school districts. *The Journal of Educational Administration, 24*(2), 213–236.

Murphy, Jerome. (1989). The paradox of decentralizing schools. *Phi Delta Kappan, 70*(10), 808–812.

Murphy, Joseph. (1991). The "Maytag Man" of school reform. *The School Administrator, 48*(2), 32–33.

Murphy, Joseph. (1993). Changing role of the superintendent in Kentucky's reforms. *The School Administrator, 50*(10), 26–30.

Murphy, Joseph. (1994). The changing role of the superintendency in restructuring districts in Kentucky. *School Effectiveness and School Improvement, 5*(4), 349–375.

Myers, M. (1992). Effective school and the superintendency: Perception and practice. *Contemporary Education, 63*(2), 96–101.

Nicholson, L. (1990). Introduction. In L. Nicholson (Ed.), *Feminism/postmodernism* (pp. 1–16). New York: Routledge.

Noddings, N. (1984). *Caring: A feminine approach to ethics and moral education.* Berkeley: University of California Press.

Noddings, N. (1992). *The challenge to care in schools.* New York: Teachers College Press.

Ornstein, A. (1991). Problems facing school superintendents and school board presidents of large school districts. *The Urban Review, 23*(3), 207–214.

Ortiz, F., & Marshall, C. (1988). Women in educational administration. In N. Boyan (Ed.), *Handbook of research on educational administration* (pp. 123–141). New York: Longman.

Paulu, N. (1989). Key player in school reform: The superintendent. *The School Administrator, 46*(3), 8–12.

Plucker, O., & Krueger, J. (1987). Heed these common sense tips and get along with your board. *The Executive Educator, 9*(6), 26–29.

Pounder, D. (1994). Educational and demographic trends: Implications for women's representation in school administration. In P. Thurston & N. Prestine (Eds.), *Advances in educational administration Vol. III* (pp. 135–149). Greenwich, CT: JAI Press.

Probyn, E. (1990). Travels in the postmodern: Making sense of the local. In L. Nicholson (Ed.), *Feminism/postmodernism* (pp. 176–189). New York: Routledge.

Rees, R. (1991). Changing hiring patterns: A case of changing perceptions. Suitable suggestions for both board officers and woman job aspirants. *Education Canada, 31*(3), 8–15.

Restine, L. (1993). *Women in administration: Facilitators for change.* Newbury Park, CA: Corwin Press.

Reyes, P., Wagstaff, L., & Fusarelli, L. (1999). Delta forces: The changing fabric of American society and education. In J. Murphy & K. Seashore Louis (Eds.), *Handbook of research on educational administration* (pp. 183–201). San Francisco: Jossey-Bass.

Richardson, J. (1995, Nov. 22). City bound. *Education Week*, 18–23.

Rist, M. (1992a). Leadership by design. *The Executive Educator, 14*(10), 31–34.

Rist, M. (1992b). Scenes from a meeting: AASA. *The Executive Educator, 14*(5), 27–29.

Ruddick, S. (1989). *Maternal thinking.* Boston: Beacon Press.

Sarup, M. (1988). *An introductory guide to post-structuralism and postmodernism.* New York: Harvester Wheatsheaf.

Scherr, M. (1995). The glass ceiling reconsidered: Views from below. In P. Dunlap & P. Schmuck (Eds.), *Women leading in education.* Albany: State University of New York Press.

Scott, J. (1986). Gender: A useful category of historical analysis. *American Historical Review, 91*, 1053–1075.

Shakeshaft, C. (1989). *Women in educational administration.* Newbury Park, CA: Sage.

Spalding, W. (1954). *The superintendency of public schools, an anxious profession.* Cambridge, MA: Harvard University Press.

Tallerico, M. (1991). School board member development: Implications for policy and practice. *Planning and Changing, 22*(2), 94–107.

Tallerico, M. (1994). Exits from urban superintendencies: The intersection of politics, race, and gender. *Urban Education 28*, 439–454.

Tewel, K. (1994). Central office blues. *The Executive Educator, 16*(3), 34–35.

Thomas, W., & Moran, K. (1992). Reconsidering the power of the superintendent in the progressive period. *American Educational Research Journal, 29*(1), 22–50.

Tyack, D., & Hansot, E. (1982). *Managers of virtue.* New York: Basic Books.

Walker, K. (1995). Perceptions of ethical problems among senior educational leaders. *Journal of School Leadership, 2*(5), 532–564.

Walker, K., & Shakotko, D. (1996, October). *The place of values in the work of Canadian superintendents: A preliminary report.* Paper presented at the Toronto Conference: Values and Educational Leadership, Toronto.

Walker, M. U. (1995). Moral understandings. In V. Held (Ed.), *Justice and care* (pp. 139–152). New York: Teachers College Press.

Weedon, C. (1997). *Feminist practice and poststructuralist theory.* (2nd ed.). New York: Basil Blackwell.

Wesson, L., & Grady, M. (1995). A leadership perspective from women superintendents. In B. Irby & G. Brown (Eds.), *Women as school executives: Voices and visions* (pp. 35–41). Huntsville, TX: Texas Council of Women School Executives.

Wills, F., & Peterson, K. (1992). External pressures for reform and strategy formation at the district level: Superintendents' interpretations of state demands. *Educational Evaluation and Policy Analysis, 14*(3), 241–260.

Wills, F., & Peterson, K. (1995). Superintendents' management of state-initiated reform: A matter of interpretation. In K. Leithwood (Ed.), *Effective school district leadership* (pp. 85–116). Albany: State University of New York Press.

Wilson, R. (1960). *The modern school superintendent.* New York: Harper & Brothers.

Wilson, R. (1980). The anatomy of success in the superintendency. *Phi Delta Kappan, 62*(1), 20–21.

Yee, G., & Cuban, L. (1996). When is tenure long enough? A historical analysis of superintendent turnover and tenure in urban school districts. *Educational Administration Quarterly, 32,* 615–641.

Zlotkin, J. (1993). Rethinking the school board's role. *Educational Leadership, 51*(2), 22–25.

Chapter 3

Considering (Irreconcilable?) Contradictions in Cross-Group Feminist Research

Michelle D. Young

During a meeting for women's rights in Akron, Ohio, a freed slave, Sojourner Truth, responded with these words to an Anglo clergyman who argued that women were unable to vote because they were too delicate:

> The man over there says women need to be helped into carriages and lifted over ditches, and to have the best place everywhere. Nobody ever helps me into carriages or over puddles, or gives me the best place—and ain't I a woman? . . . I have plowed and planted and gathered into barns, and no man could head me—and ain't I a woman? I could work as much and eat as much as a man—when I could get it—and bear the lash as well! And ain't I a woman? (Truth quoted in Flexner, 1975, p. 91)

Just as Truth's words served to explicate the incongruency of her lived experiences with that of Southern White females a century and a half ago, contemporary feminists have problematized the adequacy of a singular definition of woman. Differing conditions of life define what constitutes being a woman.

The subject of difference and how difference should or should not be researched and represented is the focus of discussions among many feminists today (Fine, 1994; Reinharz, 1992; Sawicki, 1994). Theories of difference, of course, are not new to feminism. There has been much discussion over the years concerning the nature and status of women's differences from men (e.g., biological, psychological, cultural). Contemporary theories of gender difference have also emphasized the shared experiences of women across the divisions of race, class, age, and other differences. In such theories, the diversity of women's lives and activities have often been lumped into the category "women's experience," presumably in an effort to provide a basis for a collective feminist subject, emancipatory theory, and identity politics. More recently, however, it is the differences among women (e.g., race, class, and sexual orientation) that have moved to the forefront of theoretical discussions.

In this essay I review and analyze how qualitative researchers have approached issues of cross-group feminist research (i.e., researching across difference). First, I explore the issue of women's diversity and what is meant by cross-group feminist research. I then take up issues and concerns raised with regard to contradictions inherent in this type of research. Here I review and discuss arguments made primarily by critical, feminist, and poststructural scholars that focus on refractory epistemological, methodological, and ethical issues. In addition, I occasionally place my own concrete experiences in the text. In the third section, I review and discuss a number of attempts scholars of qualitative research have made to address problematic issues and contradictions involved in cross-group feminist research. As a middle-class, university educated, Protestant, female, feminist researcher whose race is White and who has conducted cross-group feminist research with individuals who have differed from me on one or more of these identity markers, my intent is not to convince the reader to either stop performing cross-group research or to provide a universal blessing to move forward with cross-group research. Rather my intent is to explore the complexity of this issue and the approaches qualitative researchers are taking to work within or against this complexity.

ALL RESEARCH INVOLVES CROSSINGS

> *If we begin from the world as we actually experience it, it is at least possible to see that we are indeed located and that what we know of the other is conditional upon that location. There are and must be different experiences of the world and different bases of experience. We must not do away with them by taking advantage of our privileged speaking to construct a sociological version that we then impose upon them as their reality. We may not rewrite the other's world* [italics added]. (Smith, 1990, p. 25)

Feminist research is "for women" (Harding, 1987). Among White feminist scholars, feminist research is typically described as an approach to studying women from the perspective of their own experiences to develop versions of reality that more accurately reflect their experiences. It emphasizes identification, trust, empathy, and nonexploitative relationships, and one of its primary goals is "to provide for women explanations of social phenomena that they want and need" (Harding, 1987, p. 8). In doing so, it has produced radical reexaminations of assumptions, and reconstructions of previously accepted interpretations across a broad range of disciplines.

Feminist research has also been described as "part of white culture" (Reinharz, 1992). Hooks (1984), for example, asserts that

> Much feminist theory emerges from privileged women who live at the center, whose perspectives on reality rarely include knowledge and awareness of the lives of women and men who live in the margin. As a consequence, feminist theory lacks wholeness, lacks the broad analysis that could encompass a variety of human experiences. (p. x)

Too many feminist scholars, it is argued, claim to represent "women's experiences" but root their work in the experiences of White populations and samples (Stanfield, 1993a). The appellation "feminism," some believe, misrepresents women as a whole and unified group. Reinharz (1992, p. 253) quotes Arlene Kaplan Daniels as saying that feminists often "write about the problems of white women in America [sic] as though they were generic to womankind." Further, Sawicki (1991) has argued that by representing feminism as unified, authors are depicting the struggles of all females as similarly unified. Portraying feminism and the female experience as singular or common, while useful to some researchers such as Kelly-Gadol (1987) in her research on women's history, is regarded as problematic by others, particularly women of color (Anzaldua, 1990; Laible, 1995).

What does research tell us about females and their experiences? We understand that women learn continuously from birth the behavior appropriate to their position, and as they grow older their behavior and attitudes are subtly and profoundly molded by their cultural milieu (Group for Collaborative Inquiry, 1993). Moreover, analyses of contemporary institutions (e.g., schools, family, media) indicate that expectations with regard to one's gender (among other aspects of one's identity) are communicated both explicitly and implicitly. For example, Nancy Lesco (1988), who has examined the school's role in defining the identity of females, argued that school experiences are central to the perpetuation of gender identities and inequities in American society. Those who refuse to conform to acceptable norms of behavior or who violate the social dictates of their gender face restrictions and other negative consequences.

We have also learned, however, that expectations differ for women in different contexts and cultures. The impact of culture on the ways individuals and groups enact and view their lives, for example, is apparent in culturally embedded and cross-cultural research of women. Examples extend back at least a half-century ago to Mead's (1950) work in New Guinea. She documented important variations in women's behaviors across the different cultures existing within the country of New Guinea. A similar but more recent example is Herskovitz's (1967) exploration of marital practices with the Fon of Dahomey. Herskovitz reported that the Fon had 12 types of marriages and that one involved a woman marrying a woman, a practice common to a number of groups in Africa. In the United States, Moreno (1999) has explored how Latina mothers' involvement in their children's education differed from the White middle class norm. Furthermore, Ladner (1987) explored how the salient differences in the life experiences of many Black women as compared to middle-class White women is reflected in the gendered expectations of the Black adolescent females. These young females expected Black women to take a strong family role and to be economically independent, educated, resourceful, and self-reliant. Ladner explained that "The resources which adolescent girls have at their disposal combined with the cultural heritage of their communities, are crucial factors in determining what kinds of women they become" (p. 80). Similarly, hooks (1984) and Morrison (1971) have noted important differences between the concerns of the Black woman and her White counterpart. For instance, Morrison (1971) noted "it is a source of amusement . . . to Black women to listen to [White] feminists talk of liberation while somebody's nice Black grandmother shoulders daily responsibility of child rearing and floor mopping" (p. 64). Thus, from issues of nurturing to parenting practices and from values and beliefs to workforce participation, research on women has demonstrated a diversity of views, experiences, and concerns.

In addition to documenting difference, some feminist research has sought to interrupt common misrepresentations of women of color. Zinn (1982), for example, argued that Hispanic women are often depicted as resigned, quiet, simple women, dependent on macho men. However, careful investigation suggests that "Chicanas can be active, adaptive human beings despite their subordination" (p. 260) and that their oppression is a function not only of cultural tradition but also of contemporary institutional discrimination that excludes them from public life. In an attempt to emend the misrepresentation of Native American women, Green (1980) argued that we must consider Native American women and their issues within the context of Native American life. In this context, they are largely responsible for maintaining "the resilient intratribal and pan-Indian networks . . . on and off reservation, networks which keep migratory and urban Indians working, educated and in touch with their Indian identities" (p. 266). Feminists who work with women from developing countries are similarly concerned with misrepresentation. Spivak (1988), however, sees misrepresentation as quite unavoidable because the academic feminisms operating in developing countries have been, in large measure, framed by Western thought. She maintains that Western paradigms have provided both the framework and the origin for understanding.

Although race and ethnicity constitute important and frequently studied areas of difference among women, feminist researchers have also considered how women differ with regard to age, ability, social class, family background, educational attainment, sexual orientation, religion, sociopolitical perspectives, and other factors (see for example Caulfield, 1984; Linden, 1993; Moss, 1984; Rollins, 1985; Romero, 1992). Each of these categories of difference, when acting on a woman's life, combine in various ways to create very different women.

The previously cited scholars, among others (see also Chow, 1987; Davis, 1978; Dill, 1979; Hurtado, 1989), have exposed myths regarding what it means to be or behave as "a woman" and have raised awareness concerning the inadequacy of viewing "woman" as an essentialized category. "Our emphasis on 'sisterhood,' on the common oppression of all women by male domination, has contributed to ethnocentrism [among other –isms] in our movement" (Caulfield, 1984, p. 375). "While it is evident that many women suffer from sexist tyranny, there is little indication that this forges 'a common bond among all women'" (hooks, 1984, p. 4).

Albeit much of the early White feminist research made use of essentialized categories of gender, contemporary feminist researchers have increasingly recognized the importance of the differences that exist among women and of the multiple sources of identity that affect individual women. According to Harding (1991), feminists have approached issues of difference in three primary ways: (1) some see race, class, and other aspects of identity or positionality as secondary to gender; (2) some view all status and identity markers as creating different experiences for women; and (3) some view particular identity markers, such as race or class, as more important for some women than gender. Although most feminists fall into the first category, a growing number have adopted the latter two approaches.

Increased recognition of the importance of identity and positionality markers beyond gender have led some feminist researchers to question their ability to adequately understand the experiences of or to tell the stories of other women, particularly without sliding into essentialism (e.g., Alcoff, 1991; Behar, 1993; Goldman, 1993; Laible, 1995, this volume; Lather, 1994; Middleton, 1984; Patai, 1988; Smith, 1992).[1] In addition to

40   *Michelle D. Young*

questioning their ability to adequately understand the Other, these and many other scholars understand that "who is speaking to whom turns out to be as important for meaning and truth as what is said; in fact what is said turns out to change according to who is speaking and who is listening" (Alcoff, 1991, p. 12). It is also generally understood that even individuals who are very similar to us are not wholly the same and that we cannot ever assume sameness or full understanding. No researcher has the ability to see and understand exactly as the participant sees and understands. All research, thus, involves crossing.

Indeed, all research is cross-group research. When a White adult researcher studies students of color, when a middle-class researcher with no children of her own studies homeless mothers, when a researcher with no identified disabilities studies individuals with disabilities, when a feminist researcher studies nonfeminist women, these individuals are involved in cross-group research. Even when women or men with seemingly identical characteristics, backgrounds, and experiences are involved in research, some form of crossing will occur. Crossings can involve, among other things, researching across race, ethnicity, citizenship, ability, social class, age, religion, gender, family background, sexual orientation, education, and parenthood. Crossing can also involve one's theoretical perspective or worldview (see Smulyan, 2000). Furthermore, we are rarely involved in a single crossing; rather research typically involves multiple crossings, some of which we may not even be aware, and given that one's positionality is multiple and being affected by myriad and evolving factors, the nature of the crossings themselves will change over time and across contexts. The term "cross-group research" is riddled with the ambiguity and complexity of the many different experiences it implicates.

It is important, however, to note that although all crossings involve problems of understanding, interpretation, and representation, some crossings will be, for different researchers, more difficult than others. Race, for many researchers, myself included, involves one of the most difficult forms of crossings. And there are few areas within the social sciences that can rival research across race and ethnicity in terms of the heated methodological and philosophical debates that have been generated (e.g., Connolly & Troyna, 1998; Gordon, Miller, & Rollock, 1990; Scheurich & Young, 1997). Like Millman (1986) who argued that male sociologists have a serious handicap when researching women because they cannot take the role of their female subjects, Laible (this volume) argues that middle-class, Euro-American females can only see theory through middle-class, Euro-American female lenses. For her, researching beyond these identity markers—particularly to study the racial Other—is epistemologically problematic. She states:

Considering (Irreconcilable?) Contradictions   41

As I conducted research with/on adolescent females of color I was, albeit unknowingly, reshaping the girls' experiences (the Other) to either positively or negatively fit with my notions (the Same) of what it means to be an adolescent, a female, and a Mexican-American. . . . My epistemology is Western, modern, and racially-biased. (p. 184)

Other researchers argue that difficult crossings occur any time the researcher is a member of a more privileged[2] group(s) than the researched (Harding, 1987; Millman , 1986). The determination of which crossings are more difficult than others will certainly differ (sometimes significantly) depending on who is being asked and who, what, or when they are researching. The specific difficulties of cross-group research are taken up in the following section.

PROBLEMS IN CROSS-GROUP FEMINIST RESEARCH

The recent intensification of attention to the importance of difference in feminist research can be understood as a reaction to the misrepresentation of women as a unified category as previously described (Olesen, 1994).[3] Similarly, feminists may be raising questions about cross-group research because they have recognized contradictions in their work that is supposed to support women (Wolf, 1996). It may also be linked to what Alcoff (1991) refers to as "the problem of speaking for others" (p. 5), what Lather (1991) refers to as the "postmodern questioning of the lust for authoritative accounts" (p. 85) or to what Denzin and Lincoln (1994) call the "double crisis of representation[4] and legitimation" (p. 11). Indeed, feminist and other qualitative researchers are voicing important concerns and asking penetrating questions about cross-group research. Four are particularly compelling for feminist researchers—issues of representation, counter-productivity, power imbalances, and writing conventions. Each of these concerns, which potentially contradict the overarching aims of feminist research, will be examined in turn in this section.

Representation

The understanding that qualitative researchers can provide fairly accurate representations of the researched and discover meaning in the written, verbal, and observed expressions gained through the research process, has come under attack. Moreover, there is a growing understanding that "one's location is epistemically significant" (Alcoff, 1991, p. 5). That is, whether we focus our research on the researcher, research participants, data collection, analysis, or knowledge production, one's location affects the meaning-making[5] that occurs through the research process. One can never clearly view the inner life of another; rather one's views are filtered.

> [O]ntology, epistemology, and methodology. Behind these terms stands the personal biography of the gendered researcher, who speaks from a particular class, racial, cultural, and ethnic community perspective. The gendered, multiculturally situated researcher approaches the world with a set of ideas, a framework (theory, ontology) that specifies a set of questions (epistemology) that are then examined (methodology, analysis) in specific ways. That is, empirical materials bearing on the question are collected and then analyzed and written about. Every researcher speaks from within a distinct interpretive community, which configures, in its special way, the multicultural, gendered components of the research act. (Denzin & Lincoln, 1994, p. 11)

Not only is it argued that "our locations are inscribed in our interpretations of others, even as we strive to anchor texts in 'native points of view' [and that] Ethnography 'from the native's point of view' is actually an oxymoron" (Linden, 1993, p. 73), it is also argued that the researcher as outsider has not had the same types of experiences or socialization as the researched (insiders), and therefore cannot develop a true understanding of the researched (Blauner & Wellman, 1973; Merton, 1972). Culture, experience, and socialization determine to a large extent what researchers see, how they analyze data, and how they write up their findings (Stanfield, 1994).

When representing or speaking for or about others, we are representing them in certain ways, just as we are representing their needs, goals, and situations. This is the case for feminist researchers—who as mentioned earlier tend to describe their approach as studying women from the perspective of their own experiences to reveal versions of reality that more accurately reflect their experiences—just as it is the case for other qualitative researchers. Such representations are products of interpretation (Alcoff, 1991). They are not pure reflections of " eality."

Writing on a similar issue, Eisner (1992) describes the knowledge production process as transactional. He argues that what we know is "a function of a *transaction* between the qualities of the world we cannot know in their pure, nonmediated form, and the frames of reference, personal skills, and individual histories we bring to them" (p.12, emphasis in original). In my "feminist" research with homeless mothers, for example,

Considering (Irreconcilable?) Contradictions

I interpreted their lives, their struggles, their relationships, and their possibilities (Young, 1997). With regard to roles, I articulated my understanding of "public mothering" and the "grateful beneficiary" role. These interpretations, I believed, best helped me communicate some of the complexities involved in mothering children and interacting with adults under the watchful and often judgmental eye of social service agents and volunteers. Although these interpretations may have both made sense to the mothers when we discussed them and reflected (at least part of) their experience, the interpretations certainly did not reflect how the mothers would have described their experiences a priori nor what elements they felt most accurately captured the essence of their experience. Although I felt I had come to know the mothers well and that I had "traveled" to their world (Laible, this volume), fully knowing them, how they thought, and what they felt and wanted was not possible. The findings I presented were representations of my creation based on my understanding of their situation, experiences, feelings, and desires. Just as Laible reshaped what it meant to be a female Mexican American adolescent for the participants in her dissertation research, I reshaped what it meant to be a homeless mother.

Counterproductivity

The questions of whether knowledge is discovered, created, achieved, or constructed and of just how much of the researcher's influence is acceptable are issues of little consensus within either feminist circles or the broader field of qualitative inquiry. For those who are concerned with issues of representation, other questions arise, such as "What are the impacts of our representations?" The ways researchers represent their participants and what they learn from their participants can have an impact that lies anywhere between incredibly helpful to seriously destructive (regardless of intent) and, thus, counterproductive.

It is the potential for destruction that concerns many feminist researchers (although determination of what counts as helpful or destructive, among other possible results, also differs among scholars). Trebilcot (1988) describes the act of speaking for others as a form of discursive violence waged against one's participants and their beliefs. She explains that attempting to speak for another often results in cutting off the ability or willingness of one's participants to develop meaning for themselves. Similarly, the act of representing the Other has been described by Said (1985) as an act of violence because it always involves "some degree of reduction, decontextualization, and miniaturization" (p. 4).

The issue of race illustrates well the need to be concerned with representational issues in cross-group feminist research. People of color have been studied for countless decades through traditional social science techniques and perspectives.

> To the extent that ethnic models of research have filtered through the mainstreams of social sciences, they have mirrored pathological and culture-of-poverty interpretations of people of color and of the poor in conformity with historically specific folk beliefs in the dominant societal culture. (Stanfield, 1994, p. 178)

Social science researchers have made similar arguments concerning other nondominant groups. Specifically they have argued that the perspectives underlying traditional social sciences are biased toward White, middle-class, physically able, heterosexual, Christian males and against the Other. The development of feminist and standpoint epistemologies and feminist research methods was, in part, a response to an understanding that traditional epistemologies and methodologies—not just poor use of them but the actual epistemologies and methodologies—tended to distort the lives of women. For example, examination of the social and educational research knowledge bases relative to women in administration indicated that these sciences have traditionally attempted to understand the experiences of women from an androcentric perspective (Shakeshaft, 1987). Banks (1993), Barkan (1992), Gordon, Miller and Rollock (1990), and Scheurich and Young (1997) are among those who have made similar arguments with regard to race.

One result is that distortions are often enculturated into those who are the victims of the distortions (hooks, 1990; Rebolledo, 1990; Shakeshaft, 1987), necessitating "painful struggle[s] of accepting and rejecting internalized negative and disenabling self-conceptions" (West, 1993, p. 270; see, also, Banks, 1993). Such counterproductive effects occur because negative distortions of the Other frequently pass into the dominant culture as "truth," and become the basis of individual, group, and institutional attitudes and decisions. Thus, well-meaning researchers, including feminist researchers with privileged locations who speak for or on behalf of less privileged persons, can unwittingly contribute to increasing or reinforcing the oppression of the group spoken for (Alcoff, 1991). And while reflexivity is considered an important practice among many feminist researchers, few researchers, it is argued, reflect seriously on the effects that their identities and their research perspectives and tools might have on what they see and interpret in cross-group research (Connolly, 1998; Harding, 1991; Mohanty, 1991; Scheurich & Young, 1997, 1998). Furthermore, many mainstream and some feminist researchers fail to critique the dominant research epistemologies out of which they work—epistemologies that are

Considering (Irreconcilable?) Contradictions

based on White, male, and Western understandings of knowledge, knowing, and knowers—and use them unquestioningly to examine and assess the lives and experiences of the Other (Scheurich & Young, 1997; Wolf, 1996). Stanfield (1994) argues that

> The experiences that construct paradigms in sciences and humanities are derivatives of cultural baggage imported into intellectual enterprises by privileged residents of historically specific societies and world systems. This is important to point out, because it is common for scholars to lapse into internal analyses while discussing paradigms and thus to ignore the rather commonsense fact that sciences and humanities are products of specific cultural and historical contexts that shape the character of intellectual work. (pp. 181–182)

Serious reflection on issues such as one's identity and the origin of one's research perspectives and tools is important. Not only are our findings, in the absence of such reflection, often erroneous (e.g., the misapplication of White cultural masculinity and femininity concepts to Asian Americans and other people of color), but actions taken based on our misconceptions may be wrongheaded. For example, Laible (1995) wondered aloud if her research on Mexican American female students and teachers in border schools might have negative consequences. She stated,

> I realize that my life is, in many ways, different from the girls' teachers and administrators I will be studying. Hence, not only do I run the risk of mis-representing my "subjects," but I may also, unintentionally, be promoting policies and educational practices which further oppress them due to my inability to fully understand their situation. (p. 4)

Careful attention must be given to the claims we make, and to the contexts within which these claims will be dispersed. According to Alcoff (1991) researchers must analyze the effects (possible and probable) that their research reports might have. "One must look at where the speech goes and what it does there" (p. 26). This issue will be taken up again later in this chapter.

Power Imbalances

Research, according to many scholars, occurs in a context of power relationships.[6] From one perspective, the orthodox

46 *Michelle D. Young*

> scientific worldview is the product of the Enlightenment and represents a liberating step for human society in releasing itself from the bonds of superstition and Scholasticism. From another perspective, it is a movement to narrow our view of our world and to monopolize knowing in the hands of an elite few, and is fueled by patriarchy, alienation, and materialism; it is the product of a society committed to the domination of nature and of other peoples. (Reason, 1994, p. 324)

Even some forms of qualitative inquiry, according to this perspective, qualify as hierarchical, undemocratic, and/or inequitable.

For most feminists, the greatest dilemma in the research process is the imbalance of power. At least three types of power imbalances are identifiable. One involves the different positionalities or identities of the researcher and the researched. A second type of power imbalance is discernable during the defining and carrying out of the research. A third form stems from the researcher's paradigm and perspectives.

The first type of power imbalance, which was introduced earlier in this chapter, involves the identities and positions of the researcher and the researched. The hierarchies that are created from positionalities can have potentially powerful impacts on the research process, the data, the findings, and, most importantly, the people involved. According to Wolf (1996), "'studying up'—studying those with more power than the researcher—is perhaps one way to subvert this particular power hierarchy" (p. 2).

The second type of imbalance occurs when researchers maintain all or most of the control over the design and carrying out of the research. Even feminist researchers who incorporate collaborative practices into their research may, unintentionally, create or reinforce power imbalances. Moreover, little evidence exists that feminist scholars are actually exercising research strategies that substantially reduce their control over "their" research (Wolf, 1996).

> By maintaining this control and distance, most feminist scholars end up benefiting the researcher more than those studied and furthering the gap between the researcher and the researched. This behavior undercuts some of the goals set forth by feminist researchers and reproduces aspects of mainstream academic research. (Wolf, 1996, p. 3)

The third type of power imbalance, which is intimately related to the first and second, is the researcher's paradigm and perspectives. The way researchers understand their own world and that of the Other as well as what counts as, for example, feminism depends in large measure on the researcher's paradigm and perspectives. Taking the example of what counts as feminism, a researcher may or may not consider participants' struggles as feminist, while the participants may define it as such. Mohanty (1991) challenges feminist scholars to critically examine their understandings and their potential misunderstandings of participants' actions as well as the linkages between the power of their own location and their ability to define the Other.

Tandon (1982), a scholar who practices participatory action research, delineates similar critiques of the power imbalances involved in traditional research. His "elitist" critique is particularly helpful here. This critique holds that the traditional research paradigm is available to a limited number of people (i.e., scholars and researchers) who themselves occupy an elite status and conduct their research to benefit their class. The critique also supports the understanding that researchers occupy a privileged position in relation to their participants (with very few exceptions). The researcher speaks and works under the mantle of two indivisible foundations of authority: knowledge and power (Said, 1978). Knowledge of (i.e., knowing) colonized people has been the most formidable tool of economic and political colonization. Said argued that during the time of widespread British colonialism, the Western way of knowing enabled imperial dominance (just as imperial dominance supported Western ways of knowing) and became the means by which colonized people increasingly came to know themselves—as Other/subordinate. Stanfield explains the relationship between power and Western ways of knowing this way: "[K]nowledge becomes the official way of interpreting realities through the ability of a privileged subset of the population to exert its will on others through its control of . . . major institutions and resources" (Stanfield, 1985, p. 389). Thus, the socially legitimated or constructed reality (ontology), and the legitimate way or ways we know that reality (epistemology), emerged primarily from the dominant group and its social and historical experiences (Scheurich & Young, 1997; Stanfield, 1994). These arguments resonate for contemporary feminist researchers concerned with knowledge–power dynamics (e.g., Anderson, 1993; Anzaldua, 1990; Chase, 1995; Collins, 1990; Shakeshaft, 1989).

One further result of the power imbalances in research and social relations is that researchers are much more likely than the researched to have their perspectives heard by others in positions of privilege and power. According to Alcoff (1991), one's location "can serve either to authorize or disauthorize one's speech" (p. 7). This understanding (which will be discussed further in a later section of this chapter) highlights the complex nature of cross-group research.

Writing Conventions

One space in which the problems of representation and power imbalances in research are visible is in written accounts of research. Attention within recent years has been given to the ethics of qualitative writing, particularly to issues of representation and the relationship between authority and authorship. Traditional social science texts, according to Smith (1989), tend to reinforce relations of inequality by distorting or neglecting to include women's voices in the text. Moreover, when voices are included within traditional texts, they tend either to be used merely to reflect the beliefs and behaviors the authors (i.e., researchers) argue their words represent, or to be presented as disconnected from both sociopolitical contexts and relations of power (Fine, 1992).

Standing (1998) presents a similar critique of feminist writing strategies. She asserts that the way many feminists write and the way they represent the words of their participants may reinforce or contribute to power imbalances. First, she argues that if we edit participants' language in our manuscripts, we homogenize their words and take away their "distinct ways of speaking, which reflects their background and culture, and [we] make standard English the 'normal' means of communication" (p. 191). Doing so, she indicates, simply reinforces power imbalances by identifying one way of speaking (that of the dominant group) as better than others. Her second argument concerns the language conventions of academic discourse. She asserts that when feminist researchers present the experiences of their participants through academic discourse, not only is the knowledge detached from their participants' lives but the manuscripts themselves are often inaccessible for many of the participants and other nonacademics.

A different critique of writing conventions concerns the absence of researcher from her or his texts, creating the image of an objective authoritative voice. Van Maanen (1988) discusses four different writing conventions used within realist tales (the type of tales frequently told by feminist scholars): experiential authority, documentary style, culture members' point of view, and interpretive omnipotence. In each case, the scientific and objective authority of the researcher is rhetorically displayed. Richardson (1994) asserts:

> In these traditional texts, the researcher proves his or her credentials in the introductory or methods section, and writes the body of the text as though the quotations and document snippets are naturally there, genuine evidence for the case being made, rather than selected, pruned, and spruced up for their textual appearance. (p. 520)

Considering (Irreconcilable?) Contradictions   49

This understanding of research contrasts with feminist perspectives, which seek to be inclusive, relevant, contextual, and subjective.

The starting point for many critiques of traditional writing conventions is the understanding that there is no neutral or perfect way to represent the researched or their contexts. Although traditional (positivist and to some degree postpositivist) researchers tend to assume they can unproblematically enter a context, study a problem, understand the context, discover relationships, gather and interpret data, and eventually provide a report that accurately (or at least closely) reflects the phenomena in question, researchers working out of feminist, critical, constructivist, interpretivist, and poststructural paradigms hold very different understandings. Although the understandings held by these scholars are by no means the same, they tend to have a consistent theme: One enters the research process with particular theoretical frames and research traditions that lead the researcher to adopt certain understandings of participants, their behaviors, and their contexts (Young, 1999).

The representation of the Other in feminist writing, however, has been critiqued. The ideas brought together by Clifford and Marcus (1986) in their book *Writing Culture* served to substantially increase awareness of the impact of textual representations within qualitative writing. For example, their work along with that of Said (1978, 1985, 1989) and Spivak (1988) increased understanding of the Othering that frequently occurs in qualitative texts. It is argued, for example, that the classic texts of anthropology inscribed major distinctions between the writer and the Other and endowed the writer with a

> privileged gaze that reproduces the authorial omniscience characteristic of many examples of narrative fiction. The text brings actors and culture together under the auspices of a single, all-encompassing point of view. By contrast, the Other is rendered solely as the object of the ethnographer's gaze. The voice of the ethnographer is privileged, that of the Other is muted. (Atkinson & Hammersley, 1994, p. 256)

The ways in which women from developing countries have been represented by feminist researchers from developed nations provide model examples. For years White feminist researchers have been engaged in writing about and misrepresenting women from developing nations (Mohanty, 1991). Mohanty notes that these women are frequently compared to women from developing countries and then found deficient in terms of education, literacy, and access to power and resources, that is, the Other (the researched) is described in opposition to the Self (the researcher). Collins

50   *Michelle D. Young*

(1990) makes a similar argument about feminist research on women of color in the United States.

In addition to the creation of descriptive and interpretive distortions, Othering also creates a degree of separation between the researcher and the researched, which some believe is an artificial one. Indeed, Laible (this volume) asserts that our very subjectivity is dependent on the Other. And as Fine (1994) so aptly stated, the "Self and Other are knottily entangled" (p. 72).

> When we opt, as has been the tradition, simply to write about those who have been Othered, we deny the hyphen. . . . We inscribe the Other, strain to white out the Self, and refuse to engage the contradictions that litter our texts. (Fine, 1994, p. 72)

The relationships between Self and Other, however, are typically obscured in traditional social science texts.

"WHAT IS TO BE DONE?"

Feminists may raise concerns and point out contradictions other than those I have described or they may pose them differently or with greater or lesser emphasis. However, from this discussion it should be obvious that some find cross-group research to be highly problematic. People of color, feminists, and a number of other researchers who practice outside traditional social science norms have argued that researchers cannot assume to be able to transcend their own positionality, that the results of cross-group research are often counterproductive, that cross-group research usually involves significant power imbalances, and that research and writing conventions have a significant impact on the research results. Those who feel strongly about these problems advocate for the termination of cross-group research. Alcoff (1991) provides an example of a group of Native Canadian writers who, after deciding that the work of a White Canadian author was disempowering, asked that she "move over." Other researchers, like Trebilcot (1988) and Laible (this volume), have renounced for themselves the act of speaking for (certain) others.[7]

Some would claim, however, that insisting on the termination of cross-group research goes too far. In the area of race it has been argued, for example, that banning White researchers from research with racially different individuals and groups assumes a "congruence of interests between black researchers and subjects which disguises internal conflicts and suggests an artificial harmony" (Rhodes, 1994, p. 556). Other dimensions of researchers' and participants' identities, it is argued, are ignored regardless of the impact or import they have on the people involved in the research. Mirza (1998), for example, describes some of the problems involved in assuming the importance of racial symmetry and ignoring other competing dimensions of identity. Although she is a South Asian woman who researches South Asian girls and women, she found that her own identity as a South Asian woman was not enough to develop reciprocal relationships and understanding with her participants. Rather, for many reasons, she found that her participants considered her an outsider.

Another argument holds that multiple perspectives of issues and phenomena provide for a more in-depth and multifaceted understanding (Anderson, 1993; Capper, this volume; Young, 1999).[8] Anderson (1993), who works with women of color and differing social statuses, argues that cross-group research is useful not only because she, as a White, middle-class woman, generates questions that are much different from those a Black researcher might study, but also because "moving previously excluded groups to the center of our research and teaching produces more representative accounts of society and culture" (p. 43). Although she acknowledges that the Black women with whom she works may respond to her much differently than they would to a Black interviewer, she asserts that this difference "does not make the accounts any less true" (p. 51). She further argues that cross-group research will result in the availability of multiple perspectives through which we can view an issue and, thus, heighten understanding. Tixier y Vigil and Elasser's (1976) work makes a convincing case for multiple perspectives. Tixier y Vigil, who is a Chicana, and Elasser, who is White, interviewed the same group of Chicana women and found that on certain topics (e.g., discrimination) they were more forthcoming with Tixier y Vigil, but on other topics (e.g., sex) they were more open with Elasser. These scholars argued that they each, because of their ethnicity, received valuable but different information. Similarly, Reinharz (1992) discusses men who label themselves feminist and claim to do feminist research. Like Alcoff (1991), she notes that while a researcher's identity might bear on meaning and truth, it does not determine meaning and truth. Kandal writes "although a man cannot experience what it means to be a woman, this does not preclude making a contribution to the sociology of women" (Reinharz, 1992, p. 14). Kelly-Gadol (1987) also discusses the utility of having men performing feminist research. She indicates that in addition to bringing a different perspective, men can bring a degree of prestige and authenticity to feminist research.

Fine (1992) extends this argument to the issue of authority. She argues that in some cases it is important for outsiders with more privileged positions to speak for insiders. She notes, for example, that as researchers, men are often viewed as having more objectivity and credibility than women doing feminist research. This too is the case, she argues, in other arenas.

> I (white, academic, elite woman) represent the words and voices of African American and Latino, working-class and poor adolescents who have dropped out of high school, in texts, in court, and in public policy debates. . . . My raced and classed translation grants authority to their "native" and "underarticulated" narratives. . . . The power of my translation comes far more from my whiteness, middle-class-ness, and education than from the stories I tell. (Fine, 1994, p. 80)

Reflecting on the authority of the privileged voice, Alcoff raises the question "if I don't speak for those less privileged than myself, am I abandoning my political responsibility to speak out against oppression, a responsibility incurred by the very fact of my privilege?" (p. 8). Similarly Caraway (1991) worries about the stance of some scholars who claim that no one may speak for Others. She problematizes assumptions hidden in standpoint epistemology that claim "that people act rationally in their own interest, that the oppressed are not in fundamental ways damaged by their marginality, and that they themselves are somehow removed from a will to power" (p. 181), and she argues the responsibility of White feminist researchers to engage in "crossover" conversations about race and racism.

Others, however, question both the assumptions underlying the "authority of the more privileged voice" argument as well as its effects. Alcoff (1991) for example, notes that

> The procurement of such authorization does not render null and void all attendant problems with speaking for others. One is still interpreting the other's situation and wishes (unless perhaps one simply reads a written text they have supplied), and so one is still creating for them a self in the presence of others. Moreover, the power to confer such authorization, and to have power over the designated representative, is rarely present in the instances where one is being spoken for. (pp. 10–11)

Furthermore, hooks resists the idea of being defined or represented by White researchers, pointing out that White researchers who study Blacks are often assumed "to know us better than we know ourselves" (p. 22). Similarly, Lorde (1984) warned Black women that if they do not define themselves that they will be defined by others—"for their use and to our detriment" (p. 432).

Considering (Irreconcilable?) Contradictions 53

Although continuously struggling with these issues, a number of feminist researchers believe that cross-group research can and should be performed. Consequently, they have searched for and developed methods and processes for confronting their respective inability to accurately understand and represent the experiences of others when undertaking cross-group research projects that they believe are important and meaningful. In the remainder of this section, I will discuss five approaches feminist researchers have taken to respond to critiques of cross-group research: reflexivity, collaboration, evaluation techniques, speaking with/through, and textual strategies. To provide a contributive discussion of each, however, I have used the work of some researchers who do not directly discuss their work in terms of cross-group feminist research.

Reflexivity

Reflexivity involves self-reflection on one's research process and findings, self-awareness of one's social positionality, values, and perspectives, and self-critique of the effects of one's words and actions on the individuals and groups being studied. Using reflexivity in one's research indicates a departure from traditional assumptions concerning researcher objectivity and the relationship between the researcher and the researched. For some researchers, reflexivity also indicates a departure from traditional notions regarding the nature of knowledge production. Lather (1991) asserts,

> While we cannot but be engulfed by the categories of our times, self-reflexivity teaches that our disclosure is the meaning of our longing. . . . How we speak and write tells us more about our own inscribed selves, about the way that language writes us, than about the "object" of our gaze. The trick is to see the will to power in our work as clearly as we see the will to truth. (p. 119)

Thus, reflexivity provides researchers an opportunity to connect their research (i.e., how they are doing it, why they are doing it, and what they are finding) with their values, commitments, and theoretical frameworks. It also provides an opportunity to examine the dynamics that are occurring between the researcher and the researched and to explore how these dynamics are effecting the research project and participants (including the researcher).

Researchers who value reflexivity[9] have developed strategies for including it in their research designs and practice. Lather's (1991) reflexivity, for example, involves developing research designs that allow researchers to reflect on "how our value commitments insert themselves into our empirical work" (p. 80). Smith's (1993) reflexive strategies, which she refers to as critical examination, include the following activities: reflecting self-consciously on institutional racism and the way it shapes one's research; questioning how one's privileged position shapes the research experience; questioning the assumption that the knower is the ultimate authority on the lives whom she or he studies; taking multiple views of our research subjects; and acknowledging our limitations. Like Smith, Laible's (1995) reflexive strategies also involved self-interrogation. Foremost, she questioned her relationship with the Mexican American teachers, administrators, and girls with whom she was working, and she considered the impossibility of fully knowing the experiences of her participants. She argued that her self-reflexive strategies kept her "honest" and "ever mindful of the effects of my actions and words upon those persons I study" (pp. 6 & 7).

In my own work, I have used Alcoff's set of four interrogatory practices to aid my reflexivity. Alcoff (1991), argues that anyone who studies or speaks for others should only do so after an analysis of the power relations and discursive effects involved. First, we must ask ourselves why we wish to study or speak for another. Second, we must ask how our location and context affect what we end up seeing and saying. Third, we must analyze the probable or actual effects of what we present on the discursive and material context, particularly in terms of those we have studied. Finally, we must ensure that we remain accountable for the findings we ultimately share. Similarly, Anderson (1993) asserts that researchers doing cross-group research "can develop and utilize tensions in their own cultural identities to enable them to see different aspects of minority group experiences and to examine critically majority experiences and beliefs" (p. 42).

The problematics of cross-group feminist research, it is argued, may increase when researchers fail to use sufficient reflexivity. For example, in studies with small groups of participants, lack of reflexivity may leave factors such as race and class underthematized (Cannon, Higginbotham, & Leung, 1991). Lack of reflexivity may also lead one to fail to take into account other hidden structures and relations of oppression, particularly those involved in the research process.

Regardless of ones' reflective activities, however, there will still be instances in which understanding is incomplete, absent, or affected. Laible (this volume), for example, wrote:

> Well, I collected good data, I thought; the girls seemed to open up to me, and I was able to write up my findings in a way that

added to the literature. It was at my defense, however, that a committee member, Dr. Lonnie Wagstaff, asked me, "Julie, what is success for these girls (e.g., the Mexican-American girls in my study)? Whose definition of success are you using when you discuss best educational practices that lead to their success in schools?" I was taken aback and eventually responded, "I suppose that it is my definition of success and, perhaps, of some of the Mexican-American educators in those schools who have been successful based upon middle-class, Euro-American standards." Thus, despite my Chicano peer debriefers and reflexive research journaling, I had conducted the study using a Euro-American, middle-class definition of success. My epistemology was racially-biased. (p. 9)

Gebhardt (1982) explains that such occurrences are inevitable. He asserts that our entire research project, from what data we collect to what findings we develop are affected by why we wanted to collect the data. "If we collect them [data] under the hypothesis that a different reality is possible, we will focus on the changeable, marginal, deviant aspects—anything not integrated which might suggest fermentation, resistance, protest, alternatives—all the 'facts' unfit to fit" (p. 405).

Collaboration

Feminist researchers, particularly those concerned with cross-group research, reject the contention that objectivity, detachment, and neutrality should guide social science research. Ladner (1987), for example, asks "why should anyone think it good to be 'objective' (indifferent, disinterested, dispassionate, value neutral)" (p. 74). Oakley (1981) similarly argued that it is impossible to demarcate one's role as an observer from one's role as a human being. She describes her research approach as "interactive . . . a collaborative approach to the research which engages both the interviewer and respondent in a joint enterprise" (p. 44). As a woman and a mother, Oakley suggested it would be unconscionable for her not to work closely with, take a personal interest in, and even form relationships with some of her research participants as they explored issues of motherhood together. Indeed, Oakley argued that

when a feminist interviews women . . . it becomes clear that, in most cases, the goal of finding out about people through interviewing is best achieved when the relationship of interviewer and interviewee is non-hierarchical and when the interviewer is prepared to invest his or her own personal identity in the relationship. (p. 41)

As the work of Ladner and Oakley suggests, the pendulum in qualitative feminist research has been swinging toward a redefinition of relationships with the researched that stresses relationships of collaboration, and in some cases "friendship, equal footing and reciprocity" (Wolf, 1996, p. 19). Developing egalitarian relationships and friendships during the research process is an important goal for many feminist researchers. It is believed that such relationships will not only increase the participants' willingness to share but may reduce the exploitative nature of research. Practices such as answering informants' questions or providing information about oneself are common.

Although feminist qualitative researchers differ in the extent to which participants are involved in the inquiry process, many have argued the importance of collaborating with the individuals they are interested in knowing about or from. Collaborative research can dynamically alter the roles of people involved in research to achieve (it is hoped) a more egalitarian and responsive relationship, one that will lead to deeper and clearer understanding[10] (Reinharz, 1992). Reason (1994) describes collaborative research as "an emerging worldview, more holistic, pluralistic, and egalitarian, that is essentially participative. . . . This worldview sees human beings as cocreating their reality through participation" (p. 324). The difficulties involved in cross-group feminist research may differ for researchers depending on the amount and type of collaboration that occurs within the research process as well as on the amount of time spent with research participants and the roles they play or are perceived to play with their informants.

For some, collaborative research is seen as an avenue for contributing to the social and political struggles of oppressed groups (e.g., women, people of color, the working poor, the disabled). Because collaborative research is often local and because subjects may participate in defining the research topic, there is greater possibility that the results will be useful for those involved. Feminists, who are concerned with issues of exploitation and inclusion, may engage their participants both as co-researchers, sharing discourse, reflection, and idea generation about a collective project, and as co-subjects, participating in the issues or phenomena being studied. They might also involve their participants in making sense of the data. For example, Laible (1995) worked to develop "meaningful relationships" with her participants who were racially, culturally, and economically different from herself through a loving form of dialogue (p. 7). She quotes Freire (1972) as writing "Dialogue cannot exist . . . in the absence of a profound love for the world and for [human beings]" (p. 62). This form of dialogue

Considering (Irreconcilable?) Contradictions 57

required a sense of humility, respect, and faith. It also required that Laible reflect on how the girls, teachers, and administrators in her study influenced her and her writing as much as she influenced them and their responses to her.

Dialogue is a key ingredient in collaborative work. Here, the researcher and participants together explore a phenomenon and through dialogue generate a process of reflection and understanding. With regard to cross-group research, Alcoff (1991) argues that researchers "should strive to create wherever possible the conditions for dialogue and the practice of speaking with" (p. 23). Similarly, Fine (1994) asserts that given the risk for "imperial translation" researchers need "communities of friendly critical informants" that they can turn to for help in thinking through which voices and analyses to front and which ones to background (p. 80).

Like self-reflexivity, Laible (1995) argued, collaboration strives to blur the self/other or subject/object divisions that have been the legacy of traditional social science research. In traditional research, an important distinction is argued to exist between the researcher and his or her participants, securing privilege and distance. In collaborative research however, this distinction is blurred. The Self and Other are seen in more relational terms, and attention is given to what exists or is possible between the Self–Other binary.

Some feminist researchers who conduct collaborative research argue that certain likenesses between themselves and their research participants support the blurring of the Self–Other binary and enhance the collaborative process, providing a means for identification and better understanding (Collins, 1990; Millman, 1986). "Where both share the same gender socialization and critical life-experiences, social distance can be minimal" (Oakley, 1981, p. 55). However, others have cautioned that these links or likenesses are temporal and do not provide researchers with epistemological privilege (Sawicki, 1994).

Although many see collaboration and relationship building as important strategies for lessening the problems of cross-group feminist research, others believe that practices such as these are exploitative and can create fraudulent relationships—where participants are initially given the impressions of true friendships but later find that their relationship with the researcher was based on convenience. Furthermore, Reinharz (1992) explains that feminists should not confuse the use of empathy or the desire for equity with the need to build friendships and relationships. Finally, it is important to remember that merely working with rather than objectifying research participants does not make us immune to our socialization as researchers. "Unconsciously, we impose our stereotypes and ways of knowing upon those of different races, classes, genders, and cultures that we study—even as we attempt to collaborate with them" (Laible, 1995,

Evaluation Strategies

p. 13). There is little doubt of the need for researchers to continuously rethink and reflect on the relationships between themselves, their research participants, and their practice.

Evaluation Strategies

The factors involved in cross-group research and representing the Other call into question traditional criteria for evaluating and interpreting qualitative research (e.g., objectivity, validity, and reliability) (Denzin & Lincoln, 1994; Fonow & Cook, 1991; Smith, 1992). Concern with objectivity or bias, for example, is misplaced with qualitative feminist research because what a logicopositivist would consider a bias, a qualitative feminist researcher would see as a resource (Olesen, 1994). A self-reflexive understanding of one's identity is a necessary part of understanding the impact of one's presence and perspective on the research. Indeed, many feminists would argue that objectivity, as traditionally conceptualized, would decrease rather than increase the credibility of a study. It is how the biases are used (i.e., reflexively used) that is of concern for many qualitative feminist researchers. "What is required . . . is sufficient reflexivity to uncover what may be deep-seated but poorly recognized views on issues central to the research and a full account of the researcher's views, thinking, and conduct" (Olesen, 1994, p. 165). Thus "sufficient reflexivity" constitutes both a strategy for reducing the problematics of cross-group research and a factor to consider when evaluating cross-group feminist research.

Sufficient reflexivity is similar to what Reason calls "critical subjectivity" (p. 327), a state of consciousness that draws self-reflexive attention to ourselves and our understandings. It requires that our primary subjective experience be acknowledged and that we understand and accept that how and what we know is dependent on a particular epistemological perspective. It also requires sharing our understanding of how and what we know in our communication with others. Reason provides a set of guidelines to facilitate a researcher's ability to monitor their often unintentional projection of their subjective understanding onto the context and people they are studying.

> These include cycling and recycling between action and reflection so that issues are examined several times in different ways, exploring the authenticity of participation within the group, using self-development methods to look at the impact of unacknowledged anxiety, and establishing norms whereby group members can challenge unwarranted assumptions. (Reason, 1994, p. 327)

Considering (Irreconcilable?) Contradictions

A strategy that is similar to sufficient reflexivity and critical subjectivity is dialogue. As mentioned previously, dialogue is a key component of collaboration. It can also be used as an evaluation tool. For example, we can cross-check our work through member checks. Member checks typically involve sharing one's data, findings, or written reports with one's participants. It is hoped that the feedback gained from participants will increase the validity of the written report. Olesen (1994) notes, however, that although member checks have "been widely discussed, along with cautions about its use, it has not been used as often as perhaps one might expect in feminist research" (p. 166). Indeed, scholars who have used and written about this strategy seem torn between their wish to speak truth to their participants' experiences and the unenthusiastic and even hostile reactions their participants have had (Wolf, 1996).

Other researchers, including myself, frequently involve colleagues in reading field notes, interview transcripts, and interpretations. Although these collaborative efforts are often informal and used as needed, communities of research associates or like-minded scholars can also be involved in an ongoing dialogue that scholar members find mutually beneficial. Piantanida and Garmen (1999), for example, describe such a group and the group's ongoing process of discursive deliberation. Although it could be argued that participation in the research would provide for "better" (i.e., more informed) discussions and feedback, it is not a necessary condition.

Another way in which scholars have approached issues of evaluation is the creation of new criteria for adequacy within qualitative studies. Such efforts include ensuring that findings are contextually embedded, the researcher takes responsibility for the research process and its results, participants' voices are heard, and roles of researcher and participant are explicated. New forms of validity have also been proposed. Lather (1993), for example, developed four types of validity that she feels more accurately approach validity needs in qualitative research: catalytic validity, voluptuous validity, simulacra/ironic validity, and situated validity. Richardson (1994) discusses validity in another way. Using the metaphor of a crystal, "which combines symmetry and substance with an infinite variety of shapes, substances, transmutations, multidimensionalities, and angles of approach" (p. 522), Richardson argues, is more useful than using the metaphor of a triangle (as in triangulation) because what we see depends on how we look at it. Our perspectives, like facets, create different images each as valuable as the other. This differs from traditional views on validity (and triangulation) in which only one image is validated. It also makes the issue of validity more complicated and emphasizes the postmodern "doubt that any discourse has a privileged place, and method or theory a universal and general claim to authoritative knowledge" (Richardson, 1994, p. 173).

60 *Michelle D. Young*

A third type of equity that has recently been proposed is equity validity. In a discussion of the racial bias embedded in the dominant research epistemologies, Scheurich and Young (1998) argued:

> Given the deep and pervasive racism in the U.S. society and the historical record of incorporation of that racism into research and research processes, education research, in an effort to be perennially vigilant about destructive racial biases (in an effort to avoid validity threats, you might say), ought to have long ago developed a kind of validity that could be called *race-equity validity* as a common research practice applicable to social science research. (p. 29; emphasis in original)

Like other validity criteria, equity validity could be used to evaluate whether or not we can rely on the research findings and all aspects of the research to be free of racial, gendered, heterosexual, and classed biases.

A final technique for evaluating cross-group research to be discussed here is "traveling" (Laible, this volume). Traveling is different from immersion where the researcher changes his or her location but not necessarily her- or himself. As Laible describes it, traveling involves becoming an outsider-within. It

> is a way of identifying with them [the Other] because by traveling to their "worlds" we can understand what it is to be them and *what it is to be ourselves in their eyes!* Only when we have traveled in each other's worlds are we fully subjects to each other. (p. 190)

Although identifying with and attempting to see and understand as the Other sees and understand may not provide an absolute change in the situatedness of one's knowledge, it may provide for deeper understanding and create more sensitive, relevant, and contextually embedded results.

Speaking With/Through

"Deeply implicated in the very foundations of feminist research lies the question of voice" (Olesen, 1994, p. 167). As noted before, the location of both the speaker and the hearer may affect what is heard and how it is understood. In many situations when individuals from less privileged groups speak, the presumption is against them; however, when a person from a privileged group speaks, the person is typically taken seriously (Alcoff, 1991; Scheurich & Young, 1997). This understanding has com-

Considering (Irreconcilable?) Contradictions 61

pelled a number of authors who are committed to antiracist, antisexist, anti-classist, and emancipatory, critical social science to continue their cross-group research. Many of these same researchers, however, are not conducting their research unaware of the ethical and political problems involved in cross-group research and speaking for others. Rather, they are seeking ways of speaking and creating texts that legitimize the voices of the typically less-privileged individuals with whom they work.

Working from the notion that "how what is said gets heard depends on who says it, and who says it will affect the style and language in which it is stated, which will in turn affect its perceived significance" (Alcoff, 1991, p. 13), Fine (1994) argues for speaking through our participants and writing against Othering. She argues that qualitative researchers must listen to our participants as primary informants on Othering rather than as Others who we aim to adequately describe. She uses the work of Crenshaw (1992), Austin (1989), Rollins (1985), Miller (1976), and Matsuda (1993) as examples of how this might be done. These scholars, Fine argues, are committed to interrupting Othering in their texts and to allowing the reader "to hear the uppity voices of informants and researchers who speak against structures, representations, and practices of domination" (p. 78).

> Sometimes explicitly trading on race/class privilege, in these instances researchers understand the hyphen all too well. Bartering privilege for justice, we re-present stories told by subjugated others, stories that would otherwise be discarded. And we get a hearing. (Fine, 1994, p. 79)

These re-presented stories may be seen as more legitimate, less biased, and sufficiently distanced though they are at the same time "draped in white colonizing science" (Fine, 1994, p. 80) and a "discursive imperialism" (Alcoff, 1991, p. 17).

Lather (1991), however, questions the notion of speaking with or through the Other, noting that in such work "Enlightenment goals are unproblematized, especially the excessive faith in the powers of the reasoning mind. Subjects are theorized as unified and capable of full consciousness" (p. 84). Countering arguments like Lather's, Spivak (1988) argues that such critiques essentialize the oppressed as nonideologically constructed subjects and conceal the authorizing power of retreating intellectuals, who in their retreat consolidate a particular conception of experience.

Alcoff's (1991) work presents a different critique of Fine's argument. She is less certain that there is a tenable difference between speaking for, about, or through the Other.

> When one is speaking for others one may be describing their situation and thus also speaking about them. In fact, it may be impossible to speak for others without simultaneously conferring information about them. Similarly, when one is speaking about others, or simply trying to describe their situation or some aspect of it, one may also be speaking in place of them, that is, speaking for them. (Alcoff, 1991, p. 9)

Moreover, Alcoff (1991) does not see all instances of speaking for as altogether adverse. Arguing that a total retreat from speaking for others will not encourage effective listening, she indicates that in some instances "speaking for" others may be politically efficacious. However, she cautions that when doing so, one must not be "naive or unaware of the dangers and difficulties of speaking for others" (p. 19).

The act of speaking for, about, or through one's research participants also has at its very core a need to address accountability and responsibility (Alcoff, 1991)—accountability and responsibility to those for or through whom one speaks and about which one speaks. Part of accountability and responsibility resides in intent. What is the intent of doing cross-group research? Is the research for the individuals or groups under study? Why does the researcher feel it is important that she or he engages in cross-group research? As hooks (1990) stated, "it is not just important what we speak, but how and why we speak" (p. 151).

Fine (1994) addresses the issue of how and why by arguing that we should "engage in social struggles with those who have been exploited and subjugated" (p. 72).[11] She refers to this form of engagement as working the hyphens between the self and other. Here the researchers

> probe how we are in relation with the contexts we study and with our informants, understanding that we are all multiple in those relations. I mean to invite researchers to see how these "relations between" get us "better" data, limit what we feel free to say, expand our minds and constrict our mouths, engage us in intimacy and seduce us into complicity, make us quick to interpret and hesitant to write. (p. 72)

Other researchers (e.g., Behar, 1993) have included within their texts discussions of the how and why, thereby laying the intent and development of their research before the eyes and judgment of the reader.

Another aspect of responsibility is reflected in the work of Collins (1990). Collins, in defining the contours of her Afrocentric Feminist Epistemology, includes as the final dimension an ethic of personal accountability. She argues, "Not only must individuals develop their knowledge claims through dialogue and present them in a style proving their concern for their ideas, but people are expected to be accountable for their knowledge claims" (pp. 217–218). This involves two related understandings. First, in opposition to traditional beliefs that one can separate oneself from one's core beliefs, Collins considers it important for researchers to explore and understand their core beliefs as well as the relationship between their beliefs and their knowledge claims. Second, researchers must hold themselves accountable for their knowledge claims and the results of their knowledge claims. This is similar to Alcoff's understanding of responsibility.

> In order to evaluate attempts to speak for others in particular instances, we need to analyze the probable or actual effects of the words on the discursive and material context. One cannot simply look at the location of the speaker or her credentials to speak, nor can one look merely at the propositional content of the speech; one must also look at where the speech goes and what it does there. (Alcoff, 1991, p. 26)

The context within which the speaking occurs is also important to consider. It is composed of a diversity of individuals and groups motivated by various ideals and interests who pursue various goals through different strategies, thus the group or individuals being represented are rarely homogenous. I find this to be true in much of my research. The homeless mothers with whom I worked may have had similar experiences while in the homeless shelter where I worked with them, but their strategies and goals regarding what they needed to do next differed. There was no one best way for them to support their families or fight their way out of homelessness. One mother's strategy, for example, involved divorcing her husband whose financial problems she believed had pushed them into the streets, gaining marketable job skills, and starting over with her daughter. Another's strategy was limited primarily to keeping herself and her three children hidden from her abusive husband. A third mother's strategy involved convincing a relative to let her and her children stay with them while she developed a plan for making it on her own. This diversity of interests, concerns, and strategies made it difficult to develop a list of best practices for helping homeless mothers and their families move off the streets and out of shelters.

Some form of representation occurs in all cases of speaking, whether it is for or through or about, even when one does not explicitly claim to speak for or through. The author of the text is still interpreting the Other's situation and wishes, and "creating for them a self in the presence of others. ... When we sit down to write, or get up to speak, we experience ourselves as making choices" (Alcoff, 1991, p. 10). Thus, the original speaker loses some of her or his control over the meaning of her or his utterances, regardless of the researcher's intent. Spivak (1988), consequently, advocates a "speaking to" rather than through or for. In this case, the researcher neither presumes an authentic representation of the oppressed nor abnegates her or his role. Rather, the researcher "allows for the possibility that the oppressed will produce a 'countersentence' that can then suggest a new historical narrative" (Alcoff, 1991, p. 23).

Textual Strategies

The written account, which is intimately linked to the question of voice, has also been examined as a potential tool for lessening the problems of cross-group feminist research. Indeed, in the hands of many qualitative researchers, textual strategies no longer serve merely aesthetic or methodological purposes, but have ethical and political implications as well (Atkinson & Hammersley, 1994). New textual styles, which include writing against Othering, centering or decentering the author, inscribing the author into a telling that simultaneously provides multiple voices, and textually providing multiple versions of a story, have been discussed as potential means for addressing the dilemmas of cross-group research.

Writing against Othering

One form of textual distortion, discussed previously, is Othering. As argued previously, Othering occurs quite frequently in social science texts, particularly when those we are studying are different from ourselves in important sociopolitical or cultural ways. In an effort to explore how we might interrupt the process of Othering, Fine (1994) proposed that "When we construct texts collaboratively, self-consciously examining our relations with/for/despite those who have been contained as Others, we move against, we enable resistance to, Othering" (p. 74). She argues that by self-consciously working the hyphen between Self and Other, researchers will be better situated to dissect the boundaries of their relationships with their participants, to understand the politics involved in their work and to seek ways of resisting or interrupting Othering. In her discussion on working the hyphen, Fine presents three examples of how researchers have written about Othering: "Rupturing Texts With Uppity Voices" (p. 75), "Probing the Consciousness of Dominant Others" (p. 78), and "Social Research for Social Change" (p. 79).

One example of the first strategy, rupturing texts with uppity voices, is provided by Matsuda (1993) who re-creates conceptualizations of law from the perspective of the Other. She writes "the desire to know history from the bottom has forced . . . scholars to sources often ignored, journals, poems, oral histories, and stories from their own experiences of life in a hierarchically arranged world" (p. 11). Thus, the voice and perspective of traditionally Otherized voices are positioned instead as key informants. Lewis and Ketter (1999) provide an example of the second of Fine's strategies. Their work, instead of focusing on racialized others, explores how White senior high students in the Midwest make sense of their Whiteness (i.e., studying up). The third category which involves "interrupting Othering by forcing subjugated voices in context to the front of our texts and by exploiting privileged voices to scrutinize the technologies of Othering," is a strategy I have used in my work (Fine, 1994, p. 79). For example, my work with Eddie Moore Jr., an African American doctoral student and diversity trainer, seeks to center the experiences and voices of racially isolated African American adolescents in predominantly White Midwestern public schools (Young & Moore, 1999). Here our translations of the students' perspectives on their schooling experiences are supported by our educations, professional experiences, social statuses, and my Whiteness. Public educators and policymakers are, as was argued previously, much more likely to listen and hear credentialed academics than the students themselves. The possibility for resisting Othering through any of these three writing strategies as well as for having more helpful than harmful results, depends, at least in part, on a self-conscious understanding of the politics involved in research and representation. Even with such an awareness and good intentions, however, there are no guarantees.

> Herein lie the very profound contradictions that face researchers who step out, who presume to want to make a difference, who are so bold or arrogant as to assume we might. Once out beyond the picket fence of illusory objectivity, we trespass all over the classed, raced, and otherwise stratified lines that have demarcated our social legitimacy for publicly telling their [the Others'] stories. And it is then that ethical questions boil. (Fine, 1994, p. 80)

Centering/Decentering the Author

Over the last decade we have seen an infusion of first-person narratives in articles and books. Researchers, some who are retreating from misrepresenting their research participants, have begun representing themselves from inside the research situation. "We become actors in our own dramas rather than a disengaged director of a play" (Tierney, 1995,

p. 382). Attempting to avoid Othering, Shostak (1981), for example, provided a verbatim account of her discussion with Nisa, her key informant. Behar (1993) took a different approach. That her participant, Esperanza, was part of the Indian and non-Indian world in Mexican society led Behar to believe the telling of Esperanza's story needed to be in a novelistic, episodic narrative style. Behar explained this style blurred the boundary between fiction and nonfiction but allowed Esperanza's story to be better told because emphasis was placed on her own words, inflections, and the order in which she said them. Stoller, recognizing the difficulty of representing the story of the Songhay community he studied, changed the focus and format of his text (Stoller & Oakes, 1987). In the form of a memoir, Stoller became the central character of his research experience concerning the world of Songhay sorcery. Similarly, Ellis and Bochner (1992) and Kreiger (1991), among others, have included personal stories (sometimes called narratives of the self) among their writing strategies.

In contrast, other researchers have determined that decentering the author, where monologue is replaced with dialogue, allows for multiple voices to be heard. Kreiger (1983) for example, created a text in which her participants' voices are presented as a polyphonic chorus. Kreiger's own voice, however, was not included. Other examples of multi-voiced texts include Butler and Rosenblum (1991) and Schneider (1991) as well as Dwyer's (1982) self-conscious use of a dialogic textual format. Similarly, Lather (1991) notes, "In my own writing, the accumulation of quotes, excerpts and repetitions is also an effort to be 'multi-voiced,' to weave varied speaking voices together as opposed to putting forth a singular 'authoritative' voice" (p. 9). According to Tyler (1986), the postmodern researchers' use of dialogue seeks to dissolve the disjuncture between the observer and observed and distance and familiarity and to front the collaborative nature of research.

Somewhere between centering and decentering the author, one can also find accounts written by both the researcher(s) and their participant(s). These accounts (e.g., Light & Kleiber, 1981; Shostak, 1981), which are fairly uncommon, tend to reflect many voices and seek to textually demonstrate the collective nature of the data collection, analysis, and writing. They may be uncommon because writing together can be difficult and, at times, politically dangerous. "Due to the geographical inaccessibility of some groups, problems with mail delivery, potential risks in mailing such a text, and the problem of illiteracy, the sharing can often only be done in person" (Wolf, 1996, p. 33). In the end, the research and the written publication may ultimately benefit the researcher more than the researched. Still, the practice of coauthorship may lessen the exploitative nature of cross-group research.

Considering (Irreconcilable?) Contradictions — 67

Textual Multiplicity

In an effort to present voice more reflexively and/or with more complexity, some researchers have advocated for or used writing strategies that involve multiple subtexts or genres within a single text. According to Richardson (1994), when using textual multiplicity

> The scholar draws freely in his or her productions from literary, artistic, and scientific genres, often breaking the boundaries of each of those as well. In these productions, the scholar might have different "takes" on the same topic, what I think of as a postmodernist deconstruction of triangulation. (p. 522)

Marjorie Wolf (1992), for example, included three versions of an event that occurred during her field work in Taiwan in a single book: a piece of fiction, an excerpt from her field notes, and a traditional social science article. Accuracy of representation was not the issue here. Through these multiple texts, she was able to represent herself, her participants, and the research context and events in a complex and perhaps more honest manner.

During a presentation at the University of Texas, Lather (1994) discussed the use of multiple texts. She described a method of presenting her work on women who are HIV positive in three ways: the participant's direct quotations, her interpretation of the research, and the participant's reaction to her interpretations. Each of these subtexts would appear within the same text, either in succession (like that of Margery Wolf) or perhaps all three on the same page. She explained that these textual strategies would provide the reader with multiple choices for reading, interpreting, and understanding.

It was ideas like those of Richardson (1994), Wolf (1992), and Lather (1994) that spurred me to develop and use a similar strategy in my work with Mexican American mothers (Young, 1999). Akin to what Wolcott (1994) describes as the "Rashomon Effect" (p. 21),[12] I conducted a two-staged research project that involved the use of two theoretical frames to investigate the same phenomena. The findings of each stage were written separately and later discussed in common. This strategy, I believe, provides not only multiple reading possibilities but also emphasizes the constructed nature of research findings and renderings.

Experimental Writing

Richardson (1994) presents a number of experimental writing strategies that scholars who undertake cross-group research may find helpful. Fictional and poetic representations are included among her suggestions. Richardson (1992) herself has used poetry to present the findings of her research. She argues that poems are not only closer to human speech than

68 *Michelle D. Young*

prose, but that poetry also emphasizes the constructed nature of research texts. She asserts, "When we read or hear poetry, we are continually nudged into recognizing that the text has been constructed. But all texts are constructed—prose ones, too; therefore, poetry helps problematize reliability, validity, and 'truth'" (p. 522).

Clough (1992), however, criticizes scholars who view new forms of writing as a way to address the crisis of representation because she sees no true line of demarcation between the research and writing processes. Rather, she sees the field-workers' texts developing from the field experience. She argues that

> While many sociologists now commenting on the criticism of ethnography view writing "as downright central to the ethnographic enterprise" (Van Maanen, 1988, p. xi), the problems of writing are still viewed as different for the problems of method or fieldwork itself. Thus the solution usually offered is experiments in writing, that is, a self-consciousness about writing. It is only when writing is seen to provide the mechanisms of scientific conception itself . . . that it becomes clearer that it is this insistence on the difference of writing and field methods that must be deconstructed if the general function of ethnography is to be analyzed as well as the relationship of social science and mass media communication technologies. (p. 136)

By creating a written text from one's research findings, regardless of form, one is making a claim to moral and scientific authority. One is making the claim that the world of the researched can still be represented, if only in the form of a poem, a fictional account, or a multi-voiced text.

CRITICAL CONSIDERATIONS

> *No longer can social science hide behind the ivy-covered walls of academia and their research laboratories assuming they can study whomever they want to, whenever they please* [italics added]. (Stanfield, 1993b, p. 33)

I have endeavored here to sketch an overview of the problems and potential contradictions involved in cross-group feminist research that researchers should consider in pondering the ethical, political, and methodological implications of their research as well as the suggestions that have been put forth for addressing these problems and contradictions. The context within which we currently work is a propitious one, providing an opportunity for us to review, critique, and rethink our research and representational practices. The arguments of the scholars cited challenge feminist qualitative researchers to rethink assumptions, research methods, issues of diversity and identity, relationships, analytical strategies, and modes of representation and writing, and they make clear that decisions to engage in or retreat from cross-group research are entangled in both problematic ethical and political dilemmas.

Not all of the scholars previously cited are involved in cross-group feminist research; however, their research practices provide possibilities for producing less problematic cross-group feminist research. We can, through reflexivity, collaboration, and certain writing and evaluation strategies, create less problematic and perhaps more helpful representations of our research findings and participants.[13] Regardless, the issues researchers face when conducting cross-group research will undoubtedly be constituted by ambiguity.

Ambiguity, however, may breed creativity and innovation. "We are in a new age where messy, uncertain, multivoiced texts, cultural criticism, and new experimental works will become more common as will more reflexive forms of fieldwork, analysis, and intertextual representation" (Denzin & Lincoln, 1994, p. 15). "The greater freedom to experiment with textual form, however, does not guarantee a better product" (Richardson, 1994, p. 523). Researchers must also review, critique, and renew reflexive practices, collaborative approaches to their research, attempts to speak with/through their participants, and evaluation techniques.

Unfortunately, these practices can be risky undertakings in the academy today (Olesen, 1994; Richardson, 1994; Tierney, 1995). At present, few dissertation or tenure and promotion committees value collaborative research or experimental texts. During a recent discussion of the content and format of qualitative dissertations, a colleague of mine (with tenure and substantially more institutional power than I or the students with whom we were talking) facilely dismissed the importance of attempts to create more reflexive texts. Furthermore, few journals (*Qualitative Studies in Education* [QSE] is an important exception) are willing to publish work that utilize nontraditional presentation formats (e.g., multiple or split texts).[14] Richardson (1994) writes:

> One thing for us to think about is whether writing experimentally for publication is a luxury open only to those who have academic sinecure. Can/should only the already tenured write in experimental modes? Are the tenured doing a disservice to students by introducing them to alternative forms of writing? Will teaching them hereticisms "deskill" them? Alienate them

70 *Michelle D. Young*

from their discipline? These are heady ethical, pedagogical, and practical questions. (p. 523)

It is important to remember, however, that regardless of textual style or research approach, one must critically consider the results of researchers who cannot place themselves "in the same class, race, culture, and gender-sensitive critical plane as [their] subjects of study" (Harding, 1987, p. 11). Although all research involves crossings, this fact should not discount the difficulties involved in researching across difference(s) (e.g., representation, power imbalances, writing conventions, and counterproductivity).

The potential difficulties involved in cross-group feminist research, though, are not the only issues to be grappled with here. Although it has been established (at least within some discourse communities) that researchers simply cannot assume to speak with authority on the perceptions of the researched, it has also been argued that multiple perspectives produce more representative accounts of society. For some, these understandings recast the question of whether feminists should engage in cross-group research to how one might conduct such research in a non- or less-exploitative manner and reemphasize the question raised by hooks (1989) of whose interpretation should be taken as most authoritative.

I would like to speculate about how the strategies presented in this chapter might come together in a research effort to study across difference. Imagine a feminist scholar concerned with changing the representation of a certain group of women in the superintendency. Recognizing that all research involves crossings, this scholar might begin her project with self-reflexive work, examining various aspects of her identity, belief systems, and perspectives. This reflexivity would continue throughout the research process, expanding to include the researcher's interactions with and understandings of her participants. Before actually beginning the research with her participants, this scholar might meet with them and together attempt to define their common areas of commitment and interests. They would move through cycles of dialogue, reflection, and planning. As she was involved in this cyclical process the scholar would consider the role and impact of each participant's (her own included) social positions and identifications with particular social groups on the development of relationships, the data gathered, and the research process in general.

Part of planning and dialogue would include designing the research project, determining the roles participants would play, and identifying strategies for evaluating the research findings. Furthermore, given the collaborative nature of the research project, the group could infuse some forms of evaluation strategies throughout the research process. For example, as data is collected, discussed, analyzed, and interpreted, group members could apply an equity validity criterion to ensure the group's awareness and avoidance of developing misrepresentations or essentializations.

As the group moved closer to developing representations of the research findings, discussions might then shift to strategies for writing and representation. At this point, the group would be faced with, among other things, questions of sharing authorship, speaking with/through, and targeting certain audiences with certain messages. Multiple decisions, of course, might be made. For example, the group might decide that a particular piece of the research should be written in one way for one audience while a more comprehensive overview of the findings should be developed for a different audience. This is, of course, but one way researchers might make use of the five strategies discussed in this chapter. There are many other ways in which a researcher could use the strategies discussed in this piece and other strategies when undertaking cross-group feminist research.

In closing, let me be clear that my personal and professional commitment is to contribute to a more socially just society for the children and adults who learn and grow within it. I write this piece as an advocate of research that contributes to such a society; however, at times it is difficult to determine what forms of research and representations as well as what kinds of researchers might make such a contribution. I, like many others, continue to search for insights into the questions and issues addressed in this chapter. I hope that this piece will contribute to the important discussions going on today concerning cross-group research and how to develop strategies for more equitable and just research and representational practices. I recognize this chapter has provided no answers. Indeed, it appears that there are no easy or unproblematic solutions. Each individual researcher will have to come to her or his own conclusions.

NOTES

1. Some feminist scholars who hold that members of subordinated groups have unique viewpoints have developed standpoint theories. Feminist standpoint theory holds that only women can fully understand other women and that researchers and their informants are located in specific sociohistorical settings that set limits on understanding (Anderson, 1993; Wolf, 1996).

2. By privileged I am referring to one's social position. A privileged position is one that is more favorable vis-à-vis the structures of power in a society. For example, in the United States the male position is more privileged than the female position, just as the wealthy are more privileged than the poor. It is important to note however that a particular person may have a privileged position with regard to some aspects of her or his identity and less privileged positions with regard to other aspects (e.g., a working-class White male). Thus, the nature of privilege may be relationship- and situation-specific.

3. There are, of course, researchers who are less concerned or unconcerned about issues of cross-group research. For example, those influenced by hermeneutics and other perspectives that emphasize drawing on the researchers' own experiences and cultural knowledge to reach understanding may not be as concerned about representational issues (Atkinson & Hammersley, 1994). Furthermore, Wolf (1996) notes that some feminists reject the "simplistic dichotomy of insider–outsider" (p. 16), and Tuana (1993) questions why we assume the perspectives of marginalized insiders are better rather than simply different.

4. Some researchers have expressed concern over what they consider the overemphasis on the "crisis of representation." Patai (1988), for example, wrote "The crisis in representation notwithstanding, babies still have to be cared for, shelter sought, meals prepared and eaten. People who stay up nights worrying about representation should consider what would happen if all the sewers in their city were stopped up, or if garbage collection ceased for three weeks. They should ask themselves whether the crisis in representation is a crisis in the same sense as the crisis in Bosnia" (p. 65).

5. It is interesting to note, in addition to the understanding that the beliefs and experiences of the researcher shape how the researcher sees the world and works within it, others have argued that research participants are rarely able to give full and accurate explanations of their actions or intentions (e.g., Denzin & Lincoln, 1994).

6. A power dynamic that is not discussed in this chapter is that of scientific paradigms. The experiences of the powerful have constructed the dominant social science paradigms in use today. See Stanfield, 1994, pp. 181–182, and Scheurich & Young, 1997.

7. Alcoff (1991) describes this practice as the "retreat" response, which she explains is motivated by the desire to recognize difference (p. 17). For a discussion of the problems related to the retreat response see Alcoff (1991), particularly pages 20–23.

8. Other researchers have argued that arguing for the termination of cross-group research is not only impossible because all research involves a crossing, but that it is also unhelpful (see, for example, Merton, 1972).

9. For more information on using reflexivity in research, see Lather (1991), particularly chapter 4 in which she discusses feminist efforts to create empowering research designs.

10. Researcher roles are best thought of as shifting along a dynamic continuum dependent to some degree on what a researcher does and what participants think about the researcher and what she or he does (or vice versa). For a comprehensive discussion of collaborative feminist research, see Wolf (1996).

11. In the past and to a lesser degree in the present, qualitative research has been directed toward contributing to disciplinary knowledge production rather than toward improving practice. The relationship between research and practice assumed by many in the field of education, however, tends to reflect a desire to carry out research that is specifically designed to address and contribute to practice. For some, like Fine (1994), this involves actively engaging in struggles with participants. For others, indeed for many, the engagement is less active.

12. Wolcott takes this name from a film produced in 1950 by Japanese director Akira Kurosawa. This film depicts a violent event as seen from the perspective

of four witnesses. Kurosawa effectively demonstrates the vast differences in seeing, experiencing, and interpreting that different people can have of a single event.

13. Wolf (1996) discusses a few other approaches feminists have used to lessen the problems involved in cross-group feminist research. These include reciprocity and action research among others.

14. Tierney (1995) points out, however, that "such hurdles are not insurmountable barriers, they are simply problems that we must recognize and work to change" (p. 386). He argues that the structure will eventually change and therefore we should clarify our concerns so that they will be taken into consideration. He makes similar arguments regarding the paper sessions of professional associations.

REFERENCES

Alcoff, L. (1991). The problem of speaking for others. *Cultural Critique 19*, 5–32.

Anderson, M. (1993). Studying across difference: Race, class and gender in qualitative research. In J. Stanfield & R. Dennis (Eds.), *Race and ethnicity in research methods* (pp. 39–52). Thousand Oaks, CA: Sage.

Anzaldua, G. (Ed.). (1990). *Making face, making soul/Creative and critical perspectives by feminists of color.* San Francisco: Aunt Lute Books.

Atkinson, P., & Hammersley, M. (1994). Ethnography and participant observation. In N. K. Denzin & Y. S. Lincoln (Eds.), *The handbook of qualitative research* (pp. 248–261). Newbury Park, CA: Sage.

Austin, R. (1989). Sapphire bound! *Wisconsin Law Review, 3*, 539–578.

Banks, J. A. (1993). The canon debate, knowledge construction, and multicultural education. *Educational Researcher, 22*(5), 4–14.

Barkan, E. (1992). *The retreat of scientific racism: Changing concepts of race in Britain and the United States.* Cambridge, UK: Cambridge University Press.

Behar, R. (1993). *Translated woman: Crossing the border with Esperanza's story.* Boston: Beacon.

Blauner, R., & Wellman, D. (1973). Toward the decolonization of social research. In J. Ladner (Ed.), *The death of white sociology* (pp. 310–330). New York: Vintage.

Butler, S., & Rosenblum, B. (1991). *Cancer in two voices.* San Francisco: Spinsters.

Cannon, L., Higginbotham, E., & Leung, M. (1991). Race and class bias in qualitative research on women. In M. M. Fonow & J. A. Cook (Eds.), *Beyond methodology: Feminist scholarship as lived research* (pp. 107–118). Bloomington: Indiana University Press.

Caraway, N. (1991). *Segregated sisterhood.* Knoxville: University of Tennessee Press.

Caulfield, M. (1984). Imperialism, the family and cultures of resistance. In A. Jagger & P. Rosenthal (Eds.), *Feminist frameworks* (pp. 374–379). New York: McGraw-Hill.

Chase, S. (1995). *Ambiguous empowerment: The work narratives of women school superintendents.* Amherst: University of Massachusetts Press.

74 *Michelle D. Young*

Chow, E. (1987). The development of feminist consciousness among Asian American women. *Gender & Society, 1*, 284–299.

Clifford, J., & Marcus, G. (Eds.). (1986). *Writing culture: The poetics and politics of ethnography*. Berkeley: University of California Press.

Clough, P. T. (1992). *The end(s) of ethnography: From realism to social criticism*. Newbury Park, CA: Sage.

Collins, P. H. (1990). *Black feminist thought: Knowledge, consciousness and the politics of empowerment*. New York: Routledge.

Connolly, P. (1998). Introduction. In P. Connolly & B. Troyna (Eds.), *Researching racism in education: Politics, theory and practice* (pp. 1–11). Philadelphia: Open University Press.

Connolly, P., & Troyna, B. (1998). *Researching racism in education: Politics, theory and practice* . Philadelphia: Open University Press.

Crenshaw, K. (1992). *Intersectionality of race and sex*. Unpublished manuscript.

Davis, A. Y. (1978). Rape, racism and the capitalist setting. *Black Scholar, 9*, 24–30.

Denzin, N. K., & Lincoln, Y. S. (1994). Introduction: Entering the field of qualitative research. In N. K. Denzin & Y. S. Lincoln (Eds.), *The handbook of qualitative research* (pp. 1–17). Newbury Park, CA: Sage.

Dill, B. (1979). The dialectics of black womanhood. *Signs, 4*, 543–555.

Dwyer, K. (1982). *Moroccan dialogues: Anthropology in question*. Baltimore: Johns Hopkins University Press.

Eisner, E. (1992). Objectivity in educational research. *Curriculum Inquiry, 22*, 9–15.

Ellis, C., & Bochner, A. (1992). Telling and performing personal stories. In C. Ellis & M. Flaherty (Eds.), *Investigating subjectivity: Research on lived experience* (pp. 79–101). Newbury Park, CA: Sage.

Fine, M. (1992). *Disruptive voices: The possibilities of feminist research*. Ann Arbor: University of Michigan Press.

Fine, M. (1994). Working the hyphens: Reinventing self and other in qualitative research. In N. K. Denzin & Y. S. Lincoln (Eds.), *The handbook of qualitative research* (pp. 70–82). Newbury Park, CA: Sage.

Flexner, E. (1975). *Century of struggle*. Cambridge, MA: Belknap.

Fonow, M. M., & Cook, J. A. (1991). Back to the future: A look at the second wave of feminist epistemology and methodology. In M. M. Fonow & J. A. Cook (Eds.), *Beyond methodology: Feminist scholarship as lived research* (pp. 1–15). Bloomington: Indiana University Press.

Freire, P. (1972). *Pedagogy of the oppressed*. New York: Continuum.

Gebhardt, E. (1982). Introduction to Part III: A critique of methodology. In A. Arato & E. Gebhardt (Eds.), *The essential Frankfurt School reader* (pp. 371–406). New York: Continuum.

Goldman, A. (1993). Is that what she said? The politics of collaborative autobiography. *Cultural Critique*, 177–204.

Gordon, E. W., Miller, F., & Rollock, D. (1990). Coping with communicentric bias in knowledge production in the social sciences. *Educational Researcher, 19*(3), 14–19.

Green, R. (1980). Native American women. *Signs, 6*, 248–267.

Group for Collaborative Inquiry. (1993). The democratization of knowledge. *The Adult Education Quarterly, 43*(4), 1–8.

Harding, S. (1987). Introduction: Is there a feminist method? In S. Harding (Ed.), *Feminism and methodology* (pp. 1–14). Bloomington: Indiana University Press.

Harding, S. (1991). *Whose science? Whose knowledge? Thinking from women's lives.* Ithaca, NY: Cornell University Press.

Herskovitz, M. (1967). *Dahomey*, vol. 2. Evanston, IL: Northwestern University Press.

hooks, b. (1984). *Feminist theory from margin to center.* Boston: South End.

hooks, b. (1989). *Talking back: Thinking feminist, thinking black.* Boston: South End.

hooks, b. (1990). The politics of radical black subjectivity. In b. hooks (Ed.), *Yearning: Race, gender, and cultural politics* (pp. 15–22). Boston: South End.

Hurtado, A. (1989). Relating to privilege: Seduction and rejection in the subordination of white women and women of color. *Signs, 14,* 833–855.

Kelly-Gadol, J. (1987). The social relation of the sexes: Methodological implications of women's history. In S. Harding (Ed.), *Feminism and methodology* (pp. 15–28). Bloomington: Indiana University Press.

Kreiger, S. (1983). *The mirror dance: Identity in a woman's community.* Philadelphia: Temple University Press.

Kreiger, S. (1991). *Social science and the self: Personal essays on an art form.* New Brunswick, NJ: Rutgers University Press.

Ladner, J. (1987). Tomorrow's tomorrow: The black woman. In S. Harding (Ed.), *Feminism and methodology* (pp. 74–83). Bloomington: Indiana University Press.

Laible, J. (1995, April). *Crossing borders: The use of self-reflexivity and collaboration by a Gringa as she speaks for others in Texas/Mexico border schools.* Paper presented at the annual meeting of the American Educational Research Association, San Francisco, CA.

Lather, P. (1991). *Getting smart: Feminist research and pedagogy with/in the postmodern.* New York: Routledge.

Lather, P. (1993). Fertile obsession: Validity after poststructuralism. *Sociological Quarterly, 34*(4), 673–693.

Lather, P. (1994, February). *A curriculum of angels: On (not) writing about the lives of women with HIV/AIDS.* Presentation conducted at the University of Texas, Austin.

Lesco, N. (1988). The curriculum of the body: Lessons from a Catholic high school. In L. Roman, L. Christian-Smith, & E. Ellsworth (Eds.), *Becoming feminine: The politics of popular culture* (pp. 123–142). Philadelphia: Falmer Press.

Lewis, C., & Ketter, J. (1999, April). *The construction of whiteness in readings of multicultural young adult literature.* Paper presented at the annual meeting of the American Educational Research Association, Montreal, Canada.

Light, L., & Kleiber, N. (1981). Interactive research in a feminist setting. In D. A. Messerschmidt (Ed.), *Anthropologists at home in North America: Methods and issues in the study of one's own society* (pp. 167–194). Cambridge, UK: Cambridge University Press.

Linden, R. (1993). *Making stories, making selves: Feminist reflections on the Holocaust.* Columbus: Ohio State University Press.

Lorde, A. (1984). Scratching the surface: Some notes on barriers to women and loving. In A. Jagger & P. Rosenthal (Eds.), *Feminist Frameworks* (pp. 432–436). New York: McGraw-Hill.

Matsuda, M. (1993). Public response to racist speech: Considering the victim's story. In M. Matsuda, C. Lawrence, R. Delgado, K. Crenshaug (Eds.), *Words that wound* (pp. 17–52). Boulder: Westview.

Mead, M. (1950). *Sex and temperament in three primitive societies.* New York: Mentor.

Merton, R. (1972). Insiders and outsiders: A chapter in the sociology of knowledge. *American Journal of Sociology, 78,* 44–47.

Middleton, S. (1984). On being a feminist educationist doing research on being a feminist educationist: Life history analysis as consciousness raising. *New Zealand Cultural Studies Working Group Journal, 8,* 29–37.

Miller, J. B. (1976). *Toward a new psychology of women.* Boston: Beacon.

Millman, M. (1986). *Such a pretty face: Being fat in America.* Berkeley, CA: Berkeley Publishing Co.

Mirza, M. (1998). Same voices, same lives? Revisiting black feminist standpoint epistemology. In P. Connolly & B. Troyna (Eds.), *Researching racism in education: Politics, theory and practice* (pp. 79–94). Philadelphia: Open University Press.

Mohanty, C. (1991). Cartographies of struggle: Third world women and the politics of feminism. In C. Mohanty, A. Russo, & L. Torres (Eds.), *Third world women and the politics of feminism* (pp. 1–47). Bloomington: Indiana University Press.

Moreno, R. (1999, April). *Predictors of parental involvement among Latina mothers and its relation to their children's school outcomes.* Paper presented at the annual meeting of the American Educational Research Association, Montreal, Canada.

Morrison, T. (1971, August). What the black woman thinks about women's lib. *New York Times Magazine,* 14–15, 63–64, 66.

Moss, Z. (1984). It hurts to be alive and obsolete: The aging woman. In A. Jagger & P. Rosenthal (Eds.), *Feminist frameworks* (pp. 66–69). New York: McGraw-Hill.

Oakley, A. (1981). Interviewing women. In H. Roberts (Ed.), *Doing feminist research* (pp. 30–61). New York: Routledge & Kegan Paul.

Olesen, V. (1994). Feminisms and models of qualitative research. In N. K. Denzin & Y. S. Lincoln (Eds.), *Handbook of qualitative research* (pp. 158–174). Thousand Oaks, CA: Sage.

Patai, D. (1988). Constructing self: A Brazilian life story. *Feminist Studies, 14*(1), 143–166.

Piantanida, M., & Garmen, N. (1999). *The qualitative dissertation.* Thousand Oaks, CA: Corwin Press.

Reason, P. (1994). Three approaches to participative inquiry. In N. K. Denzin & Y. S. Lincoln (Eds.), *Handbook of qualitative research* (pp. 324–339). Thousand Oaks, CA: Sage.

Rebolledo, D. (1990). The politics of poetics: Or, what am I, a critic doing in this text anyhow? In G. Anzaldua (Ed.), *Making face, making soul haciendo* caras: *Creative and critical perspectives by feminists of color* (pp. 346–355). San Francisco: Aunt Lute Books.

Reinharz, S. (1992). *Feminist methods in social research.* New York: Oxford University Press.

Rhodes, P. (1994). Race of interviewer effects in qualitative research: A brief comment. *Sociology, 28*(2), 547–548.

Richardson, L. (1992). The consequences of poetic representation: Writing the other, rewriting the self. In C. Ellis & M. Flaherty (Eds.), *Investigating subjectivity: Research on lived experience* (pp. 125–140). Newbury Park, CA: Sage.

Richardson, L. (1994). Writing: A method of inquiry. In N. K. Denzin & Y. S. Lincoln (Eds.), *Handbook of qualitative research* (pp. 516–529). Thousand Oaks, CA: Sage.

Rollins, J. (1985). *Between women: Domestics and their employers.* Philadelphia: Temple University Press.

Romero, M. (1992). *Maid in the USA.* London: Routledge.

Said, E. (1978). *Orientalism.* New York: Pantheon.

Said, E. (1985). In the shadow of the West. *Wedge, 7/8,* 4–5.

Said, E. (1989). Representing the colonized: Anthropology's interlocutors. *Critical Inquiry, 15,* 205–225.

Sawicki, J. (1991). Foucault and feminism: Toward a politics of difference. In M. Shanley & C. Pateman (Eds.), *Feminist interpretations and political theory* (pp. 217–231). University Park: Pennsylvania State University Press.

Sawicki, J. (1994). Foucault, feminism and questions of identity. In G. Gutting (Ed.), *The Cambridge companion to Foucault.* Cambridge, UK: Cambridge University Press.

Shakeshaft, C. (1987). *Women in educational administration.* Newbury Park, CA: Sage.

Scheurich, J. J., & Young, M. D. (1997). Coloring epistemologies: Are our research epistemologies racially biased? *Educational Researcher, 26*(4), 4–16.

Scheurich, J. J., & Young, M. D. (1998). In the United States of America, in both our souls and our sciences we are avoiding white racism. *Educational Researcher, 27*(9), 27–32.

Schneider, J. (1991). Troubles with textual authority in sociology. *Symbolic Interaction, 14,* 295–320.

Shostak, M. (1981). *Nisa: The life and words of a !Kung woman.* Cambridge, MA: Harvard University Press.

Smith, D. (1989). Sociological theory: Methods of writing patriarchy. In R. Wallace (Ed.), *Feminism and sociological theory* (pp. 34–64). Newbury Park, CA: Sage.

Smith, D. (1990). *The conceptual practices of power: A feminist sociology of knowledge.* Boston: Northeastern University Press.

Smith, D. (1992). Sociology from women's experience: A reaffirmation. *Sociological Theory, 10,* 88–98.

Smith, D. (1993). High noon in Textland: A critique of Clough. *Sociological Quarterly, 34,* 183–192.

Smulyan, L. (2000). Feminist cases of nonfeminist subjects: Case studies of women principals. *International Journal of Qualitative Studies in Education, 13*(6), 589–609.

78 Michelle D. Young

Spivak, G. (1988). Can the subaltern speak? In C. Nelson & L. Grossberg (Eds.), *Marxism and the interpretation of culture* (pp. 280–316). Urbana: University of Illinois Press.

Stanfield, J. (1985). The ethnocentric basis of social science knowledge production. *Review of Research in Education,12,* 387–415.

Stanfield, J. (1993a). Epistemological considerations. In J. Stanfield & R. Dennis (Eds.), *Race and ethnicity in research methods* (pp. 16–36). Thousand Oaks, CA: Sage.

Stanfield, J. (1993b). Methodological reflections: An introduction. In J. Stanfield & R. Dennis (Eds.), *Race and ethnicity in research methods* (pp. 3–15). Thousand Oaks, CA: Sage.

Stanfield, J. (1994). Ethnic modeling in qualitative research. N. K. Denzin & Y. S. Lincoln (Eds.), *The handbook of qualitative research* (pp. 175–188). Newbury Park, CA: Sage.

Standing, K. (1998). Writing the voices of the less powerful: Research on lone mothers. In J. Ribbens & R. Edwards (Eds.), *Feminist dilemmas in qualitative research: Public knowledge and private lives* (pp.186–202). Thousand Oaks, CA: Sage.

Stoller, E., & Oakes, C. (1987). *In sorcery's shadow: A memoir of apprenticeship among the Songhay of Niger.* Chicago: University of Chicago Press.

Tandon, R. (1982). A critique of monopolistic research. In B. Hall, A. Gillette, & R. Tandon (Eds.), *Creating knowledge: A monopoly? Participatory research in development* (pp. 79–84). New Delhi: Society for Participatory Research in Asia.

Tierney, W. (1995). (Re)presentation and voice. *Qualitative Inquiry, 1*(4), 379–390.

Tixier y Vigil, Y., & Elasser, N. (1976). The effects of the ethnicity of the interviewer on conversation: A study of Chicana women. In B. DuBois & I. Crouch (Eds.), *Sociology of the language of American women* (pp. 161–169). San Antonio, TX: Trinity University Press.

Trebilcot, J. (1988, Summer). Dyke methods, or principles for the discovery/creation of the withstanding. *Hypatia, 3,* 1–14.

Tuana, N. (1993). With many voices: Feminism and theoretical pluralism. In P. England (Ed.), *Theory on gender/feminism on theory* (pp. 122–140). Berkeley: University of California Press.

Tyler, S. (1986). Post-modern ethnography: From document of the occult to occult document. In J. Clifford & G. Marcus (Eds.), *Writing culture: The poetics and politics of ethnography* (pp. 122–140). Berkeley: University of California Press.

Van Maanen, J. (1988). *Tales of the field.* Chicago: University of Chicago Press.

West, C. (1993). *Keeping faith: Philosophy and race in America.* New York: Routledge.

Wolcott, H. (1994). *Transforming qualitative data: Description, analysis, and interpretation.* Newbury Park, CA: Sage.

Wolf, D. (1996). Situating feminist dilemmas in fieldwork. In D. Wolf (Ed.), *Feminist dilemmas in fieldwork* (pp. 1–55). Boulder, CO: Westview Press.

Wolf, M. (1992). *A thrice-told tale: Feminism, post-modernism and ethnographic responsibility.* Stanford, CA: Stanford University Press.

Young, M. D. (1997, April). *Homeless mothers and their children's education.* Paper presented at the annual meeting of the American Educational Research Association, Chicago, IL.

Young, M. D. (1999). Multifocal educational policy research: Toward a method for enhancing traditional educational policy studies. *American Educational Research Journal, 36*(4), 677–714.

Young, M. D., & Moore, E. (1999, April). *Pretty in print: The failure of Iowa's MCNS policy in addressing the educational needs of Black adolescent females.* Paper presented at the annual meeting of the American Educational Research Association, Montreal, Canada.

Zinn, M. (1982). Mexican-American women in the social sciences. *Signs, 8,* 259–272.

Chapter 4

The Linguistic Production of Genderlessness in the Superintendency

Jennifer Scott

I'll tell you how men see me. . . they see me as a creature from another world.

(Female Superintendent in Study)

A number of factors converged to bring me to conduct this research, not the least of which was a fairly well-known quote about leadership: "It remains undefined, but you know it when you see it." If that is true, then there exists a general, unified conception of what constitutes successful leadership. My own experiences with gender discrimination led me to seek knowledge about how leadership and gender intersect and to question how successful women superintendents defined themselves, how they constructed notions of gender, and how they resolved the tensions, if any, that resulted from being both a woman and the highest authority in an organization. My questions revealed my assumptions and beliefs that women superintendents were different from men superintendents, that the superintendency was constructed as "male," and that there was a tension that resulted from being a woman in a man's world. Now you see, from the tenor of these questions, as I did, that I the researcher am not immune to the disease of gender polarization. These dichotomies limited my vision, and my initial study findings were simply an epiphenomenon of these misguided questions.

As I evolved in my understanding, my findings became insights and learnings that had no finality but were simply a point of time and space.

For every "finding" that emerged from this research there existed a counterexample that disrupted any attempts to generalize. I misrecognized gender as a unified subject, discovering that fragmentary constructions of power, femaleness, and genderlessness are not inherent but are negotiated daily in the workplace through interactions with others. I discovered complexity, ambiguity, and fragmentation that did not fit into the androcentric educational leadership discourse consisting of cause-and-effect diagrams, flow charts, reductive explanations, lists of best practices, or statistical analyses.

But I am getting ahead of myself. Permit me to share with you my argument about the linguistic production of genderless in the superintendency. My argument begins with a description of how the superintendency has been defined in the research over the past thirty years, and how it has been normatively linked to the masculine gender. Next, I discuss ways in which gendered identity is acquired and produced through negotiation in specific social contexts (in this case, the superintendency) and performed in compliance with or in resistance to socially constructed norms. Then, in the chapter subsection "The Intersection of Gender and the Organization," I describe how gender is defined and produced in the arrangements of the social structure of the workplace, where the masculine and the universal are conflated with genderlessness. For women, existence in this world requires a separation of self into two sets of consciousness that correspond to the world of the local and the particular and the outside world of the rational. This fragmentation of self causes internal tensions. With this groundwork laid, my argument then turns to the literature on language and gender. I explain how gender is performed through speech acts such as the linguistic and paralinguistic co-optation of power speech. I then make the argument, supported by examples from my own research with women superintendents, that those who use these linguistic and paralinguistic forms in the workplace index masculinity. Indeed, the participants in my study consciously deployed linguistic conventions such as power discourse, the dislocation of emotion, and the banishment of stereotypical female practices from the workplace to be successful in their work. In the end, I conclude that although these strategies did enable success by reproducing the women superintendents as genderless, they did so at a terrible price.

BACKGROUND AND THEORETICAL FRAMEWORK

Although the educational profession is heavily female, men dominate the administrative ranks in schools. The underrepresentation of women in the highest office in public schools, the superintendency, is sobering; from 1910 to the present, with the exception of a few years fol-

The Linguistic Production of Genderlessness   83

lowing World War I, about 10 percent of superintendents have been women (Blount, 1998). Although approximately the same percentage of corporate chief executive officers is female (Deal & Stevenson, 1998), corporations are not as heavily laden with female employees as are schools. In Texas, where I live and work, although women comprise 75 percent of the teachers, only 8.4 percent of superintendents are female (Meier & Wilkins, 2002). An interesting finding is that these numbers are not easily available; although the accumulation of gender statistics is de rigueur in research on students and educational programs, most states and the U.S. Department of Education do not keep historical data on gender in the superintendency (Blount, 1998). Gender in the superintendency has been historically invisible.

Over the past three decades, studies highlighted the lack of women in educational administration and attempted to define the barriers that precluded women from assuming leadership roles. These studies led to the formulation of "difference, deficit, and dominance" models (Cameron, 1996), including theories of how sex-role differences, leadership styles, organizational structure, lack of females in the pipeline, and sex-role stereotyping accounted for the underrepresentation of women in the superintendency. Much of this research was conducted from within the positivist vein, resulting in "an organization theory which has developed an almost incestual conversation with its own voices—monologue, rather than a dialogue, and one which was conducted in methodical insulation from the conversation of organizational life" (Clegg, 1977, p. 11). These works omitted discussions of conflict, inequity, disharmony, and power; assumed that sex and gender are stable, unified, dichotomous categories; and ignored the ambiguities, multiplicities, and contradictions inherent in sexual and gender identity (Eagly, Karau, & Makhijani, 1995).

During the 1990s a body of work framed from feminist and critical perspectives emerged that interrogated the authenticity or applicability of an organizational theory infused with an androcentric bias. These works deconstructed categories of male and female as naturally inherent, stable entities and viewed gender as a socially constructed convention. Theories from this perspective hold that privilege models and shapes reality, a situation that is invisible until women fail to follow the agenda of the dominant culture. First, the superintendency, as overwhelmingly populated by white males, is associated with a number of "desirable" leadership descriptors that are identified as masculine: powerful, authoritative, decisive, politically astute, and competent (Blount, 1998; Brunner, 1998; Grogan, 1996; Skrla, 1998). Second, women superintendents are expected to adopt practices and behaviors in compliance with these socially constructed normative behaviors associated with the superintendency. Third, women who adopt these "masculine" attributes pay a terrible price when they disrupt expectations associated with the female gender. Conversely, women whose leadership style is "feminine," that is, collaborative, cooperative, and caring, often are viewed as weak and ineffective. This research concludes that women superintendents who cannot strike a delicate balance between these polarities face impossible conditions that result in a number of damaging psychological phenomena, not the least of which is a sense of self-defeat, demoralization, and psychic dysfunction (Blackmore, 1993; Curcio, Morsink, & Bridges, 1989; Kanter, 1977; Koonce, 1997; Korabik, 1990; Scott, 1999; Skrla, 2000; Tallerico, Poole, & Burstyn, 1994).

The recognition and interrogation of these power, dominance, and privilege discourses has created space to locate divergent narratives that describe the everyday life of women superintendents and their struggles to survive. These works have contributed enormously to the understanding of how individuals, whether male or female, are molded, stifled, and sometimes destroyed by adopting the socially constructed, normative expectations of behavior associated with the superintendency.

The Production of Gendered Identity

It is important to understand that the attributes and characteristics assigned to the male and female genders are not inherently biological but are socially constructed. In Western society, gendered identity is enculturated, constructed, and internalized by "situating people in a culture whose discourses and social practices are organized around the lenses of androcentrism and gender polarization" (Bem, 1993, p. 143). Gender polarization bifurcates the population into two genders and imposes culturally based, oppositional definitions of gender appropriateness that are associated with males and females. These lenses of gender polarization are internalized from birth by the developing child, who is predisposed to construct an identity that is consistent with them. However, because society adopts an androcentric lens as well, the individual becomes more than a carrier of gender polarization; rather, the internalization of androcentrism makes the individual an unwitting collaborator in the social reproduction of patriarchy, which is in turn reinforced by existing cultural discourse and practices.

Masculine traits are more highly valued than are feminine traits in almost every society (Gal, 1995); in fact, gender inequalities are one of the few cultural universals. Women who adopt "masculine" leadership qualities are viewed negatively because the cultural construction of maleness is based on what is not female (Theweleit, 1977, 1989). Women are constructed as a "lack of"—that is, less competent, independent, logical, and objective. These conventional gender constructions of maleness include several explicit and implicit assumptions:

> First, masculinity and maleness are defined oppositionally as what is not feminine or female. Second, gendered identities implicitly depend on the social acquisition of appropriate attributes. Third, anatomy, learned behavior and desire are conflated so that "normal" sexual orientation and identity are heterosexual. Lastly, through biological, sexual, and social connotations, the idea of masculinity is reified and universalized. Masculinity appears as a commodity, which can be measured, possessed, or lost. (Cornwall & Lindisfarne, 1994, pp. 11–12)

Gendered identities thus result from repeated acts within one's surroundings, either in resistance to or in compliance with local expectations. These repeated acts impart a (false) semblance of gender identity as a unified subject or monolithic entity (Butler, 1990; Cameron, 1996). Therefore, as Butler (1990) suggests, gender, through these repeated acts, becomes *performative*. It is both purposeful and contingent on shifting meanings that socially and historically are constructed through discourse. In other words, the actions of women (and men) do not spring from who they are, but rather who they are depends on their repeated performance of acts that constitute their identity over time. This way of thinking about gender "focuses not on dichotomous differences expected under polarized, categorical roles of feminine and masculine, but on the fluid enactment of gender roles in specific social situations" (Bergvall, 1996, p. 175).

If gender is viewed as an open-ended category, which is analyzed according to the social construction of difference framed by local discourses of "agency, causation, personhood, and identity" (Cornwall & Lindisfarne, 1994, p. 41), masculinity and femininity become part of a system for producing difference. Individuals absorb influences from their surroundings, and in turn, release substances that influence the constructions of others, resulting in a "composite" identity. Gender difference and inequality become negotiated through interactions that are repetitious but not identical. These negotiations are sites of contestation, resistance, conformance, and permeability (Cornwall & Lindisfarne, 1994).

The Intersection of Gender and the Organization

Women enter the superintendency not merely as women but as subjects in an institutional world that is ordered, shaped, and regulated by a set of practices, or discursive fields, that define notions of what is expected and normal. These discursive fields are revealed in a number of ways, including the language superintendents use (and do not use) when talking about their identity as professionals and as women (Chase, 1995). The adaptation to and adoption of such socially constructed, normative behaviors and practices in a profession that is heavily dominated by males is well documented in the organizational and anthropological literature (see, for example, McElhinny, 1995, 1996).

The adoption of discursive practices, however, is not so much an act of agency as it is constitutive of the available socially and culturally constructed strategies. That is, although the discursive alignment of leadership style and attributes with masculine stereotypes may be a conscious strategy by women superintendents, the narrow range of options available defines that particular choice. These discursive fields are bound in the workplace by the arrangement of business, the hierarchical structure of the bureaucracy, and practices that reinforce detachment, rationality, compartmentalization, and order. Although women and men in the workplace tend to view these discursive fields as gender-neutral, they are constituted as both male and universal (Smith, 1989). De Beauvoir argued that men and women are "like two electric poles, for man represents the positive and the neutral . . . whereas woman represents only the negative" (Smith, 1989, p. 20). These orderings are based on an institutional knowledge constituted by patriarchal assumptions, language, and patterns of relating that reproduce and reinforce gender polarization, and hence, inequality.

On the other hand, unlike men, women exist in a private sphere of relations that is ordered by a different set of discursive practices and expectations. The gender socialization of females requires that they respond to behavioral expectations in this arena as well, but the skills and attributes required to successfully meet these expectations require a different sort of consciousness than the public world previously described. It is a world of the "local and particular" (Smith, 1989, p. 6), a world in which women attend to endless details of home and family. In general, women's work routines do not allow opportunities for directing projects, controlling processes, or demonstrating mastery. Smith argues "what is required is a subordination of attentiveness to self and a focus on others . . . and an openness and attentiveness to cues and indications of others' needs" (p. 66). Women are not the center of the action, so to speak; their world revolves around the schedules and enterprises of others as they coordinate and hold the threads of many lives together. Although the private sphere consists of these "episodic discontinuities" (p. 67), the public sphere is characterized by the hierarchical, the rational, and the compartmental. Women, then, are fragmented subjects located within both of these discourses; to survive in each requires a bifurcation of consciousness and an ability to transform boundaries between two very differently structured social locations.

I do not mean to imply that women have two simple identities set in the public and private sphere. The boundaries between these discourses are fluid rather than solid, and passage between the two is not easily navigated. These constructions within and the passages between these realms are marked with ambiguity, resistance, and dissonance (Morris, 1995). Hence, the multiplicity of identity and absence of a unified subject directly relates to the tensions experienced by women in roles of leadership. The constitution of gendered identity in these two worlds is evident in language.

Gender, Language, and Power

Like early work in organizational theory, sociolinguistic studies have long focused on differences between men and women. Theorists have "taken gender for granted by treating it as a demographic category that is given in advance" (Cameron, 1996, p. 44). Early research identified different linguistic forms apparent in everyday talk that were linked to gender. This linkage is known as *indexing*. In other words, the meaning of certain forms of language depends on their reference (indexing) to some other concept or category, in this case, gender. Certain linguistic forms, then, are viewed as indexical to the female gender, such as hesitation, tag questions, lack of interrupters, and silence, while others, such as forceful speech, were indexed to the male gender. This led to the formulation of the cultural difference, or the "two cultures" model of gendered speech, which has grown into a cottage industry as exemplified by Deborah Tannen's work on speech differences between men and women, and popular books such as John Gray's *Men are from Mars, Women are from Venus*. This "two cultures" model, based on data from studies of White, middle-class participants, has persisted despite more recent research that links speech usage to context or topic. Clearly, the persistence of the "two cultures" model in popular culture demonstrates the pervasiveness of gender polarization. Society assigns value, hierarchy, and status to ways of speaking depending on whether the form of speech is indexical, or indirectly linked, to the male or female gender. In this way, gender hierarchies and ideologies are displayed and sustained through verbal practices that reflect communities of practice in social groups.

This stable, dichotomous role theory has been problematized in recent research that promotes more complex understandings of gender differences in everyday speech forms (Bergvall, 1996; Cameron, 1996; Freed, 1996; Gal, 1994, 1995; Goodwin, 1990; Greenwood, 1996; Lutz, 1990; Ochs, 1992). Gal (1994) argues, "gender is better seen as a system of culturally constructed relations of power, produced and reproduced in interaction between and among men and women" (p. 408). These interactions are frequently the site of contestation and power struggles.

For example, silence is a linguistic form indexed to the female gender and generally deplored by feminists in the West. Silence is viewed as a convention representing power differentials, passivity, and lack of control. Yet as Gal (1995) notes, after Foucault, silence may also be paradoxically used as a source of power, especially in institutional settings where the relations of coercion are reversed as in police interrogations, bureaucratic interviews, and religious confessions, or as a defense against those in power, as utilized by the Apache to exclude the White outsider. Silence, then, "gains different meanings and has different effects within specific institutional contexts, and within different linguistic ideologies" (p. 172). Clearly, linguistic practices are ambiguous and contradictory, reflecting discourses of both dominance and resistance.

Researchers, then, have gained a greater, more sophisticated understanding that speech may be multiply indexical, combining features of race, class, and gender, the meaning of which is confounded by social situation and context. Indexicality is not direct, but referential. Ochs (1992) argues that:

> The relation between language and gender is not a simple straightforward mapping of linguistic form to social meaning of gender. Rather the relation of language to gender is constituted and mediated by the relation of language to stances, social acts, social activities, and other social constructs. (pp. 336–337)

Thus, the usage of certain linguistic forms indexes social meanings, which in turn constitute gender meanings. For example, Freed (1996) found that males and females in conversations about friendship equally used "female" patterns of speaking. Different ways of speaking, then, are associated not so much with gender as with expectations held for the speaker within a certain context. "Gendered" talk in the context of a relationship does not originate in the female gender, but is located in socially constructed expectations of speech patterns congruent with the role of wife, mother, lover, or friend. A position of power and authority, such as the superintendency, produces expectations of "power" speech.

The culturally constructed linkages between gender, language, and power indicate that some linguistic strategies are more authoritative than others are, such as academic discourse and formal register. These genres reflect cultural definitions of institutional life that privilege the interests of those in authority, sometimes at the expense of others. Through the use of

The Linguistic Production of Genderlessness   89

these linguistic practices, speakers may exercise power and authority or even impose symbolic domination on others.

In the next section, I demonstrate how the successful women superintendents in my study used linguistic conventions in accordance with social expectations to negotiate meaning, acceptance, and identity. I begin with a snapshot of the two women so that the reader can make his or her own conclusions about generalizability. Next, I discuss the unique context of the superintendency so that the relationship between power, language, and the organization is made explicit. Finally, I show how the participants' use of power speech resulted in the development of a contextual gender identity that was conflated with the masculine and the universal, and therefore rendered the women superintendents in this research as genderless. Their genderlessness was reinforced through both dislocation of emotion and development of a bifurcated consciousness to house their divided worlds. The use of particular linguistic conventions, consciously chosen by the women superintendents, enabled them to cope, survive, and excel in their jobs—but at a heavy price.

INSIGHTS AND LEARNINGS

Thus far, research on women superintendents has tended to focus on those aspiring to or those who have exited from the superintendency. The research on which this chapter is based focused on two successful, exemplary women superintendents in their workplaces. The importance of context and observation of the workplace dictated an ethnographic approach to this research. In addition to conducting numerous interviews with staff, parents, and community members, I shadowed the women superintendents themselves in order to observe them in a number of institutional and private situations. Because the reluctance of women to discuss gender issues has been well documented (Bell, 1995; Chase, 1995; Smulyan, 1998), I drew heavily on feminist research methods to guide my approach. For example, the importance of relationships with the participants dictated that I establish an atmosphere of trust, not only with the superintendents, but also with their staffs (Lather, 1992; Lincoln, 1995; Olesen, 1994; Reinharz, 1992).

Both women superintendents were in their fifties and White, possessed terminal degrees, and had been in the superintendency for at least ten years. One participant, whom I shall identify as *E*, arrived there via the slow track, entering the superintendency only after leaving a district where she had worked for seventeen years in almost every conceivable campus administrative position. The other participant, whom I shall identify as *J*, rapidly ascended to the superintendency, having been promoted into positions of increasing responsibility despite her lack of experience or formal training. Thus, almost immediately my findings diverged from research that cites long career paths for women who aspire to the superintendency.

Both women were intense and driven; they possessed a strong presence, a quiet air of competence and confidence, and an enormous amount of energy. They were generally held in high esteem by their staffs, boards, and constituencies for their intelligence, resilience, political shrewdness, and strength. Yet, they were also problematically viewed by some of their female colleagues as aggressive, cold, aloof, insensitive, and uncaring.

The women were highly cognizant that the superintendency is a unique position. As one said, "It's another world you enter when you enter the superintendency, and it's not like anything else that's out there. It's not being an assistant superintendent, it's not like being a principal. It's just different." The difference is that the superintendency is charged with politics and conflict to a far greater extent than are other roles in education, and the ability to address issues that emerge from conflict are inextricably linked to constructions of power and authority. The women describe it thusly:[1]

> J: The school superintendency is a political balance, not only with the seven board members that you have, because they all want different things, and you have to try to juggle that and keep them satisfied. But then the public also wants different things, because there are so many special interest groups.
>
> E: If you are going to make a difference as a superintendent you are going to lose your job . . . because the children that you have to make the difference with are *not* the children that the power structure values. When you help those children, you inevitably alienate yourself to some level from the power structure by meeting the needs that your conscience and your intellect and your moral responsibility tell you *must* be met. If you look out and see a district where there's a lot of student success, too often you see a superintendent under siege or in the process of losing their jobs because the things you do to get students to a high level of success are not popular with the people who elect boards, and that's sad.

The women superintendents, then, had no illusions about the nature of the superintendency and the impossibility of unqualified success. Because the exercise of power is constructed as a male prerogative, an authority figure who is female becomes problematic in the eyes of the school and public communities when she attempts to exercise authority. The women superintendents revealed that successfully coping with power, conflict, and authority issues, both internal and external, was crit-

The Linguistic Production of Genderlessness 91

ical to their survival. Unlike other women superintendents who have exited the superintendency and whose innocence was destroyed by the clash of gender and politics, E and J possessed a pragmatism that provided a source of strength. The women saw things as they were, not as they wished them to be. Their strategies for coping with politics, conflict, power, and gendered expectations are discussed in the following sections. They include the purposeful adoption of genderless discourse, the removal of emotional speech, and the relegation of those conventions indexed to the female to the private sphere.

Managing the Perceptions of Others through Professional (Genderless) Discourse

The women superintendents I studied framed their public lives in a professional discourse that indexed masculine behaviors associated with successful leaders, and employed linguistic and paralinguistic features that reinforced constructions of themselves as authoritarian. When asked about one superintendent's sense of power and authority, the school board president stated that she "has both . . . very authoritative . . . power is following through . . . and she's been very good about getting [things] to happen." One assistant superintendent in the same school district, when asked about the use of authority, stated:

> She uses it. Like I say, waving that magic wand and . . . she does have authority, she knows she has authority. People around her know it so there is no dealing, there is no issue there. She uses it wisely. She uses it intellectually by collecting data. There is no question about who's in charge.

In the minds of the women, this authoritative discourse was gender-neutral. Those with whom they worked mirrored these perceptions. One assistant superintendent claimed:

> I see our management in the school district as kind of gender-neutral. I'm not sure when we go into a meeting that there's much, at least conscious, thought that that person is a women or that person is a man. We've evolved to a point that we are relatively gender-neutral and I have high respect for some women and high respect for some men.

The community members I interviewed corroborated the perception of gender neutrality. One parent stated, "I don't think she comes across as masculine or feminine to people. Maybe that's why they are so accepting of her."

Furthermore, the superintendents were described by their staffs as "no-nonsense," women who "come to the point, to the heart of the issue" and "get down to brass tacks pretty quick." They were seen as leaders who were "driven and fearless." As one employee related to me, "We are saving public education. We don't have a lot of time to do it." These traits fall under the rubric of task initiating in the leadership literature, displaying an instrumentality indexical to a masculine style of leadership, as opposed to a concern with relationships and consideration. One superintendent was described by a male employee as "a remodeler . . . she is not a redecorator. She is going to take and move the walls and structurally do some major changes." This discursive framing of change reveals a masculine fondness for "what works, and for what man can make, whether it helps to build or to destroy" as opposed to a feminine commitment to "resourcefulness in peacekeeping" (Bem, 1993, p. 158).

For instance, both superintendents resolved to stay focused on "what the object is . . . to improve the school district." They met conflict and challenge to authority "head on." Both women adopted assertive and sometimes aggressive behaviors, especially in resolving conflict. Interestingly, the men in both districts saw their behavior as assertive and positive; the women, for the most part, saw them as aggressive, tinged with negativity. One participant commented:

> I don't really see myself that way [as aggressive] . . . but people criticize you and you look at it. . . . I think that sometimes the part of me that's very aggressive and assertive has done some very good things . . . so maybe they don't like it, but I happen to value it, so that's okay.

Another superintendent in the study related a story about a debate between a male superintendent and her:

> I was at the Center for Creative Leadership . . . and I was the only woman, and they [the men] kept asking me how uncomfortable I was, and I said, "I'm not at all uncomfortable." . . . When I became *very* assertive to a couple of men who were just doing some incredibly stupid things, they didn't know how to take it, and they came back to me and said, "You need to not be that assertive, you're coming on way too strongly". . . [and] you hurt us because you were a woman. . . . I am a very assertive female, and I'm not afraid to go after the devil, and if I see something that I think is wrong, then I'm going to tell you if I think

The Linguistic Production of Genderlessness

> you can handle it. I never go after someone that I don't think can handle it, and I thought those men were pretty strong . . . very aggressive, very boss management, very tough, and so when I went after one . . . we got into a pretty strong conversation [and] volleyed back and forth, and I thought great, great conversation. I felt very good. I'm not afraid of conflict, and I thought that was a terrific interchange. . . . He told me that he felt such a strong presence from me that he thought we were either going to get into a battle or fight or he was going to have to acquiesce or whatever . . . they see me as strong. . . . They think I make them look bad. . . . They see me as a creature from another world.

This passage demonstrates the location of self in a professional discourse of control, not as someone who merely adopts an assertive style, but as the ultimate aggressor and winner. The superintendent here related her reflections on the interplay of gender, social expectations, and the negotiation of meanings. Ironically, she located her superiority in gender as well as a professional discourse: a source of her strength lies in the surprise attack on the men, who are uncomfortable with her aggression. While she co-opted the masculine behavior traits of aggression and competency for her own ends, she also located herself in a realm beyond the understanding of men.

This superintendent is engaged in a linguistic performance that locates her identity as genderless. She is simultaneously male and female, and neither male nor female. She is alien, genderless, "a creature from another world." To say that she is locating her identity as genderless does not mean that she is simply managing a delicate mixture of male and female. This is where my argument diverges from the gender tightrope theory. Obviously, in the preceding passage, J is disrupting social expectations of female gender performances, but with no accompanying penalty. The "masculine" traits she has co-opted are perceived by the superintendent as being genderless. To recount De Beauvoir's argument, the masculine, and the professional discourse used in the patriarchal workplace, are conflated with the universal and the neutral, which is neither male nor female. By describing herself as "alien," J is not only locating herself beyond the understanding of men, but also beyond gender. This genderlessness is the misrecognition of the unified subject and the fulfillment of Lacanian desire, or the knowing of the unknowable.

The linguistic production of genderless leadership is sprinkled throughout the transcripts of both superintendents. Speech patterns indexical to the female gender, such as hesitation, tag questions, and lack of interrupters were used in situations such as conversations with teachers and female staff, to indicate caring and compassion. Conversely, the women used speech patterns indexical to the male gender, such as forceful speech and floor management strategies (e.g., lack of questions and pauses) in situations that demanded a projection of authority. The participants, cognizant of different social expectations with diverse communities, made conscious, strategic choices of speech and discourse style.

This linguistic production of genderless leadership was paralleled in the paralinguistic cues that the women employed. The women expressed dominance through the use of physical space, extending and encroaching on the space of others without penalty. Their body comportment also reinforced their position of authority. For example, whenever possible, they placed themselves at the head of the table—the seat of authority—in meetings. In conversational interactions, eye contact and gaze established the women as dominant; they both initiated and ended the contact. Further, their conversational partners adjusted their position to the superintendents; that is, others attending the meetings would inch their chairs around until they were facing the women, thus signaling readiness and accommodation to the dominant status of the women.

Both verbal and nonverbal accommodation, or deference from a lower-ranking or less powerful person to a higher-ranking or more powerful person, denotes social hierarchies in the workplace and constitutes social meanings. The women, by consciously choosing speech patterns and body comportment indexical to the authoritarian, universal male, achieve a unified identity in the organizational environment as genderless. This identity is reinforced through the relocation of emotion, which I discuss in the next section.

Relocating Emotion—The Rhetoric of Control

Emotional speech is gendered as female, "typically viewed as something natural rather than cultural, irrational rather than rational, chaotic rather than ordered, subjective rather than universal, physical rather than mental or intellectual, unintended and uncontrollable, and hence often dangerous" (Lutz, 1990). Emotions are construed as both weak and powerful; on the one hand, emotion is perceived as some sort of character defect to rise above (as "getting a grip on one's emotions"). Alternately, emotions are the source of great passion that "fires people up" and charges them to act beyond the ordinary. These are the "good" emotions connected with commitment to children. It is the source of the "drivenness" that enabled the women superintendents to get things done and to motivate others. However, district staff, particularly the males, generally regarded emotions, even the "good" ones, as something to be controlled, handled, or contained within the stolid walls of a masculine gendered identity. The following excerpt typifies the many examples of how the women were perceived:

> I've never seen her angry in public. Well let me rephrase that. I think I've seen her angry in public but not to the extent that somebody who didn't know her would realize she was angry in public. And I think she understands the benefit of not losing control and not losing respect in public. So she doesn't express anger, as a general rule, in public. She expresses anger appropriately in private. She understands that she can say "I'm angry" and that's okay. But she doesn't let that dominate or control her actions.

In this passage, "dangerous" or "uncontrolled" emotion is relegated to the private sphere, behind closed doors, where it can be expressed "appropriately." Expressing "dangerous" emotion is viewed as losing control, and as a result, respect. When discussing this superintendent's leadership style, the employee maintained that her ability to control her emotions is the source of her success. She does not "dramatically overreact," internalizes conflict, and remains open to ongoing discussion.

The silencing of emotion has been theorized as a rhetoric of control, which is a reproduction of women as being in need of control. This discourse governs women and establishes a boundary within which emotion is contained (Foucault, 1990). This inner boundary establishes an edge, a location within which emotion can be safely located. Lutz (1990) notes that "a discourse that is concerned with the expression, control, or repression of emotions can be seen as a discourse on the crossing back and forth of that boundary between inside and outside" (p. 73). The relegation of emotion to the private sphere is one more consciously chosen, though again circumscribed, strategy that contributes to an identity construction that seems "genderless."

The relegation of emotion to the private sphere was further evidenced in the women's talk about the criticality of toughness to survival in the superintendency. One participant discussed how she sheared away her emotional side: "I had insulated myself [so that] I could deal with situations. A part of me was very sad because I felt like I had lost a certain level of empathy, and that was a loss." Yet she justified her mental shift by comparing herself to a physician: "it can't be unlike what a doctor has to do . . . when you help them they are going to have to suffer . . . you can't help them by just leaving their pain . . . you cannot help people and make it easy at the same time."

These exemplary women superintendents, then, relegated "dangerous" emotion to the private sphere, co-opted a genderless organizational discourse, and through consistent and repeated practices, linguistically and paralinguistically, created a genderless identity that formed the bedrock of their acceptance by others as persons of power and authority.

Crossing Borders and the Bifurcation of Consciousness

The depth of my study and the relationships I formed with the women superintendents allowed exploration of much more than the workplace. Both women demonstrated two types of consciousness, one associated with the public world as exemplified by the workplace, and one associated with the private world as exemplified by the home. These worlds coexisted, but not peacefully. I observed the struggle for dominance, and the discursive tensions that resulted from the shift in thinking as borders were crossed linguistically between the public and private spheres of both women superintendents. Unlike women, men do not undergo the same shifts in thinking. Their public and private worlds are unified constructions (Smith, 1989). For these women superintendents, the quasi-emotionless world of the workplace stands in sharp relief to the emotional world of home and family.

For example, J revealed her sense of guilt in regard to her adolescent children, somewhat relieved by a "corporate husband" who helped with homework, attended athletic events, and addressed the basic needs of her children. The children's attitudes toward their mother were ambivalent; on the one hand, they seemed to recognize that their mother needed an outlet for her energy, talent, and intellect; on the other hand, they had to cope with her physical absence and unpleasant, public criticisms of her, which caused them a great deal of pain. When discussing her children, the participant's words were suffused with emotion, citing examples of "argumentative meals," where anger, disagreements, and frustrations explode, but issues eventually are resolved; she revealed her private anguish through details of conversations with her daughter, who advised her to "calm down, Mom, it's no big deal, you are blowing this way out of proportion." Her family accommodated and supported her superintendency; yet, when I asked what accommodations or sacrifices were made by her for the family, she replied "none." I asked, "So your family came second, basically. Was that the source of your guilt?" "Yes," she replied. "Yes." Later she clarified her initial statement: "It isn't so much that my job came before my children. It was that when I'm here, I give 150% and when I'm with my kids I try to give that too . . . at a cost to me." The private sphere of the women was characterized as a space in which the pain associated

The Linguistic Production of Genderlessness

with the superintendency was too great and could only be endured silently, miserably, through restless nights, self-doubts, second-guessing, and turbulent thoughts.

Their descriptions of the superintendency as a difficult occupation were peppered with emotional words and phrases. For example, the women stated:

> J: I get depressed occasionally, and that depression is not truly as much job-related as it is job-related, wife-related, family-related, finance-related . . . all those multitudes of things, and *that* is the depression more than anything. It's just if I have all cylinders going wrong, then sometimes I think what are you doing, and I really get depressed and say can I, do I want to do this, and do I really understand this.
>
> E: It is the emotional drain of the superintendency that I think would add the complexity . . . it's the intensity and complexity of the issues that you deal with. They're deeper and harder, I mean that's why the job is the harder job and the bigger job and the tougher job, because there aren't easy answers. If they are easy problems, they don't come to you; if they are tough, unsolvable, gut-wrenching, that's what comes to the superintendent.

This discourse contrasted sharply with the neutralized discourse of the professional. The excerpts indicate that both women felt at times out of control and overwhelmed; yet, these thoughts were private, not public ones. These "dangerous" or "uncontrolled" emotions were relegated to the private sphere. The emotion expressed in the public sphere was connected to their passion, commitment, energy, and urgency for the well-being and education of all children. Note, however, that these public emotions are not about competency, and although the concern for children was deeply and truly felt, the women deployed this rhetoric to control the internal politics of the district, and subdue the rhetoric when manipulating the external politics that were controlled by the power structure of each community. This passion, then, can be interpreted as controlled, purposeful, and strategic.

In sum, the women superintendents regarded emotions, even the "good" ones, as something to be controlled, handled, or dealt with. They relegated "dangerous" or "uncontrolled" emotion to the private sphere, and used a rhetoric of control when discussing emotion in the public sphere, resulting in an identity construction that allowed the women to be perceived by others as "genderless." The price they paid for this was a psychological one, resulting in a sense of loneliness and despair that never could be acknowledged in the sphere in which it occurred, a sense of

98 *Jennifer Scott*

inadequacy that never could be expressed, a sense of guilt that could never be assuaged, and a sense of fragmented identity.

CONCLUSIONS

The second wave of feminism in the 1960s was accompanied by an outpouring of literature that brought women's ways of knowing from the margin to the center. In countermanding simplistic stereotypes, oppositional constructions were erected that essentialized women's experience as relational or collaborative. The women in this study employed complex gender identities that cannot be explained using difference, deficit, or dominance models.

In many ways, these women superintendents did not disrupt gender expectations. They were wives and mothers, but they were also superintendents, which is the ultimate position of power and authority in a school district. These women adopted a professional discourse that indexed power and authority. This notion is not new; androgyny theory notes that successful female leaders often display a task orientation. However, there is an enormous difference between a focus on competence and task completion and wearing the mantle of power comfortably. The political and conflictive nature of the superintendency requires that those who assume the role adopt the socially expected norms of a professional discourse that indexes the stereotypically masculine qualities of toughness, aggression, and coolness under pressure. Emotion is relegated to the private sphere, or to personal conversations. The women I studied were not only aware that these expectations must be met, but strategically deployed these constructions, with stunning virtuosity, to exercise power and authority.

Because they used power in ways that are expected of superintendents, reinforced their authority linguistically and paralinguistically, and performed the role of the superintendent through repeated acts of authority, they seemed "genderless" to those with whom they work. The individual, fragmentary constructions of power, femaleness, and genderlessness are hidden, congealed in an amorphous mass that resembles a unified identity, achieved by an incredible sleight of hand.

Indeed, this was borne out by the reluctance of people in the school districts and communities to acknowledge gender issues. This verbal hygiene, or "diverse set of normative metalinguistic practices based on a conviction that some ways of using language are functionally, aesthetically, or morally preferable to others" (Cameron, 1996, p. 36) was evidenced in the defensive posture adopted by some district personnel who claimed to be "women's libbers." Others chose to see gender bias not as a societal problem but as an artifact from a lower evolutionary rung. These constructions are effects of the socialization, context, and communities in which these individuals reside and represent constructions that are mutually shaped through interactions with the women superintendents. The gender-neutral constructions, so prevalent in both districts, signaled that the two women superintendents were extraordinarily successful in performing appropriate male (genderless) and female behaviors in compliance with locally derived expectations.

Yet, their success came at a price. Navigating the fluid boundaries of these multiple constructions of identity resulted in great anguish, exhaustion, isolation, illness, guilt, and sacrifice. The greedy demands of the superintendency produced intense emotions, which could only find expression in the private lives of the women. The cost of this emotional suppression was written upon their bodies and revealed through low-pitched conversations about the fragmentary nature of their lived experiences. The tensions felt by the women did not result from their inability to meet the expectations of the external world. They did that beautifully. Instead, the tensions resulted from the internal pressures and fragmentation they felt in performing multiple roles.

I continue to struggle with the notion that I have essentialized these women and their experiences with a point-and-click mentality. Yet, I find that, paradoxically, to ignore the reality of the constructed and essentialized existence of the female or the male is a kind of wishful thinking on my part that mirrors the delusion of a unified self. These experiences must be brought to light so that we can begin to understand the complexity of human relationships. I prefer to think that the deployment of the subjectivity of these women superintendents was not essentializing because it was strategic, conscious, contingent on social context, and momentary. Their subjectivities assumed a primacy that was fluid and unstable. Is this not the essence of complexity, contradiction, and destablization? The unboundedness of identity, in all its both/neither gender performances, and the disruption of the myth of a unified self, is a fractal, a metaphor of the uncontainable female body. It is *lebensraum*— space for life and growth.

NOTES

I wish to thank the editors, Linda and Michelle, for their constant encouragement and the insightful suggestions they shared with me during the process of completing this work.

1. Although I completed a linguistic analysis of the superintendents' transcripts, for the readability of the quotes I use the standard mode of reporting text. However, their emphasis on certain words is italicized.

100 *Jennifer Scott*

REFERENCES

Banks, C. A. M. (1995). Gender and race as factors in educational leadership and administration. In J. A. Banks & C. A. M. Banks (Eds.), *Handbook of research on multicultural education* (pp. 65–80). New York: Simon & Schuster Macmillan.

Bell, C. S. (1995). "If I weren't involved in schools, I might be radical": Gender consciousness in context. In D. M. Dunlap & P. A. Schmuck (Eds.), *Women leading in education* (pp. 288–312). Albany: State University of New York Press.

Bem, S. (1993). *The lenses of gender.* New Haven, CN: Yale University Press.

Bergvall, V. (1996). Constructing and enacting gender through discourse: Negotiating multiple roles as female engineering students. In V. Bergvall, J. Bing, & A. Freed (Eds.), *Rethinking language and gender research: Theory and practice* (pp. 173–201). New York: Addison Wesley Longman.

Blackmore, J. (1993). 'In the shadow of men': The historical construction of educational administration as a 'masculinist' enterprise. In J. Blackmore & J. Kenway (Eds.), *Gender matters in educational administration and policy: A feminist introduction* (pp. 27–48). Bristol, PA: The Falmer Press.

Blount, J. (1998). *Destined to rule the schools: Women and the superintendency 1873–1995.* Albany: State University of New York Press.

Brunner, C .C. (1998). *The new superintendency: Power and decision-making.* Paper presented at the annual meeting of the American Educational Research Association, San Diego, CA.

Butler, J. (1990). *Gender trouble: Feminism and the subversion of identity.* New York: Routledge.

Cameron, D. (1996). The language–gender interface: Challenging co-optation. In V. Bergvall, J. Bing, & A. Freed (Eds.), *Rethinking language and gender research: Theory and practice* (pp. 31–53). New York: Addison Wesley Longman.

Chase, S. (1995). *Ambiguous empowerment: The work narratives of women school superintendents.* Amherst: University of Massachusetts Press.

Clegg, S. (1977). Power, organization, Marx and critique. In S. Clegg & D. Dunkerley (Eds.), *Critical issues in organizations* (pp. 9–21). London: Routledge & Kegan Paul.

Cornwall, A., & Lindisfarne, N. (1994). Dislocating masculinity: Gender, power and anthropology. In A. Cornwall & N. Lindisfarne (Eds.), *Dislocating masculinity* (pp. 11–47). New York: Routledge.

Curcio, J., Morsink, C., & Bridges, S. (1989). Women as leaders: Moving beyond the stage of powerlessness. *Educational Horizons, 67*(4), 150–155.

Deal, J., & Stevenson, M. (1998). Perceptions of female and male managers in the 1990s: Plus ca change. *Sex Roles, 38* (314), 287–300.

Eagly, A. H., Karau, S. J., & Makhijani, M. G. (1995). Gender and the effectiveness of leaders: A meta-analysis. *Psychological Bulletin, 117,* 125–145.

Foucault, M. (1990). *The history of sexuality.* Vol. I. New York: Vintage.

Freed, A. F. (1996). Language and gender research in an experimental setting. In V. Bergvall, J. Bing, & A. Freed (Eds.), *Rethinking language and gender research: Theory and practice* (pp. 54–76). New York: Addison Wesley Longman.

Gal, S. (1994). Between speech and silence: The problematics of research on language and gender. In C. Roman, S. Juhasz, & C. Miller (Eds.), *The women and language debate: A sourcebook* (pp. 406–431). New Brunswick, NJ: Rutgers University Press.

Gal, S. (1995). Language, gender, and power: An anthropological review. In K. Hall & M. Bucholtz (Eds.), *Gender articulated: Language and the socially constructed self* (pp. 169–182). New York: Routledge.

Goodwin, M. H. (1990). *He-said-she-said: Talk as social organization among Black children.* Bloomington: Indiana University Press.

Greenwood, A. (1996). Floor management and power strategies in adolescent conversation. In V. Bergvall, J. Bing, & A. Freed (Eds.), *Rethinking language and gender research: Theory and practice* (pp. 77–97). New York: Addison Wesley Longman.

Grogan, M. (1996). *Voices of women aspiring to the superintendency.* Albany: State University of New York Press.

Koonce, R. (1997). Language, sex, and power: Women and men in the workplace. *Training and Development, 51*(9), 34–39.

Korabik, K. (1990). Androgyny and leadership style. *Journal of Business Ethics, 9,* 283–292.

Lather, P. (1992). Critical frames in educational research: Feminist and post-structural perspectives. *Theory into Practice, 31*,(2), 87–99.

Lincoln, Y. A. (1995). Emerging criteria for quality in qualitative and interpretive research. *Qualitative Inquiry, 1*(3), 275–289.

Lutz, C. (1990). Engendered emotion: Gender, power, and the rhetoric of emotional control in American discourse. In C. Lutz & L. Abu-Lughod (Eds.), *Language and the politics of emotion* (pp. 61–92). Cambridge: Cambridge University Press.

McElhinny, B. (1995). Challenging hegemonic masculinities: Female and male police officers handling domestic violence. In K. Hall & M. Bucholtz (Eds.), *Gender articulated: Language and the socially constructed self* (pp. 217–244). New York: Routledge.

McElhinny, B. (1996). An economy of affect: Objectivity, masculinity, and the gendering of police work. In A. Cornwall & N. Lindisfarne (Eds.), *Dislocating masculinity: Comparative ethnographies* (pp. 158–171). London: Routledge.

Meier, K., & Wilkins, V. (2002). Gender differences in agency head salaries: The case of public education. *Public Administration Review, 62*(4), 405–411.

Morris, R. C. (1995). All made up: Performance theory and the new anthropology of sex and gender. *Annual Review of Anthropology, 24,* 567–592.

Ochs, E. (1992). Indexing gender. In A. Duranti & C. Goodwin (Eds.), *Rethinking context: Language as an interactive phenomenon* (pp. 337–358). Cambridge: Cambridge University Press.

Olesen, V. (1994). Feminisms and models of qualitative research. In N. K. Denzin & Y. S. Lincoln (Eds.), *Handbook of qualitative research* (pp. 158–174). Thousand Oaks, CA: Sage.

Reinharz, S. (1992). Conclusions. In *Feminist methods in social research* (pp. 240–269). New York: Oxford University Press.

Scott, J. (1999). *Constructing identity through power and discourse in exemplary women superintendents.* Paper presented at the annual meeting of the American Educational Research Association, Montreal, Quebec.

Skrla, L. (1998). *The social construction of gender in the superintendency.* Paper presented at the annual meeting of the American Educational Research Association, San Diego, CA.

Skrla, L. (2000). Mourning silence: Women superintendents (and a researcher) reflect on speaking up and speaking out. *International Journal of Qualitative Studies in Education, 13*(6), 611–628.

Smith, D. E. (1989). *The everyday world as problematic: A feminist sociology.* Boston, MA: Northeastern University Press.

Smulyan, L. (1998). *Feminist cases of nonfeminist subjects: Case studies of women principals.* Paper presented at the annual meeting of the American Educational Research Association, San Diego, CA.

Tallerico, M., Poole, W., & Burstyn, J. N. (1994). Exits from urban superintendencies: The intersection of politics, race, and gender. *Urban Education, 28,* 439–454.

Tannen, D. (1994). *Talking from 9 to 5: How women's and men's conversational styles affect who gets heard, who gets credit, and what gets done at work.* New York: William Morrow.

Theweleit, K. (1977). *Male fantasies: Volume I: Women, floods, bodies, history.* Minneapolis: University of Minnesota Press.

Theweleit, K. (1989). *Male fantasies: Volume II: Male bodies: psychoanalyzing the white terror.* Minneapolis: University of Minnesota Press.

Chapter 5

Mourning Silence:
Women Superintendents
(and a Researcher)
Rethink Speaking Up and
Speaking Out

Linda Skrla

PROLEPSIS

Given that I have chosen to compose a piece that does not conform completely with traditional academic writing styles, I have included some initial explanatory material to provide a guide for the reader as she or he moves through my text. In looking for a way to provide this explanation that would fit well with my idea of what I am about in this work, I came across the term *prolepsis*, which can be understood to mean "the anticipation of possible objections in order to answer them in advance" (Infoplease, 1999). This prolepsis, then, lays out my approach to this work in a way that provides some signposts for the reader as well as anticipates some of the objections that could be raised about the way I have done things.

First of all, this chapter is about female public school superintendents, women who work in what the U.S. Department of Labor has described as the most gender-stratified executive position in the country (Björk, 1999). A second theme of this piece is silence—institutional silence, political silence, personal silence, even silence about silence—multiple and intertwined silences all related to absent, stifled, or prohibited speech about women's unequal position in society in general and the superintendency in particular. The third, and central, focus of the chapter is on what Derrida (1994) called the work of mourning: "Mourning . . . consists always in attempting to ontologize remains" (p. 9).[1] It is philosophical mourning of which Derrida wrote, and the remains to which he referred were the traces, the scraps, the leftovers of concepts that had been deconstructed. In other words, the work of mourning is what follows in the wake of understanding that concepts no longer fulfill their promise (Lather, 1998). That is, once concepts have been troubled or problematized, we must work to recuperate our thinking. The new thinking, though, will inevitably bear the traces of the concepts, the thinking that came before, even if the concepts and thinking have been deconstructed, rejected, discarded, killed off. Thus, "Mourning is about things neither present nor absent" (Lather, 1999, p. 136); that is, it is neither possible to fully recoup the remains nor to be free from them. "As a 'loss,' the remains are not there for us. . . . Yet the trace . . . remains in the act of mourning" (Cornell, 1992, p. 73). It should be pointed out here that the philosophical concept of mourning does not necessarily carry with it the sadness or grief associated with conventional definitions of mourning. Thus, the work of reontologizing the remains of problematized concepts may be positive and productive.

The primary connection between these three themes—women superintendents, silence, and mourning, as the title indicates—is the mourning work done by three female superintendents who were participants in one of my earlier research projects. Their mourning work followed speaking up in research interviews about their experiences with sexism, discriminatory treatment in the public school superintendency and, thus, breaking their career-long silence about these issues; their mourning work is discussed in the second half of this chapter. There is other mourning work going on in this piece, however—my own mourning work about research. This is where I begin the text that follows, with the evolution of my thinking about women in the superintendency and what it means to do feminist research about/with them. This evolution could be thought of as successive waves of my own mourning work. I chose this as a beginning point because I believe, with Blackmore (1999), that "The representation of self emerges as an issue in the messy nexus of research, theory and feminist practice" (p. 62). The remaining sections of this chapter are organized in a way that may not necessarily match the expected structure for academic writing (here I am anticipating some of the objections mentioned earlier). By this I mean that introductions, elaborations, and explanations are provided at the point they become necessary (in my view) in the flow of the text rather than where they might customarily be expected.

THE RESEARCHER'S MOURNING WORK

Background and Context

At first, we ignored their presence. Then, we counted them numerically and reported their numbers as neutral assessments of truth (Blount, 1995). Then, we questioned them in our positivist surveys and aggregated their responses with men's, assuming their views and experiences were the same as men's. After many years, we realized that they might be different, so we designed research that focused specifically on them, but our methods still were androcentric and our questions still were based on male views (Bell, 1988, 1995; Shakeshaft, 1987, 1999). Eventually, we consciously sought to use feminist methods and appropriately empathic interview techniques in our research with them—but often we found that they would not or could not talk to us about the discrimination they faced (Beekley, 1994; Bell, 1995; Chase, 1995).

The they/them about whom I write are women public school superintendents—arguably the most marginalized group in educational administration. Women hold less than 7 percent of superintendencies (Glass, 1992), yet 75 percent of the teaching force from which superintendents come is female (National Center for Education Statistics [NCES], 1997).[2] This situation is not new; in fact, the 7 percent figure has remained virtually unchanged for the past 40 years. These numbers, by themselves, do not tell us much about the intensely complex situation in U.S. society and in our schools that produces and sustains such a staggering degree of gender stratification in public school leadership. Further, the numbers tell us nothing about the work lives of the relatively few women who inhabit the superintendency role. Unfortunately, research in educational administration about women superintendents has failed to meaningfully identify, let alone address, the problems these women face. This failure is due to educational administration research's particularly unsavory history with respect to women that has been well documented by Banks (1995), Bell (1988, 1995), Blount (1995, 1998), Chase (1995), Shakeshaft (1987, 1999) and others. Because research on the superintendency has, until quite recently, used male-dominated samples and male-biased attitudes and methods, much is still unknown about "what women's ambitions and perspectives are [and] how women perceive and experience their work" (Bell, 1988, p. 35).

There has been, however, some small progress toward gaining insight on women's work lives as superintendents within the past decade as qualitative studies of women's experiences in the superintendency have begun to appear in the literature (see, for example, Brunner, 1994, 1997; Chase, 1995;

Grogan, 1996; Tallerico, Burstyn, & Poole, 1993). This type of research has provided some knowledge of what women superintendents experience, including glimpses of sexism and discriminatory treatment that continue to disgrace the profession (Scheurich, 1995), but even in these studies, barriers have persisted in getting women to talk openly. For example, Beekley (1994) in her study of women's exit from the superintendency mused:

> Why did these women fail to acknowledge the prejudice and discrimination they experienced? They really did not talk at length about the problem. Was it because they just accepted it as part of the job, or were they so accustomed to it they didn't find it unusual? Did they ignore it as a way of managing the work they had to do? Is it not socially acceptable to talk about it? (p. 149)

Numerous researchers have explained this self-silencing behavior on the part of women superintendents and other female administrators as a by-product of the male-dominated culture of educational administration in which women learn that they are out of place and should keep quiet (West & Zimmerman, 1991). The phenomenon has been variously described as "downplaying isolation and sexism" (Marshall, 1993, p. 173), failing to comprehend how gender serves as a segregating factor (Schmuck & Schubert, 1995), a myth of neutrality that keeps administrators from confronting sexism (Rizvi, 1993), and discriminatory social constructions that make certain phenomena unobservable (Anderson, 1990; Hyle, 1991).

This cultural silencing, according to Mary Daly (1978), is a strategy employed (or deployed) by the dominant (androcentric) culture to stifle and erase women's voices and prevent the possibility of women speaking out against sexism and discrimination. Foss, Foss, and Griffin (1999) elaborate:

> Silencing takes many forms, but it centers on the creation of fear in the minds of women should they speak out against the foreground [dominant societal views]. Calling women *sick*, *selfish*, *sexless*, or *man-haters* when they raise the issue of women's oppression . . . threaten[s] women into silence. . . . Such labels effectively silence women because of their negative connotations in the foreground. Silenced, women are then prevented from speaking against foreground practices and policies and on behalf of their woman-identified Selves. (p. 143)

Such silencing is prevalent throughout U.S. society, but the overwhelmingly male-dominated culture of educational administration has created a situation in which the silencing of women's views is particularly acute (Clair, 1998; Jaworski, 1993). In fact, Susan Chase (1995) has argued persuasively that structural conditions and discursive possibilities in educational administration effectively prevent the formation of feminist activist discourse.

Further, this silencing has been so effectively accomplished that it is itself invisible to the vast majority of those who work in educational settings—teachers, administrators, principals, superintendents, board members, professors, administrative students, and so on. The silence on women's issues in educational administration, thus, is a feature, a product, an effect of the normal situation—what Daly (1978) labeled "numbing, dumbing normality" (p. 19) and Foucault (1980) termed "the procedures of normalization" (p. 107).

Research Stage I

In 1996, prompted by research findings about the silence on women's issues in educational administration, and specifically by the inability and/or unwillingness of female superintendents to talk openly about their experiences, I developed a study that was designed to get past this barrier of inhibited speech. I wanted to get behind, below, and beyond what I saw as women superintendents' silence about their experiences with sexism in the superintendency. As a practicing public school administrator, aspiring superintendent, and doctoral student researcher with strong feminist convictions, I was persuaded by my reading of Lather (1991) and others that the "goal of feminist research in the human sciences [was] to correct both the *invisibility* and *distortion* of female experience in ways relevant to ending women's unequal social position" (p. 71).

Therefore, I designed a study that used a three-stage qualitative research design—an "empowering research methodology" (Lather, 1987, 1991)—that was intended to get women who had been superintendents to feel free and safe enough in a research interview setting to talk openly about their lives in this male-dominated role. A key feature of this empowering methodology was my deliberate attempt to conduct interviews in a way that I felt was closer to conversing with colleagues than to traditional interviews in which an "expert" researcher questioned research "subjects." Mishler (1986) described this interview approach as "accept[ing] interviewees as collaborators, that is, as full participants in the development of the study and in the analysis and interpretation of the data" (p. 126). By using such an approach, I hoped to reach beneath the surface-level discourse on gender that is ordinarily filtered by "social regularities that . . . operate like a grid that generates what may be seen and talked about" (Scheurich, 1994, p. 445), and thus produce study findings that would contribute in some substantive way to the research about women superintendents.

After completing the study, I had been, I felt, successful in reaching my goal of getting beyond women superintendents' silence, and I have written and presented about the results of that study (see Skrla, 1998, 2000, and Skrla, Reyes, & Scheurich, 2000). The title of one of the articles that came out of the study, "Sexism, Silence, and Solutions: Women Superintendents Speak Up and Speak Out," is descriptive of the study findings. Through the course of two rounds of individual interviews and one group interview, my three study participants grew increasingly comfortable talking about, and eventually became quite vocal about the sexism and discrimination they faced as superintendents. They also talked candidly about their own silence and the silence of the educational administration profession on these issues and proposed their own solutions for some of the problems women superintendents face.

Research Stage II

Often since the completion of that study, however, I have wondered about the aftereffects of this research for the women who were the participants. Although I took the usual precautions for care of my participants that qualitative researchers take—informed consent, member checks, triangulation of meaning achieved through sequential interviews, use of pseudonyms in the final report—I still felt a vague but lingering sense of unease that grew stronger as I read more "post" (McWilliam, 1997), i.e., postmodern, poststructural, postcolonial, writing about the research process (e.g., Alexander & Mohanty, 1997; Blackmore, 1999; Britzman, 1995; Moya, 1997; Scheurich, 1992, 1997; St. Pierre, 1997; Smith, 1999; Visweswaran, 1994). I grew more troubled by what Lather (1998) described as "unproblematized assumptions about the role of 'transformative intellectuals,' ideology critique, a voluntarist philosophy of consciousness and pretensions toward 'emancipating' or 'empowering' some others" (p. 6). Eventually, these readings and my own reflections "brought forward my own 'liberatory' assumptions and [I] was forced to examine them" (McWilliam, 1997, p. 225).

In other words, I had achieved my objectives in my research in that I had gotten women who were, by their own descriptions, not feminists, who had maintained silence about the discrimination they experienced throughout their professional careers, who wanted to "get past the gender issue" (Skrla, Reyes, & Scheurich, 2000) to acknowledge to themselves and to talk openly with each other and with me about the sexism that permeated the culture of the public school superintendency. I had accomplished successfully what Visweswaran (1994) described as the normative ethnographer's task: "We exhort tales and confessions from reluctant informants; we overcome the resistance of recalcitrant subjects" (p. 60). Then, having gotten what I came for, I went off to write my representation of these women's lives as superintendents, and I left my participants to deal with the aftermath of their participation in my research. Beyond the ordeal of the research itself, these women had to deal with broken silence and the resultant collapse of paradigms that had served them apparently well for their entire professional careers. My study participants were left with the task of reconstructing their thinking about their lives and their work in the face of "concepts [now] understood as no longer fulfilling their promise" (Lather, 1998, p. 3)—what Derrida (1994) calls the work of mourning. My participants, thus, were faced with the work of mourning their broken silence.

I am certainly not the first researcher to wrestle (albeit after the fact) with issues surrounding the gathering of interview data and textual representation of such data. For example, Kamala Visweswaran's (1994) question "Does not my puncturing of a carefully maintained silence replicate the same moves of a colonial anthropology?" (p. 60) resonated with me, and I found it troubling. In my desire to contribute in a positive way to the (in my view severely flawed) research literature on women superintendents, I had been seduced by the notion of using feminist qualitative methods that "promise[d] to deliver voices that have been previously shut out of normative educational research and to remedy the ways educational research normalizes populations through its imposition of categories that situate individuals as the site of the problem" (Britzman, 1995, p. 235). In designing my study to get past the individual and institutional silence about sexism and discrimination in the public school superintendency, I had neglected to attend to my own presumptions of empowerment toward my participants.

Furthermore, I had not sufficiently considered other troubling methodological issues such as what Elizabeth St. Pierre (1997) termed "the disjunction between the theory of the researcher and the theory of her participants" (p. 378). As a researcher who leaned toward feminist poststructural interpretations, St. Pierre described being "floored" by the complexity of describing the lives of women who had lived for decades within humanist understandings of their world using her own theoretical frame that was "committed to the persistent critique of all claims to truth, including the truth of their lives" (p. 377). Other feminist researchers (e.g. Smulyan, 2000; Visweswaran, 1994) have grappled with this same dilemma. Deborah Britzman (1995) also reported struggling with the notion that

[Poststructural] theorizing may not make sense to the people behind my text. . . . Most, if not all, of my participants were deeply invested in the humanistic notion of an essential self. . . . I am getting at the inevitable tension, born from the theories that structured my narrations, that my interpretation will agonize what they take as their lived experience. And if ethnography authenticates representation, what does it mean to employ theories that call into question promises of representation and belief? (p. 236)

Like these other researchers, I found that I was no longer sure what to make of or how to write about the stories my participants told me. As I became more convinced that the stories these women told (and the silence that prevented their telling) had less to do with my participants' individual choosing selves and more to do with patriarchal and hegemonic forces and discourses (Clair, 1998) at work in the culture of educational administration, I became less sure how to represent these stories without "falling into arguments regarding true and false consciousness" (Britzman, 1995, p. 236) or how to deal responsibly with the fact that "academic researchers . . . are required to theorize our respondents' accounts and lives and locate them within wider academic and theoretical debates" (Mauthner & Doucet, 1998, p. 141).

The only way I could think of to attempt to quiet my unquiet thoughts about these issues was to go back to my participants and talk to them again. This time, my motivation for interviewing these women was both different and the same as it had been two years earlier. It was different because I had lost some of my naive emancipatory zeal, although I was now mindful that I was probably still equally naive about a whole host of other methodological and epistemological issues I did not yet know enough about to recognize. For this interview, I wanted to focus on how the women had reconstructed their thinking on both personal and professional issues after the breaking of what we all termed their silence about the discriminatory treatment they faced as superintendents. My motivation was the same as two years previously, however, in that I had not entirely given up my desire to work through my research toward promoting change in educational administration, to "provide a critical space for pushing thought against itself" (Britzman, 1995, p. 237) about the situation for women in the superintendency.

Two years elapsed between the end of the original research study and the time I invited my three original participants to get back together as a group for another interview. I was uncertain about whether or not they would be willing to participate in another interview, but all three women agreed. The discussion in the next section of the chapter is drawn from

Mourning Silence

data gathered during the re-interview of my three original study participants. The interview was conducted as a focus group using open-ended questions. The session was tape-recorded and transcribed; the transcript served as the primary source of data for this chapter. Additionally, attending to the fact that in research interviews multiple things happen simultaneously, many or most of which go unnoticed (or are unknowable) by the researcher or the participants (Scheurich, 1997), the graduate assistant with whom I work, Dawn Hogan, observed the interview (with permission of the participants) and made notes on her observations. Her notes (and debriefing conversations I had with her following the interview) served as additional sources of data. I have attempted to write this chapter in a way that is consistent with how I now view research interviewing and the text that comes out of such interviews. I have been influenced by Delgado-Gaitan (1993); Fine (1994); Fine, Weis, Wesseen, and Wong (2000); Lather (1997, 1998); Lincoln (1993); Peshkin (1988); Scheurich (1992, 1997); St Pierre (1997) and others to think that any text can only approximate, at best, an unreliable representation of some small part of what comes out of the intensely and messily complex human interactions, what Scheurich (1997) terms the "wild profusion," that are research interviews.

To help the reader better understand what came out of my conversation with the three women who had been my study participants, some introduction to them and the setting in which they served as public school superintendents would likely be helpful. Leslie Conrad, Amanda Hunter, and Emma Wilburn[3] are all White women of middle age. These women, at the time of the original research study, had all exited the superintendency for work in other education-related fields. The choice of exiters rather than currently practicing superintendents was a strategy I employed to promote the likelihood of candid conversations, given the oppressive effect the culture of public school administration has on dissenting voices. Because the number of women who have been superintendents is small and the number who have exited the profession is even smaller, it is important to protect the details of these women's lives that might be most telling. Therefore, following Morse's (1994) suggestion, the descriptions of the participants' experiences and work settings that follow are presented as aggregates "so that identifiers (such as gender, age, and years of experience) are not linked (making individuals recognizable) and are not consistently associated with the same participant throughout the text, even if a code name is used" (p. 232).

The study participants had a broad range of experiences in school administration and the superintendency. The school districts for which these women served as superintendents were all located in the South and could be termed medium sized (between 2,000 and 6,000 students). The participants' districts served student populations that were economically and racially diverse. Only one of the participants was born and raised in the state where she served as superintendent; another was born in a different southern state; the third participant was born in the North and spent most of her career there before moving to the South to work as a superintendent. For two of the women, the superintendency they exited was their first. The third woman who participated in the study was one of the pioneer women superintendents in her state and had served as superintendent for three districts.

One of the participants was recruited for her most recent superintendency by a search consultant hired by the school board. The two others were promoted from within the district, one from the position of business manager and the other from the role of assistant superintendent for instruction. All of the women had been superintendent for more than five years in the district from which they exited the superintendency. At the time of the original interviews, one had left the superintendency less than six months earlier, another had been out of the role for one year, and the third had exited two years before. During the six-month period in which the original interviews took place, all three women were working in education-related fields other than public schools. Two of the participants were still working in the same jobs during the follow-up interview. One of the participants had returned to the superintendency on an interim basis. Two of these former superintendents held doctoral degrees. All three were married, and one had school-aged children. All of the women belonged to their state administrator organizations, but none of them belonged to any women's organizations or groups. Two participants knew one another slightly before participation in the research project; neither knew the third participant.

What would traditionally be known as the "findings" or results section of this chapter follows. It is generally organized into categories consistent with three broad themes that the participants and I explored during our most recent interview. We talked about the mourning process, that is, the evolution of their thoughts and how they now think two years after "speaking up and speaking out," about (a) the present situation for women in general in the superintendency, (b) their own experiences in the superintendency, and (c) their experiences as participants in the original research project. However, while writing within these themes, I have attempted to do so in a way that conveys some of the complexity and uncertainty of interaction among four humans.

THE PARTICIPANTS' MOURNING WORK

The three women former superintendents who participated in my original study and in the follow-up interview spent their entire careers in public school administration adhering to norms that prevented their noticing or speaking out about gender-related issues, sexism, and discrimination. They were, by their own descriptions, silent and largely unaware. Emma said it was "unusual for me to think that way [about gender]." Leslie described herself as "ignorant of a lot of it" and said she performed her duties as superintendent as if "gender were not involved." Amanda put it this way: "I didn't see it. Or, if I did see it, I acknowledged it; I knew it was there, but I wanted to be better than that. I wanted to get past the gender issue."

Despite this career-long silence and unawareness, during the course of my original research study that involved two rounds of extended individual interviews and a group interview, the three women became more open to examining and talking about their experiences as superintendents through the lens of gender. Eventually, especially in the final, focus group interview, the participants spoke quite candidly about the sexism and discrimination that they had experienced in their careers. These women talked at some length about experiencing specific manifestations of sexism and discriminatory treatment, including continual questioning of their competence, sex-role stereotyping (perceptions about malleable personalities, assumptions about appropriate activities, and expectations of feminine behavior), and intimidation.[4]

I should point out here that I do not mean to imply that these women's descriptions of their experiences with sexism and discrimination in the superintendency, exhorted after the fact in research interviews, corresponded with any externally verifiable reality. I am now, and was during the original interviewing process, of the opinion that these research interviews represented, as Britzman (1995) found, "a contradictory process whereby the past is reinvented and textualized through the discourses and practices of the present" (p. 234). In fact, the stated goal of the original research was to study the social constructions of gender and the public school superintendency from the perspectives of women superintendents.

My three participants' constructions of gender and the superintendency, though, changed through the course of and as a result of the original research interviews. In other words, I openly and intentionally set up the process expecting that women who had remained silent throughout their work lives on issues of sexism and discrimination and gender would break that silence and talk to me about these things. In doing so, however, the ways in which they produced their own identities (Britzman, 1995; Scott, 1999) and made sense of their experiences and themselves were altered by their participation in my research. This, of course, leads to the focus of the current piece—what came after "speaking up and speaking out," the mourning work that followed the ruptured silence. As a researcher, I am hopeful that useful understandings, both about research process and about women's experiences in the public school superintendency, may emerge from the conversation I had with my participants during our follow-up interview that occurred two years after the original project. That is, in reconstructing their thinking about the superintendency and about themselves as women after breaking their silence, different understandings may emerge that were impossible before. These understandings, though, will be colored by the traces, the remains, the morsels, of the thinking that came before. As Lather (1998), drawing from the work of Judith Butler, emphasized, "concepts understood as no longer fulfilling their promise do not become useless. On the contrary, their very failures become provisional grounds and new uses are derived" (p. 3). Thus, through the work of mourning both their broken silence and their previous conceptualizations of themselves and of the superintendency, in picking up and examining and putting down again their old thinking, healing may occur and new thinking may be generated that was previously impossible. That is, "The future, the beyond, is revealed in the remembrance of the remains; the chance for the future, in other words, is preserved in the work of mourning" (Cornell, 1992, p. 75).

Mourning the Superintendency

I began my most recent interview with my participants by asking them if they thought anything had changed over the past two years with respect to the overall situation for women in the superintendency. Leslie replied: "I see the situation as just the same. I don't think the system has changed. . . . There are just the same stories repeated over and over and over and over." The conversation seemed quickly to shift then to a discussion of the contradictory way in which the superintendency is commonly thought of and the way, in the participants' views, it actually is. I saw this as a discussion of some of the fictions of the superintendency that the three women seemed formerly to believe and now saw as myths. This, to me, was the first area of mourning that arose in the discussion—mourning of myths, illusions, naivetes about the role of the superintendent.

The fiction that featured most prominently in our discussion had to do with the notion that the most important requirement for success in the superintendency was doing the job well as traditionally defined—attending to the finances, facilities, and instructional program of the district, doing "what is right and good by kids," as Amanda described it. Examining their experiences in hindsight, through the distance of between three and five years since their exits from the superintendency, and after participating in my original research project, Leslie, Emma, and Amanda drew sharp distinctions between the previously stated view of what being a superintendent was all about and how they now viewed it in terms of the

Mourning Silence   115

power, prestige, and politics that are inherent parts of the role. Emma put it this way:

> It's been interesting as I've looked back and have tried to tell people not to make the same mistakes I think I made. I was being so task oriented and thinking what I was getting into was a job. What I was getting into was a role. . . . You get so focused on making the right decisions. . . . I don't think I understood exactly the significance of being *The Superintendent*. I never thought of myself in terms of the power and prestige, and I didn't use that as well as I could have because I was focused on doing the job. . . . I think that was a major mistake because I didn't see myself as being that important to people.

Amanda characterized herself in much the same way (saying to Emma): "I'm like you; I never saw myself as anything—anyone any different than just someone who played a part in the school. . . . I did not understand it until after the fact." The same type of view of herself as someone who eschewed the power, prestige, and politics associated with the role (thus conforming to feminine norms) and focused on providing educational benefits for children (also in line with gendered expectations for "caring" leadership) was echoed by Leslie:

> When I think back to what I was doing, I was probably still focused on reaching this goal for the kids, and I didn't take time to understand the emotional perspective of a lot of the board members—in terms of their reaction to what I was proposing. . . . I'm beginning now to think through and reflect.

Later in the interview conversation, the participants themselves linked their naivete about this particular fiction to gender-related factors including societal norms and female socialization. Ferguson (1984) pointed out that this type of naivete is widespread among women working in bureaucratic organizations: "Belief in an 'individual solution,' ironically pursued *en masse* by legions of ambitious candidates, is the great American illusion. . . . The naivete of many women [lies] in believing that ability and achievement are the bases for reward" (pp. 183–184). Amanda described her current understanding of the situation, in contrast to her previous view, this way:

> The issues were crossing that gender line and doing what a man would do. Everyone wanted to categorize you as "a soft woman would not do something like this." So I think it's

crossing those lines and standing up for what you know is right, well, they can't understand that, they can't support that. ... It is not the side [of a woman] that the public wants to see, or the board wants to see, or school people want to see. I never even considered that. I really don't think I considered the public perception. I just considered what I thought was right. I thought that what would win out is what is right and good for kids. And that is not what wins out. That's probably what my biggest misconception was.

Here I heard Amanda draw a clearly-stated contrast between her former views of the superintendency as a sort of meritocracy, where competence would be an absolute defense against politics (Blackmore, 1999), even gendered politics, and her current understanding that gender did indeed operate in her past experiences as superintendent.

Emma talked in much the same way about looking back on her experiences as a superintendent and seeing that gender colored others' perceptions of her performance as superintendent:

I think that as I look back—at the time I don't think I felt as much that it was a gender issue—but looking back, there really were things. They [constituents] don't really want a woman to be competent across the board. My strength (in my mind) was curriculum and instruction, but because I had a business background in the district, people wanted to assume I knew nothing about instruction. I was not supposed to be competent in everything. You're just not supposed to be competent in everything. You're supposed to need somebody to help you in something. And if you're really good and look like you don't need help, I think that, as a woman, that invites, that just gets at people. It gets at other women; it gets at other men. I think it almost causes you more trouble with women than with men. Men will just come at you. Women—you look back and you're bleeding from the back and you never know you were stabbed. You know, little thin stilettos that go in there and all of the sudden you've bled to death. I think part of my lack of doing well on the job was some things that I should have done differently.

Emma's comments seemed to indicate that she had reconstructed her views of the operation of gender in her work life as superintendent to include the understanding that many people with whom she worked, both men and women, found her competence as a female superintendent threatening. That is, in satisfying the expectation for competency as a superintendent (in finance as well as the more traditionally female realm of curriculum and instruction), she violated normalized expectations of femininity.

Mourning Their Own Careers

A second area of mourning work that my study participants and I discussed was their thinking (both past and present) about their own careers as female superintendents. Several strands or themes seemed to run through this part of the interview conversation. Two that I have pulled from the transcript to explore here are isolation and return.

The first of these, isolation, is a familiar theme from recent qualitative research with women superintendents. Colleen Bell (1995) described this isolation that women superintendents experience as resulting from cultural pressure to "de-feminize," or disaffiliate from other women to prove themselves as professionals. This creates a situation in which every woman superintendent deals alone with the institutional sexism and discriminatory treatment. As Susan Chase (1995) put it, "In this profession, a lonely, isolated struggle against inequality is the requirement and cost of professional success" (p. 33).

Amanda described her dawning awareness of her own isolation and individualized internalization of her experiences in the superintendency by relating her reaction (and her husband's) to reading the transcript of the group interview from the original study:

> I read the transcript after we were done the first time and my husband also read it. He asked me, "Which one was you?" It was like an echo of the same things. He knew I was doing this but didn't know anything of the content. I never even discussed it at home. So I brought it home one evening and I said, "You know, just read this." And he got to reading it, and he read the whole thing, and he said, "I thought this was just you." It was a real eye-opener for him as it was for me that, God, I'm sick that it's the same thing [for other women superintendents].

I found this part of Amanda's talk with the group powerfully moving. When she said that her husband of many years could not pick out which parts of the transcript from the group interview in the original study were her words and which belonged to the other two women, and she then talked about how amazed they both were by this, I was struck anew by the force of what I saw as the normalizations that circulate and operate in educational administration discourses.

118   *Linda Skrla*

The individualization, isolation, and loneliness that suffuse the work lives of women superintendents were also the focus of data that Leslie provided, although this was not verbal data from the interview; it came several months later via e-mail. At the end of the interview, I encouraged the participants to call or e-mail if they had any additional thoughts they wanted to contribute to this research effort. I knew that at least one of the women wrote poetry, so I also invited them to send poetry if they had some that fit with the subject of the research. Here is a poem Leslie sent.

> Thoughts after a long day by a new superintendent
> Leslie Conrad
> **L**onely . . .
> **O**stracized. Why? Because I'm an
> OUTsider and a woman?
> **N**ew to most people in the community?
> **E**xcellence, they said, "Focus on
> academic excellence.
> **L**ead and we will follow."
> **Y**es, I have led and I am very lonely.

In repeated readings of Leslie's poem, first in the e-mail and numerous times since, I have been strongly affected by at least two things. First, I have been struck by the force of the emphasis, both in the structure of the poem and from its overall effect, on loneliness. Leslie sent specific instruction in her e-mail that the first letters of the lines were to be set in bold type, I assumed to emphasize that the letters spell out the word *lonely*. This word also begins and ends the poem.

The second thing that affected me about this poem was that it seemed to reveal something more of Leslie's thoughts, feelings, and constructions about her experiences in the superintendency than was available through interview conversations. Perhaps this something more is similar to what Maxine Greene (1995) described as releasing the imagination through artistic forms. To illustrate, a facet of this poem that stood out for me was the word *ostracized* and its link to outsider status and femaleness. Leslie was probably the participant most reluctant to discuss gender-related issues in her superintendency during the original study. She described herself as operating as if "gender were not involved" during her long and successful career as a public school superintendent. Nowhere in the transcripts of any of the original interviews or the follow-up interview on which this chapter is based did Leslie use such a forceful word as *ostracized* in relation to gender. It seemed to me that this poem, following as it did months after the latest interview, indicated that the work of mourning continues (at least for Leslie) and that it continues to produce reconstructed concepts and understandings.

The second area of mourning work around the participants' own careers as superintendents that stood out as a recurring theme was the question of whether or not each of the women would return to the superintendency at any point in the future. Although one of the participants seemed sanguine about her choice to exit the field, there appeared to be a great deal yet unresolved about this issue for the other two women. Amanda, particularly, returned to the topic several times at different points in the interview conversation. Each time she emphasized that she had no doubts of whether she could do the job again and said that she was happy with her choice to pursue another career path (though one still related to public education). This excerpt from the transcript is typical of Amanda's talk on this issue:

> I think [the superintendency] is wonderful, I'm glad that I was a part. Then I wonder sometimes why don't I want to be a part again? Maybe that's not good. But I've never, not one time, looked in the job bulletin for the superintendents' jobs and thought, "Hey, I'm going to try for that." . . . I don't want it. Because I know that I can do it. . . . I try to stay as positive as I possibly can because I had five great years and I have good memories. . . . I think it's really important to stay positive. Otherwise, who is going to want to go and do that job? . . . Where I still struggle is that the [women superintendent aspirants] out there that can't wait to get into this type of role and I think, "You are going to crash and burn. You are too strong willed; you are going to struggle." And I don't like that feeling.

Dawn commented in her observation notes that Amanda seemed to her to be "continuing to mull over the whole thing [her superintendency experience]."

Amanda also spoke specifically about the role mourning work following the original research project played in shaping her thinking about her decision to exit the superintendency:

> It helped me. As I drove home [from the group interview in the original study], you know I thought, "That was neat. That was what I needed." I needed to know, and it also helped me because I was feeling right then that maybe I was afraid to go

back in there [the superintendency] because I wasn't applying for any superintendencies that first year. And I felt really safe where I was, and I liked what I was doing. But it [the research] was a time for me to say, "Hey, this [the current position] is what I'm good at, this is a job I like every part of. Where in that other one [the superintendency] there were things that I did not like, and I did not like me doing some of those things . . . I think that [participating in the research] really worked for me.

Leslie, in contrast, seemed quite comfortable with her decision to leave the superintendency and pursue other work. (Dawn's notes describe her demeanor as peaceful when talking about this issue.)

I have no desire [to return to the superintendency]. I'm really happy doing what I'm doing. I took my file drawer of all my stuff that I had kept for a couple of years; I threw it all in the trash. I mean, it was time.

Emma, after listening to the other two participants speculate about returning, described her situation this way:

I am less resolved. I am still more beat up. I don't know if I'll ever get over it. And yet, I am the only one [of the three participants] that would like to go back to it. . . . I feel like I have a gift for administration, and I miss using that gift. I've not found anything I get as passionate about as I did about being superintendent.

For at least two of the participants (Amanda and Emma), their decisions to exit the superintendency permanently seemed to be an issue around which there was much mourning work yet to be done.

The three women had clearly thought about their decisions to exit a great deal since the original research study, and it seemed as if their new understandings about issues explored in the earlier section on the superintendency (politics, power, prestige, and gender) both provided some resolution and created new tensions. The participants talked about both things—that gaining a "better" understanding of their experiences in the superintendency through participation in the original research helped them to let go of their decision to exit (as previously illustrated), and that these same new understandings caused them to speculate how they could have done the job better while still in the superintendency, how they might do it better if they returned, or how the situation could be improved for future women superintendents.

Mourning the Research

All three study participants, when I initially approached them about the original research project, expressed reluctance or uncertainty about participating. I openly shared the feminist nature of the project with them at that time; perhaps because of this, but likely due to other complicated factors as well, all three said they had anxieties about participating, although they agreed to do so. Thus, I was interested to hear how the women thought about having been participants in my original study now that two years had passed since its completion. As I discussed in the introduction to this chapter, I was concerned about what the aftereffects were, from the view of my participants, of my "empowering" research design. I was also interested in hearing their views on qualitative research versus the quantitative variety that the two women who held doctorates had done for their own dissertations.

During the final section of our interview conversation, I asked several questions about these issues. Amanda, Emma, and Leslie expressed uniformly positive views of having been participants in the study. Of course, given the nature of the interview setting and the relationships that had formed between the study participants and me and among the women themselves, I am unsure about how comfortable they might have felt about expressing negative sentiments. All three participants, though, clearly seemed to have given the study and their participation in it a great deal of thought.

One word they all used frequently was *reflective*. They talked about how this study gave them a space and a place and forced them, in some cases, to think about their experiences and, in the group interview, to process these same experiences in the company of other women who had also been superintendents. Leslie described her experience as a study participant this way:

> It wasn't just me. Even though I read the literature [about women superintendents], hearing it from real life people that had the same experience made a difference. Sort of like an AA group. To help you feel a little better, maybe also help give some more direction for where you need to go. I think it works both ways; it gives you some perspective in terms of looking back over your shoulder. It makes you feel more whole. . . . I think being reflective can do nothing but help.

Similarly, from Amanda:

> I probably wasn't that reflective until we all had met together. I mean we had talked [during the individual interviews] and I still

122   *Linda Skrla*

had some emotions about the whole thing, but it wasn't until I heard other people. . . . It helped me. As I drove home, you know, I thought it was neat. That was what I needed. . . . This is an extremely reflective time; it made me even think about things that I probably didn't want to think about; it was good.

Emma described it this way:

> It [the research project] was very good for me. . . . From this I realized that I had made a mistake in not having a network to help me. . . . So, this for me really made me aware of what a gap I had created for myself. . . . Just sitting here with both of you [Amanda and Leslie], I have learned so much, and so, for me, it was a very good experience.

It seemed to me that what I have characterized from a researcher's view in the chapter as the work of mourning—reconstruction work following the problematizing of concepts (Lather, 1998)—my participants thought of in more humanist terms as reflection. And they saw this reflection triggered by participation in the original research study as needed and productive work—work that went undone while they were still in their superintendent roles.

In response to a question from me about having been participants in a qualitative research study, Emma and Leslie (Amanda had left for an appointment by this point in the interview) spoke strongly positively about the experience. From Emma:

> Isn't there someone who's talked about the research, the interaction of the researcher and the people they are researching—that research does not occur without impacting those researched? . . . It's like what you did with us. You got research information, but we also grew and were impacted by the research, so it was a much more dynamic process versus a static process. And I don't think that is something that happens in quantitative research. I am immensely different than I would have been if I had not participated in this.

Leslie put it this way:

> If you had done a survey about my views on these things, I mean, you wouldn't have anything. The richness definitely would not be there, nor the learning for us, or the healing, or whatever you want to call it.

Mourning Silence

What I want to call it, and have called it throughout this chapter is mourning, the philosophical, intellectual, and emotional work of three women in reconceptualizing themselves and their work lives following the breaking of career-long silence on issues of sexism and discriminatory treatment in the public school superintendency. My participants called it (variously) reflecting, learning, growing, and healing. Their terminology suggests to me that they saw this work, and the research study that prompted it, as personally beneficial, which I must admit, as an anxious researcher, I found reassuring. I am concerned, though, that the implications for the educational administration profession of what was discussed in the aftermath of these women's silence not be lost in the satisfactory warmth of my participant's reassuring comments.

By this I mean that in sifting through the remains of the three women's former thinking about their lives as superintendents, in picking through the scraps and sewing together the story that was told here, a patchwork has been created that stands as a particular kind of counterpoint to traditional normalized narratives about the superintendency. This patchwork of remains, as Cornell (1992) explains, "'exhibits what it should hide, dissimulacras what it signals.' The part is not lost in the whole. The remains are not grasped as simply the expression of a greater system. Yet the remains cannot be known in and of themselves" (p. 74). In other words, the different pieces of Amanda's, Emma's, and Leslie's thoughts about the superintendency, their careers, and the original research project that have been sewn together in this chapter can be understood in multiple and particular ways that do not represent any master story about women superintendents. Yet each of these pieces of thought is built on the experience of the thinker having been a female superintendent and, therefore, it cannot be understood apart from that experience. Thus, the silences, the myths, the isolation, the loneliness that were the focus of this mourning work, in addition to being important and compelling pieces of these three women's individual stories, form a larger patchwork or mosaic (Cornell, 1992) that is a damning picture of women's experiences in the public school superintendency. This is a picture that continues to be largely excluded from the mainstream exhibitions of the educational administration profession. That is, our journals, textbooks, university classrooms, professional organizations, state education agencies, and local boardrooms persist in displaying only the normalized view of the public school superintendency. I (and, I suspect, Amanda, Emma, and Leslie) would argue that the best hope for working to change the current grossly gender-stratified situation in the public school superintendency lies in replacing the normalized view of the superintendency with views like the patchwork pieced together from the mourning work that has been described here.

124 Linda Skrla

NOTES

I would like to thank Jim Koschoreck, Patrick Slattery, Jennifer Scott, and Dawn Hogan for their thoughtful comments and constructive suggestions on earlier drafts of this chapter. I am also grateful to Michelle Young for her focused and insightful editorial work. Finally, I would like to express my deepest appreciation to Jim Scheurich for his patient and consistent support of my scholarly work and his constant encouragement to push the limits of my thinking about research and about women superintendents' issues.

1. The inspiration for this chapter and specifically for the use of Derrida's (1994) concept of mourning came from Patti Lather's paper "Troubling Praxis: The Work of Mourning," which she delivered at the symposium *Mourning Marxism? Philosophical Explorations in Feminism, Poststructuralism, and Educational Research* sponsored by the Philosophical Studies in Education Special Interest Group (SIG) at the 1998 American Education Research Association (AERA) meeting in San Diego.

2. For the 1995/96 school year, the ratio of male superintendents to male teachers in U.S. public schools was 13,901/553,984 (.025) and the ratio of female superintendents to female teachers was 982/1,610,016 (.0006). Because "virtually all school administrators are initially recruited from the ranks of teachers" (Banks, 1995, p. 70), the odds of a male teacher becoming superintendent are one in 40; for a female teacher, the odds are one in 1,667. In other words, men are more than forty times more likely than women are to advance to the superintendency from teaching (Skrla, 1999, p. 3).

3. All participants' names are pseudonyms.

4. For extended discussion of these issues, see Skrla (1998, 2000) and Skrla, Reyes, & Scheurich (2000).

REFERENCES

Anderson, G. L. (1990). Toward a critical constructivist approach to school administration: Invisibility, legitimization, and the study of non-events. *Educational Administration Quarterly, 26*(1), 38–59.

Alexander, M. J., & Mohanty, C. T. (1997). Introduction: Genealogies, legacies, movements. In M. J. Alexander & C. T. Mohanty (Eds.), *Feminist genealogies, colonial legacies, democratic futures* (pp. xii–xiii). New York: Routledge.

Banks, C. A. M. (1995). Gender and race as factors in educational leadership and administration. In J. A. Banks & C. A. M. Banks (Eds.), *Handbook of research on multicultural education* (pp. 65–80). New York: Macmillan.

Beekley, C. X. (1994). *Women who exit the public school superintendency: Four case studies* [CD-ROM]. Abstract from: Ovid File: Dissertation Abstracts Item: AAC 9500864

Bell, C. S. (1988). Organizational influences on women's experience in the superintendency. *Peabody Journal of Education, 65*(4), 31–59.

Bell, C. S. (1995). "If I weren't involved with schools, I might be radical": Gender consciousness in context. In D. M. Dunlap & P. A. Schmuck (Eds.), *Women leading in education* (pp. 288–312). Albany: State University of New York Press.

Björk, L. G. (1999). Collaborative research on the superintendency. *AERA Research on the Superintendency SIG Bulletin, 2*(1), 1–4.

Blackmore, J. (1999). *Troubling women: Feminism, leadership, and educational change.* Buckingham, UK: Open University Press.

Blount, J. M. (1995). The politics of sex as a category of analysis in the history of educational administration. In B. Irby & G. Brown (Eds.), *Women as school executives: Voices and visions* (pp. 1–5). Austin: Texas Council of Women School Executives.

Blount, J. M. (1998). *Destined to rule the schools: Women and the superintendency 1873–1995.* Albany: State University of New York Press.

Britzman, D. P. (1995). "The question of belief": Writing poststructural ethnography. *International Journal of Qualitative Studies in Education, 8*(3), 229–238.

Brunner, C. C. (1994). *Emancipatory research: Support for women's access to power.* Paper presented at the annual meeting of the American Educational Research Association, New Orleans, LA. (ERIC Document Reproduction Service No. ED 373 440)

Brunner, C. C. (1997). Working through the "riddle of the heart": Perspectives of women superintendents. *Journal of School Leadership, 7*(3), 138–162.

Chase, S. (1995). *Ambiguous empowerment: The work narratives of women school superintendents.* Amherst: University of Massachusetts Press.

Clair, R. P. (1998). *Organizing silence.* Albany: State University of New York Press.

Cornell, D. (1992). *The philosophy of the limit.* New York: Routledge.

Daly, M. (1978). *Gyn/ecology: The metaethics of radical feminism.* Boston: Beacon.

Delgado-Gaitan, C. (1993). Researching change and changing the researcher. *Harvard Educational Review, 63*(4), 389–411.

Derrida, J. (1994). *Specters of Marx: The state of the debt, the work of mourning, and the new international.* New York: Routledge.

Ferguson, K. E. (1984). *The feminist case against bureaucracy.* Philadelphia: Temple University Press.

Fine, M. (1994). Working the hyphens: Reinventing self and other in qualitative research. In N. K. Denzin & Y. S. Lincoln (Eds.), *Handbook of qualitative research* (pp. 70–82). Thousand Oaks, CA: Sage.

Fine, M., Weis, L., Wesseen, S., & Wong, L. (2000). Qualitative research, representations, and social responsibilities. In N. K. Denzin & Y. S. Lincoln (Eds.), *Handbook of qualitative research* (2nd ed.). Thousand Oaks, CA: Sage.

Foss, K. A., Foss, S. K., & Griffin, C. L. (1999). *Feminist rhetorical theories.* Thousand Oaks, CA: Sage.

Foucault, M. (1980). Two lectures. In C. Gordon (Ed.), *Power/knowledge: Selected interviews & other writings 1972–1977* (pp. 78–108). New York: Pantheon.

Glass, T. E. (1992). *The 1992 study of the American school superintendency.* Arlington, VA: American Association of School Administrators.

Greene, M. (1995). *Releasing the imagination: Essays on education, the arts, and social change.* San Francisco: Jossey-Bass.

Grogan, M. (1996). *Voices of women aspiring to the superintendency.* Albany: State University of New York Press.

Hyle, A. E. (1991). *Women and public school administration: Invisibility and discrimination.* Paper presented at the annual meeting of the American Educational Research Association, Chicago, IL. (ERIC Document Reproduction Service No. ED 335 770)

Infoplease. (1999). [On-line]. Available: http//:www.infoplease.com

Jaworski, A. (1993). *The power of silence: Social and pragmatic perspectives.* Newbury Park, CA: Sage.

Lather, P. (1987). *Feminist perspectives on empowering research methodologies.* Paper presented at the annual meeting of the American Educational Research Association, Washington, DC. (ERIC Document Reproduction Service No. 283 858)

Lather, P. (1991). *Getting smart: Feminist research and pedagogy with/in the postmodern.* New York: Routledge.

Lather, P. (1997). Creating a multilayered text: Women, AIDS, and angels. In W. G. Tierney & Y. S. Lincoln (Eds.), *Representation and the text: Reframing the narrative voice* (pp. 233–258). Albany: State University of New York Press.

Lather, P. (1998). *Troubling praxis: The work of mourning.* Paper presented at the annual meeting of the American Educational Research Association, San Diego, CA.

Lather, P. (1999). The places in which we thought then. *Journal of Curriculum Theorizing, 15*(2), 133–138.

Lincoln, Y. (1993). I and thou: Method, voice, and roles in research with the silenced. In D. McLaughlin & W. G. Tierney (Eds.), *Naming silenced lives: Personal narratives and processes of educational change* (pp. 29–47). New York: Routledge.

Marshall, C. (1993). Gender and race issues in administration. In C. Marshall (Ed.), *The new politics of race and gender: The 1992 yearbook of the Politics of Education Association* (pp. 168–174). Washington, DC: Falmer.

Mauthner, N., & Doucet, A. (1998). Reflections on a voice-centered relational method: Analyzing maternal and domestic voices. In J. Ribbens & R. Edwards (Eds.), *Feminist dilemmas in qualitative research: Public knowledge and private lives* (pp. 119–146). London: Sage.

McWilliam, E. (1997). Performing between the posts: Authority, posture and contemporary feminist scholarship. In W. G. Tierney & Y. S. Lincoln (Eds.), *Representation and the text: Reframing the narrative voice* (pp. 219–232). Albany: State University of New York Press.

Mishler, E. G. (1986). *Research interviewing: Context and narrative.* Cambridge, MA: Harvard University Press.

Morse, J. M. (1994). Designing funded qualitative research. In N. K. Denzin & Y. S. Lincoln (Eds.), *Handbook of qualitative research* (pp. 220–235). Thousand Oaks, CA: Sage.

Moya, P. M. L. (1997). Postmodernism, "realism," and the politics of identity: Cherríe Moraga and Chicana feminism. In M. J. Alexander & C. T. Mohanty (Eds.), *Feminist genealogies, colonial legacies, democratic futures* (pp. 125–150). New York: Routledge.

National Center for Education Statistics (NCES). (1997). *Digest of education statistics 1997* [On-line]. Available: http://nces.ed.gov/pub/digest97/98015.html

Peshkin, A. (1988). In search of subjectivity—One's own. *Educational Researcher, 17*(7), 17–21.

Rizvi, F. (1993). Race, gender, and the cultural assumptions of schooling. In C. Marshall (Ed.), *The new politics of race and gender: The 1992 yearbook of the Politics of Education Association* (pp. 203–217). Washington, DC: Falmer.

Schmuck, P. A., & Schubert, J. (1995). Women principals' views on sex equity: Exploring issues of integration and information. In D. M. Dunlap & P. A. Schmuck (Eds.), *Women leading in education* (pp. 274–287). Albany: State University of New York Press.

Scheurich, J. J. (1992). *Doxological bricolage: Methodology in the postmodern: The politics of research theory in education*. Unpublished doctoral dissertation. Ohio State University, Columbus, OH.

Scheurich, J. J. (1994). Policy archaeology: A new policy studies methodology. *Journal of Education Policy, 9*(4), 297–316.

Scheurich, J. J. (1995). The knowledge base in educational administration: Postpositivist reflections. In R. Donmoyer, M. Imber, & J. J. Scheurich (Eds.), *The knowledge base in educational administration: Multiple perspectives* (pp. 17–31). Albany: State University of New York Press.

Scheurich, J. J. (1997). A postmodernist critique of research interviewing. In J. J. Scheurich, *Research method in the postmodern* (pp. 61–79). London: Falmer.

Scott, J. (1999). *Constructing identity through power and discourse in exemplary women superintendents*. Paper presented at the annual meeting of the American Educational Research Association, Montreal, Quebec.

Shakeshaft, C. (1987). *Women in educational administration*. Newbury Park, CA: Sage.

Shakeshaft, C. (1999). The struggle to create a more gender inclusive profession. In J. Murphy & C. S. Lewis (Eds.), *Handbook of research on educational administration* (2nd ed.) (pp. 99–118). San Francisco: Jossey-Bass.

Skrla, L. (1998). *Women superintendents in politically problematic work situations: The role of gender in structuring conflict*. Paper presented at the annual meeting of the American Educational Research Association, San Diego, CA.

Skrla, L. (1999). *Femininity/masculinity: Hegemonic normalizations in the public school superintendency*. Paper presented at the annual meeting of the American Educational Research Association, Montreal, Quebec.

Skrla, L. (2000). The social construction of gender in the superintendency. *Journal of Education Policy, 15*(3), 293–316.

Skrla, L., Reyes, P., & Scheurich, J. J. (2000). Sexism, silence, and solutions: Women superintendents speak up and speak out. *Educational Administration Quarterly, 36*(1), 44–75.

Smith, L. T. (1999). *Decolonizing methodologies: Research and indigenous peoples*. New York: St. Martin's Press.

Smulyan, L. (2000). Feminist cases of nonfeminist subjects: Case studies of women principals. *International Journal of Qualitative Studies in Education, 13*(6), 589–609.

St. Pierre, E. A. (1997). Nomadic inquiry in the smooth spaces of the field: A preface. *International Journal of Qualitative Studies in Education, 10*(3), 365–383.

Tallerico, M., Burstyn, J. N., & Poole, W. (1993). *Gender and politics at work: Why women exit the superintendency.* Fairfax, VA: National Policy Board for Educational Administration. (ERIC Document Reproduction Service No. ED 361 911)

Visweswaran, K. (1994). *Fictions of feminist ethnography.* Minneapolis: University of Minnesota Press.

West, C., & Zimmerman, D. H. (1991). Doing gender. In J. Lorber & S. A. Farrell (Eds.), *The social construction of gender* (pp. 13–37). Newbury Park, CA: Sage.

Part II

Reconsidering Feminist Epistemologies in Educational Leadership

This part begins with Chapter 6 by Cynthia Dillard, who proposes a different approach to feminist dilemmas in research. She shares with her readers what she calls an endarkened feminist epistemology. Cynthia informs the development of this alternative epistemology with an examination of the cultural genesis and meanings of the lives of African American women leaders and researchers. Cynthia develops an endarkened feminist epistemology, which embodies a distinguishably different cultural standpoint, located in the intersection of the cultural constructions of race, gender, and other identities and the historical and contemporary contexts of oppressions and resistance for African American women.

The next chapter, chapter 7, "Chicana Feminism and Educational Leadership," by Sylvia Méndez-Morse, contains an exploration of the utility of three facets of Chicana feminist epistemology for conducting research in educational leadership. These three facets are a Pan-American perspective; an assertion of multiple oppressions caused by the intersections of gender, class, race/ethnicity, religions, language, and sexual orientation; and an emphasis on advocacy for social justice.

Chapter 8 is the text of a speech written by Julie Laible as a keynote address for the Campus Ministers' Association Faith Seeking Understanding Lecture in Tuscaloosa, Alabama, shortly before she was killed in an automobile accident in March 1999. Julie was a courageous and loving scholar whose research and practice focused keenly on issues of equity and social justice. As an assistant professor at the University of Alabama, Julie taught courses and conducted research that aimed to improve educational opportunities and to create supportive environments for all children. The content of her chapter shares an exploration of what Julie held critical in her life, faith, and profession and how she arrived at these understandings. Grounding her ideas in feminist and critical theory and theology, Julie also outlines the contours and content of a loving epistemology. As Julie notes in her text, her work in this area emerged through research she conducted in the Texas–Mexico borderland. Julie began her research in educational leadership by examining practices that increased the success of Mexican American female students. As she developed as a scholar, her focus shifted. She started to question the validity and ethics of her work with the Other and her ability to fully or accurately understand Others' experiences, and she searched for more ethical ways of producing knowledge about other human beings. It was during this time of critical reflective work that she began to explore the development of a loving epistemology. This theoretical work, which she sketches for us in her speech, contributes to the evolving discussions concerning the development and use of alternative epistemologies.

Following Julie's piece are three responses (chapters 9, 10, and 11) that highlight the meaningful guidance Julie's work provides for feminist and nonfeminist researchers alike. Each of the respondents makes sense of Julie's work and uses her lessons in different ways. Colleen Capper (in chapter 9) shares five lessons that she gained through engaging with Julie's work: lessons about belief and faith, lessons about our academic work, lessons about our work and faith, lessons about time, and lessons about epistemology. She then focuses on the contours of Julie's loving epistemology, offers some additional ideas, and creates fertile ground for the further discussion and development of a loving epistemology.

The second response to Julie's work, chapter 10 by Michelle Young and Linda Skrla, discusses the implications of a loving epistemology for the practice of educational leadership by women. Michelle and Linda extend the three contours of Julie's loving epistemology to apply them to the current need to reexamine feminist research in educational leadership.

In the third response (chapter 11), Catherine Marshall, inspired by Julie's discussion of epistemological and methodological advances, reflects on the evolution of research and policy approaches to the problem of women's underrepresentation in educational leadership theory and practice, and on the evolving right of scholars to insert values into their research agendas. Catherine ends her piece by urging her readers to action based on the knowledge accumulated through decades of research on women in educational leadership.

Chapter 6

The Substance of Things Hoped for, the Evidence of Things Not Seen: Examining an Endarkened Feminist Epistemology in Educational Research and Leadership

Cynthia B. Dillard

According to Stanfield (1993), "epistemological concerns in cultural research in the social sciences cannot be divorced from concerns regarding the functions of culturally hegemonic domination in knowledge production and dissemination and in the selections and rewarding of intellectual careers" (p. 26). Additionally, the underlying understanding of the nature of reality and the forms of discourse one employs to construct realities in research on leadership (or is encouraged or permitted to employ) significantly impacts not only what can be said and how it is said, but where it is said. Nowhere is this truer than in the interpretation and representation of educational inquiry, especially as we engage more artistic modes of research (Austin, 1994; Eisner, 1979; Greene, 1978; Walker, 1996; Yenne-Donmoyer & Donmoyer, 1994). As we see a gradual "opening up" of the uses of Black vernacular and more indigenous references in pop culture representations in theater, music and the like (although still primarily controlled and attended by predominantly White audiences), it seems reasonable to assume that the educational leadership research community might also be ready to examine more culturally indigenous ways of knowing research and enacting leadership in the academy. In this way, such voices are provided legitimation, not of their existence, but as analytic, conceptual, and representational tools that explicate deep meanings of the very bases of educational research and leadership, its ontologies, epistemologies, pedagogies, and its ethical concerns.

I will argue here that when we begin to move beyond race/ethnicity and gender as biological constructions to more culturally engaged explanations of being human, and when we seek to examine the origins of such knowledge constructions of the very nature of how reality is known (its patterns of epistemology),[1] we will find that what constitutes knowledge depends profoundly on the consensus and ethos of the community in which it is grounded. Given the shifting demographics and recent interest in "multicultural" communities and people of color, it is not only an ethical imperative for researchers/leaders, but also a compelling possibility to engage a differing metaphor of research, one that profoundly disrupts the idea of neutral relationships and structures in inquiry and points instead to the complex nature of research when it maintains allegiance and substantive connections to the very communities under study. Thus, alternative epistemological truths are required if educational researchers and leaders are to be truly responsible, asking for new ways of looking into the reality of others that opens our own lives to view—and that makes us accountable to the people, interests, and needs of whom we study.

As an African American feminist scholar, I will examine in this chapter what I call an endarkened feminist epistemology. In defining an endarkened feminist epistemology, I have deliberately sought language that attempts to unmask traditionally held political and cultural constructions/constrictions, language that more accurately organizes, resists, and transforms oppressive descriptions of sociocultural phenomena and relationships. In this vein, Asante (1988), Morrison (1992), Thiongo (1986) and others have suggested that language has historically served—and continues to serve—as a powerful tool in the mental, spiritual, and intellectual colonization of African Americans and other marginalized peoples. They further suggest that language itself is epistemic, that it provides a way for persons to understand their reality. Thus, to transform that reality the very language we use to define and describe phenomena must possess instrumentality: It must be able to *do* something toward transforming particular ways of knowing and producing knowledge.

Therefore, in contrast to the common use of the term *enlightened* as a way of expressing new and important feminist insights (arising historically from the well-established canon of White feminist thought), I use the term *endarkened* feminist epistemology to articulate how reality is known when based in the historical roots of Black feminist thought, embodying a distinguishable difference in cultural standpoint, located in the intersection/overlap of the culturally constructed socializations of race, gender, and other identities and the historical and contemporary contexts of oppressions and resistance for African American women. Such attention to the epistemological levels of research and leadership also implies a shift in the research metaphors and an uncovering of the ideologies that we have taken for granted, those that have traditionally left unproblematized our goals, purposes, and practice in educational research. To articulate an endarkened feminist epistemology, it is important that I first address the shifting ground of educational research and the prevailing metaphors that have [mis]guided us in our research endeavors.

CHANGING METAPHORS, CHANGING IDEOLOGIES: THE SHIFTING CULTURAL GROUND OF RESEARCH

All research is social construction and a cultural endeavor. A major contribution of feminist, ethnic, and cultural studies to the educational research community has been the reframing of the research endeavor as an ideological undertaking, one deeply embedded within the traditions, perspectives, viewpoints, cultural understandings, and discourse style of the researcher (Dillard, 1995; James & Farmer, 1993; Lather, 1986; Packwood & Sikes, 1996; Scheurich & Young, 1997; Stanfield, 1993). Packwood & Sikes (1996) argue convincingly that these ideologies are reflected in the metaphors that we use to conceptualize both the processes and the epistemological bases of research. Ironically, however, they suggest that even in the current plethora of narrative accounts of research (see Casey, 1995 for a comprehensive review of narrative research in education), the most pervasive metaphor characterizing the final product (the research paper or published article), is still that of research as recipe. They suggest further that

> this is not only an implicit metaphor, it is also an implicit myth. The metaphor is that the process of research is to follow a recipe, and the myth is that this is the truth. These are illusions that researchers perpetuate. We perpetuate them by the way we present our final research texts and by the way we carefully delete the voice of the researcher, our own voice, from the text. (p. 336)

We can see from the metaphor of research as recipe that the relationship between the researcher (as "knower") and the researched (as "known" or "to be known") is one of detachment: The researcher is set apart from the subject (the recipe) so that knowledge (the final outcome) is "objective." While much has been written on the virtues and pitfalls of positivistic quantitative social science, one could argue that much qualitative work also rests on similar conceptions of "truth." I would further add that regardless of research paradigm, if educational research is to truly change or transform, it will only be because we are in the midst of a "far-reaching intellectual and spiritual revisioning [and articulation] *of reality and how we know it"* (Palmer, 1983, p. xvii, emphasis mine)—in other words, a transformation at the epistemological level.

From my standpoint as an African American woman, moving away from such a metaphor is critical, not simply as a move against objectivity or one "right way" to engage in educational research. At its epistemic core, it is for me a move away from the fundamentally wrongheaded assumptions that undergird such a metaphor in my work and the work of others, and toward a recognition of my own African-centered cultural identity and community. This necessitates a different relationship between me as the researcher, and the researched—between my knowing and the production of knowledge. This is also where Black feminist knowledge[2] provides an angle of vision from which to construct an alternative version of this relationship and a new metaphor in educational research, one that moves us away from detachment with participants and contexts and their use as "ingredients" in our research recipes and toward an epistemological position more appropriate for work within such communities.

Thus, a more useful research metaphor arising from an endarkened feminist epistemology is *research as a responsibility,* answerable and obligated to the very persons and communities being engaged in the inquiry. Because the purpose of this chapter is to articulate an endarkened feminist epistemology, the metaphor of research as a responsibility is a central assumption—and an invitation to the reader to become aware of multiple ways of knowing and doing research available to those serious enough to interrogate the epistemological, political, and ethical level of their work. It is also the intent to enter and, it is hoped, to push forward Scheurich and Young's (1997) challenge toward a "lively discussion" about the "racial" in our research in two important ways: first, by placing the narratives of African American women leaders at the center of this discussion of an endarkened feminist epistemology and articulating this epistemological position through these voices; and second, through illuminating the important meanings of the metaphor of research as responsibility in the enactment of an endarkened feminist epistemology.

ENACTING REPRESENTATION: NARRATIVE RESEARCH AS CULTURAL IDEOLOGY

Engaging an endarkened feminist epistemology has strong implications for the ways in which written texts are displayed and discussed. I have chosen in this chapter to explore the possibilities of narrative representations called life notes (Bell-Scott, 1994). Seen as a part of the body of research literature commonly known as narrative research, life notes refer broadly to constructed personal narratives such as letters, stories, journal

Substance of Things Hoped for, Evidence of Things Not Seen 135

entries, reflections, poetry, music, and other artful forms. However, as a form of narrative, life notes may be seen as embodying the meaning and reflections that consciously attend to a whole life as it is embedded in sociocultural contexts and communities of affinity. How such meaning is represented takes on importance here, with life notes holding the common trait of being relatively "unedited, uncensored, woman talk" (Bell-Scott, 1994, p. 13). An important assumption guiding this representational move is that African American women's "theory" has not been broadly utilized in mainstream educational research, even as it has been continually and constantly constructed and utilized within African American communities and contexts to give sense and meaning to one's life (Brown, 1988; Gordon, 1985; hooks, 1989, 1995; Some, 1994). Finally, I suggest that African women's voices embodied in life notes can be seen as specialized bodies of knowledge which, while legitimate and powerful, have been excluded from the reified bodies of knowledge and epistemological roots undergirding most social science research literature and practice. This has led to the expression, self-definition, and validation of Black female understandings and knowledge production in alternative sites—that is, in music (such as in the African American blues traditions), poetry, literature, and daily conversations, to name just a few (Collins, 1990). I made the choice to represent data in this way to at least begin to gesture toward the confluence of the aesthetic, female, cultural sensibilities that are often stifled in traditional modes of representation and discourses, mostly because they require (but rarely receive) translation from one context to the other, which denaturalizes, reduces, and diminishes their richness and meaning. Further, the attempt within these narratives is to illustrate the relationships of power, the contexts of opportunity (or lack thereof) and to highlight the epistemological roots and their consequent local meanings in my life and in the lives of Black women researchers more generally.

In this chapter, I enact what one of Lightfoot's (1994) participants, Katie Cannon, refers to as the "epistemological privilege of the oppressed (p. 59)": I speak truth to research and leadership as it is known by three prominent African American women leaders/researchers. The hope, through utilizing life notes as a form, is that readers of these texts will experience them as "overheard conversations, in addition to actual literary texts" (Bethel, 1982, p. 180), conversations that embody a particular and explicit standpoint. In this way, these narratives may be viewed as at least part of the "evidence of things not seen," demystifying African American feminist ways of knowing, in moments of reflection, relation, and resistance: Black women's spaces where one can know who we are when we are most us.

Data were collected primarily through the use of interview, but also through the analysis of texts and written documents produced by three

African American women. The first narrative is that of a graduate student in her second year of socialization and course work toward a doctoral degree in higher education administration. The second is that of a secondary school principal in an urban school district. The final narrative is an autobiographical narrative written by me, as a college-level administrator at a predominately White university. Multiple rhetorical styles are used to represent these women's voices in narratives. Although this representational move is mine alone, it was done in an attempt to both mirror and honor the style and substance of the data as it was shared with me. However, the reader should keep in mind a major purpose of this chapter: To explore, at the level of representation, an endarkened feminist epistemology. In other words, in what is literally and metaphorically the chapter's center (and within the inherent confines of a book chapter), I enact the ways that narrative research texts about leadership are also cultural ideology through three narrative life notes, positioned not as Other but as center, given "a society full of institutionalized and violent hatred for both [our dark] skins and [our] female bodies" (Bethel, 1982, p. 178). It is precisely at this point of representation, when the pressures to conform to the "norms" of "proper" scientific research are most difficult to resist that I seek to recognize the cultural genesis and meanings of the lives of African American women researchers and to disrupt and unsettle the taken-for-granted notions surrounding the very goals and purposes of educational research.

LIFE NOTES NARRATIVES: THREE VOICES

Narrative #1: The Opening

> Where the road goes from paved to gravel is the place where
>   my life is
> Right in that spot, that line, that crack—
>   There is the wormhole of who I be.
> I be me in that space
>   Dark and quiet—
> And Whole—
> Wholly me and made of all that is me
> Journeying to the edges
>   Spilling over to pavement or gravel—
> Sustaining this entity through movement and talk
> Folding into itself facing attack
> Turning out onto the street facing struggle
> Being me
>   Being Whole

Being me again
Ever re-creating
    clarifying
    pushing the edges
So that this Third Space
    between paved and gravel becomes . . .
and Becomes more than a crack (break yo' mama's back)
        a line (problem of the twentieth century)
        a spot (see it run)
    but Becomes . . .
and is becoming   whole (philosopher)
        integrated (transgressive)
        critical (-ly important)
        VOICED (heard)

Narrative #2: Leading With her Life: A Day in the Life of a Black Woman High School Principal

I grew up here in Easely, right over in the South district. At that time there weren't too many of "us" [African Americans] so I knew everyone in the city who was Black. Schools? I went to Catholic schools all my life—even college! That's funny to me because even though I went to Catholic schools, and I wore a uniform, and the nuns and things, I actually got a really good education. It was about the only way to get an integrated education in Easely, especially in the '50s. And that was important to my parents.

My Dad was an eighth-grade graduate and was one of the first African American barbers on the Easely-to-Chicago train route. My Mom had two years of college. She was a teacher too. One, my oldest sister, went to college in the convent and one still is a practicing nun. My brother, who's only ten months younger than me, is the only one of us kids who didn't go to college. Education was really a priority for my family. Getting an education was important. My Dad used to say that we had to do better [than our White counterparts] because we're never good enough and we'll never be good enough. An education would help us to deal with that.

My Daddy used to make us sit there and watch the news, for hours. At first we wanted to go run the streets with our friends, but then it got really interesting. It got real. We discussed those things at the dinner table. We knew there was racism here in Easely too, but it didn't take the same form. It was much more subtle. That's why my parents put such emphasis on getting a good education, to better prepare us to combat the racism we might face . . .

You may not know it, but I'm a teaching principal. It's really unusual but I did it because I'm not gonna take just anyone into my school. Yea, it means a lot more work for me. But I did it because those available for the position in the surplus pool were less than desirable. And there weren't any [Black] folks in the pool either. The only way to get around that is not to open it up. So I started out just teaching one semester. Now I've been teaching for three years. It's just one of those things that you have to do with this job. And you know something? It shuts the faculty up. They can't say I don't know anything about the plight of teachers. . . .

I came to the district a long time ago. At that time Rosefield was all White. When they sent me here the school was more than 50 percent minority. That's part of the reason I'm here. My *promotion* [emphasis hers] was that I was brought here to Rosefield to clean up this *mess* [emphasis hers]. And it was a mess. But now [two years later] we're doing a lot better. But we're changing. The ninth grade class is about 60 percent White again and I think this is a trend. Eventually, I'll be reassigned somewhere else. The community, the teachers, they will want a White principal again. That's just the way it is. You just have to go with it. . . .

I don't need to have my own children because I've got 1,000 of them five days a week, six hours a day. There was this one student—she didn't do very well her first few years. She'd been in foster home after foster home. Finally, I got her into the Upward Bound program. Then she was selected as a Natural Helper. After a while, she began to really get into her classes. But then she would be disappointed when she got her report card. Her cumulative GPA was so low and as a senior, she thought she couldn't catch up. But I kept pushin' her. Her last two quarters she got a 4.0. For graduation, I got her a gift certificate to a local department store. She actually went on to university, over there where you are, I think! You need to look her up! . . .

You know, as the principal, I go through all of the report cards and write notes on them before they are given to the kids—all 800 of them. All students with 4.0 get stamps saying "excellent"—and I write a little note, too. All kids with a 3.0

get a different stamp. And all the Black kids with a 3.0 get another special stamp, And then any kid who shows improvement gets a stamp, too! It takes me a long time, but it's important to recognize their achievements. . . .

"Yes. Rachelle Smith? This is Gloria Natham, the principal at Rosefield, Issac's school. Well, Ms. Thomas. I need to tell you that we were under the understanding that Issac picked up his transcripts [from his previous school]. We have been working with the counselor. He's been playing around and now since he didn't register, we can only get him a second- and third-period class. He was up here on registration day, but he didn't bother to go through registration. So this is what we're gonna do. He's gonna go immediately into the Learning Assistance Center [a special student study hall/tutorial]. He came in here playing and we need to let him know that we take his education seriously. He will also have a contract. That means he signs in every day with each of his teachers and a progress report is sent to you every other week. Now, Issac does not need any help or encouragement with ways to help him make excuses. If he has a dental appointment or something, then you need to write him a note. But we do not excuse students for sleeping in or being late. And we do not have to accept all of his notes either. See, it's just like a job. They only let you be absent or late one or two times and then you're out. So, I'll get the counselors together so we can make him a schedule. He'll have the progress report and attendance card every week. He [now] knows that you know he has it so there's none of that. See, what we're trying to do here is get him through school. Bye-bye."

Some people grumble because I really don't have an open-door policy. I don't want folks to visit me like they'd visit their hairdresser or their psychiatrist. I don't have time for that. I have better things to do with my time. They should know how to teach. . . .

I have been into each teacher's class during the first two weeks of classes. I just want to see what they're doing. When I came to Rosefield, the kids weren't in class. They were walking the halls. And almost every kid walking the halls were Black and Hispanic kids. They'd still be there happy as clams if we didn't get after them and the teachers whose class they were suppose to be in. Now the halls are clean and there are more of our Black and Asian and Hispanic kids in those higher-level classes. Part of the reason is that you're standing right in their faces [some of the traditional White teachers]. That kind of presence helps them to realize that you're not letting them off the hook. They've got to teach all of the kids. . . .

I just put my foot down. If it's not good for kids, it's not good for Rosefield. I just say this is what we did and why we did it. It's as simple as that. But I have very good relationships with the [teacher's union]. I talk with them a lot! One of the guys named William Dudley, ya' know, he's Black. And he just tells me the law. He came out here to Rosefield last year and came to some interesting perceptions himself [about what Natham sees as "old guard" faculty]. But what that means is that it puts us on one hand as friends. We're usually not in adversarial roles. But sometimes we are. But no matter whether it's positive or negative, you always wonder if the grievance or issue would be the same if you were a White principal. It's hard.

Narrative #3: A Memorandum of Understanding

MEMORANDUM

TO: Those who want to know at least part of the
        reason why Black women leaders might have an
        "attitude" in the academy
FROM: Author #2
RE: Some Real Colleague Blues[3]
DATE: April, 1995

I am looking for real colleagues
I am looking for real, honest colleagues.

Not folks who assume from jump street that I've arrived in the Dean's office or the academy solely because of affirmative action, but folks who don't think that my leadership and teaching, particularly at a "prestigious" university, requires an extraordinary explanation for my being there.

I am looking for real honest colleagues who assume that my ways of being (my culture), my ways of knowing (my theory), and my ways of leading (culturally engaged) are not any less rigorous or righteous or real than their own but instead a place from which I center and make sense of my work as an African American woman. These real colleagues do not see a conflict between theory and cultural/experiential explanations as principles that guide thought and action, but recognize that it is that sort of didactical framing that inherently continues to advance a traditionally racist and sexist agenda, particularly in leadership and educational research.

Substance of Things Hoped for, Evidence of Things Not Seen   141

In other words, I am looking for colleagues who do not believe that the bell curve really exists.

I am looking for real honest colleagues. Colleagues who are comfortable enough with their own constructions of their own humanity to respect mine. Who aren't scared of talking about the ways that racism, or classism, or sexism, or homophobia shape our decisions about policies and programs within education. Folks who know that those are the very conversations that will breath life into an academy that thrives on reproducing privilege and inequality at every turn.

I am looking for good honest colleagues who will not ask the question: "what is it like to be a Black woman administrator? Oh yea, I've got about five minutes," but instead will, over a glass of wine, cup of coffee, or a meal (and as a *regular* ongoing part of their lives), engage in the *reciprocal* dialogues and struggles necessary to actually hear my response—the blood, sweat, and tears, as well as the joy, the sensuality, the hopefulness, the spirit-filled nature of my being in and choosing administration as part of my academic life.

I am looking for colleagues who will understand why many Black women do not separate our "academic" work from the rest of our life's work, from advocacy work on behalf and in the very communities of color and women who nurture us, who take us in, who patch us up after what feels like a lifetime of struggle to survive the often brutal realities of the professorate. We are intimately connected to our communities and must give homage to those whose work it has been to sit with us, talk with us, feed us, bandage us up, hug us, and remind us of the legacy of strong women and men of color who have come before us. It is only then, after we have been "pushed back to strength" as sister Gloria Wade Gayles would say, that our communities of care send us away from these home places, better and stronger advocates for the struggle of opportunity and human rights, especially in educational contexts.

I am looking for colleagues who can see that there are deep connections between being Black academics and leaders, mothers and lovers, and researchers and scholars that inform our work. These colleagues must recognize too that inherent in being one of the too few sisters who have successfully navigated a way through the maze of higher education leadership, I have a higher moral responsibility that transcends being widely published in the top journals, beyond being "politically correct." In other words, women leaders of color and consciousness, while fully cognizant of and attentive to the requirements of tenure, promotion, and a scholarly life, must also pay attention in our research, teaching, and leadership to Alice Walker's call for "each one to pull one [or more]."

In this vein, I am particularly looking for some leadership colleagues who "don't believe you're ready for a promotion to full-time

Associate Dean" but two months later, after learning that I am a finalist for a Deanship at a prestigious private university suddenly discover my enormous talent and value to the institution. "An associate deanship is yours if you'd like it. . . ."

Yea, I am looking for some real honest colleagues.

I am yearning for some honest colleagues who know there is no such thing as an acceptable joke about race or gender or sexual orientation/affiliation and other honest colleagues who will "go off" without my being there;

I am seeking some I-am-equally-responsible-for-engaging-and-dialoging-in-the-most-honest-ways-I-can kinds of colleagues;

I am looking for, searching for (and in some cases, I am fortunate enough to have found) honest colleagues who are not intimidated or confused by the power and magic of women of color, who choose to be leaders. Especially articulate, bright, well-published, successful, gorgeous, connected, righteous Black women intellectual leaders who do not want to be rendered invisible to be accepted or acceptable in higher education. Do you know any colleagues like that?

THE SUBSTANCE OF THINGS HOPED FOR: THEORIZING THROUGH AN ENDARKENED FEMINIST EPISTEMOLOGY

> *You know where the minefields are . . . there is wisdom. . . . You are in touch with the ancestors . . . and it is from the gut, not rationally figured out. Black women have to use this all the time, of course, the creativity is still there, but we are not fools . . . we call it the "epistemological privileges of the oppressed." How do you tap that wisdom—name it, mine it, pass it on to the next generation?* [italics added] (Lightfoot, 1994, p. 59)

These life notes provide a glimpse of the complexity of issues, identities, and politics that influence and shape particular conceptions and world views, and ultimately our lives as educational leaders and researchers. The intention here is not to present Black woman victimized, unable or unwilling to recognize even our own complicity at times, especially at times when we resist "talking back" within the racist, sexist, and homophobic institutions where we work. It is further not the intention to present our selves and our lives as "always acting from the position of powerlessness that white supremacy defines as our place" (hooks, 1995, p. 269). The legacies raised up in life note narratives—of precious mentors, mothers, comrades, and colleagues—suggest a strong historical ethos of commitment to transformative work through our research, teaching, and leadership, in honor to named communities of affinity and support. The final intention here is not to present race, ethnicity, or gender as being essentialist, unchangeable or immovable. Instead, these positionalities must be seen as shifting and dynamic sets of social relationships that embody a particular endarkened feminist epistemological basis. Through utilizing multiple and complex representations, our ability to understand, construct, and negotiate between and among these multiple relations and realities can continue to unfold (McCarthy & Critchlow, 1993; Omi & Winant, 1986).

Although these narratives offer versions of feminists and feminisms often unheard, they also articulate a conscious struggle in our attempt to do as Golden and Shreve (1995) suggested: To "fess up" to the ambiguity often tied up in the chasm between biological–material and ideological–epistemological definitions of feminism, its constitutive theories and elements, and the complexity and range of representation and responses. However, an inclusive and transformative possibility of any/all feminist thought must fundamentally take into account the special and particular ways of seeing that Black and other marginalized female scholars bring to the knowledge-production process, not as biological constructions but as historical, political, and cultural constructions, under constant and vigilant negotiation, and conceptualized to disrupt at least, and possibly "to dismantle the master's house" (Lorde, 1984, p. 112).

Although there is no easy way to "analyze" these narratives, embodied within them are specialized knowledges that theorize a dismantling standpoint of and for African American women and that encompasses a coherent and dynamic epistemology: A place from which to theorize the leadership and research realities of Black women through situating such knowledge and action in the cultural spaces out of which they arose. Thus, in articulating an endarkened feminist epistemology and a new metaphor for research (as responsibility), I first examined patterns and themes that were found in common between the three narratives and placed those in the context of the literature on Black feminist/womanist thought, and also of my own experiences and research findings as an African American woman leader and scholar. Then I raised several questions that helped me to do two things: (1) to conceptualize, theoretically ground, and put forth alternative methodology and representational moves around which I could arrange these African American women leaders' voices, articulating an endarkened feminist epistemology, and; (2) to offer broadened understandings for those in the research community who engage inquiry around culture and the often slippery constructs of race, ethnicity, and gender— and who find their current epistemological positionings and more widely known research traditions unpalatable. The questions were these: Does the

144 *Cynthia B. Dillard*

multiplicity of our modes of knowing representationally suggest a similar multiplicity in our understanding of the very nature of the realities of leadership? Said another way, are there patterns of epistemology that can help us to decipher the patterns of leadership lives, those situated political struggles and personal passions that lie at the nexus of scholarship and activism? For African American women leaders and researchers living within our highly racist, sexist, and class-conscious society, how do we use experiences of racism, sexism, and other oppressions to inform our research as well as our leadership? Might the discourses we employ—and their patterns of epistemology—differ from what is traditionally known or spoken as "academic?" If so, how are they different? Most important, what do particular standpoints make possible in educational inquiry and how might that assist the entire research community in conceptualizing our work beyond often simplistic, biological and didactic notions of identity, politics, and the like to more useful cultural ones? In other words, how do the insights engaged in being and living as an African American woman leader and researcher open up new possibilities for the research and leadership community to see phenomena in new ways?

Given this analysis, what then are the assumptions of an endarkened feminist epistemology? Maybe more important, within a cultural view of narratives, what might such assumptions tell us about the partial, situated nature of any claims to knowledge, given the dynamic shifts and even contradictory nature of research experiences and explorations of cultural identity?

Before discussing these assumptions, several caveats are in order. Fine (1992) suggests that the study of gender differences may be safe within the context of education and particularly feminist research, but this focus makes us deploy and legitimate essentialist understandings of gender (Chodorow, 1978) and "reproduce dualities/beliefs about gender, sexuality, and race and ethnicity" (p. 8). Patricia Hill Collins (1990) suggests further that Black feminist ideology "does not mean that all African American women generate such thought or that other groups do not play a critical role in its production" (p. 22): Being biologically female (or male) does not automatically a feminist thinker make. Self-conscious, determined examination and struggle is often required to reject distorted and oppressive perceptions of women in general and African American women particularly, and to value human thought and action from self-defined standpoints. As Stanlee James further suggests, this consciousness work is itself a form of "theorizing"[4]:

> Although Black women are often characterized as victims, theorizing is a form of agency that provides them with opportunities to learn, think, imagine, judge, listen, speak, write, and

act—and which transforms not only the individual (from victim to activist, for example) but the community, and the society as well. (James & Busia, 1993, p. 2)

Such "theorizing" is confounded by the vigilant need for African American scholars and leaders not simply to study and read written texts, "but [to read] the situation we [are] in . . . to understand the necessity for studying the terrains of hierarchy and power and hypocrisy and authenticity." (Omolade, 1994, p. xii)

The contours, politics, and research implications for engaging an endarkened feminist epistemological basis and related ways of research need to be explicated, particularly for those seeking to engage research in more alternative ways. However, I want to be clear about the viewpoint forwarded here, recognizing the reductionistic, flattening problematics inherent in "outlining" the assumptions of an epistemological stance. First, I do not subscribe to substituting a dominating White male version of science with a Black female version, reinscribing the same positivistic view of science. The social critique that endarkened feminist assumptions engage is focused on the violence perpetrated in the universal generalization from the particular White male knowledge of the nature of reality to describe everyone's realities, including those Black and female. This brings me to the second point: There is a need to resituate our research endeavors in their cultural and historical contexts, to reclaim their personal and social roots or origins. Thus, the fundamental questions in research should not be whether one epistemological basis is logical (all cultural groups develop logical thought, albeit differently from one another). Rather, as Palmer (1983) suggests, the questions should be

> Whose voice is behind the thought? What is the personal and communal reality from which that thought arises? How can I enter and respond to the relation of that [those] thinker[s] to the world? (p. 64)

As a Black feminist researcher, I utilize both African–African American and feminist literature in theorizing these assumptions, reflecting the representation (conceptual and epistemological) of elements of both traditions in articulating an endarkened feminist epistemology. Although I draw heavily on Collins' (1990) core theories of Black feminist thought and Harding's (1987) elements of feminist psychology respectively, I have also drawn on Palmer's (1983) work on spirituality in education. Although rarely mentioned in discussions of educational research and teaching (see Dillard, Abdur-Rashid, & Tyson, 2000, for an examination of spiritual concerns in teacher education), spirituality is intimately woven into the

146   *Cynthia B. Dillard*

ethos of an endarkened feminist epistemology. The convergence of these three bodies of literature, along with my examination of the narratives presented here, provide primary contexts for imagining and theorizing these assumptions.

Finally, as Stanfield (1993) suggested at the outset of this chapter: "Epistemological concerns in cultural research in the social sciences cannot be divorced from concerns regarding the functions of culturally hegemonic domination in knowledge production and dissemination and in the selections and rewarding of intellectual careers" (p. 26). Thus, articulating these assumptions of an endarkened feminist epistemology is important for a number of reasons: first, in raising awareness of the power relations played out in our academic careers as researchers; second and more pragmatically, to provide guidance (and courage) to members of tenure committees' publication review boards who may better recognize the "validity" of the work of African American women within and outside of the academy, based on these alternative sets of assumptions; third and finally, to challenge the all-too-prevalent idea that there is a unitary way to know, do, and be in educational research endeavors.

Assumption #1: Self-Definition Forms One's Participation and Responsibility to One's Community

From an endarkened epistemological ground, all views expressed and actions taken related to educational inquiry arise from a personally and culturally defined set of beliefs that render the researcher responsible to the members and the well-being of the community from which their very definition arises. For example, in the narrative of the principal, she talks passionately about being responsible to African American and other students of color particularly—and students, more generally. However, as she describes the motivation for that sense of responsibility, she takes us back to her childhood and her own schooling experiences as a source of self-definition.

According to Collins (1990), although race and gender are both socially constructed categories fraught with problematics, one could argue that constructions of gender rest on clearer biological criteria than those undergirding race (Appiah, 1992; Bell, 1992; Omi & Winant, 1993; West, 1993). However, although united by biological sex, women as a category do not construct the same meaning of woman, given distinct her-stories, geographic locations, origins, cultures, and social institutions. Although most feminist scholars would recognize and subscribe to at least some common experiences based in culturally engendered experiences of being female, the experiences are qualitatively different for those who stand outside the circle of "acceptable" women, most particularly African American women (King, 1988). This is not meant to suggest that an additive analysis is ever useful in educational research—that is, that the greater the multiplicity of oppressions, the purer the vision of group members on marginalization or subjugation. Instead, what is suggested is that the struggle for a self-defined feminist consciousness for African American women in our roles as scholars seems to require embracing both a culturally centered worldview (in this case African-centered) and a feminist sensibility, both necessary in embracing and enacting an endarkened feminist epistemological stance. Through such praxis, an alternative ideology and cultural meaning for research is articulated, one that reflects elements of both traditions, a both–and standpoint (Collins, 1990) deeply rooted in the everyday experiences of African American women. In the narratives, even with the variability that was articulated in the unique individual versions of who we are as Black women researchers, coherence is realized in our collective refusal to be reduced to someone else's terms—to give voice to silenced spaces as an act of resistance.

Defining oneself in relation to one's cultural and social community also defines one's participation within that community, both one's connection and affiliation as well as one's responsibility. Thus, if one claims that one is *of* the group (that is, chooses to conduct research, and makes assessments of claims to knowledge of the group, however distant or intimate those claims), there must be a simultaneous assessment of a person's character, values, motives, and ethics in relation to that group.[5] In other words, regardless of the identity position claimed (e.g., Black, White, male, female, etc.), from an endarkened feminist epistemological standpoint, the researcher would necessarily and carefully examine his or her own motives, methods, interactions, and final research "reports"—and seek understanding and meaning-making from various members of the social or cultural community under study. In essence, each of the three voices here unabashedly claimed an identity standpoint and cultural positionality as Black women (e.g., "I be me in that space/Dark and quiet—And Whole"). However, it is through the voice of the principal in narrative 2 that we can clearly see self-identity and responsibility to the students and staff at Rosefield enacted in her refusal to allow "undesirable" teachers into her building and taking the vacant teaching position herself, increasing the number of African American teachers in the building. This allowed her to create a self definition—and a socially constructed definition as well amongst teachers—as an African American woman teaching principal. Such a definition formed both how she participated in the community of teachers, the manner that she would respond to that community, and maybe most important, the manner in which the community responded to her.

148 *Cynthia B. Dillard*

From an endarkened epistemological ground, all views expressed and actions taken related to educational inquiry arise from a personally and culturally defined set of beliefs that render the researcher responsible to the members and the well-being of the community from which their very definition arises: To know something is to have a living relationship with it, influencing and being influenced by it, responding to and being responsible for it.

Assumption #2: Research is Both an Intellectual and a Spiritual Pursuit, a Pursuit of Purpose

An endarkened feminist epistemology draws on a spiritual tradition, one in which the concern is not solely with the production of knowledge (an intellectual pursuit) but also with uncovering and constructing truth as the fabric of everyday life (a spiritual pursuit). Thus the "theories" of knowing that have guided research as a value-free social science are directly challenged when an endarkened feminist epistemology is articulated, as suggested here by Collins (1990):

> Alternative knowledge claims are rarely threatening to conventional knowledge. Such claims are routinely ignored, discredited, or simply absorbed and marginalized in existing paradigms. . . . [However] much more threatening is the challenge that alternative epistemologies offer to the basic process used by the powerful to legitimate their knowledge claims. If the ideology used to validate knowledge comes into question, then all prior knowledge claims validated under the dominant model become suspect. . . . The existence of [an endarkened] feminist ideology calls into question the content of what currently passes as truth and simultaneously challenges the process of arriving at that truth. (p. 219)

As suggested in the final narrative, "I am looking for colleagues who do not believe the bell curve really exists." African American women have historically and contemporarily addressed our multiple oppressions (personal and societal) through versions of spirituality (James & Busia, 1993; Lightfoot, 1994; Richards, 1980; Vanzant, 1996; Wade-Gayles, 1995). However the educational research literature by or about African American women researchers' and teachers' spiritual concerns, though often unnamed, are pervasive (see exemplars in Foster, 1990; hooks, 1994; Ladson-Billings, 1994). While these works are deeply intellectual, several conditions or elements are embedded within their purpose that imply research as a spiritual pursuit. First there is an explicit, very powerful sense of self in the role of researcher/teacher, directly linked to an explicit sense of purpose for whatever research moves are made. There are often multiple levels of vulnerability in the research endeavor. An endarkened feminist epistemology enacts "stepping out on faith," whether traversing tenure and promotion, publication, unequal power relations or just being present in the academy, or being "pushed back to strength" as we heard in the narratives. Finally, there is a relationship of reciprocity and care apparent in the relationships of the research project embodying three major components. First, there is the recognition that each individual as a unique expression of a common spirit inherent in all of life (James & Busia, 1993; Paris, 1995; Richards, 1980; Some, 1994; Vanzant, 1996; Wade-Gayles, 1995). Such spiritual concerns are articulated epistemologically in that value is placed on individual expressiveness; individual differences are not seen as detracting from but as enriching to an endarkened feminist epistemology, the foundations and processes of our work. We see an example of such expressiveness in the simple line from the poem/narrative: "There is the wormhole of who I be." Emotions are considered not only appropriate but necessary in determining the validity of an argument (Collins, 1990). Finally, developing the capacity for empathy in research is critical for attempting to recognize the value of another's perspective, whether or not one agrees with that perspective. Simply put, perspectives have merit and standing simply because they exist, and our role as educational researchers becomes one of recognizing and embracing them as such. In this way, we are encouraged to welcome the conflict inherent in our diversity (of paradigms, methodology, representation), to live within its sometimes seeming ambiguity, and to develop the purpose in research of not just honoring our own version of the praxis and politics of research as truth, but to seek to honor the truth that is created and negotiated in and between ourselves, in relationship with one another as researchers.

Assumption #3: Only Within the Context of Community Does the Individual Appear (Palmer, 1983) and, Through Dialogue, Continue to Become

This endarkened feminist epistemological assumption suggests that dialogue is key in both conducting research and in assessing knowledge claims: That there is value in the telling, in invading those secret silent moments often unspoken, to be understood as both participating in and responsible to one another as researchers. Further, there is value in being connected, in seeking harmony and wholeness as a way to discern "truth." In the narratives presented previously, the intention was partially to raise up the evidence of things not seen in the lives of African American women in the academy, while concomitantly inserting our voices into the research community in dialogic ways that insist that we exist, with language giving form to an endarkened feminist epistemology. These narratives might be seen as a dialogic offering for members of the educational research community whose work may be informed by what are equally valid ways of inquiry and knowledge production, embodied in the wisdom and knowledge of Black women's lives.

A number of researchers (Asante, 1988; Morrison, 1993; Thiongo, 1986) point to the importance of instrumentality in the languages and discourses used to create relationships based on equality, that is, in dialogue that transforms or provides a new way to understand our reality and communal responsibility as women researchers, teachers, and scholars of color. "Dialogue implies talk between two subjects, not the speech of a subject and an object. It is humanizing speech, one that challenges and resists domination" (hooks, 1989, p. 131). This is the sort of dialogue implied and desired in the third narrative ". . . over a glass of wine, cup of coffee, or a meal . . . engage in the reciprocal dialogues and struggles necessary to actually hear my response—the blood, sweat, and tears, as well as the joy, sensuality, and the hopefulness, the spirit-filled nature of my being." Thus, through awareness of an endarkened feminist epistemology, all involved in the conversation can resist and challenge entrenched ways of thinking about their research lives, and provide new ways to "be" researchers.

Assumption #4: Concrete Experiences[6] within Everyday Life Form the Criterion of Meaning, the "Matrix of Meaning-Making" (Ephraim-Donker, 1997, p. 8)

In African American communities, what happens in everyday life to individuals within the community is critical to "making sense" of particular actions, expressions, experiences and community life in general. Collins (1990) suggests that this underlies two aspects of knowing that are particularly important to this fourth assumption of an endarkened feminist epistemology: knowledge and wisdom. She further elaborates:

> Women of color cannot afford to be fools of any type, for our objectification as the Other denies us the protection that white skin, maleness, and wealth confer. This distinction between knowledge and wisdom, and the use of experience as the cutting edge dividing them, has been key to [our] survival. In the context of race, gender, and class oppression, the dis-

tinction is essential. Knowledge without wisdom is adequate for the powerful, but wisdom is essential to the survival of the subordinate. (p. 208)

Thus, in our scholarship and research, African American women often invoke our own concrete experiences and those of other women and communities of color in our selection of topics for investigation and for the methodologies that we engage (Collins, 1990). We "study" the concrete experiences and acts of African American or people of color, while at the same time striving to understand and explicate the wisdom contained in those meanings. As Collins states further:

These forms of knowledge allow for subjectivity between the knower and the known, rest in the women themselves (not in higher authorities), and are experienced directly in the world (not through abstractions). (p. 211)

Thus, concrete experiences—uniquely individual while at the same time both collective and connected—lend credibility to the work of African American women engaged in transformative research and inquiry, as well as suggest the presence of an endarkened feminist epistemology that grounds such work.

Assumption #5: Knowing and Research are Both Historical (Extending Backwards in Time); To Approach Them Otherwise is to Diminish Their Cultural and Empirical Meaningfulness

An endarkened feminist epistemology both acknowledges and works against the "absent presence" of women of color from the shaping of the rules that have historically guided formal educational research, the system of knowledge production within higher education, and the meanings and legitimacy surrounding research processes. In other words, Black feminist thoughts, although not a part of the original canon of theories, rules, and perspectives that surround what gets perpetuated today as educational research broadly defined, attempts to both highlight what's missing from these definitions as well as to extend these definitions through the inclusion of African women's knowledge. However, important to this assumption of an endarkened feminist epistemology is that such omissions have led to what Wynter (1992) and others aptly describe as a distorted empirical reality fundamentally based on inclusion and exclusion as a way to maintain White and male superiority and as an organizer for our hierarchical social

152   *Cynthia B. Dillard*

structures in education and society (Ani, 1994; Appiah, 1992; hooks, 1989; James & Farmer, 1993; Stanfield, 1994).

The disciplines of Black and other ethnic studies and women's studies have opened the way for multiple theoretical and epistemological readings in the fields of educational research. A major contribution of these fields is that feminists and scholars of color (and those of us who identify as both) have argued that we members of marginalized groups have unique viewpoints on our own experiences and provide a needed critique as well as an "endarkenment" on society as a whole. (Anderson, 1993; Foster, 1990; Haraway, 1988; Harding, 1982; Ladson-Billings, 1994; Lorde, 1984). Such standpoints suggest that race, class, gender, and other identity formations are both origins and subjects of particular knowledges. Accordingly, a feminist standpoint "preserves the presence of the active and experiencing subject (Smith, 1987, p. 105)." Standpoint theory also recognizes that researchers and subjects are located in specific and particular positionalities (Tierney, 1994). Within and against these locations, researchers engage in social relationships with research participants, and the process and work of research acknowledges and embraces the presence of the researcher.

However, an unexpected outgrowth of this body of work has been both an increasingly monolithic notion of various cultural identity groups (Stanfield, 1993) and often essentialist notions of who is capable, based on their own life histories, to conduct research with/in various populations. Although I will argue vehemently that Black women as a cultural group "theorize" and embody extensive life experiences that, while diverse, shape a coherent body (as we saw in the life notes), what I am attempting to advance here is the notion that, in educational research, such theoretical and conceptual standpoints are cultural; they are not inherent in one's biology:

> Talk of race is particularly distressing for those of us who take culture seriously. For, where race works—in places where "gross differences" of morphology are correlated with "subtle differences" of temperament, belief and intention—it works as an attempt at metonym for culture, and it does so only at the price of biologizing what is culture, *ideology* [emphasis mine]. (Appiah, 1992, p. 45)

We must recognize that the forms of discourse and literatures that have defined the claim of an epistemological universality (that which the talk of "theory" inevitably implies) inhibit both our ability to examine with necessary clarity (not to mention attention to ethical and moral concerns) and to interpret the complexity of human cultural thought and action that we study in educational research. In short, researchers who accept the relevance of poststructural, postmodern, feminist, and critical race theories have reason to be at least uncomfortable with extending these theories to contexts, peoples, methodology, texts, and work outside this tradition. In other words, one's epistemological basis for research must engage in relevant cultural understanding and "theorizing" that is informed by the insights of those experiencing the world as the very phenomena being explored.

Thus, when research work is engaged within the cultural, social, political, and historical milieu of its creation—from its epistemology to the research experience to its report—we stand to get closer to what Appiah (1992) calls a productive mode of reading, a space and a way of seeing that creates the opportunity to rethink the meaning of the whole experience of research as an epistemological and cultural text.

Assumption #6: Power Relations, Manifest as Racism, Sexism, Homophobia, and so on, Structure Gender, Race, and Other Identity Relations within Research

Whether concerns over research legitimacy, tenure and promotion, publication, or professional acceptability, asymmetrical power relations, particularly as they influence the work of women in the academy, have been well studied and articulated (see Bannerji, 1991; Fine, 1992; Harding, 1987; Harris, 1990; James & Farmer, 1993). However, although African American women are more present in the academy today, the racist, sexist, and classist structures and belief systems around us remain relatively unchanged. The consequences of such stability are even more extreme when we Black women seek to situate ourselves into spaces of feminist discourse only to find that:

> In a racist society like this one, the storytellers are usually white and so "women" turns out to be "white women." Why in the face of the challenges from "different" women and from feminist method itself is feminist essentialism so persistent and pervasive? In my view, as long as feminists, like theorists in the dominant culture, continue to search for gender and racial essences, Black women will not be anything more than a crossroads between two kinds of domination, or at the bottom of a hierarchy of oppressions; we will always be required to choose pieces of ourselves to present as wholeness. (Harris, 1990, p. 589)

Thus, an endarkened feminist epistemology has as its research project the vigilant and consistent desire to "dig up" the nexus of racial/ethnic,

154 *Cynthia B. Dillard*

gender, and other identity realities—of how we understand and experience the world as Black women. For feminist research to truly embrace such an epistemological stance, gender, race, class and other constructed identities (what some have despairingly referred to as "personal experiences"), as well as experiences and meanings within power asymmetrics (Harding, 1987) that have historically been constructed through unequal access and in contexts of power must be at the center of the research project. As the student said in the first narrative: ". . . Sustaining this entity through movement and talk/ Folding into itself facing attack/ Turning out onto the street facing struggle/ Being me/ Being Whole/ Being me again. . . ." These stories, when shared and heard by White researchers, are often unbelievable at worst, painful fodder for contexts of White guilt at best. However, these cultural ideologies are the exact stories that "endarken" the epistemology at work, that expose the relations of power that disproportionately exclude how and what we know the world to be as Black women, how we know racism and sexism and identity politics influence and shape the contexts of our lives, in contrast to being told how they operate from perspectives outside of ourselves. But at the same time, an endarkened feminism seeks to resist and transform these social arrangements as well, seeking political and social change on behalf of the communities we represent as the purpose for research, versus solely the development of universal laws or theories for human behavior.

A FINAL NOTE

> *Race is the tar baby in our midst; touch it and you get stuck, hold it and you get dirty, so they say. But anyone who reads these [life notes] will discover only premeditated ruminations designed to cleanse, complete, and free. The aching honesty, the willingness to critique and unveil the mark . . . is testimony to the bounty we could all share if we tried as hard to see each other as we try not to, or to "fess up" rather than be nice* [italics added]. (Marita Golden [Golden & Shreve, 1995], p. 3)

It is with more than a little trepidation that I commit these private conversations and their analysis to more public spaces, especially in what seems often daunting and exclusionary dialogues around race, class, and gender in educational research generally, and leadership more particularly. Like other Black feminist scholars, I have come to know intimately the angst that Critchlow (1995) speaks of: the outsider-within position (Collins, 1990) of being a Black women scholar, and like most, relying on formal academic training designed to encourage us to decontextualize our

Substance of Things Hoped for, Evidence of Things Not Seen   155

deeply raced/gendered/classed/sexualized lives and alienate ourselves from our communities, families, and even ourselves to do "legitimate" scholarship; attempting to work within such sites is fraught with immeasurable contradictions and exaggerations.

In the Christian biblical tradition, the underlying scripture from which the title is taken (Hebrews 11:1) relates to the importance of faith: "Faith is the substance of things hoped for, the evidence of things not seen." Although critical of racism and sexism in higher education and unexamined epistemological assumptions that pass as universal truths in educational research, one might suggest that, simply by continuing to believe that such a dialogue might be possible and useful is an exhibition of the extraordinary faith we still manage to have for the possibility of engaging our collective humanity, even in the academy. Thus, this chapter is dedicated to those who work diligently to transform these often alienating positionalities, and to those who "theorize" African American lived realities in ways that shape a more radical and transformative feminist politic in educational research. Envisioning research as responsibility might just be one of the shifts we need.

NOTES

The author wishes to gratefully thank Daa'iyah Abdur-Rashid, Dionne Blue, Dafina Lazarus Martin, Carmen Medina, Carolyn Simpson and Cynthia Tyson for their thoughtful critique and comments on various versions of this chapter.

1. I use the phrase "patterns of epistemology" to suggest that epistemology (how we know reality) is not a monolithic body, but is instead the ways in which reality is a deeply cultured knowing that arises from and embodies the habits, wisdom, and patterns of its contexts of origin.

2. With early roots in the work of Barbara Smith, Akasha Hull, Audrey Lorde and more recently of Patricia Bell-Scott, Katie Cannon, Joy James, Ruth Farmer, Barbara Omolade and Patricia Hill Collins, Black feminist voices argue that the very presence and positionality of Black women scholars and researchers gives us a coherent and distinctive cultural, analytical and ideological location through which a coherent epistemology—and a different metaphor for educational research—can be articulated.

3. This chapter was presented as part of a symposium of the same name at the 1995 American Education Research Association Annual Meeting. Many thanks (and maybe apologies) to Pearl Cleage (1990) whose essay, "Good Brother Blues," inspired the form of these life notes; the power and poetry of her language best captures both the frustration and the joy of my working life as an African American woman in the predominantly White male world of the academy.

4. One of my current struggles, given the instrumentality of language suggested here, is with the term *theory* and the relationship it implies in the research endeavor. From the Greek *theoros* or spectator, it suggests explanations at a

156   *Cynthia B. Dillard*

distance, with the researcher's positionality not accounted for as an integral part of the contours of the construction of reality. Although I recognize the contradiction in using this term from an endarkened feminist epistemological space, I am currently searching for a more integrative and accessible term to use in its place.

5. Given this discussion, the reader may assume that I am making an essentialist move here, a move arguing that self-definition is only "a Black [woman's] thang." And indeed, as a self-identified African American woman researcher, I choose to study African American women and communities and to be informed by African-centered theories and experiences. However, my stance relative to self-definition and responsibility is that, regardless of the race, gender, or other identity positions claimed by educational researchers, we all define our Selves as either insiders or outsiders of the communities that we study. Thus, while there should be no doubt that an endarkened feminist epistemological standpoint arises from the voices of African American women whom I've studied, it is offered here as an alternative framework in the research community, useful to anyone who has the courage and desire to understand and embrace the metaphor of research as responsibility (in this case, to the African American women and communities I study) and who seeks to be informed—and challenged—by their research practices.

6. Both standpoint theory and the meanings (or even existence!) of concrete experiences in postmodern times may be problematic for some readers. Although I do see involvement with the postmodern discussion as a way to draw attention to and examine the manner in which African American women's lives research themselves and are re-searched, I agree with Lubiano's (1991) notions that an African American feminist postmodernism "insists on the representation of history in the present moment" (p. 157) and "[needs] to be politically nuanced in a radical way, focus[ing] on such differences' implications especially in moments of oppositional transgressions" (p. 160). She goes on to suggest that "one of the things that an African American presence in postmodernism generally can offer [is a] constantly reinvigorated critique (p. 153). My modest critique is my conscious choice to engage alternative cultural discourses other than postmodern in this chapter, a discourse more in keeping with the spirit of an African ethos.

REFERENCES

Anderson, M. L. (1993). Studying across difference: Race, class, and gender in qualitative research. In J. H. Stanfield, (Ed.), *Race and ethnicity in research methods* (pp. 39–52). Newbury Park, CA: Sage.

Ani, M. (1994). *Yurugu: An African-centered critique of European cultural thought and behavior.* Trenton, NJ: Africa World Press.

Appiah, K. A. (1992). *In my father's house: Africa in the philosophy of culture.* New York: Oxford University Press.

Asante, M. K. (1988). *Afrocentricity.* Trenton, NJ: Africa World Press.

Austin, D. A. (1994, May). African-American success stories: Three narrative journeys. Paper presented at the Stone Symposium, University of Illinois, Urbana, IL.

Bannerji, H. (1991). *Unsettling relations: The university as a site of feminist struggles.* Boston: South End Press.

Bell, D. (1992). *Faces at the bottom of the well: The permanence of racism.* New York: Basic Books.

Bell-Scott, P. (1994). *Life notes: Personal writings by contemporary Black women.* New York: W.W. Norton & Company.

Bethel, L. (1982). "This infinity of conscious pain": Zora Neale Hurston and the Black female literary tradition. In G. T. Hull, P. B. Scott, & B. Smith (Eds.), *All the women are White, all the Blacks are men, but some of us are brave* (pp. 176–188). New York: Feminist Press.

Brown, E. B. (1988). African-American women's quilting: A framework for conceptualizing and teaching African-American women's history. In M. R. Malson, E. Mudimbe-Boyi, J. F. O'Barr, & M. Wyer (Eds.), *Black women in America: Social science perspectives* (pp. 39–52). Chicago: University of Chicago Press.

Casey, K. (1995). The new narrative research in education. *Review of Research in Education, 21,* 211–253.

Chodorow, N. J. (1978). *The reproduction of mothering: Psychoanalysis and the sociology of gender.* Berkeley: University of California Press.

Cleage, P. (1990). *Mad at Miles.* New York: Ballantine.

Collins, P. (1990). *Black feminist thought: Knowledge, consciousness, and the politics of empowerment.* New York: Routledge.

Critchlow, W. (1995, 16 April). *Presentation.* Presentation given at The Ohio State University College of Education Annual Research Retreat, Columbus, OH.

Dillard, C. B. (1995). Leading with her life: An African American feminist (re)interpretation of leadership for an urban high school principal. *Educational Administration Quarterly, 31*(4), 539–563.

Dillard, C. B., Abdur-Rashid, D., & Tyson, C. A. (2000). My soul is a witness: Affirming pedagogies of the spirit. *International Journal of Qualitative Studies in Education,13*(5), 447–462.

Eisner, E. (1979). *The educational imagination: On the design and evaluation of school programs.* New York: Macmillan.

Ephraim-Donker, A. (1997). *African spirituality: On becoming ancestors.* Trenton, NJ: Africa World Press.

Fine, M. (1992). *Disruptive voices: The possibilities of feminist research.* Ann Arbor: University of Michigan Press.

Foster, M. (1990). The politics of race: Through the eyes of African American teachers. *Journal of Education, 172*(3), 123–141.

Golden, M., & Shreve, S. R. (Eds.). (1995). *Skin deep: Black women and White women write about race.* New York: Doubleday.

Gordon, B. (1990). The necessity of African American epistemology for educational theory and practice. *Journal of Education, 172,* 88–106.

Greene, M. (1978). *Landscapes of learning.* New York: Teachers College Press.

Haraway, D. (1988). Situated knowledge: The science question in feminism and privilege of partial perspective. *Feminist Studies, 14*(3), 575–599.

Harding, S. (1982). Is gender a variable in conceptions of rationality? *Dialectica, 36,* 225–242.

Harding, S. (1987). *Feminism and methodology: Social science issues.* Bloomington: Indiana University Press.

Harris, A. (1990). Race and essentialism in feminist legal theory. *Stanford Law Review, 42*(3), 581–616.

hooks, b. (1989). *Talking back: Thinking feminist, thinking Black.* Boston: South End Press.

hooks, b. (1994). *Teaching to transgress: Education as the practice of freedom* (pp. 168–184). New York: Routledge.

hooks, b. (1995). Feminism in Black and White. In M. Golden, & S. R. Shreve (Eds.), *Skin deep: Black women and White women write about race.* New York: Doubleday.

James, J., & Farmer, R. (Eds.) (1993). *Spirit, space, and survival: African American women in (White) academe.* New York: Routledge.

James, S. M., & Busia, A. P. A. (Eds.). (1993). *Theorizing Black feminisms: The visionary pragmatism of Black women.* New York: Routledge.

King, D. K. (1988). Multiple jeopardy, multiple consciousness: The context of a Black feminist ideology. *Signs, 14*(1), 4–72.

Ladson-Billings, G. (1994). *The dreamkeepers: Successful teachers of African American children.* San Francisco: Jossey-Bass.

Ladson-Billings, G. (1996). For colored girls who have considered suicide when the academy's not enough. In P. Peterson & A. Neumann (Eds.), *Research and everyday life: The personal sources of educational inquiry* (pp. 168–184). New York: Teacher's College Press.

Lather, P. (1986). Issues of validity in openly ideological research: Between a rock and a soft place. *Interchange, 17*(4), 63–84.

Lightfoot, S. L. (1994). *I've known rivers: Lives of loss and liberation.* Reading, MA: Addison-Wesley.

Lorde, A. (1984). *Sister outsider.* Freedom, CA: The Crossing Press.

Lubiano, W. (1991). Shuckin' off the African-American native other: What's "po-mo" got to do with it? *Cultural Critique, 18*, 149–186.

Maher, F. A., & Tetreault, M. K. (1994). *The feminist classroom.* New York: Basic Books.

McCarthy, C., & Critchlow, W. (Eds.). (1993). *Race and representation in education.* New York: Routledge.

Morrison, T. (1993). *Playing in the dark: Whiteness and the literary imagination.* New York: Vintage.

Omi, M., & Winant, H. (1986). *Racial formation in the United States: From the 1960s to the 1990s.* New York: Routledge.

Omi, M., & Winant, H. (1993). On the theoretical concept of race. In C. McCarthy, & W. Critchlow (Eds.), *Race and representation in education* (pp. 3–10). New York: Routledge.

Omolade, B. (1994). *The rising song of African American women.* New York: Routledge.

Packwood, A., & Sikes, P. (1996). Adopting a postmodern approach to research. *Qualitative Studies in Education, 9*(3), 335–345.

Palmer, P. (1983). *To know as we are known: Education as a spiritual journey.* San Francisco: Harper.

Paris, P. J. (1995). *The spirituality of African people: Toward a moral discourse.* Minneapolis: Augsburg Fortress Press.

Richards, D. M. (1980). *Let the circle be unbroken: The implications of African spirituality in the Diaspora.* Lawrenceville, NJ: The Red Sea Press.

Ryan, M. (1988). The theory of ideology reconsidered. *Cultural Studies, 2*(1), 57–66.

Scheurich, J. J., & Young, M. D. (1997). Coloring epistemologies: Are our research epistemologies racially biased? *Educational Researcher, 26*(4), 4–16.

Smith, D. E. (1987). *The everyday world as problematic: A feminist sociology.* Boston: Northeastern University Press.

Some, M. P. (1994). *Of water and the spirit: Ritual, magic, and initiation in the life of an African shaman.* New York: G. P. Putnam's Sons.

Stanfield, J. H. (1993). Epistemological considerations. In J. H. Stanfield, (Ed.), *Race and ethnicity in research methods* (pp. 16–38). Newbury Park, CA: Sage.

Stanfield, J. H. (1994). Ethnic modeling in qualitative research. In N. K. Denzin & Y. S. Lincoln (Eds.), *Handbook of qualitative research* (pp. 175–188). Thousand Oaks, CA: Sage.

Thiongo, N. W. (1986). *Decolonizing the mind: The politics of language in African literature.* Portsmouth, NH: Heinemann.

Tierney, W. G. (1994). On method and hope. In A. Gitlan (Ed.), *Power and method: Political activism and educational research* (pp. 97–115). New York: Routledge.

Vanzant, I. (1996). *The spirit of a man.* New York: Harper Collins.

Wade-Gayles, G. (Ed.). (1995). *My soul is a witness: African American women's spirituality.* Boston: Beacon Press.

Walker, A. (1996). *The same river twice: Honoring the difficult.* New York: Scribner.

West, C. (1993). *Race matters.* Boston: Beacon Press.

Wynter, S. (1992). *Do not call us Negros: How multicultural textbooks perpetuate racism.* San Francisco: Aspire Books.

Yenne-Donmoyer, J., & Donmoyer, R. (1994, April). *In their own words: A reader's theatre presentation of middle school students writing about writing.* Script presented at the annual meeting of the American Educational Research Association, New Orleans, LA.

Chapter 7

Chicana Feminism and Educational Leadership

Sylvia Méndez-Morse

The inclusion of women in studies of educational leadership has yielded insights on administrative socialization, discriminatory hiring practices, underrepresentation of women and people of color, myths about gender and leadership, and the impact of traditional theories of leadership on the lives of women in educational administrative ranks. This book's focus on reexamining critical feminist research in educational leadership and the accompanying questions it raises about theories, methodologies, and epistemologies—how these impact the women whose lives are investigated, the ethical and political implications of such work, how feminist researchers attempt to reconcile methodological and epistemological problems, and the development of alternative ways of framing, looking, questioning, and knowing—lead to a more sensitive, more accurate, and more inclusive application of these reconceptualized theories, methods, and epistemologies. More important, such a focus also invites challenges to these critical and contested areas of scholarship and, thus, demonstrates committed, critical reexamination of feminist research in educational leadership. Although not present in all feminist educational leadership discourse, a discussion of the role of race and ethnicity, in addition to gender, is beginning to emerge in this area. One source of such a perspective that has been minimally explored is Chicana feminist thought.

Chicana feminist scholarship offers an alternative epistemology not only to the discussion of gender, including its construction and its impact on the lives of women, but also to the continuing conversation on educational leadership. It is a means of knowing and conceptualizing a broader gestalt of leadership. Three characteristics of Chicana feminism provide unique contributions to educational leadership theory: a Pan-American perspective; an assertion of multiple oppressions caused by the intersections of gender, class, race/ethnicity, religion, language, and sexual orientation; and an emphasis on the advocacy for social justice. Before describing these three aspects of Chicana feminist thought, a brief explanation of the word *Chicana* and some description of the history of Chicana feminism are in order.

To begin a discussion of Chicana feminist thought, it is important to start with the term *Chicana*, because the word itself is controversial. *Chicana* is a word used by some women of Mexican descent to describe themselves as culturally and politically conscious and/or active individuals. Delgado Bernal (1998) asserted that the term included an "identity of resistance" (p. 556). For many Chicana feminists, the meaning of the term *Chicana* includes resistance to sexism and other institutional and individual practices that contribute to the alienation, exclusion, or marginalization of women of Mexican descent. However, the word *Chicana* also includes the acceptance of, as well as pride in, cultural and linguistic attributes of these women. For many, this label "rejects the idea that we must deny our Mexican heritage in order to be a 'real' American" (Gallardo, 1999, Who are Chicanas, ¶2). Use of this word can also be considered as a response to White feminists who want "women of color to do the impossible: to choose between being a female and being a person of color" (Blea, 1992a, p. 6). Thus, a women who describes herself as a Chicana is one who embraces selected cultural aspects of her ethnicity, who promotes bilingualism and/or the maintenance of the Spanish language, and who rejects and resists discriminatory practices that limit her participation and that either ignore or exclude her contributions.

Several Chicana feminist scholars have asserted that Chicana feminism has its roots in the work of female activists during the Chicano civil rights movement of the 1960s and 1970s. (Blea, 1992a; Pesquera & Segura, 1993). Chicana activists confronted Latinos and their chauvinistic attitudes and many of these women became instrumental in establishing Chicana Studies as a legitimate and separate area within the Chicano or Mexican American Studies movement on university campuses across the nation. However, recent publications by yet other Chicana feminist scholars include previously undocumented stories of women of Mexican descent in social change activities (Delgado Bernal, 1997; Méndez-Morse, 2000; Rodriguez, 1994; Vera, 1998). These emerging presentations of Latinas' lives contain challenges not only to the ethnic stereotyping of Latinas, but also to the notion that Latina feminist activities began during the Chicano civil rights movement. Moreover, Chicana feminist scholarship, regardless of its historical roots, contains a minority woman's perspective as both the "researcher" and the "subject" and, as

Chicana Feminism and Educational Leadership   163

such, provokes self-reflection and analysis of Latina scholars as "border" researchers.

Thus, consideration of Chicana feminist thought has much to offer to the reconsideration of theories, methodologies, and epistemologies, not only in studies of gender, but also to investigations of educational leadership. It is the intent of this chapter to begin a dialogue between Chicana feminists and educational leadership feminist scholars. Although not all three characteristics of Chicana feminism—a Pan-American perspective, an assertion of multiple oppressions, and an advocacy for social justice—are applied in this chapter, a brief discussion of these is included and presented next. This is then followed with the main focus of this chapter, which is a discussion of multiple or "interwoven" oppressions and how they contribute to the educational leadership discourse.

THREE CHARACTERISTICS OF CHICANA FEMINISM

A survey of Chicana feminist work reveals that it encompasses a Pan-American perspective. It is a perspective that is strongly influenced by geographic location yet not constrained by political borders. *Aztlan*, a concept popular during the Chicano civil rights movement of the 1960s and '70s, was/is an assertion of a Chicano homeland that encompassed the geographic areas of northern Mexico, the southwestern states of California, Arizona, New Mexico, and Texas, and extended as far north as Colorado. For many Chicanos, Aztlan was/is wherever Hispanic people formed communities. It is this identity with a physical location, Aztlan, and an accompanying tendency to overlook the "borders" but accommodate or adjust to the political boundaries, that resonates with many Mexicans and Mexican Americans.

Chicana feminist Gloria Anzaldua (1987) has provided the concept of "border consciousness," a frame of mind that is able to accommodate, adjust, and interact with, within, and between borders or cultures. Anzaldua asserted that because Mexican American women live and work within two cultures, they have formed a third culture, a border culture. She posited that the ability to "cross borders" is an aspect of Chicanas' skill to handle multiple identities, which facilitates tolerance for contradictions and ambiguities. Rodriguez (1994) stated that this border consciousness is distinctly metaphysical and that crossing or functioning within more than one culture is a "most ordinary thing in Mexican American women's lives" (p. 63). The Pan-American perspective of a Chicano homeland that transcends a political border that separates two countries coupled with the concept of border consciousness—the ability to switch between living in one culture and then crossing the border to be in an "other" culture—

contributes to further understanding the lives of women, particularly women of color. As Blea (1992a) asserted,

> Minority women tend to have a more holistic view of the world because they recognize their lives have been shaped by a number of factors that do not affect other women ... their experience has been different, even unique, since being a female is complicated by being a minority. (p. 4)

A third aspect of this broad Pan-American perspective is the reclaiming of, and for some an introduction to, the lives of Mexican and Mexican American female leaders and an insertion of a possible alternative construction of leadership into the conversation. The leadership actions of women of Mexican descent are often found in local community efforts. They are/were women—mothers, *tias,* sisters, cousins, *abuelas*—in non-positional leadership roles who are known within their local community or families. Chicanas who study the lives of Latinas have frequently cited the contributions of women throughout the history of Mexico and the United States (Delgado Bernal, 1997; Gaspar de Alba, 1998; Méndez-Morse, 2000; Pardo, 1999; Rodriguez, 1994; Vera, 1998). For example, Chicana feminists can claim the writings of the first published feminist in the "New" World—Sor Juana Inés de la Cruz. She is well known for her poem, *Sátira Filosófica,* which begins with the words, "Hombres necios"—annoying men (my translation). Sor Juana wrote during the seventeenth century and during this time was often publicly "criticized for being too 'masculine,' that is, for indulging her mind too much, for speaking out, for reading and writing, for not being submissive to her superiors" (Gaspar de Alba, 1998, p. 139). This characteristic of Chicana feminist thought, a Pan-American perspective, includes the concept of Aztlan (one homeland, two countries), provides the construct of a border consciousness (recognition of the skill to function in various arenas or cultures), and supplies an arena where Chicana feminist scholars (and others) can regain the work of many Latinas who have defied sexist attitudes and practices. It allows for a means to claim the leadership legacy that is part of the history of Mexican and Mexican American women, even though it is often ignored or minimally acknowledged.

The second characteristic of Chicana feminism is the assertion that there are multiple oppressions caused by the intersections of gender, class, race/ethnicity, religion, language, and sexual orientation (Blea, 1992a; Castillo, 1994; Delgado Bernal 1998; Garcia, 1995; Pesquera & Segura, 1993; Segura, 1986, Vera, 1998). It is the inclusion of these additional characteristics of Mexican and Mexican American women to discussions of sexism that most distinguishes Chicana feminism, as well as other minority feminists, from White feminism. Chicana feminists challenge the White feminist paradigm because of its primary focus on the impact of patriarchal practices and maintain that this fundamental characteristic distracts from seriously considering the influence of racism and classism when examining sexism (Blea, 1992b; Castillo, 1994; Delgado Bernal, 1998; Pesquera & Segura, 1993). This specific characteristic of Chicana feminist thought is the primary focus of this chapter.

Finally, because of the multiple oppressions that are present in the lives of many in the Latino community, a third characteristic of Chicana feminist thought is the assertion of the need for active participation in challenging and changing institutional structures, policies, and practices that inhibit the full engagement of people of color in a democratic society. This recognition of the necessity to struggle for social justice is evident in many areas of Latina activism, such as participation in strikes for improved conditions for farm workers and lobbying for appropriate educational practices such as bilingual education. Chicanas, both feminists and non-feminists, have consistently been active participants in various social movements. Examples can be found in Pardo's (1998) book about the work of Mexican American female activists in resisting state-sponsored and commercial projects in East Los Angeles and Monterrey Park, which would have adversely affected the lives of the people in those communities. Additional descriptions of Latinas' activities in social change efforts can be found in sociological and historical studies of events such as the Finck Cigar strike in San Antonio, Texas, the efforts of cannery row workers in California, and the protests of seamstresses in Farrah factories in New Mexico and Texas (Ruiz, 1987, 2000; Talgen, & Kamp, 1993; Zavella, 1987). These and other studies of grassroots Chicana leaders are emerging. These investigations not only challenge portrayals of Mexican and Mexican American women but, by reporting on these women's contributions to social change efforts, provoke a reconsideration of leadership (Delgado Bernal, 1997; Méndez-Morse, 2000; Rodriguez, 1994).

The preceeding three characteristics of Chicana feminism provide unique and important contributions to the discussion of leadership, and contribute to the conversation about educational leadership specifically. This chapter contains a discussion of how Chicana feminism informs and expands the construction of educational leadership. The primary focus of the remainder of this chapter is an application of the second characteristic—multiple oppressions—to the conversation of educational leadership. Additionally, this discussion includes an assertion that, although the intersections of gender, class, race/ethnicity, sexual orientation, religion, and language do combine to form compounded means of discrimination for women of Mexican descent, within these variables there are also sources of hidden, unrecognized strengths and talents.

INTERWOVEN OPPRESSIONS

Chicana feminists include the intersections of race/ethnicity, class, religion, language, and sexual orientation—not just gender—when studying the lives of Mexican and Mexican American women. Chicana feminist scholars emphasize that, similar to the work of fellow feminists of color, an "endarkened" feminist epistemology contributes to understanding the experiences of women. Blea (1992a) described this as an ability of minority women to have a broader worldview because "they recognize their lives have been shaped by a number of factors that do not affect other women. . . . Being a female is complicated by being a minority" (p. 4). Chicana feminist scholars have "challenged the historical and ideological representation of Chicanas, relocated them to a central position in the research, and asked distinctively Chicana feminist research questions" (Delgado Bernal, 1998, p. 559). Thus, as female scholars of color, we ask different questions, contribute a different perspective, and maintain that the factors of race/ethnicity, sexuality, class, religion, language, *and* gender have a profound impact on our lives.

The dimensions of gender, class, race/ethnicity, religion, sexuality, and language interact not as multiple forms of discrimination, but rather as interwoven forms of oppression that are connected. They are interwoven as in a fabric, one thread laid on top of another, reinforcing the other. In attempting to understand the dynamics of gender, class, and race/ethnicity in the lives of minority women, a perspective of interwoven oppressions is appropriate because each strand acts on the others to strengthen the aspects of the other threads. Each thread intertwines and becomes mutually involved with others to form something else—a cloth. This model may be viewed as the strand of race/ethnicity next to the thread of class on top of the fiber of gender, or gender on top of class beside race/ethnicity; the placement of the threads of oppression does not matter. What matters is that together they form a cloth of oppression that is difficult to tear. For many Chicanas, the added threads of Catholic religious subjugation, homophobic attitudes toward sex, and language proficiency, specifically English language abilities, form a tighter woven fabric of oppression.

By examining each thread individually, it is easier to discern how it contributes to the total strength of a confining mantle worn by many Mexican and Mexican American women. Looking at the interaction of the various threads of the interwoven oppressions that many women of Mexican descent encounter, feminist or not, is challenging. However, it is the unique attributes of Chicana feminist thought, particularly experience with crossing borders, that facilitates and encourages the attempt to do so.

Chicana Feminism and Educational Leadership   167

Recent and emerging voices in Chicana feminism provide guidance. For example, application of theoretical perspectives such as Delgado Bernal's (1998) "cultural intuition," which she described in her article on Chicana feminist epistemology, is particularly cogent. She asserted that cultural intuition is a "complex process that acknowledges the unique viewpoints that many Chicana scholars bring to the research process" (p. 555). It is this aspect of Chicana feminist thought, border consciousness, that facilitates the examination of the individual strands and a holistic analysis of the fabric of interwoven oppressions. The task of unraveling the woof and warp of the interwoven threads of oppression experienced by many women of Mexican descent is necessary and enlightening.

UNRAVELING THE CLOTH OF INTERWOVEN OPPRESSIONS

As has been previously mentioned, Chicana feminists have consistently maintained—it is not just gender. In an effort to understand the interwoven oppressions that impact Mexican and Mexican American women, Chicana feminist scholars have also explored the impact of class (Baca Zinn, 1975), of race/ethnicity (Blea, 1992a, 1992b; Delgado Bernal, 1997; Mirandé & Enriguez, 1979; Pesquera & Segura, 1993; Segura, 1986; Vera, 1998), of religion (Castillo, 1994; Medina, 1998), of homophobia and lesbianism (Anzaldua, 1987; Perez, 1998; Trujillo, 1998), and of English language proficiency (Blea, 1992a) on the lives of women of Mexican descent. It is not an attempt to ignore or diminish the importance of gender but, rather, an endeavor to understand what makes gender—this simple common denominator of half of a large minority population—so powerful when it is interwoven with class, race/ethnicity, religion, sexual preference, and language.

The first fiber that is noticed in this cloth is sexism and patriarchy. Chicana feminists recognize that gender is a powerful characteristic that influences the lives of women, all women. Moreover, many Chicana scholars have documented the Mexican culture's strong influence on the appropriate roles for women and how these limit the life opportunities of Mexican and Mexican American girls and women (Anzaldua, 1987; Mirandé & Enriguez, 1979). As many Chicana feminist scholars have reported, women of Mexican descent often confront chauvinistic attitudes not only from members of their families but also in their work place (Ruiz, 1987; Soldatenko, 2000; Zavella, 1987). These Chicana scholars have documented the struggles of Latina factory workers to form unions and confront the industries' owners to improve their working conditions. Throughout, these women encountered actions and attitudes that demonstrated, as Soldatenko (2000) stated, "women of color do the work; white men lead" (p.139). Gender discrimination is part of the oppression that many Mexican and Mexican American women endure.

The second thread to explore is race/ethnicity or, more specifically, the issue of color. Chicana feminist scholars have remarked on the discrimination that exists because of skin color, both outside of and within the Mexican and Mexican American culture. Frequently noted within Chicana literature are descriptions of the higher value placed on fair skin and light hair by some Mexican and Mexican Americans. Many Latinas can recognize the label *morena* (dark skin) and the admonition of *vente por la sombrita*, which can be translated as "stay in shade or to stay out of the sun so as to not get dark/darker." Moraga (1995) described this higher regard for the lighter shades of hair and skin color with these words, "no one ever quite told me this (that light was right), but I knew that being light was something valued in my family" (p. 16). Often it is difficult to separate culture from ethnicity/race, but skin color is a physical characteristic that is quickly noted. Chicana feminists recognize that skin color, as well as race/ethnicity and subsequent racist or discriminatory practices, further limit and influence the life experiences of a person. The inclusion of race/ethnicity with discussions of the impact of skin color within Chicana feminism and Chicana literature contributes to further understanding how oppression, based on skin color, is present not just between different racial or ethnic groups, but also within such groups.

This acknowledgment of the influence of color is an aspect of the interwoven oppressions characteristic of Chicana feminism. Its strength is its ability to facilitate linkages to other minority groups, such as African Americans and Native Americans, that are strongly impacted by discrimination based on skin color both within and outside of their racial or ethnic groups. For example, within the African American community there is the term "passing," which indicates that an individual is light enough to pass for a White person. Within many Spanish-speaking communities, the words *güera* and *güero* are used to describe a person who could pass for at least a non-Latina or White person. This is one example based on linguistic dimensions of racial/ethnic groups that demonstrates a connection between Chicana feminist scholars discussions of color and other minority groups not only in the United States but also to other people of color throughout the world.

Acknowledgment of the influence of color also promotes a better understanding of the strength of cultural icons. This is evident in the power of the Virgen de Guadalupe, with her dark skin, to connect with Mexicans, especially the darker members of this population. Chicana feminists have explored how this powerful religious and cultural icon demonstrates a connection to indigenous roots, the culture of native peoples in

Chicana Feminism and Educational Leadership 169

Mexico. This connection to Meso-American cultures, in turn, provides exemplars of strong females when looking at the indigenous religions and their inclusion of goddesses such as Tonatzin in Aztec mythology, the goddess of childbirth. Thus, when Chicana feminist scholars consider the role of race and ethnicity in conjunction with the impact of color in the construction of race/ethnicity, they are able to recognize the influence of race/ethnicity/color as a limitation, and to connect with the alternative representations of female power that are common in many non-Western, non-White cultures in the Americas.

The next strand to examine in the cloth of interwoven oppressions is class. Many Chicana scholars have examined the working lives of Latinas and have documented how these women's success is often limited because of their gender and ethnicity (Hurtado, 1989). These researchers have documented how many women of Mexican descent work in labor markets where they are frequently relegated to the most menial positions, where their upward mobility is limited, and where they are once again victims of patriarchy. Additionally, studies have documented the reduced earning power of women of Mexican descent that is strongly influenced by the level of education attained. Thirty-six percent of women of Mexican descent earn a high school diploma and six percent graduate from college. Latinas, as other people of color in the United States, are predominantly of working-class backgrounds (Hurtado, 1989). Certainly the limited educational levels attained by this population diminishes the earning abilities and opportunities of these women. This, in turn, contributes to the fact that many Mexican and Mexican Americans have a working-class background.

The working-class background of many women of Mexican descent does not necessarily indicate lessened opportunities for demonstrating leadership abilities, however. Pardo (1999) reported on the community-building experiences of Mexican American women in California. She discussed how the women worked as volunteers in church activities and how this contributed not only to an increased sense of agency for themselves but also an increased advocacy for the nuns with whom they worked. Pardo stated,

> Some women thought nuns should be entitled to more authority in the parents' group. . . . The women perceived that their volunteer work, which supplemented the costs of parochial schooling, justified their right to have a "say-so" about the use of funds. This meant they directly negotiated with the priest in charge of the school. (p. 287)

Chicanas, like other women, are influenced by patriarchal attitudes of where their work emphasis should be—their homes. Nonetheless, many

170   *Sylvia Méndez-Morse*

of these women are working outside of the home, sometimes defying the patriarchy but more often simply contributing to the welfare of their families. Whatever the motivation, many of these women contend with the dual job of being a worker and the primary homemaker. However, many Latinas do not follow the prescribed role, and when they are working outside of their homes, often there is support for their dual responsibilities. That is, although there is evidence that Latinas have this double burden, there are also reports of the support and encouragement of their family (Avery, 1982; Fernandez, 1989; Gándara, 1982; Herrera, 1987, Méndez-Morse, 1997). Both immediate and extended family members and spouses were sources of support and assistance in areas such as child care and encouragement for pursuing educational as well as career goals.

The fourth fiber of interwoven oppressions experienced by many Latinas to explore is the influence of language, particularly English language proficiency. It is common knowledge in Latino communities that lack of English proficiency is a detriment to any progress or success. In addition, there are documented examples of groups both within and outside of the Latino community that insist on English only for immigrant peoples in the United States and suggest that reluctance to reject their native languages is un-American and a refusal to become completely engaged in American society (Rodriguez, 1994). Many Mexicans and Mexican Americans recognize and urge the acquisition of English but are also reluctant to abandon their native language. It is difficult to let go of the language of mothers, fathers, and grandparents. Ironically, recent global economic realities have demonstrated the advantages of conducting business in the native languages of customers. Despite such an awareness of the benefits and power of bilingualism or multilingualism, a majority of Americans adhere to their English-only mindset and lack respect for and oppose educational programs that promote academic development of a language other than English.

Chicana feminist scholars have documented how Latinas have been restricted because of limited English proficiency. However, there have been almost no studies to examine if, and how, bilingual skills have assisted these women. Nevertheless, there is at least one example of Mexican American female community leaders whose bilingual skills assisted their efforts in mobilizing community members. Pardo (1999) reported that many of the women she studied used their bilingual Spanish–English skills to inform other community members of issues that had a wide impact on the local neighborhood. These skills proved significant in building strong and united community efforts to address concerns that many in the area had.

We next look at the thread of religion, specifically the impact of Catholicism with its strong patriarchal paradigm and the restrictive role it places on women. Chicana feminist scholars have written about their recognition of oppression from Christian, primarily Catholic, religious practices that maintain the supremacy of patriarchy (Castillo, 1994; Medina, 1998; Rodriguez, 1994). Some Chicana feminists argue that this aspect of the Spanish conquest of the New World introduced the second-class status of women, which had not been experienced in indigenous cultures. The truth of this claim appears especially evident when comparing the mythology of native people throughout Mexico and the southwestern United States. Chicana feminist scholars have questioned, in particular, the continued virgin–whore duality prevalent in Catholicism and its impact on how religious leaders view women. "The Virgin Mary—who was a virgin and a mother, but never a sexual being—is presented as an important role model for all Hispanic women" (Espin, 1995, p. 424). Despite the contradictory messages that the church gives women about sexuality, Chicana scholars have reported that Latina women find means for accommodating religious teachings with their personal, and sometimes conflicting, beliefs. For example, Medina (1998) found that the Chicana women in her study were able to replace "patriarchal religion with their own cultural knowledge, sensibilities, and sense of social justice" (p. 189).

Although these negatives can be damaging to many women, religion can also have a positive side. For example, even within the restrictive roles that are imposed on women, such as women's work being within the home and with the family, the church has provided an outlet for Mexican and Mexican American women in organized groups such as Las Hijas de Guadalupe. It is within these church groups that many women have been active in their local communities and such involvement has facilitated the leadership development of women. More importantly, because of historical and cultural links to indigenous peoples and their mythologies, there is the recognition of feminine power as a significant component of these frameworks (Blea, 1992b; Delgado Bernal, 1997; Mirandé & Enriquez, 1979; Pesquera & Segura, 1993; Segura, 1986; Vera, 1998).

Finally, the strand of sexual orientation is considered as a component of the interwoven oppressions experienced by lesbian Latinas. This strand is closely related to the thread of religion, given the Catholic Church's stance toward homosexuality. Chicana feminist scholars have focused on the prevalent homophobia that exists within the Latino community (Anzaldua, 1987; Perez, 1998; Trujillo, 1998). Not only is there a strong reluctance to accept homosexuality but, as Espin (1995) discussed, even "politically aware" Latinos and Latinas demonstrate a "remarkable lack of understanding of gay-related issues . . . [and] Hispanics who consider themselves radical and committed to civil rights remain extremely traditional when it comes to gay rights" (p. 427).

HOW CHICANA FEMINISM CAN CONTRIBUTE TO
RESEARCH ON WOMEN IN EDUCATIONAL LEADERSHIP

The aforementioned unraveling of interwoven oppressions demonstrated how different forms of discrimination and oppression simultaneously impact women educational leaders of Mexican descent. It also demonstrated that, although the intersections of gender, class, race/ethnicity, sexual orientation, religion, and language combine to form compounded means of discrimination for women of Mexican descent, within these variables there are also sources of hidden, unrecognized strengths and talents. The question for us at this juncture is, "what can an application of Chicana feminism, and specifically the lens of interwoven oppressions, contribute to research on women in educational leadership?"

Few studies of educational leaders have taken into consideration the impact of more than one source of difference (e.g., race, class, gender, language, ability, sexual orientation). Indeed, examinations of some forms of difference, like sexual orientation and the role it plays in the lives and practice of educational leaders, have only recently begun to appear in the literature. Thus, an examination of educational leaders that takes into consideration more than one form of difference, it seems, would be truly groundbreaking. Moreover, such a line of inquiry could inform and expand the current construction of educational leadership and what it means and what it is like to be a female educational leader.

To illustrate, one area that has been explored is that of gender and culture. A powerful contrast to traditional patterns of chauvinistic behaviors appears to exist in the families of Mexican and Mexican American educational leaders. That is, in studies of Latina educational leaders, the typical patriarchal stance toward women, which results in no support from spouses, is not found. On the contrary, some Latina educational leaders receive encouragement and support from their husbands to pursue their career goals (Avery, 1982; Carranza, 1988; Colon Gibson, 1992; Méndez-Morse, 1997). Colon Gibson (1992), for example, reported that the Hispanic administrators in her study credited their husbands as sources of encouragement and other forms of support, such as accommodating schedules so that the women could study at home or assisting with housework, shopping, and childcare. Similarly, Avery found that "support from the husband for extra-family activities and achievements was important and valued" (1982, p. 18). In Méndez-Morse's (1997) study of four Mexican American female superintendents, she reported that these women benefited from continual and consistent spousal support throughout their administrative careers. Although it cannot be assumed that non-Hispanic female leaders do not enjoy the support and encouragement of their husbands or that all Latina leaders do, these studies,

Chicana Feminism and Educational Leadership 173

which investigated different types of Hispanic female leaders, indicate that spousal support is a significant component in these women's lives. These findings trouble traditional stereotypes of Mexican and Mexican American men and the treatment of women of Mexican descent, raising interesting questions for research.

Although these women mentioned did not appear to experience sexist attitudes with their husbands, these Latina educational leaders did face gender discrimination and were able to confront it. As Méndez-Morse (1997) found in her study of Mexican American female superintendents, women leaders faced gender discrimination more often than racism. One woman reported how a school board president instructed her not to apply for a superintendent's position, even though she was the acting superintendent at the time, because the board would not consider a female for the position. This is an example of overt gender discrimination. This same woman reported incidents of being treated like an administrative assistant (e.g., being asked how to contact the superintendent) while she was working in her—the superintendent's—office; a more subtle but equally serious example of gender discrimination.

A second area that has been explored, though to a lesser extent, is that of gender and skin color. In their discussions of discrimination based on skin color, both within and outside of the Mexican and Mexican American culture, and the higher value placed on the lighter shades of hair and skin, Chicana feminist scholars have asserted that an awareness of such values facilitates an understanding of racial discrimination experienced both by Latinas and by other minority group members. Is this true? And if so, how would this inform the discourse on educational leadership?

Studies on minority educational leaders, both female and male, report a high occurrence of assignment to campuses with large minority student populations. Are such placements made on the assumption that similar racial or ethnic backgrounds (and skin color) would benefit the campus leader and the students? Whatever the explanations, they will be informative at individual and organizational levels. Do such assignments produce increased or improved leadership effectiveness? How would this relate to school reform efforts? Would there be evidence of addressing social justice problems?

My own investigations of the experiences of Latina educational leaders provide some interesting findings worth considering. One Chicana campus leader, Dr. B., shared the following story. A teacher was describing the need to report to central office administrators about a group of students she had taught previously. The teacher stated that what she could remember most about the class was that "they were a very hyper group. Just a bunch of Mexican jumping beans." Dr. B. stated that she attempted to get clarification from the teacher about her characterization of the students loaded with such a racist term without immediately confronting the teacher as a racist. In her attempt, Dr. B. explored various forms of discussion to help the teacher recognize the racism in her remarks. Her attempts, however, were to no avail. Within a few days, the teacher delivered to Dr. B. a "gift"—a package of Mexican jumping beans. Clearly, Dr. B's experiences with ethnic discrimination alerted her to the teacher's attitude toward the Mexican American students in her care and influenced this Latina educational leader's attempts to point out the racism the teacher exhibited, even though her efforts failed.

Simply reporting the incident to a *comadre*, a fellow Chicana who studies women like Dr. B, began a long period of self-reflection for this Chicana campus leader and the researcher. Their dialogue, once reported in academically appropriate channels and heard, will contribute to the conversation on educational leadership, feminist or otherwise.

A third and final area I would like to mention is that of gender and social class. Various Chicana feminist scholars have commented on the prevalence of Mexicans and Mexican Americans being economically at the working-class or poverty level. Studies on Latina educational leaders indicate that many of these women also came from such economic backgrounds. Current research reveals that Mexican American female educational leaders confirm that having come from working class or poverty-stricken families themselves helps and encourages them to aggressively meet the needs of similar-background children in their schools. In addition, these women described how their working-class backgrounds facilitated their efforts to inform their teachers about poor students' circumstances and how this influences these students' school performance. Still further, these Mexican American female school leaders reported that their "humble beginnings" assisted them in relating to parents and family members more easily.

What can be gained from these research examples that look at more than one form of difference? Perhaps the main benefit is avoiding the risk of oversimplifying the lives of women educational leaders. Certainly other female school and district leaders can inform us about how being different from their constituencies in areas such as class or race/ethnicity influences their work. We would also learn from lesbian educational leaders and their experiences. Yet another contribution of considering more than one form of difference is a clearer understanding of how these other dimensions are not only restraints but also benefits at both individual and organizational levels. The interwoven oppressions model presented in this chapter begins a dialogue for reconsidering difference in the lives and work of female educational leaders, and for reflecting on the implications of difference for educational leadership theories, methodologies, and epistemologies.

CONCLUSIONS

With the inclusion of a Chicana feminist perspective and its three characteristics, the notion of interwoven oppressions was presented as a model for reconsidering what studies of Latina educational leaders have reported. It is more than an attempt to participate in the conversation about educational leadership and feminism. It is a contribution rich with some insights about the work of these women, but it is also laden with questions.

Perhaps the primary question this area of inquiry addresses is: do minority female educational leaders confront sexism and patriarchal practices similarly to White women? Studies are beginning to investigate the relationship between the matched racial and/or ethnic background of these two groups. Inclusion of gender when exploring the influence of the educational leaders' race and ethnicity certainly would enrich the examination of the impact of these characteristics. Does either characteristic matter when implementing reform efforts?

Investigations of Chicanas' interwoven oppressions, their border consciousness, raise other questions as well. For example, investigating what role (if any) this consciousness plays in facilitating or impeding Chicanas' interactions with the many constituencies in their work arenas would inform the construct of educational leadership. Can Mexican and Mexican American women community activists inform leadership development programs? Does having bilingual or multilingual language skills contribute, for example, to effective community relations? Does previous experience as a bilingual teacher influence the campus leader's work with implementing appropriate instructional strategies of language-minority students?

This chapter is a foundational attempt at (1) reconsidering the various threads in the cloth of interwoven oppressions that is often placed on women of Mexican descent as well as (2) considering what such a reconsideration means when focusing specifically on female educational leaders of Mexican descent. This glance at the *género* of this mantle of gender *and* race/ethnicity/color *and* class *and* religion *and* language, though nascent, reveals a texture and a pattern that, when looked at differently, shows a *tejido*, an interweaving of threads, that singularly and collectively is extremely valuable.

REFERENCES

Anzaldua, G. (1987). *Borderlands/La frontera: The new mestiza.* San Francisco: Aunt Lute Books.

Avery, D. M. (1982). *Critical events shaping the Hispanic woman's identity.* Chicago: Chicago State University, Center for Woman's Identity Studies.

176 *Sylvia Méndez-Morse*

Baca Zinn, M. (1975). Political familism: Toward sex role equality in Chicano families. *Aztlan, 6*(1), 13–26.

Blea, I. I. (1992a). Chicana scholarship and third world perspectives. In *La Chicana and the intersection of race, class, and gender* (pp. 1–20). Westpoint, CT: Praeger.

Blea, I. I. (1992b). Theoretical perspectives on the intersection of gender, class, and ethnicity. In *La Chicana and the intersection of race, class, and gender* (pp. 117–130). Westpoint, CT: Praeger.

Carranza, R. (1988). Research findings on marriage, income, and stress of professional women, *Intercambios Femeniles, 3*(1), 6–9.

Castillo, A. (1994). *Massacre of the dreamers: Essays on Xicanisma.* New York: Penguin.

Colon Gibson, F. (1992). *A profile of Hispanic women administrators in New Jersey public schools: Their entry and retention in educational administration.* Unpublished dissertation, Temple University.

Delgado Bernal, D. (1997). *Chicana school resistance and grassroots leadership: Providing an alternative history to the 1968 East Los Angeles blowouts.* Unpublished dissertation, University of California, Los Angeles.

Delgado Bernal, D. (1998). Using a Chicana feminist epistemology in educational research. *Harvard Educational Review, 68*(4), 555–582.

Espin, O. M. (1995). Cultural and historical influence on sexuality in Hispanic/Latin women: Implications for psychotherapy. In M. L. Andersen & P. H. Collins (Eds.), *Race, class, and gender: An anthology* (pp. 423–428). Boston: Wadsworth.

Fernandez, M. A. (1989). *Hispanic women school administrators: Critical reflections on their success.* Unpublished dissertation, University of San Francisco.

Gallardo, S. (1999). *Making face, making soul . . . A Chicana feminist Web page.* http://chicanas.com/huh.html

Gándara, P. (1982). Passing through the eye of the needle: High-achieving Chicanas. *Hispanic Journal of Behavioral Sciences, 4*(2), 167–179.

Garcia, A. M. (1995). The development of Chicana feminist discourses. In A. Kesselman, L. D. McNair, & N. Schniedewind (Eds.), *Women images and realities: A multicultural anthology* (pp. 406–413). Mountain View, CA: Mayfield.

Gaspar de Alba, A. (1998). The politics of location of the tenth muse of America: An interview with Sor Juana Inés de la Cruz. In C. Trujillo (Ed.), *Living Chicana theory* (pp. 136–165). Berkeley, CA: Third Woman Press.

Herrera, R. Y. (1987). Professional development, *Intercambios Femeniles, 2*(6), 21.

Hurtado, A. (1989). Relating to privilege: Seduction and rejection in the subordination of White women and women of color. *Signs: Journal of Women in Culture and Society, 4*(4), 833–855.

Medina, L. (1998). Los espíritus siguen hablando: Chicana spirtualities. In C. Trujillo (Ed.), *Living Chicana theory* (pp. 189–213). Berkeley, CA: Third Woman Press.

Méndez-Morse, S. E. (1997). *The meaning of becoming a superintendent: A phenomenological study of Mexican American female superintendents.* Unpublished dissertation, University of Texas at Austin.

Méndez-Morse, S. (2000). Claiming forgotten leadership. *Urban Education, 35*(5), 584–596.

Mirandé, A., & Enriquez, E. (1979). *La Chicana.* Chicago: University of Chicago Press.

Moraga, C. (1995). La güera. In M. L. Anderson & P. H. Collins (Eds.), *Race, class, and gender: An anthology* (2nd ed., pp. 15–22). Boston: Wadsworth.

Pardo, M. S. (1998). *Mexican American women activists: Identity and resistance in two Los Angeles communities.* Philadelphia: Temple University Press.

Pardo, M. S. (1999). Creating community: Mexican American women in Eastside Los Angeles. In N. A. Naples (Ed.), *Community activism and feminist politics: Organizing across race, class, and gender* (pp. 275–300). New York: Routledge.

Perez, E. (1998). Irigaray's female symbolic in the making of Chicana lesbians *Sitios y lenguas* (Sites and discourses). In C. Trujillo (Ed.), *Living Chicana theory* (pp. 87–101). Berkeley, CA: Third Woman Press.

Pesquera, B. M., & Segura, D. M. (1993). There is no going back: Chicanas and feminism. In N. Alarcón, R. Castro, E. Pérez, B. Pesquera, A. S. Riddell, & R. Zavella (Eds.), *Chicana critical issues* (pp. 95–116). Berkeley, CA: Third Woman Press.

Rodriguez, J. (1994). *Our Lady of Guadalupe: Faith and empowerment among Mexican-American women.* Austin: University of Texas Press.

Ruiz, V. L. (1987). *Cannery women, cannery lives.* Albuquerque: University of New Mexico Press.

Ruiz, V. L. (2000). Claiming public space at work, church, and neighborhood. In V. L. Ruiz & C. Noriega (Eds.), *Las obreras: Chicana politics of work and family* (pp. 13–39). Los Angeles: UCLA Chicano Studies Research Center Publications.

Segura, D. M. (1986). Chicanas and triple oppression in the labor force. In T. Cordova, N. Cantu, G. Cardenas, J. Garcia, & C. M. Sierra (Eds.), *Chicana voices: Intersections of class, race, and gender* (pp. 47–65). Albuquerque: University of New Mexico Press.

Soldatenko, M. A. (2000). Organizing Latina garment workers in Los Angeles. In V. L. Ruiz & C. Noriega (Eds.), *Las obreras: Chicana politics of work and family* (pp. 137–157). Los Angeles: UCLA Chicano Studies Research Center Publications.

Talgen, D., & Kamp, J. (1993). *Notable Hispanic American women.* Detroit: Gale Research.

Trujillo, C. (1998). La virgin de Guadalupe and her reconstruction in Chicana lesbian desire. In C. Trujillo (Ed.), *Living Chicana theory* (pp. 213–231). Berkeley, CA: Third Woman Press.

Vera, M. H. (1998). *The Chicana college graduate: Community college learning experiences, coping strategies, and cultural conflicts.* Unpublished dissertation, Texas A&M University.

Zavella, P. (1987). *Women's work and Chicano families: Cannery workers of the Santa Clara Valley.* Ithaca, NY: Cornell University Press.

Chapter 8

A Loving Epistemology: What I Hold Critical in My Life, Faith, and Profession

Julie C. Laible

Good evening. It is good to see all of you here this evening—thank you for coming. I see good friends and colleagues and members of this church in which I worship in the audience. I am honored that the campus ministers' association asked me to be a part of this lecture series. When Sandy Winter, our minister, told me that I would be receiving a letter formally requesting that I be a speaker, I must admit that I was excited. What I do as a researcher and teacher on a daily basis, I like to think, is based in what I hold critical in my life and in my faith. Having to prepare this lecture during Lent, one of my favorite liturgical seasons, one in which we are encouraged to reflect on what is keeping us from God, was also, I thought, a wonderful time for me to look at my life and my profession. On the other hand, when I learned that "the last lecture I would ever give" was a part of the request, I felt a very heavy weight on my shoulders. How do I tie everything I hold critical in my life, faith, and profession into one lecture and share it in a way that would be meaningful to you? Did I need to jump 30 years ahead to what will hopefully be the end of my career and present you with a "grand work" a "perfected theory?" I decided rather quickly that wasn't possible or probable and that this, hopefully, will not be the last lecture I will ever be giving. In fact, if you asked me what I hold critical in my life, faith, and profession next year, you may very well get a different response, perhaps similar, but different nonetheless. However, for tonight, I will pretend that this is *it*, the last one. Here it goes.

Tonight I would like to talk about my role as a researcher in the university, which is, I believe, shaped by my Christianity. Specifically, I will discuss what it means to do research on or with people who are different than yourself. I conduct qualitative research, a form of research that is also called naturalistic or interpretive research, because instead of doing experiments with control and treatment groups or instead of collecting quantifiable data, we enter the natural setting (in my case, the settings are usually schools), interview and observe humans, and then interpret their actions. I am sure there are some of you in the audience who are not researchers—nor do you ever plan to be one. That's okay—we are a strange bunch; that is certain. However, I would venture to say to those of you who are not researchers, you will be researchers of human behavior of one sort or another—whether you plan to enter business, or law, or social work, communication, or K–12 education. You will interact with others—some of whom are very different than yourself, you will collect your own data (as formal or informal as that may be), and you will come to your own conclusions about those people. So, in a sense, we are all social science researchers whether we realize it or not, or whether or not we think of ourselves as such.

But first, before I talk about that, I want you to know who I am and specifically what I believe as a person of faith.

As most of you have determined by now, I am a Christian. I know two years ago in this lecture series Dr. Soresen said that every bit of his faith was chiseled out with an anvil and hammer. I will admit that I've had my moments hammering and questioning. With the Age of Reason, the Enlightenment, logic, science, being a person who believes in God is not as common in the academy as it used to be. We are socialized to not believe in anything unless it follows the logical empiricists' "verifiability principle of meaning." These logical empiricists were philosophers of science—many psychologists, whose notions of how we conduct research became deeply embedded in U.S. universities about 75 years ago. Their verifiability principle of meaning holds that the only way you can claim something is true is if you sense it through one of your five senses using the scientific method, or if it is a tautology of math or logic. *Well, God doesn't match the verifiability principle of meaning.*

Christianity, too, has been critiqued more recently by postmodernists who claim it is a metanarrative, a grand totalizing theory with a capital "T" that claims there is one truth, a claim which most postmodernists say is oppressive. And I agree with them. I agreed that history has shown us that Christianity has been oppressive to many groups of people. In fact, I would say many of its forms are today oppressive to large numbers of people. One reason, however, I did not give up my faith as these theories became known to me was a new knowledge of the historical Jesus. This knowledge came to me through a group of Jesus scholars, some Christian, some not, who have studied Jesus as a historical person,

A Loving Epistemology   181

the sociopolitical context of the early Christian movement, and the ways in which early Christianity is different, in so many ways, from some forms of Christianity of today. In addition, they also gave my modern academic "way of empirically knowing" side, something to hang my hat on, so to speak, by using the historical method to help us understand the time in which Jesus lived. Much of what they say, my good religion philosopher friend told me, was common knowledge in most philosophy of religion circles before the Jesus Seminar Scholars (in fact, at least 100 years ago, some of what they are saying was widely accepted in the academy). What these more recent scholars did, however, was bring this knowledge to a much wider public—and thank goodness that wider public included me.

Marcus Borg (1995), one of the more famous Jesus scholars, also made the claim, a claim that was incredibly comforting to me, that faith and belief are different. You may never truly know what you believe—you may always be questioning—but faith is possible, nonetheless. This is the same notion articulated by religious philosopher William James (1912). James described a version of faith in which doubt was possible. The test of this faith, according to James, was the courage or readiness to act in spite of the fact that one does not know the outcome of his or her actions.

Here is what Borg (1995) claims about Jesus. He makes four points (and you will see in a moment how this relates to my research, I promise):

1. The historical Jesus was a spirit person, one of those figures in human history with an experiential awareness of the reality of God.
2. Jesus was a teacher of wisdom who regularly used the classic form of wisdom, speech (such as parables), to teach a subversive and alternative wisdom.
3. Jesus was a movement founder who brought into being a Jewish renewal or revitalization movement that challenged and shattered the social boundaries of his day (which eventually became Christianity).
4. Jesus was a social prophet, similar to the classical prophets of ancient Israel. As such, he criticized the elites (economic, political, religious) of his time, was an advocate of an alternative social vision, and was often in conflict with authorities (both Jewish and Roman).

This last characteristic of Jesus is my favorite, and a strong part of why I am Christian—I think. Walter Brueggeman (1978), an Old Testament scholar, sums it up nicely in a statement that hangs on my computer in my office. In this statement he describes Jesus' solidarity with and compassion for marginalized people. It is important to understand that marginalized persons during Jesus' time included lepers, prostitutes, the poor, the outcast, and the Jewish peasant farmers and artisans oppressed by the Romans. Jesus' form of compassion took hurt seriously and did not accept it as a normal or natural human condition. Such compassion was not permitted in Jesus' time because such compassion, which undermines norms and taken-for-granted conditions, supports people rather than empires. In effect, Jesus' compassion was more than an emotional reaction—it was a criticism of and a challenge to a power structure that placed social control above the individual person. This description of Jesus is one that I believe in strongly and one that informs my position as an academic.

I am going to move now to discussing my work, which includes teaching, research, and service. The part I am going to focus on is the research side—the way in which I study and know other humans in the field of education. As all of you know from the announcement of this series and from Patrick's introduction of me, I teach in the department of educational leadership. We prepare teachers to become principals, superintendents, and other leaders in educational contexts. A big part of my profession includes producing knowledge and conducting research that furthers the field of education. Those of you who are professors in the audience know this expectation very well. In doing research, starting with my dissertation in graduate school, I have found some aspects of it troubling, very morally troubling—thus, for the last five years or so, I have been struggling to find a way to conduct research that is not problematic—in essence. I have been attempting to solidify a theory of knowing others that fits with my Christian beliefs and what I believe are general human imperatives of living in the world as compassionate, loving human beings.

Cornel West (1993), one of my favorite philosophers, who is a professor of Religion and Afro-American studies at Harvard University, discussed his social analytic perspective—a perspective that informs his thought, research, writing, and so on, not unlike what I am trying to do. He calls his social analytic perspective post-Marxist because it incorporates Marxist class critiques as well as racial, feminist, gay, lesbian, and ecological modes of social analysis and cultural criticism. But what West says about his faith is what I would like to quote because I agree with him strongly. He writes, "I arrive at these analyses because the moral vision and ethical norms I accept are derived from the prophetic Christian tradition. I follow the biblical injunction to look at the world through the eyes of its victims" (p. 133). This Christocentric perspective, he claims, requires that one see the world "through the lens of the cross—and thereby see our relative victimizing and relative victimization. . . . The synoptic vision I accept is a particular kind of prophetic Christian perspective that comprehensively grasps and enables opposition to existential anguish, socioeconomic, cultural, and political oppression and dogmatic modes of thought and action" (p. 133).

West does not believe, and neither do I, that this specific version of the prophetic Christian tradition has a monopoly on such insights, capacities, and motivations; yet, for now, this Christian tradition works for him, and it works for me because its moral vision and ethical norms propel human intellectual activity (such as my research and other parts of my life) to account for and transform existing forms of dogmatism, oppression, and despair.

So what is happening in my profession, specifically in my research, that hampers this vision? Indulge me for a minute as I take you back to my dissertation defense, which took place at the University of Texas in Austin. Having an undergraduate degree in the teaching of Spanish and having had teaching experiences in which I saw the ways linguistically and culturally diverse students were oppressed in schools, I always had an interest in studying ways to change that situation. So, in my dissertation, I examined educational practices that increased the success of Mexican American female students. I conducted qualitative research in two Texas–Mexico border high schools. Much of my research involved me, a Euro-American from the Midwest, interviewing Mexican American girls who had lived in the Rio Grande Valley all their lives, and for most of whom Spanish was their first language. I knew my perspective was limited, but I thought if I had colleagues who had grown up in their area, they could serve as peer debriefers, helping me understand the Mexican American female perspective. I also kept a reflective journal, trying to become aware of my own Eurocentric biases. Well, I collected good data, I thought; the girls seemed to open up to me, and I was able to write up my findings in a way that added to the literature. It was at my defense, however, that a committee member, Dr. Lonnie Wagstaff, asked me, "Julie, what is success for these girls (e.g., the Mexican American girls in my study)? Whose definition of success are you using when you discuss best educational practices that lead to their success in schools?" I was taken aback and eventually responded, "I suppose that it is my definition of success and, perhaps, of some of the Mexican American educators in those schools who have been successful based on middle-class, Euro-American standards." Thus, despite my Chicano peer debriefers and reflexive research journaling, I had conducted the study using a Euro-American, middle-class definition of success. My epistemology was racially biased (Scheurich & Young, 1997).

Let me stop here and define three words that I am going to be using a few more times: One is ontology—that is a branch of philosophy that studies the nature of existence (reality). The second one is epistemology—a branch of philosophy that investigates the origin, nature, methods, and limits of human knowledge (how do we know reality). The last one is methodology—the underlying rules and principles of a philosophical system or inquiry procedure (how we study reality). Logical empiricism and qualitative philosophy are both methodologies.

So, what I argued a few seconds ago was that my epistemology, how I come to know different realities, is racially biased—I can only see things through my Euro-American middle-class lens. My conducting this type of biased research is part of what Scheurich (1996) calls the Western knowledge project. . . . The purpose of research [the heart of the Western Knowledge Project] is to study the world (the Other), organize the world through a theory (re-form or reshape the Other into the Same), and produce a written text communicating the victory of the Same over the Other (p. 54).

As I conducted research with and on adolescent females of color I was, albeit unknowingly, reshaping the girls' experiences (the Other) to either positively or negatively fit with my notions (the Same) of what it means to be an adolescent, a female, and a Mexican American.

Bell hooks (1990), an African American scholar and cultural critic, describes this violence, the violence of radical critical thinkers, feminist thinkers, who participate in the discourse about the Other. She plays with the voice of the colonizer.

> No need to hear your voice when I can talk about you better than you can speak about yourself. No need to hear your voice. Only tell me about your pain. I want to know your story. And then I will tell it back to you in a new way. Tell it back to you in such a new way that it has become mine, my own. Rewriting you, I write myself anew. I am still author, authority. I am still the colonizer, the speaking subject, and you are now at the center of my talk. Stop. (p. 152)

The defense question haunted and continues to haunt me as an assistant professor establishing a research agenda. I have continued to read scholarly work regarding outsider research (e.g., Collins, 1990; Paredes, 1997; Stanfield, 1994) and Euro-American privilege (e.g., Barndt, 1991; Derman-Sparks & Phillips, 1997). I have also recently had frank discussions with African American colleagues, students, and friends regarding these topics. My participation in these activities has convinced me that I will *never* be able to fully or accurately understand Others' experiences. My epistemology is Western, modern, and racially biased (Khare, 1992; Scheurich, 1996; Scheurich & Young, 1997). My desire to gaze on the Other and reinscribe them in my words, in my opinion, is no longer valid or ethical. My research victimizes others, although this is not my conscious intent. Nevertheless, it is an activity I am quite certain Jesus would

A Loving Epistemology

not condone. And unfortunately, a great deal of this type of research takes place in this university by incredibly caring and well-meaning individuals and in universities just like this one. In fact, it happens in all universities—I am not singling out the University of Alabama.

I want to stop here and make two points. The first point I have already made rather indirectly. The second one is new. First, I hope it is clear by now that I believe research on Others is unethical, especially Euro-American research on people of color. Social philosopher Linda Alcoff (1991), states

> The recognition that there is a problem in speaking for others has arisen from two sources. First, there is a growing recognition that where one speaks from affects the meaning and truth of what one says, and thus that one cannot assume an ability to transcend one's location. . . The second source involves a recognition that, not only is location epistemically salient, but certain privileged locations are discursively dangerous. In particular, the practice of privileged persons speaking for or on behalf of less privileged persons has actually resulted (in many cases) in increasing or reinforcing the oppression of the group spoken for. (pp. 6–7)

So the knowledge we Euro-Americans gain is not only inaccurate, it is victimizing and oppressing those we are studying (and isn't that the last thing we Christian scholars want to do?).

The second point I want to make—and prepare yourself for this one—is that institutions in the United States, universities included, were developed in a way, and continue to function in a way, that specifically benefit one group of people. That group is Euro-American, middle- to upper-class, and usually male. On the other side of the coin, the standard operating procedures in universities tend to hurt those people (e.g., students, faculty, administrators) who do not fit the above profile. That does not mean that Euro-American, middle-class persons in the universities are bad people, evil-intended persons. Quite to the contrary. In fact, I include myself in that group, and I also include many, many good friends. I actually include most of this audience in that group—and I know for a fact that those of you who I know are caring, loving individuals. And I think it is a safe bet to hypothesize that the rest of you are, too. It is not individual evilness, but institutional evil that I am speaking of. Think of the majority of the students in your classes—who are they?—think of the majority of the professors you have—what do they look like?—think of the authors you read and the language in which you are expected to communicate—whose knowledge and ways of communicating are you validating? Again,

I am not singling out the University of Alabama; I am talking about universities all across the nation.

So, believing with all my heart the above two "facts" (there are ethical problems with research on others that are different than myself, and I am working in an institution that gives me great benefits because of my race and class and denies these benefits to others), I ask myself, "How do I continue in my profession as a Christian, particularly in an institution I know is oppressing large numbers of people?" Would Jesus dismantle universities? Probably not, but I think he would drastically change them.

During the last segment of this lecture, because I cannot talk about all the ways I would want to change universities, I am going to return to my research dilemma. There, I can make small changes in both my work and in the thoughts of colleagues who take my critique of university knowledge production seriously. For us, is there an ethical way to continue producing knowledge about other human beings? Is there such a thing as a "loving epistemology?" I will start with the work of a Jewish philosopher, then I will end with a brief discussion of the writings of a few female philosophers, specifically female philosophers of color.

First, I must discuss Emmanuel Levinas. Levinas was born in Lithuania to a prominent Jewish family. He studied the Bible in Hebrew, but spoke Russian at home. His family moved to the Ukraine during World War I, but shortly thereafter returned to Lithuania. In 1923 he left home to study in France and in Germany under two well-known philosophers, Edmund Husserl and Martin Heidegger. He became a French citizen, married, did military service in Paris, and eventually took a position in a university there. He began to publish his academic works, but in 1939 he was drafted into the French army. He served as a translator because he spoke German, French, and Russian. Because he wore a French uniform, he was sent to a labor camp, not a concentration camp. Back home in Lithuania, his parents and all of his siblings were murdered by the Nazis (Davis, 1996). I think Levinas' experiences as a victim, as an oppressed person, are critical to understand as you think about his philosophy.

Even before, but certainly after World War II, Levinas began critiquing both of his mentors, both Husserl and Heidegger, who are known as founders of phenomenology. Phenomenology, in contrast to logical empiricism, argues that we can know the natural world, not only by the scientific method and the verifiability principle of meaning, but through our consciousness. Husserl said we should inspect our own consciousness and bracket off all things from the external world that we may doubt exist. That leaves only our consciousness, a transcendental Ego. For example, when I am conscious of a tree, I may doubt the objective existence of the tree, but I cannot doubt the reality of my consciousness. The tree is only knowable through my consciousness that intends it. Levinas believed

A Loving Epistemology

Husserl broke ground on many fronts, but he did not take into account that our consciousnesses are time- and context-bound. For example, how I experience the tree depends a great deal on the time in history in which I find myself. Levinas also critiqued Husserl because his notion of consciousness does not allow for the existence of other consciousnesses (Davis, 1996; Manning, 1993; Peperzak, 1993).

Heidegger, Levinas' other mentor, built on the work of Husserl, but instead of a consciousness, Heidegger talked of a Being or Existence; the German word for this is *Dasein*, which is an event or a process; it is the mode of existence of beings. Existence can only be apprehended through the analysis and description of human "being" (Dasein), the basic mode of being in the world through participation and involvement. Being and beings, in contrast to Husserl's consciousness, are engaged in time and history. As Levinas said, "They are dominated and overwhelmed by history." So, according to Heidegger, subject (our consciousness) and object (everything in the external world) constitute and are constituted by one another in a process that denies the sovereignty and independence of either and ensures a perpetual interchange (Davis, 1996; Manning, 1993; Peperzak, 1993).

However, eventually, Levinas found fault with both Husserl and Heidegger—he believed that both thinkers subsumed the other under the authority of the Same, which is consciousness in Husserl and Existence of Being (Dasein) in Heidegger. Levinas stated that we need to go back one step before consciousness or existence to state what is pre-phenomenological, pre-ontological. In this state, we, the subjects are exposed to Others.

Levinas (1981) in *Otherwise than Being: Beyond Essence*, states that exposure to the Other is the bedrock of our selfhood; it is the condition of subjectivity, not an aspect of it. He argues that he is responsible to the Other because his existence, his very subjectivity, is dependent on his relation to the Other. See how this is different from Husserl and Heidegger, who focused on the consciousness of Existence/Being. They give little thought to the Other, and in fact, Levinas argues, their theories dominate or subsume the Other. Levinas' theory, in contrast, does not dominate or subsume the Other. Rather Levinas' work articulates a clear and extensive responsibility to and for the Other. Furthermore, his articulation of ethics for a moral person (and you may want to insert person of faith here), creates a responsibility to the Other that is absolute.

Levinas dedicated his last major work to victims of the Holocaust, though he does not mention the event in his writings. Colin Davis (1996), who writes on Levinas, indicates that although Levinas does not mention the Holocaust nor the realities that brought it on, his work is certainly informed by them. Like Levinas, Davis challenges us to foreground and listen to the voice of the Other rather than to respond to the Other with violence as some did during the Holocaust. On a large scale, violent responses to the Other cost millions of lives. Two examples are the Holocaust, in which six million Jews died, and the Middle Passage, in which 50 million Africans died. On a smaller scale, such responses have resulted in failures to understand the Other and their misrepresentation in our research. As a researcher, as a student of the philosophy of science, and as a Christian, I believe Levinas' placing of ethics before ontology and epistemology is correct.

So, the first part of my "loving epistemology" includes putting ethics before ontology and epistemology. But there are others out there who do speak of ethics in relation to epistemology. This past fall, Dr. Sheri Shuler asked me how my thoughts in developing a "loving epistemology" were different from or similar to some of the feminist-standpoint epistemologies that place women's experiences and an ethic of care at the center of the research process. I must admit that my fledgling notion of a "loving epistemology" is in many ways like their work. I especially like the work of Kathryn Addelson (1993) who writes:

> We feminist philosophers who work within the academy are ourselves part of an elite. We are makers of knowledge; we exercise cognitive authority. In the United States, the academic elite has many times operated to support the very dominance structures that the women's movement has worked to overcome. This, of course, is the reason feminists try to change philosophy, using the strategy of undermining from within. . . . The social position of feminist philosophers is a dominant one, not only over the positions of most other women, but also the positions of men of other classes, races, ages (both young and old), and even nations. In such a dangerous position, it is essential to do responsible work—and to be accountable for our work. We need to be accountable in general to all women, children, and men and responsible in particular to our sisters doing activist work outside the academy as well as our sisters in other disciplines within it. (p. 268)

She concludes that the measure of any epistemology lies in how well it allows knowledge makers to be responsible. Am I able to define what that means for each one of you? I do not think I can. Each person must make those decisions herself or himself. As I have been musing about a "loving epistemology" with friends, my friends have asked me, "So, Julie, who can I do research with or on? Only people who are my same race, class, gender, and who have a similar background and make the exact same salary as I do?" I have even, believe it or not, been gently accused of essentializing culture, of not understanding its complex nature, the hybridity of identities within cultures, the decentered subject of the post-structuralists. But as I struggle to do responsible, ethical, moral research, I realize that some forms of knowledge production are, for me and in my opinion, better than others—Researcher to Subject, Self to other Selves.

This may be the second part of my "loving epistemology." I will just give you one example. Patricia Hill Collins (1998), an African American sociologist, in her book, *Fighting Words: Black Women and the Search for Justice*, develops epistemological criteria for critical social theory. They are:

1. Does your social theory speak truth to people about the reality of their lives?
2. Does this social theory equip people to resist oppression?
3. Does this critical social theory move people to struggle?

I would have to say that my dissertation work, in which I researched Mexican American females, would definitely not meet the first criterion and was a weak affirmative to the second and third questions. Some of my more recent research, however, on Euro-American school leaders and how to develop them as antiracist leaders, comes much closer to meeting Collins' criteria.

In addition to laying out criteria for me to consider, feminist scholars of color have encouraged me to travel to other worlds. That is the last and final component of my "loving epistemology" as it stands now. *Traveling*. I first heard this notion being discussed by Collins at AERA (American Educational Research Association) last spring. In her invited address, she spoke of the life of Sojourner Truth and the ways in which her biography suggests an epistemology of empowerment. Sojourner Truth's biography speaks to the significance of her movement among multiple communities, the impact that these diverse groups had on her worldview, and the potential significance of her life for an epistemology of empowerment. Her travels through outsider-within locations may explain her remarkable ability to see things differently than others of her time did. Collins says Truth was "visionary in her ideals concerning equity and justice, yet pragmatic about the political actions needed to make justice a reality." But Sojourner Truth's traveling was different than the traveling that I and most of you that look like me need to do. Many times people like us have traveled to different worlds and have conquered them, taken their best resources, and claimed them for our own. At the very least, we have traveled and not understood.

The traveling that I am encouraging us to do is very different. And here I must give credit to Dr. Jerry Rosiek from the University of Alabama for recently pointing me to the work of Maria Lugones (1987) and her article, "Playfulness, World-travelling, and Loving Perception." In her article, Lugones states that traveling to someone else's world is a way of identifying with them because by traveling to their "worlds" we can understand what it is to be them and *what it is to be ourselves in their eyes!* Only when we have traveled in each other's worlds are we fully subjects to each other.

Knowing others' "worlds" is part of knowing them and knowing them is part of loving them. . . . Without knowing the other's world, one does not know the other, and without knowing the other, one is really alone in the other's presence because the other is only dimly present to one. Through traveling to the other's "worlds," we discover that there are "worlds" in which those who are victims of arrogant perception are really subjects, lively beings, resistors, constructors of visions, even though in the mainstream construction they are animated only by the arrogant and are perceived as pliable, foldable, file-awayable, and classifiable (pp. 17–18).

This traveling is, according to Lugones, a form of identification that she considers incompatible with arrogant perception and constitutive of a new understanding of love.

So, my advice to you, in this, my last lecture, is to travel knowing that you are responsible for others—they are a part of you—you do not exist without them. Traveling can involve actual physical movement or talking to others or reading literature by others. But travel. Jesus scholar Jonathan Dominic Crossan (1998) asks us to imagine a Jesus settled in Nazareth with family, or with Peter in Capernaum. If settled, his disciples could have brought the marginalized to him. But that would not have been an example of "loving epistemology." Jesus traveled. I wish you well on your journeys.

EDITORS' NOTE

This speech was one of the last pieces of scholarship written by Julie Laible, who in the spring of 1999 was tragically killed. Her struggles with developing a way of researching and a theory of knowing others that includes compassion and love is one of her significant legacies. Her loving epistemology should contribute substantially to research and scholarship that seeks to transform existing practices and conditions that are socially unjust.

REFERENCES

Addelson, K. P. (1993). Knower/doers and their moral problems. In L. Alcoff & E. Potter (Eds.), *Feminist epistemologies* (pp. 265–294). New York: Routledge.

Alcoff, L. (1991, Winter). The problem of speaking for others. *Cultural Critique*, *92*, 5–32.

Barndt, J. (1991). *Dismantling Racism: The continuing challenge to White America.* Minneapolis: Augsburg Press.

Borg, M. (1995). *Meeting Jesus again for the first time.* San Francisco: Harper.

Brueggeman, W. (1978). *The prophetic imagination.* Philadelphia: Fortress Press.

Collins, P. H. (1990). *Black feminist thought: Knowledge consciousness, and the politics of empowerment.* New York: Routledge.

Collins, P. H. (1998). *Fighting words: Black women and the search for justice.* Minneapolis: University of Minnesota Press.

Crossan, J. D. (1998). *The birth of Christianity: Discovering what happened in the years immediately after the execution of Jesus.* San Francisco: Harper.

Davis, C. (1996). *Levinas: An introduction.* South Bend, IN: University of Notre Dame Press.

Derman-Sparks, L. & Phillips, C. B. (1997). *Teaching/learning anti-racism: A developmental approach.* New York: Teachers College Press.

hooks, b. (1990). *Yearning: Race, gender, and cultural politics.* Boston: South End Press.

James, W. (1912). The sentiment of rationality. In P. R. Barton (Ed.), *Collected works of William James: Essays in radical empiricism* (pp. 126–141). New York: Longmans, Green.

Khare, R. S. (1992). The Other's double—the anthropologist's bracketed self: Notes on cultural representation and privileged discourse. *New Literacy History*, *23*, 1–23.

Levinas, E. (1981). *Otherwise than being: Beyond essence.* Boston: M. Nijhoff.

Lugones, M. (1987). Playfulness, "world"-traveling, and loving perception. *Hypatia*, *2*(2), 3–19.

Manning, R. J. S. (1993). *Interpreting otherwise than Heidegger: Emmanuel Levinas's ethics as first philosopher.* Pittsburgh: Duquesne Press.

Paredes, A. (1997). On ethnographic work among minority groups. *New Scholar*, *1*, 1–32.

Peperzak, A. T. (1993). *To the other: An introduction to the philosophy of Emmanuel Levinas.* West Lafayette, IN: Purdue University Press.

Scheurich, J. J. (1996). The masks of validity: A deconstructive investigation. *The International Journal of Qualitative Studies in Education*, *9*(1), 49–60.

Scheurich, J. J. & Young, M. (1997). Coloring epistemologies: Are our research epistemologies racially biased? *Educational Researcher*, *26*(4), 4–16.

Stanfield, J. (1994). Empowering the culturally diversified sociological voice. In A. Gitlin (Ed.), *Power and method: Political activism and educational research* (pp. 166–175). New York: Routledge.

West, C. (1993). *Keeping faith: Philosophy and race in America.* New York: Routledge.

Chapter 9

Life Lessons and a Loving Epistemology: A Response to Julie Laible's Loving Epistemology

Colleen A. Capper

Dear Julie,

We miss you.

I am writing in response to your last paper, your last lecture. My response to you reminds me, as Mitch Albom (1997) learned in *Tuesdays with Morrie*, that death ends a life, not a relationship. From your piece, I take five lessons that I would like to remember as gifts from your relationship with all of us: lessons about belief and faith, lessons about our academic work, lessons about our work and faith, lessons about time, and lessons about epistemology.

LESSONS ABOUT BELIEF AND FAITH

I appreciated how you outlined the differences between belief and faith. Over the years, I have wrestled with my beliefs as with alligators. I have a difficult time with this "Jesus thing." I "served" as a United Methodist Church Missionary for five years in Appalachia "answering the call" to Christian service. Within the first six months of my time there, my mom died, I fell in love with another female missionary, faced inevitable insanity or suicide with my rampant addictions, and bumped into the work of feminist theologian Rosemary Radford Reuther. I realized—after years of attending bible school, working as a church camp counselor,

193

serving as our church organist and children's choir director, participating in six years of intense bible study after high school, aiming for a career as a "foreign" Christian missionary, and being pissed that I was not Catholic because if I were then I could be a nun—that perhaps the bible was not The Truth. Of course, it was just a short walk to think that, perhaps, neither was Jesus.

Now I sit under the watchful eye of the writhing Jesus when I occasionally attend the weekly mandatory Mass with our son who attends Catholic school. Quinn loves this school, a place, he says, "where we can talk about Jesus and gays and lesbians, and it is OK." One day, during the drive home from school with my partner, he exclaimed, "Mom, if I hadn't gone to a Catholic school, how would I have learned about Jesus?" He was horrified at the thought that perhaps he would have grown up without knowing this person. He asked me to help him transform a cardboard box and towel into an altar in his bedroom, making crosses out of popsicle sticks. When I was a little girl, my altar included a candle, a bible and a picture of Jesus. In your piece, you historically situate this Jesus person and appropriate him as a radical, speaking an alternative wisdom of equity and justice in support of your own convictions and beliefs. When discussing my seminar on "Spirituality in Leadership" with other radical scholars in education, they have also shared this socially responsive view of Jesus or Christianity. My next-door neighbors, however, label themselves fundamentalist Christians and appropriate Jesus as a conservative, speaking a wisdom in support of their own convictions and beliefs. Who's to say which one is "right?" What makes a liberal socialist view of Jesus more "right," closer to "truth," than a conservative view?

LESSONS ABOUT OUR ACADEMIC WORK

I admire how you situate yourself in your writing as a researcher, unabashedly, without apology. If we do not name ourselves, others will name us for us. Sometimes the anti-intellectual sentiment of not only society but even universities, particularly those who work in professional schools, would like us not to feel good about research, that there are more practical tasks to be done. For those of us who were not bred from academic or "professional" stock, a life of the mind can be difficult to claim. Last year on my annual visit to my dad in Florida, he asked again, "Now what is it that you do at the university?" This question, after ten years as a professor. Neither of my parents finished high school, and my siblings and I knew well the hard labor of farmwork. I identify with Parker Palmer (1998) who wrote, "Long into my career I harbored a secret sense that thinking and reading and writing, as much as I loved them, did not qualify as 'real work'" (p. 22). Your last written piece and the research and writing that lay before it are examples to me again of how important this work is. And, for better or worse, our written word lasts far longer than our physical bodies.

LESSONS ABOUT OUR WORK AND FAITH

I admire how you brought your faith and belief directly to the workplace—in the theological quotes hanging on your computer and in the way you consciously sought spiritual connection. Yet you sought not just any connection, but a connection between your faith, your life work, and issues of equity and justice. Like sexuality, the language of the spirit is difficult to bring to work and we often seek to squelch those aspects of ourselves only to have them leak out of us in offending or unhealthy ways. We are fully spiritual beings and walking into our office at the university does not change that.

LESSONS ABOUT TIME

I felt a surreal energy fill me up when I first read your piece. You innocently proclaimed that ". . . this hopefully will not be the last lecture I will ever be giving." And it was. Just as when canning tomatoes with my mom six weeks before she died, I fully expected she would be there to enjoy them in the winter. The fragility of life. No life of the mind, no intellectual argument or theoretical exposition can excuse us from death.

What if? From the time I watched my mom exhale and then not inhale again, I have asked the question more often, but not often enough. What if this were my last class, what would I say? What course experiences would I find most important? In the end, will department politics really matter? I ask this about my writing. What next? In the long list of writing projects, if I had a year left to write, what would I write? I am humbled and grateful I had the chance to write this response.

LESSONS ABOUT A LOVING EPISTEMOLOGY

You argue that there are two major issues to conducting research aligned with your spiritual beliefs: One, ". . . there are ethical problems with research on others that are different from [ourselves]." Two, as academics,

196 Colleen A. Capper

we work in institutions that give us great benefits because of our race and class and that deny them to others.

To counter these two problems you advocate for a loving epistemology and you offer three contours of this epistemology. First, you believe we need to place ethics before ontology and epistemology. That is, ". . . the measure of any epistemology lies in how well it allows knowledge makers to be responsible" and to be accountable for our work. Because as academics we are in positions of power, we always have to scrutinize our work for the ways it could affect others.

Second, you believe that ". . . some forms of knowledge production are . . . better than others" and one set criteria for "betterness" is Patricia Hill Collins' (1998) criteria for critical social theory. That is, you argue that to be sure our research does not hurt others, we should measure our research against Collins' criteria as follows:

1. Does this social theory speak truth to people about the reality of their lives?
2. Does this social theory equip people to resist oppression?
3. Does this critical social theory move people to struggle [meaning to work against oppression, to care deeply about something]?

Your third aspect of a loving epistemology is to question if our epistemology allows us to travel to other worlds. You drew from Sojourner Truth as an example describing how she "moved among multiple communities, and the impact that these diverse groups had on her world view. . ."

ADDITIONAL THOUGHTS TOWARD A LOVING EPISTEMOLOGY

I would like to address each of your three contours of a loving epistemology and offer some additional ideas about this epistemology. If you believe all research conducted with others different from ourselves is unethical, then since everyone is everyone else's Other, and everyone is different from us in some way, then that means research on or with anyone is unethical—all research is unethical. Though you are searching for ways to conduct research that is "not problematic" and does not hurt others, I believe this is theoretically and practically impossible. Your goal seems to reflect the modernist idea of trying to conduct research that is "unbiased" or purely "objective." Depending on one's epistemology, what we have learned over time is that all research is "biased" or we bring a part of ourselves into all research, regardless of method. We cannot keep ourselves out, even if we try. Rather than squelching bias or keeping themselves out of the research, many scholars have discovered the benefits of having themselves be part of the research, to indeed seek to change the participants and be changed themselves by the research (Burrell & Swadener, 1999; see also Lather, 1993 on catalytic validity and more recent work on autoethnography).

Just as critical theorists sought university classroom teaching situations that were fully "safe" for all involved and allowed everyone free and equal "voice," feminist post-structuralism reminds us that no classroom situation can ever be fully safe for all involved at all times. Pretending we can create classroom experiences that are totally safe is as dangerous as not recognizing them as unsafe in the first place. Similarly, no research is "pure" or without power inequities. All research has consequences, negative and positive, for all involved, and those consequences shift over time. Rather than trying to squelch the "problems," perhaps we should conduct research that is "openly problematic." Just as we can never be fully compassionate, fully loving at all times, we cannot conduct research that on some level will not hurt others. We can work toward research that will minimize the hurt done to others and ourselves, but we can never eliminate the hurt.

You use Collins' criteria for social theory as a way to discern research that is "better" than other research. Perhaps we can define "better" to mean research that is less hurtful? Otherwise, why can't some forms of knowledge production just be different from other ways? Why do we have to position ourselves or our views as better than others? Why can't we say, "this is what works for me" and why, and respect the epistemological path that others are on? I also examine each of Collins' criteria here and offer some ideas for rethinking these criteria.

Her first question asks: Does the social theory speak truth to people about the reality of their lives? We know from basic social psychology that how people view their world determines their "reality." What is reality? Whose reality? Reality viewed through what lens? "The reality" does not really exist except in the context of an individual's reality at a particular point in time that can shift and change. I would change this first criterion to say, "Does your social theory mirror back to people *their* reality of their lives at a particular point in time?"

Second, does this social theory equip people to resist oppression? Whose oppression as defined by whom? For a loving epistemology, I would restate this criterion to say, "Does this social theory equip people to name their own pain and oppression for themselves, how they harm themselves, how they harm others, how they experience forgiveness of themselves and others and how they experience forgiveness from others?"

Collins' third criterion asks if this critical social theory moves people to struggle [meaning to work against oppression, to care deeply about something]? Collins wants people to feel the passion because "... people often feel compelled to take action against injustice when they care deeply about something" (p. 244). Again I ask, struggle against what? Oppression as defined by whom? I have witnessed the passion of individuals, people who care very deeply about issues—those who fight for justice for people of color or for sexual minority civil rights, among others. I have also witnessed the passion of other individuals, those who care very deeply about issues; for example, those who believe gays and lesbians are an abomination of God and should be killed; providing basic civil rights is out of the question. A loving epistemology would perhaps ask instead: "Does this social theory move people to question themselves and others, not to be critical, but to seek to understand? Does this social theory move people not only to struggle but also to experience joy, freedom, and happiness?"

If we are to model a loving epistemology, then we have to move beyond "good guy–bad guy" perspectives. A loving epistemology must embrace all of us, especially those whose views are opposite our own. A loving epistemology must move beyond simply reversing roles and considering it progress if we now have the Indians-against-the-Cowboys game and the Indians are winning or the goal is for the Indians to beat the Cowboys. We have to move beyond the "bad White guys" and the "poor oppressed others." A loving epistemology must be inclusive. Otherwise, we are no different from those who seek to exclude us. A loving epistemology can claim the history of oppression, it can acknowledge the individual-, institutional-, epistemological-isms that routinely inhibit some people from making the most of their gifts and talents, and we can work toward removing those barriers without seeking to erase or annihilate those we consider "in power." We must model what we wish to see in others. As such, the three epistemological questions, if we are to use them as part of a loving epistemology, must make sense and be of use to all people despite their beliefs.

Your third contour of a loving epistemology asks us to "travel to other worlds." You remind us that "many times people like us have traveled to different worlds and have conquered them, taken them, taken their best resources, and claimed them for our own. At the very least, we have traveled and not understood." You encourage us to travel to the world of others as a way to help us know another and what it is to be ourselves in their eyes. A loving epistemology would encourage us not to confine our travels to the exotic, that is seeking out those who share our ideology but whose lives appear different from us, for example, by the color of skin or the presence of physical disabilities. Although exotic travels are important, we need also to travel to the world of those who with or without intention seek to hurt us in direct or indirect ways.

Life Lessons and a Loving Epistemology   199

You showed this kind of travel as your research moved from studying Mexican American young women to Euro-American school leaders. I am encouraged by similar research that reflects how we have more to learn and know about those who are sometimes considered "oppressive" of others, and not just to expose what we consider oppressive sensibilities, but sincerely to "seek to understand." For example, James Sears (Sears & Carper, 1998), an openly gay male, has sought to create space for sustained dialogue with fundamentalist Christians and critically oriented educators on educational issues: ". . . competing factions each with self-righteous certainty, brandishing particular versions of 'the truth'" (p. 1). He writes, "As Americans, for too long we have not needed to communicate across the racial, class, gender, religious or sexual borders and so we did not—and *now* it seems we cannot" (p. 2; emphasis in original). A loving epistemology must support such sustained dialogue with multiple intersecting Others, including those traditionally in power.

In addition to traveling to exotic places and to the worlds of those who are in traditionally privileged positions, a loving epistemology would encourage us to take excursions within ourselves. It seems we know and report so much more about others than about ourselves. We become so eager to know about the other, we overlook the other within. A loving epistemology, grounded in loving our neighbors and ourselves, would encourage self-care and the gaze within.

Julie, thank you for your lessons about belief and faith, academic work, work and faith, time, and epistemology. You are now on your own travels to worlds we cannot see. I am encouraged to learn that, after a lifetime of studying death and dying, Elisabeth Kubler-Ross (1997) has decided death does not exist. As problematic as love is, we thank you so much for reminding us about love before passing over. Thank you for your being, for all you gave to us, and for all you continue to give to us. Blessed Be.

REFERENCES

Albom, M. (1997). *Tuesdays with Morrie: An old man, a young man, and life's greatest lesson.* New York: Doubleday.

Burrell, P., & Swadener, B. B. (1999). Critical personal narrative and autoethnography in education: Reflections on a genre. *Educational Researcher, 28*(6), 21–26.

Collins, P. (1998). *Fighting* words: *Black women and the search for justice.* Minneapolis: University of Minnesota Press.

Kubler-Ross, E., M.D. (1997). *The wheel of life: A memoir of living and dying.* New York: Touchstone.

Lather, P. (1993). Fertile obsession: Validity after poststructuralism. *Sociological Quarterly, 34*(4), 673–693.

Palmer, P. (1998). *The courage to teach: Exploring the inner landscape of a teacher's life*. San Francisco: Jossey-Bass.

Sears, J. T., & Carper, J. C. (1998). *Curriculum, religion, and public education: Conversations for enlarging the public square*. New York: Teachers College Press.

Chapter 10

Research on Women and Administration: A Response to Julie Laible's Loving Epistemology

Michelle D. Young and Linda Skrla

In 1991, Patricia Hill Collins published her influential book, *Black Feminist Thought: Knowledge, Consciousness, and the Politics of Empowerment*. Her theorizing in this book subsequently opened up a space for new thought and conversation about epistemologies for many other scholars, particularly women scholars of color. Collins' extensive influence on such epistemological thought and conversation is evident in several chapters of the current volume. For example, Maenette Benham, Cynthia Dillard, Julie Laible, and Sylvia Méndez-Morse all take up the relationships between identity (who one is) and epistemology (how one knows). In each of their chapters, Collins's influence is clear. However, although Maenette, Cynthia, and Sylvia follow Collins by deriving their epistemological analyses from their gender and ethnic identities, Julie's epistemology work centers on a different, and emotional, aspect of identity—love.

Julie's loving epistemology, thus, challenges traditional Western research norms of neutrality and rationality by placing emotion at the center of the knowledge-production process. She does this by describing and elaborating on three components of a loving epistemology, which include: (1) putting ethics before ontology and epistemology, (2) asking of one's research, "Does it speak truth to your participants?" "Does it enable them to work against oppression?" and "Does it push them to work against oppression?" and (3) traveling.

We find Julie's conceptualization of a loving epistemology to be very provocative. Because Julie is no longer with us, however, we cannot sit down with her and engage her in a generative discussion about her ideas as we were blessed to be able to do about so many other topics when she was alive. It is easy to imagine her, in fact—sitting on the edge of a chair in a corner of some hotel lobby at an academic conference or standing in the hallway on the third floor of the George I. Sanchez building at the University of Texas at Austin (where all three of us did our doctoral studies)—passionately explaining what this idea of a loving epistemology means to her, blue eyes sparkling, hands waving to illustrate her points, positive energy radiating all around her. It is deeply saddening that we cannot now ask Julie about specific issues or ask for her to clarify a point through example or illustration. However, her absence should not and will not prevent us from exploring her ideas or from learning from them. In this essay, we attempt to do just that. We explore each of the three contours of Julie's loving epistemology and draw from them helpful ideas for rethinking feminist research in educational administration.

PUTTING ETHICS FIRST

In describing her loving epistemology, Julie spoke of a compassion that takes "hurt seriously and does not accept it as a normal or natural human condition" (Laible, this volume, p. 182). We understand this compassion to be the foundation of Julie's ethics. Her ethics involve a responsibility to the Other, and her epistemology requires that one put this responsibility to the Other (her ethics) first when conducting research.

In engaging with Julie's discussion of ethics (component #1 of her epistemology), however, we became increasingly less sure of what she meant by putting ethics before ontology and epistemology. Does this mean that before one engages with issues of ontology and epistemology, one must have his or her ethical principals clarified or solidified? That is, is there a linear progression of choices that must be made by researchers? For example, before we choose to employ ontology B and epistemology C, must we first choose system of ethics A? If so, the implication would be that ethics supercedes our understanding of reality and our view of knowledge. Because we do not see ethics operating within such a hierarchy, and because it does not seem likely that Julie viewed ethics, ontology, and epistemology in a linear hierarchy either, we moved past this (mis)understanding of what putting ethics first means and continued in our musings.

Perhaps by asking researchers to "put ethics first," a loving epistemology stresses the primacy of ethics in research rather than imposing a hierarchy. In this interpretation, instead of having a series of choices to make about research that begin with ethics, one's ethics would envelope and guide one's thoughts and actions—permeating the entire research process like a fine mist. Researchers would work consciously and conscientiously to keep their ethical principles, their responsibilities to the Other, at the forefront of their work. This is a valuable proposition, and it is one that more and more researchers (particularly qualitative and feminist researchers) are finding important to their work (e.g., Alcoff, 1991; Lather, 1993).

Several examples come to mind of ways in which such a foregrounding (or permeation) of ethical relations with the Other could shape and guide the research process. For instance, Patti Lather (1998) described "praxis under erasure," a concept derived from Derrida's practice of writing under erasure or "sous rature," that can be understood as a process of troubling and bracketing one's ideas throughout the research process. Troubling involves constantly subjecting ideas to interrogation, while bracketing allows one to use the ideas as resources while scrutinizing their usefulness, impact, accuracy, assumptions, and so on. Praxis under erasure, then, requires accountability to those with whom we conduct research through engagement, critical reflection, and scrutiny of the processes and products of our research. Given the continuously changing nature of the educational and political contexts within which women administrators work, as well as the increasingly complex and evolving forms of oppression impacting women and their work as school and school-system leaders, the importance of a concept such as praxis under erasure is clear. Such a praxis would not only enable a higher degree of confidence in one's findings, but it would also facilitate the process of keeping one's ethical principals, one's responsibilities to the Other, out front.

Collins (1991) also discussed the importance of ethics and accountability in research. Her black feminist epistemology contains an ethic of personal accountability. According to Collins, an ethic of personal accountability requires that individuals not only "develop their knowledge claims through dialogue and present them in a style proving their concern for their ideas, but people are expected to be accountable for their knowledge claims" (pp. 217–218). For Collins, all knowledge claims are thought to derive from the thinker's core beliefs, values, and ethics. However, Collins moves beyond mere accountability to suggest that ethics be employed in assessing knowledge claims.

The idea that a researcher would have to hold himself or herself accountable for her or his knowledge claims and also be accountable to the researched challenges conventional ideas about research and knowledge production. It suggests a different measure for the legitimacy or validity of

204   *Michelle D. Young and Linda Skrla*

knowledge claims, and it is an idea we find useful to research on gender and leadership. For example, in research on women in educational administration, one's ethical principles might inform a kind of validity that could be labeled *gender-equity validity*. Like other validity criteria, gender-equity validity would be used to evaluate whether we can depend on the research findings to be critically cognizant of, and to work against as much as possible, gender biases in all aspects of research (see Scheurich & Young, 1998, for a similar discussion of race-equity validity).

Thus, as illustrated by concepts such as praxis under erasure, an ethic of accountability, and gender-equity validity, we think the contour of a loving epistemology that requires putting ethics first holds great promise. Like Julie, we believe that research requires an ethics of responsibility for and accountability to those whom we engage in the research process. However, from this understanding we do not arrive at the same conclusion as did Julie. Specifically, we do not agree that an ethic of responsibility to the Other can be enacted through disengagement with populations of which we as researchers may not be members. As argued elsewhere in this volume (Young, chapter 3), researching across identity, culture, race, sex, and so forth is clearly difficult and certainly problematic. However, disengagement, in our view, simply is not an option. Practical circumstances (i.e., a culture that is riddled with racism, sexism, homophobia, xenophobia, etc.) and ethics demand that we be present and engaged, however difficult, painful, or inevitably and unrelentingly problematic that may be. Being accountable, responsible, and ethical, in our view, involves engagement.

ASKING OF YOUR RESEARCH

Julie's call to put ethics first is embodied in the second component of her loving epistemology. Her ethical principal of responsibility permeates the three critical questions that she proposes for researchers to ask of their research. She asks that we consider the purpose, content, and results of our research with regard to how well they fit the lived experiences of those studied as well as how they enable and encourage positive change for those studied. These questions are, in essence, ethic-based measures of validity.

The first of three questions is: "Does your social theory speak truth to people about the reality of their lives?" We understand Julie's concern here to be about the accuracy, validity, or trustworthiness of one's representations and interpretations. This is an issue with which many qualitative researchers struggle (e.g., Alcoff, 1991; Denzin & Lincoln, 1994; Scheurich & Young, 1997; Skrla, this volume). As researchers, we want our research participants to read our representations of their words and their lives and to say, "Yes, that is the way I see it." We want our research to capture reality as accurately as possible. However, we recognize that complete accuracy is impossible. Our personal biographies are inscribed in our interpretations of others. How we know and what we see is always filtered by who we are.

Two other issues that are critically important to consider in posing the question about whether our research speaks truth about the reality of people's lives are *point in time* and *essentialization*. As Capper (this volume) points out about the first of these issues, point in time, the question of whether one's research or social theory speaks truth to those whose lives were researched implies an ahistorical and unitary subject. However, when we represent research participants, we are representing our understanding of them at a single point or period in time. Our representations, once written, do not have the capacity to grow as the researched grow. Similarly, although we may attempt to present different individual research participants as unitary within our descriptions, the complexities of subjectivity and the problematics of analysis and interpretation make such efforts impossible. Through interpretation and analysis we search for patterns across our data and attempt to learn something from those patterns. Inevitably, some participants will agree with the patterns we identify and our interpretation of them; others will not. This is the case whether we are engaged in these activities as solo researchers or as collaborators with participants (Wolf, 1996).

Lather's (1998) conceptualization of a praxis under erasure is again a helpful tool for addressing questions of validity such as the ones posed by Julie. Using this praxis, researchers would be attempting to capture the reality of their participants while questioning why and how well they are capturing (even for a brief moment in time) that reality. Praxis under erasure could also facilitate a researcher's efforts to address the second and third questions that Julie raises: "Does your social theory [and the results of your research] equip people to resist oppression?" and "Does this critical social theory move people to struggle?"

We understand these questions—which are overtly focused on providing individuals with tools and on infusing them with a desire to use those tools in a struggle against oppression—to be, at their core, about a form of equity validity. These issues, given their action orientation, are critical. We believe it is important that we do research for a purpose that extends beyond our desire to know and to publish what we learn. Although we understand that some researchers and theorists disagree, and we are well aware of postmodern critiques of "unproblematized assumptions about the role of 'transformative intellectuals' . . . and pretensions toward 'emancipating' or 'empowering' some others" (Lather, 1998, p. 6), we believe it is important that, as we expand our knowledge and understandings, we also consider how these products might be of use. Like Lather, we find that, despite its many significant problems, "praxis is a concept [we] cannot seem to do without" (p. 11). For example, when conducting research with women in educational leadership positions, we believe it is important that our research provides insight, that it furthers understanding, and, if possible, that it provides tools that facilitate positive change.

Therefore, before moving on to an exploration of the third component of Julie's loving epistemology, we feel it is important to focus the discussion on the actions researchers take as a result of the research they conduct. It is not advocacy itself that we are concerned with here, however. Rather, our concern is with the action a researcher takes if she or he feels she or he has done an inadequate job or if the researcher finds flaws in his or her research interpretations or analyses with validity.

We would like to revisit, for a moment, the example that Julie provided to explain her concerns about validity: "Despite my Chicano peer debriefers and reflexive research journaling, I had conducted the study using a Euro-American, middle-class definition of success. My epistemology was racially biased" (Laible, this volume, p. 183). Julie's concern, that the definition of success operating in her research was not that of the young women she researched but her own, led Julie to feel as though her research was invalid. In her estimation, the research did not speak truth to the young women about the reality of their lives. Similarly, she felt that her social theory was inadequate for either moving or preparing her participants to resist oppression. As a result, Julie decided that she would never again engage in research on Others.

Although we have struggled to understand her logic in choosing this path in her response, we remain puzzled. As we have noted above and as others have written in multiple volumes of scholarship, research never accurately captures reality. In response, researchers have devised all sorts of strategies for being vigilant about achieving higher levels of validity in their research. Furthermore, while we have no way of knowing how far off from the girls' understandings of their reality Julie was (and surely these understandings and realities were multiple and fluid), we can say with certainty that no researcher ever creates a representation or interpretation as a solo enterprise. Even when a research project is not consciously collaborative, no researcher has complete ownership of the ideas that are developed through the project. In Julie's research, the young women, their teachers, and Julie together made meaning. Therefore, although we find great value in the questions raised in the second section of Julie's loving epistemology and in its emphasis on ethics and responsibility, we cannot accept disengagement with certain populations as a means for ensuring equity, validity, and responsibility in our research.

TRAVELING

The final component of a Julie's loving epistemology is the concept of traveling. Traveling, according to Julie, is different from immersion because in immersion an individual may change his or her location but not herself or himself. When one travels, one becomes an outsider-within. Julie urges researchers to travel to the world of the Other and to place oneself in the position of learner. Here the learning one would do includes more than learning about the Other; it would also involve, as Julie pointed out, learning to see oneself through the eyes of the Other.

Traveling may indeed provide a deeper understanding of the Other, and how the other sees and understands that, in turn, could facilitate more sensitive and contextually embedded results (Young, chapter 3, this volume). As Keyes, Capper, Jamison, Martin, and Opsal (1999) suggest,

> We need to take a stand but one that ensures that the positions of all the "others" whose lives are part of that stand be considered. This rejects the notion of a unitary sense of reform that represents all students, families, and their needs. . . . We must be prepared and able to reject even our more sacred educational concepts. (p. 516)

We believe the insights that are gained by learning from those who are different from ourselves could drastically change the way we see, understand, and conduct research. We can see many benefits gained from traveling. However, we believe that we must do more than travel. We believe we must engage with others—regardless of how similar or different they are from ourselves—around issues that are essential to the development of a socially just society. At the same time, we believe we must always scrutinize our actions, motives, and impacts.

We would suggest that the notion of traveling as a component of a loving epistemology needs to be extended to include recognition of, and commitment to, reciprocity. The terminology "traveling," to us, still sounds dangerously close to older, now thoroughly repudiated, anthropological notions of visiting and studying the exotic Other (see, for example, Visweswaran, 1994). So, although gaining a deeper understanding of others and attempting to learn to see ourselves as others see us are important ethical considerations for research, we must also realize that, when traveling, we inevitably leave part of ourselves behind. We not only are changed ourselves by our interactions with the people we research, the same interactions with us change our participants as well. This means, then, more of a mutual engagement and more of a mutual struggle for understanding, mutual benefit, and mutual responsibility are required than the terminology "traveling" encompasses.

What this concept of mutual engagement means is that we as researchers must constantly consider our own complicity in power arrangements and in other oppressions that structure the lives of the people in our settings for research and that we must always ask ourselves how our presence and our research affect our participants. Furthermore, we must acknowledge to ourselves and to our participants that these effects may range from positive to neutral to strongly negative and that many or most of them may be beyond our conscious understanding or out of our control. In traveling to learn about others, we must always and inevitably remain critically conscious of ourselves and our motives and remember that "narratives of salvation and redemptive agendas [may be] ever deeper places for privilege to hide" (Lather, 1998, p. 6). Thus, in traveling to learn about other women in the practice of educational administration, we should plan to mutually engage with these women, their lives, and their struggles. With Delgado-Gaitan (1993), we think that to do otherwise would be unethical.

CONCLUSION

Within her writing on a loving epistemology, Julie stated quite plainly that what she valued in her life and in her faith drove her research. She wrote, "What I do as a researcher and teacher on a daily basis, I like to think is based on what I hold critical in my life and in my faith" (Laible, this volume, p. 179). We have considered what those values were that she referred to in her work, and we have explored the components of her loving epistemology. But we will never really know for certain how close we have come to understanding what Julie truly meant. We will never be able to fully grasp either the values or the ideas that were foundational to her epistemological beliefs. And we will never see where she might have eventually taken her ideas as she continued to engage with and develop her loving epistemology.

For this we are deeply saddened and, at the same time, intensely angry. It is unfair and an enormous loss that Julie will not have an opportunity to develop her ideas. We have learned from Julie, nonetheless, and her ideas have certainly spurred substantive responses from researchers within this volume and, we assume, among her readers as well. Thus, we are saddened and angry, but we also feel quite fortunate; Julie's ideas, like Maenette's, Cynthia's, and Sylvia's (all in this volume), step up to and challenge traditional knowledge production and validation processes (Collins, 1991), and they provide researchers with different perspectives, ideas, and tools.

Research on Women and Administration 209

Furthermore, Julie's work raises an important question for researchers, particularly those who examine populations who have been oppressed or discriminated against: What is it that drives our research? As two female researchers who study the leadership and lives of women school and school-system administrators, we found this a poignant question. Our answer: Our roles as researchers in universities are shaped and driven by issues of equity and social justice. We want our work to contribute to a socially just society. We have tried to shed our illusions of emancipating or empowering others, however, and like Julie, we are still deeply troubled by aspects of our work. Above all, however, we consider research on women in educational leadership as too important to dismiss ourselves from engagement with it.

We agree with Julie that we must each take responsibility. We also agree that we must seek ways of doing research that are more responsible than were our past ways. We believe that this is what she was searching for in her work. In its current form, her loving epistemology problematizes the way we do research and suggests an alternative perspective and approach. Although we do not agree with all of her components or all of the arguments she made, we respect her ideas and her courage and we learned a great deal by engaging with her work.

REFERENCES

Alcoff, L. (1991). The problem of speaking for others. *Cultural Critique, 19*, 5–32.

Collins, P. H. (1991). *Black feminist thought: Knowledge, consciousness and the politics of empowerment.* New York: Routledge.

Delgado-Gaitan, C. (1993). Researching change and changing the researcher. *Harvard Educational Review, 63*(4), 389–411.

Denzin, N. K., & Lincoln, Y. S. (1994). Introduction: Entering the field of qualitative research. In N. K Denzin & Y. S. Lincoln (Eds.), *The handbook of qualitative research* (pp. 1–17). Newbury Park, CA: Sage.

Keyes, M. W., Capper, C. A., Jamison, M., Martin, M., & Opsal, C. (1999). Tradition and alternative in educational practice: Three stories of epistemological conflict. *Journal for a Just and Caring Education, 5*(4), 502–519.

Lather, P. (1993). Fertile obsession. *Sociological Quarterly, 34*(4), 673–693.

Lather, P. (1998, April). *Troubling praxis: The work of mourning.* Paper presented at the annual meeting of the American Educational Research Association, San Diego, CA.

Scheurich, J. J., & Young, M. D. (1997). Coloring epistemologies: Are our research epistemologies racially biased? *Educational Researcher, 26*(4), 4–16.

Scheurich, J. J., & Young, M. D. (1998). In the United States of America, in both our souls and our sciences we are avoiding White racism. *Educational Researcher, 27*(9), 27–32.

Wolf, D. (1996). Situating feminist dilemmas in fieldwork. In D. Wolf (Ed.), *Feminist dilemmas in fieldwork* (pp. 1–55). Boulder, CO: Westview Press.

Visweswaran, K. (1994). *Fictions of feminist ethnography*. Minneapolis: University of Minnesota Press.

Chapter 11

The Emperor and Research on Women in School Leadership: A Response to Julie Laible's Loving Epistemology

Catherine Marshall

The child who said, "Yikes! that emperor has no clothes!" was like the young scholars today who are researching the issue of women in school leadership. The methodological and theoretical leaps of the past three decades lend support to those who actively research questions that challenge the emperor. The repressed truths about persistent underrepresentation of women in educational administrative positions, and the ways the scholars, the knowledge base, and the professional culture have perpetuated this repression is a naked embarrassment. Although the child, and the scholars, may be shushed for challenging hegemony, they know what they see. Emerging theoretical and methodological shifts, evoked in Julie Laible's reflections, herald the foundations and legitimacy of such challenges to repressed realities about inequities in schooling.

With Julie's discussion of epistemological and methodological advances as the inspiration, I will reflect on the evolution of research and policy approaches to the problem of women's underrepresentation. With Julie's assertions about what matters, I will reflect on the evolving right of scholars to insert values, such as "the desire to eliminate institutional evil" into their social justice research agendas. My review and reflection conclude, as Julie did, with optimistic and activist recommendations for researchers.

211

212 Catherine Marshall

THE EVOLUTION FROM NON-ISSUE TO
CONTROLLED ISSUE TO EMBARRASSMENT

In her speech, Julie had to imagine how she and her field would have evolved in 30 years. I do not have to imagine, having reviewed the research and lived with the policy effects of 30 years of research on women in educational leadership (hereinafter called WEL).[1] I try, in my reflections, to point out the paradigm that has kept scholars under control and has kept us from pointing at the emperor and his hegemonic masculinities (Blount, 1999). Note how the ideals of logical empiricism and the search for perfected theory required passion-free, sanitized research questions that built on traditions that constrained curiosity and evaded the realities of people's lives. But note, too, the emerging critiques and methodologies that transformed research on WEL. Julie's work, and her generation, can soar from this transformation.

In the 1950s and early 1960s, WEL was a nonevent, undiscussed. Gender policy issues were in the air but the concern was about giving more men positions, to be role models for boys and to give them good jobs after World War II (Blount, 1999; Tyack & Hansot, 1982). During that time, as I went through elementary and secondary school, I never saw a female school leader. The employment and power arrangements in the informal curriculum of schooling taught boys and girls that men are in charge, and differentiated sex role socialization was part of the formal curriculum in home economics and shop, physical education, and so on. Who would think to do research on WEL? Most states and professional associations did not even keep statistics on gender in education. From his data collected from teachers, Lortie (1975) concluded that women use this "semi-profession" as a way to have children and still have a job. When I read this in graduate school I was angry.[2] But as a new graduate student in 1975, my professors pronounced that I could not be a good researcher if my feelings influenced me. Good researchers should maintain analytic distance; their research questions should be built from the foundation of such previous research and would be significant if they met a need expressed by people in important positions.

A thread of research did document the few women who attained leadership positions. Surveys in the 1960s asked whether they were first-born, married, had children, and what kind and size of school or district they led. It was as if they were unnatural albino zebras who must be documented for a specimen record (and perhaps controlled before they multiplied?). Still, with the "great man" theory-in-use defining leadership, and with the increased separation between the professions of teaching and administration (Ortiz & Marshall, 1988), the women leader was quite special. Later (see the following), feminist theory and qualitative inquiry

The Emperor and Research on Women in School Leadership   213

supported research on the qualities of women leaders rather than on corralling them.

By the 1960s and 1970s, WEL was a research and policy issue, framed to understand why so few women entered and moved up in administration and whether women could be competent leaders. The management paradigm and social systems theory base of educational administration helped identify relevant categories of the organizational tasks and leadership characteristics (assessed through surveys, questionnaires, writing tasks, and in-basket simulations) for comparing men and women.

Findings about women's lack of motivation and experience in public relations, finance, and politics (and their superior experience in instructional leadership) were uncritically incorporated in well-intended programs to fix women's deficiencies. Still, by helping identify the barriers that women experienced in considering and entering leadership, these studies and programs allowed a shift from the old psychological focus on individual characteristics to a focus on the organizational and professional culture. Guess what? That's where the deficiency lay.

As for me, during years of public-school teaching, I watched tall White men catapulted into leadership and wondered why, even though Congress had passed Title IX, it was still a struggle to bring women, gender, and my new feminist insights to school. I then entered an educational administration doctoral program and finally saw women who were administrators or trying to be. Slowly, as I recognized deficiencies in the knowledge base and inquiry traditions that required deductive approaches and quasi-experiments in a search for perfect theory, I began to understand. Later still, I realized how the power to declare and frame the research question enabled powerful groups to shove alternative, challenging, and embarrassing questions and findings to the side.[3]

Still, in the 1970s and early 1980s, equity values held some sway in policy arenas. Equal-employment policies and a few programs were going to fix the WEL problem, to eliminate the barriers. Federal funding became available for programs that, for example, used the sponsor–protégé mechanism to assist women (Adkison, 1980) and developed curriculum and training materials to counteract sexist practices in schooling. However, the meager and short-lived funding and the quick-fix assumptions resulted in token efforts with token results. Liberal feminist approaches demanded equal access and pay but did not address fundamental gender-politics issues or require a fundamental reworking of the empire. Policies were not enforced and professional cultures were not altered. During the Reagan–Bush era, the funding was drastically reduced and feminists directing the federal programs were fired or reassigned. Feminist theory and the feminist movement did not make the leap from women's studies to the power and control issues in public schooling. In political science and law, feminists were expounding the feminist critique of bureaucracy and justice (e.g. Ferguson, 1984; MacKinnon, 1989), but they were not connecting their critique to the structure of schools or to the political socialization processes that occur in schools whereby children accept the relegation of private-sphere issues to females and the traditional values of patriarchal law and politics. In education, gender researchers were documenting sex-role stereotyping but seldom connecting it to the gender–power dynamics of school leadership. Too, the scholarly critique of quick-fix approaches, especially the work of (usually male) critical theorists, was diverted to publication of theoretical tomes or to issues of poverty and racism.

Education feminists (myself included) were busily continuing more research finding the organizational and professional cultural barriers to women's access, but the research was not used to reframe policy. The persistent findings showing that women's leadership was more inclusive and democratic (shown in 1950s and 1990s data, e.g. Gross & Trask, 1964; Scott, 1999) could have been incorporated in policy directives favoring women and training men to be more like them.

True, by the late 1980s and 1990s, the research was more sophisticated. Micropolitical lenses were used, for example, to explain how women and minorities learned to keep quiet about the different treatment and career opportunities that shaped their careers (see, for example, Bell & Chase, 1993; Chase, 1995; Marshall, 1993; Marshall & Mitchell, 1991). And, in the prestigious *Handbook of Research on Educational Administration*, Ortiz and Marshall (1988) stated clearly that political choices were being made to retain the practices and knowledge bases that had undermined women's access to school leadership. That pointed to the emperor's nakedness, but apparently the emperor was not embarrassed. Why would he have to read that stuff anyway—schooling, feminism and critical theory were still non-events. Women weren't mounting successful lawsuits. Women kept working hard as public educators and more and more women entered careers in the educational administration professorate (McCarthy & Kuh, 1997). True, some were leaving administrative careers in disgust and discouragement (Tallerico, 1992). Some were quietly spending lots of time with feminist and critical literature, freed from master narratives and the search for perfected theory. True, some showed signs of criticizing the elites and conflicting with authority. True, some were dabbling in narrative, discourse analysis, feminist theory, and so on. As long as women kept teaching the required courses and helping prospective superintendents get credentialed, they could be indulged. Women educators and scholars knew the emperor's power to grant tenure and promotions, to award grants, to give job recommendations, and to review publications.

Qualitative studies have shifted WEL to seek women's own views of education careers, to observe women on the job, and to look for women's

The Emperor and Research on Women in School Leadership 215

leadership where it takes place naturally—more often as activist teachers—rather than in superintendencies, where it has passed through unnatural filters (see, for example, Acker,1994; Dillard, 1995; Marshall, 1985, 1993; Weiler, 1988). Assessing women's leadership with outdated, male-normed theories and criteria of management and leadership are rendered ludicrous. Instead, by putting women at the center, we encounter the possibilities of leadership values, perspectives, goals, and behaviors from women's experience.

Research on WEL and feminist theory have a great deal to offer in these times, when educational administration policy, practice and theory are constantly challenged (Marshall, 1995; Maxcy, 1994; Slater; 1995). Previously unspeakable realities can be countenanced. Feminist theory and WEL research exposes the very real issues of educators who have tremendous anxiety over integrating their personal- and private-sphere emotions, demands, and values with the public demands on school leaders. Feminist theory and WEL research reveals the dilemmas faced by educators who see that entering administration could mean cutting off relationships and a sense of connectedness with children and teachers. Feminist and critical theory and WEL research recognize that traditional theory and professional socialization evades equity issues. By becoming accomplished professionals and bureaucrats, educational administrators rid themselves of passion and political stance. They learn to smooth over troublesome events and dilemmas (such as persistent inequities) to present a calming public face. Therefore, the shift in WEL to incorporating women's perspectives has been good for WEL and promising for urgently needed alternative models of leadership.

The critical theorist asks, "Who benefits and who loses?" when analyzing policy choices. The feminist policy analyst asks, "if we place the needs and concerns of women at the center of this policy decision, how is it altered?" And the postmodern policy analyst searches out the values stances and powerful forces at work when (seemingly objective) policy choices are made, often finding regularities in practice that exclude the needs and perspectives of marginals and reify those of dominants.

Research on WEL is irrevocably altered with the feminist critical policy analysts' questions (Marshall, 1997). Now scholars entering educational administration should be asking, "will my women (and men) educational administration students and the communities they lead really benefit from this theory?" They can ask, "what should professional socialization and leadership theory look like now that we are incorporating women's perspectives? And what policies can we create to compensate for mistaken practices?" No longer can we proceed with WEL research as if administration theory, practice and policy were gender neutral. Now that we have progressed beyond the earlier stages, any such WEL would be wheel-spinning.

216   *Catherine Marshall*

Further, it would maintain the emperor's embarrassing parade. Feminist critical policy analysis has laid bare the regularity through which women educational leaders' careers and values are excluded.

THE EMPEROR IS INCREASINGLY IRRELEVANT

By the mid 1990s, as Julie Laible and others were launching their careers, it still mattered what the emperor wore, but one could safely travel to a different country. True, traditional knowledges still dominated educational administration. True, schools of education, credentialing, and administrator-selection policy decisions were grounded in efficiency and public school choice and achievement outcomes. But Julie and many others are lured to a new country. They are smart enough to pay homage and respect to the emperor but are excited, risk-taking, and idealistic enough to move to this developing country.

By now, education feminist theory is flourishing in academia. The academic emperor doesn't read it but his eyesight and his power are fading anyway. Julie and her generation are betting on being able to work with the professional emperors by leading the way with programs and research that starts with the assumption that educators will, can, and desire to work on equitable, caring, and democratic schools. Theirs is an involved, empowering, collaborating, idealistic and generous approach, working to make change in schools while working to change theory and research. They benefit from grandfathers and grandmothers in education qualitative research like Louis Smith and Hortense Powdermaker, in education feminism like Nel Noddings and Jane Roland Martin. They ride the waves from critical, postmodern, post-Marxist and feminist educators like Bill Foster, Patti Lather, Jim Scheurich, and, I hope, Catherine Marshall, who demand that we identify the political choice being made whenever schools continue inequitable practices.

TOOLS FOR EXPLORING WHAT YOU CARE ABOUT

A loving epistemology provides comfortable tools for scholars with social activism in their belief systems. If, like Julie, one's work motivations are assisting in making a world full of empowered liberated people, we now acknowledge the possibility of activism-embedded agendas (Lather, 1991; Schram, 1995). As we worry over abusing and colonizing research "subjects," we have journals like *The International Journal of Qualitative Studies in Education* that offer open dialogue on relationships and ethics in qualitative inquiry. As we quest toward being useful, we have developed

The Emperor and Research on Women in School Leadership 217

field-based, collaborative-action, participatory research strategies that challenge us to work with the research agendas defined by our collaborators. With realizations of feminist critical-policy analysis, we can move beyond "seeing the world through the eyes of its victims" and point to the recurrent political choices being made to perpetuate inequities. With these realizations informing WEL research, with loving epistemology, we put women at center, incorporate their realities and, as Julie says, "travel knowing that you are responsible for others," so that our social theory does speak truth to people about their realities, equips people to resist oppression, and moves people to struggle.[4]

The next step will be acting rather than researching and writing. Where the emperor reigns in education programs, journals, career opportunities, certification processes, professional conference proceedings and the like, pretending that our knowledges and practices are gender neutral, we must use the perspectives laid out in Julie's paper as tools for telling the emperor to step aside.

NOTES

1. My personal/professional reflections use, but take liberties with, Tetrault's (1984) framing of the issue of women in educational leadership.

2. In fact, *I* had chosen to be a teacher in part for that reason. I must have resented this highly regarded scholar analyzing people like me so simplistically, as if our motivations could be categorized by our marital and motherhood status.

3. In separate incidents, when I told a school administrator and a professor that I might do my dissertation on why so few women were in school administration, the administrator replied, "women don't *want* administrative positions." The professor replied, "you have to come up with a significant research question and that isn't." Such responses did not fit with reality, because my fellow students were often close to 50 percent women.

4. At the 1999 American Educational Research Association (AERA) symposium called "Facing the Family Secret: Women in the Superintendency," I urged the audience to quit paying dues to organizations, like AERA Division A and the American Association of School Administrators, whose leaders provide only lipservice to women. They hold the power to take serious action based on the decades of research proving women's competence and demonstrating the ways the field excludes women.

REFERENCES

Acker, S. (Ed.). (1994). *Gendered education: Sociological reflections of women, teaching and feminism.* Buckingham, UK: Open University Press.

218   *Catherine Marshall*

Adkison, J. A. (1980). Strategies to promote women's careers in school administration. *Administrator's Notebook, 29*(2), 1–4.

Bell, C., & Chase, S. (1993). The underrepresentation of women in school leadership. In C. Marshall (Ed.), *The new politics of race and gender* (pp. 141–154). London: Falmer Press.

Blount, J. M. (1999). *WWII and the great gender realignment of school administration.* Paper presented at the annual meeting of the American Educational Research Association, Montreal, Canada.

Chase, S. (1995). *Ambiguous empowerment: The work narratives of women school superintendents.* Amherst: University of Massachusetts Press.

Dillard, C. B. (1995). Leading with her life: An African American feminist (re)interpretation of leadership for an urban high school principal. *Educational Administration Quarterly, 31*(4), 539–563.

Ferguson, K. E. (1984). *The feminist case against bureaucracy.* Philadelphia, PA: Temple University Press.

Gross, N., & Trask, A. E. (1964). *Men and women as elementary school principals.* Cambridge, MA: Harvard University Graduate School of Education.

Lather, P. (1991). *Getting smart: Feminist research and pedagogy with/in the postmodern.* London: Routledge.

Lortie, D. C. (1975). *Schoolteacher: A sociological study.* Chicago, IL: University of Chicago Press.

MacKinnon, C. A. (1989). *Toward a feminist theory of the state.* Cambridge, MA: Harvard University Press.

Marshall, C. (1985). The stigmatized woman: The professional woman in a male sex-typed career. *Journal of Educational Administration, 23*(2), 132–152.

Marshall, C. (1993). The politics of denial: Gender and race issues in administration. In C. Marshall (Ed.), *The new politics of race and gender* (pp. 168–175). London: Falmer Press.

Marshall, C. (1995). Imagining leadership. *Educational Administration Quarterly, 31*(3), 484–492.

Marshall, C. (Ed.). (1997). *Feminist critical policy analysis: A perspective from primary and secondary schooling.* London: Falmer Press.

Marshall C., & Mitchell, B. (1991). The assumptive worlds of fledgling administrators. *Education and Urban Society, 23*(4), 396–415.

Maxcy, S. (1994). Education policy centres: New priorities for the new era. *Journal of Educational Policy, 9*(4), 353–368.

McCarthy, M. M., & Kuh, G. D. (1997). *Continuity and change: The educational leadership professorate.* Columbia, MO: University Council for Educational Administration.

Ortiz, F. I., & Marshall, C. (1998). Women in educational administration. In N. J. Boyan (Ed.), *Handbook of research on educational administration* (pp. 123–142). New York: Longman.

Schram, S. F. (1995). Against policy analysis: Critical reason and poststructural resistance. *Policy Sciences, 28*(4), 375–384.

Scott, J. (1999). *Framing survival strategies: Resilience and resistance in women superintendents.* Paper presented at the annual meeting of the American Educational Research Association, Montreal, Canada.

Slater, R. O. (1995). The sociology of leadership and educational administration. *Educational Administration Quarterly, 31*(3), 449–472.

Tallerico, M. (1992, January). School board–superintendent relationships. *Urban Studies, 26*(4), 371–390.

Tetrault, M. K. (1984). *Stages of thinking about women: An evaluation model.* Paper presented at the annual meeting of the American Educational Research Association, New Orleans, LA.

Tyack, D., & Hansot, E. (1982). *Managers of virtue: Public school leadership in America, 1890–1980.* New York: Basic Books.

Weiler, K. (1988). *Women teaching for change: Gender, class, and power.* South Hadley, MA: Bergin & Garvey.

Part III

Reconceptualizing Applications of Feminist Research in Educational Leadership

This part contains three chapters that illustrate applications of reconsidered feminist research. In chapter 12, "In Our Mother's Voice: A Native Woman's Knowing of Leadership," Maenette Benham proposes a model of educational leadership that is grounded in both feminist and native/indigenous epistemological understandings. Maenette draws on her work with a group of fourteen native school leaders to articulate a leadership model called "Go to the Source," which allows for dynamic interpretation of local content and context.

In chapter 13, Linda Skrla applies a poststructural conceptualization of power—the productive effect of power through normalization—to advocate reconsideration of recent research on women in the public school superintendency. Linda argues and attempts to demonstrate in this chapter that understanding of and explanation for the perpetuation of male dominance in the superintendency might best be gained from examining underlying normalizations, particularly the normalization of femininity and masculinity, that structure the discourses and practice of educational administration, including the most recent research on women superintendents.

The final chapter in the book, chapter 14 by Michelle Young, uses a feminist-poststructural perspective to explore representations of the predicted shortage of school administrators through task force reports and policy documents. She demonstrates that two traditional representations have dominated the discourse on the leadership shortage and have left little room for alternative representations. As a result, a third representation, the shortage as a gender crisis, becomes evident only when one examines the documents for what is not included. Michelle's analysis elucidates how representations of the shortage that fail to include gender not only effectively delegitimize gender as a consequential factor in the analysis of the predicted shortage, but also how such representations are counterproductive to correcting the projected shortfall.

Chapter 12

In Our Mother's Voice: A Native Woman's Knowing of Leadership

Maenette K. P. AhNee-Benham

THE BEGINNING: THE ROOTS OF THE WORK

With the arrival of Western ideology, native/indigenous[1] peoples of North America, Hawai'i, Alaska, Australia, and Aotearoa (New Zealand) have had to suffer the trauma of assimilation, cultural deprivation, and genocide. Despite this shock, they have survived, holding tenaciously to distinct traditions and languages. Yet, these traditions and languages are still endangered because there is a continued tendency among researchers and scholars to define native/indigenous peoples from perspectives and interests that have dismissed or romanticized unique life forces. For example, an anthropologist sees an indigenous group as ripe for observation or an entrepreneur sees an opportunity to exploit cultural art forms.[2] In our schools, a nonnative teacher might view native children as academically disinterested and inept, a nonnative counselor might focus on issues of poverty and family distress, and a nonnative school nurse might see only obesity, hypertension, and diabetes (see, for example, Dehyle, 1992). Native/indigenous peoples, however, often see themselves and the issues they face differently (Benham & Cooper, 2000). Unfortunately, nonnatives have conducted much of the research about native groups that has defined educational policy and practice.[3] In light of this, much more work by native scholars with an "insider" perspective is essential for the future progress of unique native/indigenous peoples.

In particular, more study and writing must be encouraged on the topic of native/indigenous women's ways of knowing and doing educational leadership. For example, much of the literature currently available focuses on the deficits of native women, such as their poor socioeconomic status and their negative characterizations (see Green, 1990, 1992). Indeed, contemporary images of native/indigenous women have been bizarrely portrayed in the media, such as the alcoholic and neglectful mother; the spiritual, sexless medicine woman; or the exotic princess and sometime prostitute (see Benham & Cooper, 1998; Medicine, 1978, 1988). As a consequence, native/indigenous women are often misunderstood and thought to be unqualified to provide leadership (Tsosie, 1988). Although history recounts the extraordinary leadership of some native women (Allen, 1992; Foreman, 1976), there is little literature that focuses on native/indigenous women's ways of leadership. Hence, to better understand how native women have led (and currently lead) and to enhance the opportunity for native women to participate fully in educational leadership, conversations (such as the one presented in this chapter) must be supported and disseminated more broadly.

To understand native/indigenous women's ways of leadership, one must first understand the context of the native/indigenous worldview.[4] In general, native peoples, especially women, walk in many worlds, for example, inside and outside of native and nonnative lands, through professional and personal situations, and across diverse cultural boundaries. Through these multiple venues, they must wrestle with the perpetuation of their cultural heritage and the pressure to assimilate (Betz, 1991). In addition, the journey of many native/indigenous women educational leaders, teachers, and scholars is complicated by the diversity among and within native groups to the degree that preserving hundreds of languages, unique ways of life, rituals and stories is in itself a daunting task. As a native scholar, it has also required me to position native ways of knowing within the broader and more eclectic feminist discussion. What I, as a native Hawaiian scholar and teacher have learned is that native/indigenous women scholars must define an educational course and language (both are still works in progress) that speaks to (and communicates with) a broader audience about who, what, and how native women come to know and do their work as educational leaders. Despite the pressures to speak in current feminist and leadership language, native/indigenous scholars must take courage to define our own lexicon that best expresses our feminine traditions (see also Moraga & Anzaldua, 1983).

The purpose of this chapter, therefore, is to forward a native/indigenous epistemology for educational leadership from the perspective of native women in our own voices. It is my hope that the thoughts and work

In Our Mother's Voice

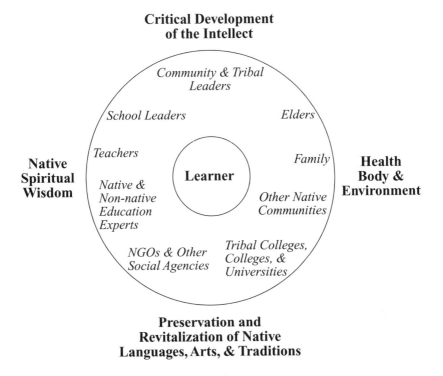

Figure 12.1 Go to the Source.

presented here will help you (the reader and advocate) to create the best possible learning environments and experiences for native children and youth. To provide some beginning context, in July 1997, 14 native school leaders (women and men) gathered to share and examine their diverse, culturally grounded epistemological foundations and principles of native/indigenous best practices and thinking around leading, learning, living and teaching. The project, entitled *Indigenous Educational Models for Contemporary Practice: In Our Mother's Voice* (Benham & Cooper, 2000), aimed to provide a forum for the articulation of these ideas. The work of the forum resulted in the model "Go to the Source" (see Figure 12.1), which best defines the ways in which we have conceptualized native women's ways of leading. This is the story of our journey to define the source of our dream, a native women's perspective of leadership for the education of our native children and youth.

BEGINNING THE JOURNEY TO THE SOURCE:
TO THE EAST AND TO THE SOUTH

Traditional native ways of knowing incorporate a balance of the social/cultural, physical/health and well-being, psychological/cultural integrity, and spiritual being of an individual, all within the complexities of a social system of roles and responsibilities.[5] The movement of living, in short, is deeply interconnected with the movements in nature. This is not a purely native feminist way of thinking, but a cultural and symbolic value that permeates the lives of a community of people. It is, therefore, a founding principle on which our model "Go to the Source" is grounded and is the foundation on which the native women and men who participated in this work conduct their professional lives. In light of this, I do not begin this work with a single dimension of leadership from a feminist perspective, for example the cognitive modification of the field of leadership, but instead, from an alternative worldview that focuses on the interconnectedness of family, community, culture, nature and spirituality.

And so, this project began with a dream during my travels east to teach an educational leadership course on community building from a native/indigenous perspective. Symbolically, the east is the place of beginnings—a place we return to many times in our life travels. The primary goal of this dream was to bring together native knowledge and best practices that support the educational success of native children and youth. In the end, this work became a journey about wholistic visioning, a special collective story that is constructed through multiple women's voices and different experiences that are about living, learning and leadership. This dream became reality during the summer of 1997 in the south, to the direction of the sun, to *Sol y Sombra* (the house of the sun) in Santa Fe, New Mexico.

The symbolism of the south is that it offers us an opportunity to become connected with other people and to share our passions and our visions. This unique forum called on the voices of 14 native school leaders who are Native Hawaiian, Maori, Okanagon, Oneida, Ojibwe, Australian Aborigine, Piegan, Cherokee, Cochiti Pueblo, and Athabaskan. Here were voices that have been hidden in the educational world (Benham & Cooper, 2000; Hallinger, 1995). This project sought to facilitate connections across native voices, to find both commonalities and differences, but primarily to address problems encountered in educational systems through a uniquely native/indigenous lens.

While there was a rich list of potential participants, only a small number could be invited to the gathering.[6] The participants were selected because they are often charged, by their communities, with educative directives which include, but are not limited to: (1) defining the areas of need for native children and youth, (2) developing both a knowledge base and instructional strategies that include the history, culture, art, and language of native children, and (3) articulating a mission that is deeply native and that advocates for equity and diversity within a mainstream Western society. The vision of their work ensures that valuable contributions are made to the intellectual, social, instructional, cultural, and ethical development of pre-Kindergarten through grade 16+[7] education.

There were, among the participants, shared understandings about schooling. For example, the participants' educational biographies and stories revealed a common belief that when a family is strong, then a community and its schools are strong. The principle of family first, of schools supporting and encouraging families to participate in the work of learning and teaching, has been supported in current research. In a preliminary survey of a little more than 1,000 native college and high-school students (Ewan, 1997), students identified little support and guidance from home as a primary factor for dropping out. A Pima student (18 years old) commented, "I personally think so many Indian youth drop out because their parents don't give them the support they need in those critical young years" (p. 28). And, a Leech Lake student (23 years old) shared, "Many Indian youth drop out because of their home life. The schools can't make them stay in classes. It's the parent's job to let their children know that education is crucial" (p. 28).

The disconnect between families and schools, Genevieve Gollnick (Oneida) suggested in one of our large group discussions during our gathering, was due in part to the effect of the boarding-school era.[8] To reverse this trend that has alienated families and dismissed traditional cultural values that support the participation of families and communities in every aspect of a child's life, Genevieve argued, educational leadership must approach schooling from an inclusive viewpoint. Susan Wetere-Bryant (Maori) echoed Genevieve's statement, sharing:

> To make our schools successful we need to involve community elders, families and cultural leaders. Our children need to know that the most important people in their lives are supportive. We must also involve community residents, businesses and their employees, and other social programs public and private. I believe that our children need to know that what they are doing in school is important not only to their families, but to the community at large. Coordinated efforts can create schools that provide the very best learning experiences to build strong leadership, provide our youth with career and life choices, and in the end help to build viable [economic] communities in the 21st century.

The participants at the gathering also shared common dilemmas in their work to promote culturally appropriate leadership, teaching and learning. For example, participants commented that they often struggle to clearly articulate, defend, and implement an institutional mission that promotes native self-determination.

Although there were many reasons for this challenge, a common barrier was the effect colonization has had that has led to feelings of isolation, alienation, and sorrow. In many cases, participants agreed, they were dealing with large communities of families and individuals who had very little self- and cultural-esteem. In the end, "There are many people who do not believe they have any choices. Given this, educational institutions must work deliberately, consistently, and with the guidance of *kupuna* (elders) to assure that a mission and vision is set and that we [educators] never lose sight of it" (Kalena Silva, Native Hawaiian).

Elgin Badwound (1991), former president of Oglala Lakota College in Kyle, South Dakota, also believes that educational institutions must have clear missions. He fears that ambiguous and undefended mission statements that do not focus on culture will result in curriculum that is detached from native values. However, what Badwound and the gathering participants have come to understand is that the task of clarifying and defending a mission that genuinely embraces native values is made more difficult by the absence of a philosophical approach to learning that presents a framework to organize the goals of a curriculum, define the content of the learning experiences, and develop appropriate teaching strategies. The challenge then to native educational leadership is to define a philosophical approach that could frame thinking, doing, and ongoing educative evaluation.

Our group came to realize, by the second morning of our meeting in the south, that this challenge would shape our continued work together. What would emerge over the following days would reveal a journey to the source, to the kiva (Cochiti Pueblo), to the piko (Native Hawaiian), to the longhouse (Iroquois and First Nations), to the dreaming (Australian Aborigine), and to the mountain (Maori) where wisdom, spirituality, and sacred covenants with nature and foundations of identity become the root of our passions that give both context and meaning to our relationships and ways of knowing and doing educational leadership.

TRAVELING TO THE SOURCE OF OUR LEADERSHIP PHILOSOPHY: TO THE WEST

We know enough about educational leadership to understand that the current knowledge base is less than distinctive, lacking any agreement regarding a content that is relevant and interesting and which substantively guides inquiry and practice around issues that are of import to native peoples (Benham & Cooper, 2000; Hallinger, 1995; Swisher & Tippeconnic, 1999). Hallinger and Heck (1996) argue that because the impact of school leadership on learning is indirect, more comprehensive models of leadership must be defined. However, as Shakeshaft (1989) maintains, leadership theory continues to be androcentric (White male), and she admonishes the field for its neglect of "other diverse" perspectives. As a result, current leadership models, which have often confused "leadership" with position occupancy (Kellerman, 1984), continue to foster a nebulous, often contradictory and narrow perspective of leadership that serves to maintain superordinate–subordinate relationships within an elitist hierarchy, thereby excluding the native voice. At the same time, scholars have busied themselves building a knowledge base which, while eclectic,[9] has focused primarily on theory and little on practice.

The work to nurture leadership[10] among native people, and especially native women, who have not traditionally held leadership positions, becomes problematic as current research, educational policy, and professional preparation programs fail to recruit and equip potential native school leaders for the possibilities and challenges of schools in the 21st century. Current efforts to revitalize the educational leadership knowledge base (see Bolman & Deal, 1995; Donmoyer, 1995; hooks, 1994; Sergiovanni, 1992) suggest that if a professional practice is to be grounded on a substantive knowledge base, then that knowledge must be useful, interesting, and include diverse views. I argue that such a knowledge base is dependent on a continued critical dialogue that allows for the introduction of new voices, such as that of native school leaders, into the conversation, which generates a more germane knowledge for native peoples. I do not suggest that this effort in any way distill a pedestrian or essentializing way of knowing. On the contrary, this work hopes to advance a distinctive knowledge base regarding the thinking and understanding, the skills and practices, and the decision making and problem solving of professional women and men deeply committed to their native lineage.

Our symbolic journey to the west to define a native/indigenous leadership model thus asked participants to peel away the layers of race/ethnicity, gender, and class and to ground themselves in the spiritual essence of their cultural and historical thoughts and prayers. What was learned was that each leader had to shed their baggage (e.g., anger and pain) and stand humble in the stories that were shared. Sam Suina (Cochiti Pueblo) guided us through this process saying, "We have been blessed with great strength, but there is sacrifice we must make, for nothing is given unless something is shared." Insight is a gift. Through ceremony (which cannot be shared in print) the participants collaboratively produced a native/indigenous leadership model of learning, living and teaching that is founded on a single commitment, "We cannot afford to lose one native child" (Armstrong, 2000).

The "Go to the Source" model was our response to the challenge to define a philosophical approach that framed learning, leading, and teaching. It is grounded on the following beliefs: (a) native/indigenous school leaders must meet the needs of an increasingly diverse native student population; (b) teaching and learning must be grounded in living native ways of knowing and doing within a broad context of school, family and community; and (c) schools that serve native youth must form professional learning communities with tribal, local, national, and global connections. The central message of the "Go to the Source" model speaks to the need and the power of self-determination and self-empowerment for all native/ indigenous peoples. That is, that native/indigenous peoples have the right and the responsibility to determine, articulate, implement and assess their educative processes. Indeed, what we have learned overtime is that self-determination is hard work because it takes both individual and collective commitment to reflect on where we have been, to work out a future that illuminates the depth of native knowing, and is inclusive of current thought and practice (see also McLaughlin, 1989).

TRAVELING TO THE MOUNTAIN: A MODEL FOR NATIVE EDUCATIONAL LEADERSHIP

To this day I am still awed by the diversity and uniqueness among our tiny group of native educational leaders who gathered at *Sol y Sombra*. Because of our linguistic and cultural differences, we were sometimes frustrated and challenged to arrive at one philosophical approach that spoke to the complexities of who we are as native/indigenous people and what we dream for our educational institutions. And yet, we found common dreams and challenges, and an unifying passion and knowledge that our work was important. The "Go to the Source" model, therefore, employs broad themes that allow for the dynamic interpretation of local content and context. We began with the question: "What do we want for our children?" In short, we agreed that what we want is for our children: (a) to be fluent in their mother tongue (in most cases to be bilingual and/or multilingual); (b) to articulate a strong, positive native/indigenous cultural self-identity, to be centered in their unique ways of knowing, and to live as proud human beings; (c) to respect the land, the place of their ancestors; and (d) to be confident that they can make choices and define what they do, to be self-determined human beings.

Knowing what we wanted for our children, we continued our work to construct a model of leadership grounded in our cultural ways of know-

In Our Mother's Voice 231

ing and best practices. We shared stories, helped, guided, prodded, healed, prayed, laughed and cried, but all the time climbing and moving toward a shared vision. Our continued work realized the necessity of grounding a culturally based leadership model on fundamental principles. The principles we collaboratively defined include: (a) native spiritual wisdom, which is guided by the hearts of our grandmothers and grandfathers; (b) critical development of the intellect, which intersects native ways of seeing and doing with modern ways of seeing and doing; (c) promotion of a healthy body and a healthy environment; and (d) preservation and revitalization of native languages, arts and traditions.

At the core of this model is the student/learner who connects us to both our past and our future. Indeed, all decisions regarding policy, practice, pedagogy, governance and organizational structure must support the learner and be grounded on four essential life elements: critical development of the intellect, healthy body and environment, preservation of language, and spiritual wisdom. Because we honor native ceremony, we must also remember that the four points must also work collectively to achieve balance at the personal, institutional, and community levels.

Locating, building, and maintaining this balance have become both a challenge and an opportunity for native school leaders. Over a century of oppression has left native/indigenous communities detached from schools, and generations of adults have been left with negative memories of schools (especially the Indian boarding-school generations; see Szasz, 1977). Additionally, contemporary values of leadership and governance create difficult situations for tribal leaders. As Twila Martin, former chairwoman of the Turtle Mountain Band of Chippewa, stated:

> There is an appreciation for how our ancestors were able to provide for our survival through leadership that emphasized the needs of the tribe and did not dwell upon the interest of individuals. They [ancestors] were able to look beyond the question, "What am I able to get out of this?" Instead, they asked, "What can I do to ensure the survival of our people?" I honestly believe that value is an innate quality and still exists within our political leaders. Now, how well they are able to maintain it is something different. The reason is that so often there are people who are pressing upon you their desires or their need to be treated differently, to be treated as individuals, provided favoritism. (cited in Boyer & Martin, 1993, p. 24)

The task of educational leadership, as the "Go to the Source" model suggests, is to weave a basket of learning potential utilizing the time and resources of individuals, families, community and cultural leaders, and businesses and other institutions in, near, and beyond the native/tribal neighborhood/land. Creating community-based collaboration in support of schools, in the words of participant Darrell Kipp (Blackfeet) requires school leaders to

> Tap into the multiple, diverse assets and resources of the people in your community—your family and friends—to surround the school and do good for the children at the school. It takes finesse to balance all this support so that you can have a healthy and productive learning environment. Many people want to help, but we need to teach them how to be of help. I think we do this by sharing with them what the vision is and how they can become a part of it, be owners of that vision.

The fundamental principles of the model and the collaborative nature of support are further illuminated in the dynamic dimensions of knowledge, community, and family. Knowledge is key to native understanding because of the belief that knowledge comes from the ancestors, is passed to us today, and moves us forward to the future. This idea challenges a native person to trust both the lessons learned from the past and to realize, or come to know, the new shapes of knowledge today. This requires a person to transcend finite (factual) knowing and enter into a more abstract, multiple layering of meaning. Vine Deloria Jr. (1991/1994) states: "Traditional knowledge enables us to see our place and our responsibility within the movement of history" (p. 23). The gathering's participants suggested that one's native language leads to understanding positionality and context because it carries the double entendre meanings of the past and is filled with metaphor, which helps define our present.

Knowledge, then, becomes the responsibility of community. Deloria Jr. (1991/1994) suggested:

> Education in the traditional setting occurs by example and not as a process of indoctrination. That is to say, elders are the best living examples of what the end product of education and life experiences should be. We sometimes forget that life is exceedingly hard and that not one accomplishes everything they could possibly do or even many of the things they intended to do. (p. 23)

The "Go to the Source" model also advocates for community involvement and responsibility in learning and teaching processes. Our conversations about community brought a striking point to the surface, that is, that community is not a birthright. Participants agreed that community

In Our Mother's Voice

could only thrive if members believe they belong and actively contribute as members of the community. Deloria Jr. (1991/1994), in support of this notion, writes:

> The old ways of education affirmed the basic principle that human personality was derived from accepting the responsibility to be a contributing member of a society. Kinship and clan were built upon the idea that individuals owed each other certain kinds of behaviors and that if each individual performed his or her task properly, society as a whole would function. (p. 21)

Knowledge and community, therefore, are enhanced by genuine involvement of the family in school-related activities. The 'ohana (Native Hawaiian meaning "extended family") is the cord that tightly weaves the "Go to the Source" model into a basket that can carry the generations of the future. The extended family is boundless, because it exists now as in the past, and will continue into eternity by connecting our generations, *na pu, na lei, na mamo* (Native Hawaiian saying meaning "our generations past, present, future"). Including the 'ohana as a primary stakeholder of schooling assures that what is culturally important will be included in the experience. More important, native students, by experiencing the interconnectivity of family and learning, can become stronger participants and contributors in their community. Deloria Jr (1991/1994, p. 23) supports this idea:

> The final ingredient of traditional tribal education is that accomplishments are regarded as the accomplishment of the family and not to the world around us, particularly the people around us, so that we know who we are and have confidence when we do things.

In addition, the circular structure of the model symbolically represents the necessity for balance between the individual, educational program, and institution. That is, the model attempts to define a balanced philosophy of native life, pedagogy and institutional practices that seek cultural dignity as well as equal participation. Our Iroquois cousins, drawing lessons from the Medicine Wheel, saw the "Go to the Source" model as holistic, forwarding the principle that community building must occur at multiple levels of the personal, the programmatic, and the community. For example, on the personal level, the model requires an individual to know her/his language, culture, and history and to live by the following principles: (a) to be ever vigilant to know what is good for yourself and what is not; (b) to daily give thanks and seek ways to be of service to others; (c) to treat guests with honor; and (d) to honor and act for the good of the collective while retaining a balance for the respect of the individual (Jeannette Armstrong and Genevieve Gollnick).

On the programmatic level, the model supports strong teacher and leader professional development to: (a) increase learning and practice of native language skills, (b) develop teaching and resource materials that enhance critical thinking and deepen cultural knowing, (c) create dynamic learning experiences in partnership with community and elders, and (d) further understand the importance of native knowing in the teaching process. On the institutional level, the model defines a new system of learning that requires a re-visioning that places at its core native/indigenous epistemologies and a commitment to distribution of decision making, connections to other social systems, and ongoing learning in multiple environmental settings.

The implication of this model on schools considers the way in which schools should function within a native community. For example, because lack of resources can diminish the efficacy of educational and community economic opportunities, appropriate financing of schools must become an important priority of the community as a whole. What we have learned from the examples provided by the Oneida Turtle School (Gollnick), the Pikani Peigan Institute (Kipp), and the Okanagon Writing Center (Armstrong) is that the "school" becomes a "place" for learning across the generations. Not only are K–12 classes held throughout the day, but intercommunity, intergenerational literacy programs, basic-skills curriculum, and cultural arts activities (to name a few) are offered in this hub of learning.

THE GIFT OF SERVICE FOUND IN THE NORTH: THE WORK OF NATIVE WOMEN LEADERS

Our symbolic journey to the north reminds us that the greatest of all lessons is found in the service of others. There were four themes that emerged from the work of each educational leader that defined the preceding model, in brief: (a) an emphasis on native-language development in both written and oral skills, and a press toward multilingualism; (b) a commitment to native understanding of culture and history, past and present, and focus on ways to address current issues; (c) articulation of a curriculum grounded in self-determination, cultural self-esteem, personal vision and passion; and (d) a central focus on teaching and learning processes that build responsibility to self, family and community, and actively involve family and community in the learning process.

All Native Educational Programs Must Emphasize Native Language Development in Both Written and Oral Skills and Press toward Multilingualism

There is general agreement among native scholars that the inclusion of cultural values and mother tongue in the formal school-learning experiences of native children and youth is essential to both an individual's cultural self-esteem and to the health and well-being of a native community. Abigail Gray (1997) wrote, "Linguistic and cultural barriers have the power to inadvertently advance the decay of the cultural fabric of organizations, communities and nations. A lack of linguistic and cultural knowledge is no longer apropos in adaptive societies" (p. 80). Aligned in spirit and practice with this statement, participants at the gathering have worked hard to hold onto and to renew, through teaching and learning, their mother tongue. Their unifying belief is that this knowing will link children and youth to rich histories and heroic ancestors. To advocate for mother-tongue language programs is a politically charged stance because it means that one believes that native sovereignty matters, that native peoples have the right to engage in matters that are purposeful, and that native communities are empowered to act on important matters.

Taking such a stand has sustained each of the gathering's participants in their community-based work to deliberately develop and implement blue-ribbon educational programs that are culturally appropriate. For example, Genevieve Gollnick shared her experiences at the Oneida Turtle School (Wisconsin) where native and nonnative teachers and staff of Oneida children and youth were required to earn an Oneida Teaching Certification. Teachers and staff attended ongoing professional development courses taught by cultural leaders, and participated in cultural events that taught the native language and philosophy. Through these experiences teachers developed curriculum, instructional tools, and pedagogical methods that were grounded in Oneida language, tribal history, and cultural ways of knowing.

In Hawai'i, children can attend public Hawaiian-language immersion schools from preschool through grade 12. Teachers and staff, fluent in the Native Hawaiian language, have developed curriculum, instruction, assessment and testing that meets both State of Hawai'i and national standards across the disciplines. And, because Native Hawaiian cultural experts and kupuna (Native Hawaiian meaning "elders") continue to be involved in developing learning initiatives and academic programs, the values, history, and cultural ways of the Hawaiian people remain core to the learning experience (see Sarah Keahi, Native Hawaiian, in Benham & Cooper, 2000). Each of these programs illuminates the journey of the "Go to the Source" model that embraces the academic disciplines of the humanities, social sciences

236 *Maenette K. P. AhNee-Benham*

and natural sciences. And, they affirm that the learning journey is inclusive of both native traditional knowledge and contemporary knowledge as it weaves a strong community basket.

The value of both mother-tongue instruction and contemporary academics is revealed in each of the four quadrants of the "Go to the Source" model. Within the spiritual, a person learns the stories, ceremonies, and art of her/his lineage that is passed through mother-tongue instruction. This spiritual strength defines a way of living that supports a native identity—cultural integrity—which builds a strong sense of affective balance. The spiritual and affective balance of self can lead to expressions of communal wholeness and stewardship expressed in the model. The third quadrant, physical health and well-being, links the importance of a healthy mind, body and spirit. Both native and nonnative language and cultural norms need to be balanced in this quadrant because individuals and communities work collectively to govern fairly and inclusively. The final quadrant, the cognitive (intellectual growth) honors a diverse knowledge base that is supportive of an individual's fluency across social venues.

All Native Education Programs Must Emphasize Native Understanding of Culture and History, Past and Present, and Focus on Ways to Address Current Issues

This theme for school leadership was a result of the participants' experiences with curricular materials that excluded or stereotyped the stories of their native communities. The essentializing and romanticism of native experience through a lackluster curriculum devalues the human spirit and leads to self-destruction (see also Bray, 1999). Although Native American children come to school with hope and enthusiasm, many begin to languish, failing to meet academic standards and eventually dropping out. The Native Americas survey of native youth (Ewan, 1997) reported that a factor for dropping out was that students could not see themselves in professional careers, hence, there was no value in the school experience. Other students reported that life hardships, created by poverty, drug abuse, alienation and despair had led them away from schools and to gang life. Not having a strong family unit has led "many young people to join gangs that ignore the values and culture of their tribe, but instead replicate the values of violent and disruptive gang behavior" (Paul Johnson, Anishnabe). Several Indian youth stated, in their survey responses, that although the dilemmas they face might make life difficult, they believed that school was important. However, they mentioned that schools could be more valuable to them if they incorporated their Native American tribal values, language, and cultural ideas into the school day, established high academic expectations for all native students, provided good counseling programs that incorporated their tribal ways and protocols, and presented positive Indian role models (e.g., their elders) for school children.

The students have it right! The commitment of native/tribal schools and its leadership should be to assure that both content and pedagogy present accurate historical retelling from the native perspective and include an intrinsic element of building civic and community responsibility (see also the work of Vine Deloria Jr., 1991/1994).

The foundation of a culturally appropriate curriculum is grounded on four foundational principles. The first, critical thinking, requires the dedication of credentialed native and nonnative teachers who not only expect high academic achievement but also work collectively with other teachers, students, and cultural leaders to generate knowledge and learning. In essence, teachers and students become the leaders of their learning classroom as they work to understand traditional cultural values and employ the skills of literacy (in both their mother tongue and English), math, and science to bridge the ways of The People and those of the larger society.

The second principle, the implementation of an idea, asks that native students of all ages be provided diverse opportunities to work collaboratively on a community-based project that not only instills the values of hard work, determination to succeed, and passion to learn, but creates valuable links between the classroom and their real world. Building on critical thinking and implementation, the third principle, taking responsibility for sharing knowledge, places the native student in a position in which he or she can capably work and interact with many different communities of people. The objective of this essential principle communicates a deeply held value among many native peoples, that is, that individual accomplishments (personal and professional) are used to help others.

The life lessons one learns over time, the contributions one makes to one's community, and the effort one has made to build bridges across cultural groups leads to the final principle, respect for those with knowledge and wisdom. This important principle completes the circle that connects the school experience to native ceremonies, values and languages and also links students to their heritage and builds their relationships with others within the tribe and throughout the world. An example of how the elements of critical thinking, implementation, sharing knowledge and respect are illuminated in a learning experience developed through the Okanagon writing program. In essence, students, in collaboration with elders and native experts (cultural artists), examine social and political issues (e.g., family violence, drug abuse, fishing rights, etc.) through creative writing and film work. Addressing contemporary issues challenges the students to

238 *Maenette K. P. AhNee-Benham*

think deeply about a problem and the ways in which they might work through the tensions of traditional and modern values to locate a healthier quality of life. These works are showcased and often lead to community social programs (see Jeannette Armstrong, 2000).

The Curriculum Must Be Grounded on Principles of Self-Determination, Cultural Self-Esteem, and Personal Vision and Passion

Like the first and second themes for school leadership, the genesis of this idea came from participants' stories and experiences in educational institutions (e.g., boarding schools) that served to dismiss the issues and concerns native children and youth brought to the classroom. Gregory Cajete (1994), a Tewa Indian scholar from Santa Clara Pueblo, asks his readers to transform the context and meaning of teaching as he explores the ceremony in teaching and learning. His work helped the participants to think more about challenging the sociocultural and political hegemony that has supported the stratification and marginalization of native children and youth.

Cajete's work is supported by numerous native scholars (see Swisher & Tippeconnic, 1999) who argue that high dropout rates and low test scores among native youth signals a need for improved understanding and involvement of native scholars in the study and development of pedagogy and content. In addition, native/tribal communities should be in control of all the elements of their children's schooling, to include: language, learning, teaching, evaluation, and research of their schools. An example of educational self-determination comes from our cousins to the north, the Inuit communities of Northern Quebec. They have designed an educational model they call *Satuigiarniq* (to reclaim) that intends to "redefine, strengthen, and reclaim a holistic educational system in Nunavik in partnership with and with direction from the people of Nunavik" (Armstrong, Bennett, & Grenier, 1997, p. 8).

Our native-based model of including community members in the process of educational development and renewal provides rich opportunity for native peoples to redefine their educational system, remain true to native/indigenous culture and values and, at the same time, prepare children and youth for the contemporary world. Placing the control of educational leadership and curricular content in the hands of native peoples, however, is a politically powerful stance that is aligned with current calls for self-determination. Pedagogical power and authority, which has not been in the hands of native communities, provides authority to define what is learned, who learns, and how learning is done. For the native edu-

In Our Mother's Voice 239

cational leader, pedagogical power recognizes that native ways of knowing are important and that both teachers and educational leaders are critical cultural brokers (see also McLaughlin, 1989).

The Work of Educational Leadership Must Center on Teaching and Learning as Processes, Which Build Generosity, Compassion, and Responsibility for Self, Family, and Community, and at the Same Time Actively Involve the Extended Family and the Native Community

This theme values the work of teachers, therefore teachers become integral to the implementation and the balance of the "Go to the Source" model. Karen Swisher (1990) and Swisher and Dehyle (1989) write that teachers of native students have the responsibility to understand and to teach the underlying philosophies and values of their indigenous culture. In essence, teaching that is linked to identity must incorporate oral stories and traditional teaching, teaching environments that honor the connection to nature and the land, and learning that is inclusive of native worldviews.

The participants of our gathering saw teachers not only as guides who pilot our children and youth through their educational journey, but more importantly as servants of the community that work to help bring balance to individuals who in turn create empowered communities. The "Go to the Source" model urges school administrators and teachers to become proactive community leaders and to develop community-based activities that integrate traditional and contemporary practices to address pressing social issues. This would include increasing opportunities for community members (e.g., elders) to participate in language and cultural events. Additionally, school leaders and teachers must partner with both native and nonnative individuals and groups to create mentoring experiences in academics, skill development, and native/tribal traditions.

In the end, from the worldviews and professional experiences of the participants at our gathering, leadership is rooted in a respect for traditional cultural ways of knowing, a commitment to social justice, and a passion for all things big and small. Several participants commented that "leadership is when one and many speak for the good and on behalf of The People. And a leader is the first person to go hungry and the last person to eat" (L. A. Napier, Cherokee). Leadership is not restricted to the school setting; in fact, being an active member of the native/tribal community not only builds one's credibility, but assures that the mission of sovereignty and social justice becomes valued throughout the community. Susan Wetere-Bryant (2000), defining leadership, shared:

240   *Maenette K. P. AhNee-Benham*

There are many struggles in the development of better learning and teaching for our indigenous children. There are many philosophies and ways of thinking that need to be thought through. Every struggle and challenge adds to our development. Central to our success is valuing ourselves through knowing ourselves. We cannot fail if we are supported to access our inner strength, inner *mana* (self power) we have to be effective in our lives. Leadership in these efforts is key. To be an educational leader is a completely absorbing responsibility. I believe that I am the instrument through which energy is channeled. In this way, I am able to engage others to support their work or to help them understand their internal and external words. I see myself as an educational leader in the Maori community and at the government level (non-Maori). My role is to understand the Maori worldview as well as the non-Maori view. Then, as the cultural negotiator, make sense of it for both sides. I traverse worlds with an insider and outsider knowing, but with a goal to advance positive thinking and action that invests in Maori people. (p. 150)

A TIME FOR REFLECTION AND MOVING AGAIN TO THE EAST: CONCLUSIONS AND CHALLENGES

So what have I, a Native Hawaiian woman, learned about educational leadership? First, that to advocate and to act to make a significant difference in educational institutions that affect the lives of native/indigenous children and youth is a tough journey. Like a marathon, there will be some trepidation because the task is great and one can only hope that you have the capacity to continue. And, at the end of the race expect to be pretty tired, but completion has its own energy and so I believe that we awake each day ready to run again. For each of the individual educational leaders who participated in this story making, their vigilance to see this journey to the mountaintop is the strength on which the "Go to the Source" model is built. Darrell Kipp, in a passionate speech to the gathering participants, reaffirmed the importance of this lesson:

We cannot dismiss our history of extermination and the removal of our people so that the White man could get to the natural resources. Assimilation through the Indian boarding schools was a large part of this history in which schools were used to acculturate and socialize new values and another way of seeing the world. Today, we see the effects of capitalization, entrepreneurs through gaming. The selling of the Native!

Through all of this we see ourselves, our young people and our old people, struggling with the negotiation between the old and the new. So, what occurs in our educational settings is extremely important! Teaching our youth how to maintain the essence and meaning of their heritage through language and cultural practices is important. And, teaching our youth how to negotiate between the traditional and the contemporary is important. Our model is important because it exemplifies a process, a natural process that acknowledges the importance of building relationships within our communities, with our environment, and with other cultures. So, education, as our model suggests, connects students to "living" in their physical, spiritual and native environments. This is important.

In essence, our movement that began in the east then moved to the south, to the west, and to the north symbolizes the importance of our participation as individuals in a universal and collaborative effort that begins with the spirit. Our message illuminates our commitment and practice as native school leaders that value the generosity of spirit, compassion, love, and joy. This leads to the "Go to the Source" model that advocates building strong educational communities that are family-centered, preserves and revitalizes native languages and cultures, and strengthens self-identity and sovereignty.

So what's next? I'd like to suggest three important tasks. First, continued efforts on the part of native scholars, policymakers, educational leaders, and communities are needed to assure culturally relevant learning experiences that validate a native student's culture, language, and home life. Second, increased development and resources need to be provided to teachers to help them assist their students to understand how school learning can contribute to their own quality of life *and* to the healthy life of their tribal community. And third, further study of educational leadership, from the perspective of native women doing the good work within a native/indigenous context needs to be started. It is through the dissemination of these ideas that we may learn more about the joy of living and the deeply held belief that embedded in one's heart, mind, and soul is the source of leadership.

NOTES

1. Native is defined in this work as native peoples who have been colonized and governed by a Western society to include: Native American Indians (U.S. and Canada), Native Alaskan Eskimos, Native Hawaiians, Maoris, and Australian Aborigines. Native and indigenous is used synonymously throughout the text.

242   *Maenette K. P. AhNee-Benham*

2. See the writings of Dr. Beatrice Medicine for a careful and comprehensive discussion of this observable fact.

3. Delegates at the White House Conference on Indian Education (WHCIE) in 1992 observed that much research has been done about Natives conducted by nonnatives. This suggests a need for a wide range of research by Natives with an "inside" view of issues.

4. It is extremely dangerous to propose a singular worldview, because native/indigenous peoples are complex, and differ across communities and histories. At this point, I speak more broadly and do not assign a particular set of cultural values.

5. There is a growing body of literature written about native/indigenous culture by native/indigenous authors. I do not attempt to list the diverse sources here; however, for Native Hawaiian cultural traditions, I would refer the reader to Pukui, et al., (1972). *Nana I ke Kumu (Look to the Source).* Hui Hanai: Honolulu, HI.

6. Here is a listing of the participants: Sarah Keahi, Native Hawaiian, educator; Sam Suina, Cochiti Pueblo, community college professor; Genevieve Gollnick, Oneida, curriculum director (K–12); Darrell Kipp, Blackfeet, cofounder and teacher in a native-language immersion program; Jeannette Armstrong, Okanagon, author, researcher, teacher; Kalena Silva, Native Hawaiian, professor of Hawaiian studies and language; L. A. Napier, Cherokee Nation of Oklahoma, assistant professor of educational leadership; Paul Johnson, Ojibwe, educational consultant; Miranda Wright, Athabaskan, anthropologist, community developer, and educator; Susan Wetere-Bryant, Maori, researcher and educational consultant; Linda Aranga-Low, Maori, K–12 educator; Kate Cherrington, Maori, educational specialist, tertiary education; Gail Kiernan, Australian Aborigine, educational consultant, political activist; Rosalie Medcraft, Australian Aborigine, K–12 educator and children's book author.

7. Pre-Kindergarten–16+ signals our recognition that formal educational experiences should be seamless, reaching into community colleges, trade and vocational schools, professional development, and higher education (post secondary).

8. Boarding schools for Native American children and youth (as well as for Canadian tribes) have been well documented; for more information, see Coleman, 1993; Lomawaima, 1994, 1995; Swisher & Tippeconnic, 1999; Szasz, 1977.

9. Drawing from a variety of disciplines to include: business, sociology, psychology, anthropology, and political science.

10. Leadership, as defined by the author and participants at the In Our Mother's Voice gathering, is not "role" specific, but shared responsibility that is grounded in native cultural principles and that moves toward a vision of schools that might be generated by teachers, building-level school administrators, parents, students and community members.

REFERENCES

Allen, P. G. (1992). *The sacred hoop: Recovering the feminine in American Indian traditions.* Boston, MA: Beacon Press.
Armstrong, E., Bennett, S., & Grenier, A. (1997). Satuigiarniq: Reclaiming responsibility for education. *Journal of Staff Development, 18*(3), 6–11.

Armstrong, J. (2000). A holistic education, teachings from the Dance-House: "We cannot afford to lose one native child." In M. Benham & J. Cooper (Eds.), *Indigenous educational models for contemporary practice: In our mother's voice* (pp. 35–43). Mahwah, NJ: Lawrence Erlbaum Associates.

Badwound, E. (1991). Teaching to empower: Tribal colleges must promote leadership and self determination in their reservations. *Tribal College Journal of American Indian Higher Education, 3*(1), 15–19.

Benham, M., & Cooper, J. (1998). *Let my spirit soar! Narratives of diverse women in school leadership.* Thousand Oaks, CA: Corwin Press.

Benham, M., & Cooper, J. (Eds.). (2000). *Indigenous educational models for contemporary practice: In our mother's voice.* Mahwah, NJ: Lawrence Erlbaum Associates.

Betz, D. (1991). *International initiatives and education of indigenous peoples: Teaching and learning to "dance in two worlds".* (RC 018320) Oklahoma City, OK: Sovereignty Symposium IV. The circles of sovereignty. The next generation. Educating the American Indian children. (ERIC Document ED 339561)

Bolman, L., & Deal, T. (1995). *Leading with soul: An uncommon journey of spirit.* San Francisco: Jossey-Bass.

Boyer, P., & Martin, T. (1993). Going to battle: Twila Martin considers the power and limitations of leadership. *Tribal College Journal of American Indian Higher Education, 5*(2), 24–27.

Bray, S. W. (1999, March). *The emancipation proclamation for Indian education: A passion for excellence and justice.* Paper presented at the Annual Conference on Creating the Quality School, Memphis, TN.

Cajete, G. (1994). *Look to the mountain: An ecology of indigenous education.* Durango, CO: Kivaki.

Coleman, M. (1993). *American Indian children at school, 1850–1930.* Jackson: University Press of Mississippi.

Dehyle, D. (1992). Constructing failure and maintaining cultural identity: Navajo and Ute school leavers. *Journal of American Indian Education, 31*(2), 24–47.

Deloria, V. Jr. (1991/1994). *Indian education in America: 8 Essays by Vine Deloria, Jr.* Albuquerque, NM: American Indian Science & Engineering Society.

Donmoyer, R. (1995, April). *The very idea of a knowledge base.* Paper presented at the annual meeting of the American Educational Research Association, San Francisco, CA.

Ewan, A. (1997). Generation X in Indian country: A Native Americas Indian youth survey. *Native Americas, 14*(4), 24–29.

Foreman, C. (1976). *Indian women chiefs.* Washington, DC: Zenger Publishing Co.

Gray, A. (1997). Modeling transcultural leadership for transformational change. *Journal for Vocational Special Needs Education, 19*(2), 78–84.

Green, R. (1990). The Pocahantas perplex: The image of Indian women in American culture. In E. C. Dubois & V. Ruiz (Eds.), *Unequal sisters: A multicultural reader in U.S. women's history* (pp. 15–21). New York: Routledge.

Green, R. (1992). *Women in American Indian society.* New York: Chelsea House.

Hallinger, P. (1995). Culture and Leadership: Developing an international perspective in educational administration. *UCEA Review, 36*(1), 3–7.

Hallinger, P., & Heck, R. (1996). Reassessing the principal's role in school effectiveness: A review of empirical research, 1980–1995. *Educational Administration Quarterly, 32*(1), 5–44.

hooks, b. (1994). *Teaching to transgress: Education as the practice of freedom.* New York: Routledge.

Keahi, S. (2000). Advocating for a stimulating and language-based education: "If you don't learn your language where can you go home to?" In M. Benham & J. Cooper (Eds.), *Indigenous educational models for contemporary practice: In our mother's voice* (pp. 55–60). Mahwah, NJ: Lawrence Erlbaum Associates.

Kellerman, B. (Ed.) (1984). *Leadership: Multidisciplinary perspectives.* Englewood Cliffs, NJ: Prentice–Hall.

Lomawaima, K. T. (1994). *They called it Prairie Lights: The story of Chilocco Indian School.* Lincoln: University of Nebraska Press.

Lomawaima, K. T. (1995). Educating Native Americans. In J. Banks (Ed.), *Handbook of research on multicultural education.* New York: Macmillan

McLaughlin, D. (1989). Power and politics of knowledge: Transformative leadership and curriculum development for minority language learners. *Peabody Journal of Education, 66*(3), 41–60.

Medicine, B. (1978). *The Native American woman.* Albuquerque, NM: Eric/Cress.

Medicine, B. (1988). Professionalization of Native American (Indian) women: Towards a research agenda. *Wicazo Sa Review, 4*(2), 31–42.

Moraga, C., & Anzaldua, G. (Eds.). (1983). *This bridge called my back: Writings by radical women of color.* New York: Kitchen Table, Women of Color Press.

Sergiovanni, T. (1992). *Moral leadership: Getting to the heart of school reform.* San Francisco, CA: Jossey-Bass.

Shakeshaft, C. (1989). *Women in educational administration.* Newbury Park, CA: Sage.

Swisher, K. (1990). Cooperative learning and the education of American Indian/Alaskan Native students: A review of the literature and suggestions for implementation. *Journal of American Indian Education, 29*(2), 36–43.

Swisher, K. & Dehyle, D. (1989, August). The styles of learning are different, but the teaching is just the same: Suggestions for teachers of American Indian youth. *Journal of American Indian Education* (Special Issue), 1–14.

Swisher, K., & Tippeconnic, J. III. (1999). *Next steps: Research and practice to advance Indian education.* Charleston, WV: Appalachia Educational Laboratory.

Szasz, M. C. (1977). *Education and the American Indian: The road to self-determination since 1928* (2nd ed.). Albuquerque: University of New Mexico Press.

Tsosie, R. (1988). Changing women: The cross-currents of American Indian feminine identity. *American Indian Culture and Research Journal, 12*(1), 1–37.

Wetere-Bryant, S. (2000). Educational empowerment for Maori people: "We are on the right path. We are on the right dreaming." In M. Benham & J. Cooper (Eds.), *Indigenous educational models for contemporary practice: In our mother's voice* (pp. 145–151). Mahwah, NJ: Lawrence Erlbaum Associates.

Chapter 13

Normalized Femininity: Reconsidering Research on Women in the Superintendency

Linda Skrla

Seventeen years ago, in a 1984 article titled "The Crisis in Excellence and Equity," Catherine Marshall summarized statistics that highlighted the gross underrepresentation of women in public school administration at that time, and she also provided strong evidence that the relatively few women who served as principals and superintendents, as a group, did a superior job. After laying out evidence of the ongoing exclusion of women from educational leadership positions in juxtaposition with evidence of women's considerable strengths and successes in those leadership roles, Marshall posed the question, "Why have policymakers and educators failed to see that women's leadership abilities, resources, and insights are valuable?" (p. 29).

Three years later, in 1987, Charol Shakeshaft published *Women in Educational Administration*, a widely read and influential book that comprehensively examined the issues surrounding women in school administration. In the chapter in which she summarized research on barriers to women's advancement into school administration, Shakeshaft commented,

> We are left wondering why, if gender is not the overriding explanation of a profession structured according to sex, are men managers and women teachers? How is it that women, more than men, are in positions low in power and opportunity? Why is it that teaching is a high opportunity profession for a man but not for a woman? (p. 93)

248 *Linda Skrla*

In 2002, fifteen years after Shakeshaft's book and nearly two decades after Marshall's article, school administration, particularly the superintendency, continues to be overwhelmingly dominated by men. In fact, the U.S. Department of Labor described the superintendency as the most male-dominated of any executive position in the country (Björk, 1999).

The enormity of this continued male domination of the superintendency can be illustrated by using data available from the Institute for Educational Leadership (IEL) and the National Center for Education Statistics (NCES). A recent IEL publication, *The U.S. School Superintendent: The Invisible CEO* (Hodgkinson & Montenegro, 1999), used a large sample of superintendents nationwide and determined that women occupied 12 percent of U.S. superintendencies in 1998. According to the NCES publication *Digest of Education Statistics 2001*, for the 1995–96 school year, there were 14,766 public school districts in the United States. By assuming that each public school district had one general superintendent and applying Hodgkinson and Montenegro's 12 percent figure,[1] it can be estimated that in 1996, there were 1772 female and 12,994 male superintendents of schools in the U.S. During this same school year, there were 2,164,000 public school teachers in the United States. Of these, 553,984 (25.6%) were men and 1,610,016 (74.4%) were women (NCES, 2001). Thus, the ratio of male superintendents to male teachers was 12,994: 553,984 (.0234), and the ratio of female superintendents to female teachers was 1772:1,610,016 (.0011). Because "virtually all school administrators are initially recruited from the ranks of teachers"[2] (Banks, 1995, p. 70), the odds of a male teacher becoming superintendent are approximately one in 40; for a female teacher, the odds are roughly one in 900.[3] In other words, men are more than twenty times more likely than are women to advance to the superintendency from teaching.[4]

Thus, the early days of the twenty-first century seem an appropriate time to reflect on this abysmal lack of progress toward equitable representation for women in the public school superintendency. Despite gradually increasing numbers of women in the "pipeline" roles that typically lead to the superintendent's office, despite the predominance of women in university educational administration preparation programs, and despite a growing feminine presence in other historically male-dominated professional fields, women have made few gains in the superintendency (Keller, 1999). In short, little has changed since Marshall and Shakeshaft wrote about these same issues in the mid-1980s. Furthermore, the staggering gender stratification in the superintendency that disgraces educational administration continues to receive little attention in the mainstream discourse of the profession (Scheurich, 1995).

These twin phenomena, a chronic and hugely inequitable situation and disinterest in addressing it in meaningful ways, suggest that there is more going on with the perpetuation of male dominance in the superintendency than earlier research on the issue has been able to reveal. The central theme of the current edited volume is reconsidering feminist research in educational leadership, and I would suggest that research on gender stratification in the public school superintendency is an area ripe for reexamination. In the remainder of this chapter, I will describe and make an initial attempt to operationalize one suggested path for such a reexamination. This reexamination responds to another question posed by Marshall (1997): "What goes on in shaping training, certification, selection and promotion of educational administrators that ensures White male dominance and leaders oriented toward bureaucratic maintenance?" (p. 1) by using a poststructural conceptualization of power—deployment of power through normalization—to provide an alternative perspective on research about women superintendents that has accumulated in the past decade. I suggest that understanding of and explanation for the perpetuation of male dominance in the superintendency might be gained by examining underlying normalizations that structure the discourses and practices of educational administration, including most recent research on women in the superintendency.

NORMALIZATIONS AS PRODUCTIVE EFFECTS OF POWER

Popkewitz and Brennan (1998) distinguish between two views of power in research for social change—power as sovereignty and power as deployment. Research incorporating the first view, power as sovereignty, "give[s] attention to what groups are favored in decision making and how the decisions distribute values to produce a context of domination and subordination—the rulers and the ruled" (p. 17). Much of the educational research literature conducted from critical frameworks (including Marxist and feminist) uses the power as sovereignty lens, and it has contributed greatly to our understanding of how discrimination, including sexism, operates. However, it is the second of Popkewitz and Brennan's definitions of power—power as deployment—that I am concerned with in proposing an alternative lens for studying sexism in the superintendency. This second view of power is based on the productive quality of power as identified in the works of Michel Foucault. According to Popkewitz and Brennan (1998),

> This productive notion of power concerns its effects as it circulates through institutional practices and the discourses of daily life. . . . Strategically, the study of the effects of power enables us to focus on the ways that individuals construct boundaries and possibilities. . . . Such reasoning has multiple

250 *Linda Skrla*

trajectories and explores the various strategies through which individuality is constructed as both disciplining and productive of power. The productive elements of power move from focusing on the controlling actors to the systems of ideas that normalize and construct the rules through which intent and purpose in the world are organized. (pp. 18–19)

Power as deployment, or the productive effect of power, then, in contrast to sovereign power, is generative or constitutive. This type of power circulates through discourses and practices and actually produces the desires and behaviors of individuals and the rules and practices of societal institutions such as schools.

An example of this view of the productive effects of power is found in Jennifer Gore's (1998) contention that remarkable sameness of schooling practices across sites and through time, and the apparent imperviousness of these practices to the most radical of educational reforms, is linked to power relations in schools. She argues that the techniques of power that Foucault identified in his study of prisons are equally applicable to the study of schools. One of these techniques, normalization, has particular applicability to the study of women's experiences in the superintendency. Gore described her use of the term *normalization* as follows:

Foucault (1997) highlighted the importance of "normalizing judgment," or normalization, in the functions of modern disciplinary power. He explained that such normalizing judgment often occurs through comparison, so that individual actions are referred "to a whole that is at once a field of comparison, a space of differentiation and the principle of a rule to be followed" (p. 182). For the purposes of my research, normalization was defined as "invoking, requiring, setting, or conforming to a standard—defining the normal." (p. 237)

In Gore's view, then, the technique of normalization is one of the productive effects of power in that it involves more than just comparisons to what is defined as normal; it operates to produce the normal through its disciplinary effects on thoughts, actions, and individual modes of being—and also important, this type of power acts to produce the normal in our research.

Additional insight on the productive effects of normalization can be gained from the work of Gordon (1980). He described these effects as operating at both individual and group (or institutional) levels:

If the general object-material for the relations and networks of power studied by Foucault is that of the concrete forms of conduct and behaviour of human beings, then one can say that operations designed to form or re-form this material articulate themselves according to broad modalities, "microscopic" and "macroscopic": techniques which effect an orthopaedic training of the body and soul of an individual, and techniques which secure and enhance the forms of life and well-being of a population or "social body." Now it is possible to effect a partial classification of programmes, strategies and technologies according to how their field of operation focuses within one or other of these modalities, and how a double epistemological–practical activity of shaping their material into a normal-normative-normalisable form is weighted toward the focus of the individual or that of the population. (p. 254)

Gordon's suggestion for a partial classification of "programmes, strategies, and technologies" (techniques of power) according to whether their "double epistemological–practical activity" of normalization is focused on the individual or the population offers great explanatory potential, in my view, for exploration of the issues surrounding women in the superintendency.

NORMALIZATIONS OF FEMININITY IN
RESEARCH ON WOMEN IN THE SUPERINTENDENCY

In the years that have passed since Marshall's and Shakeshaft's questioning of the androcentric status quo in education administration, a significant, and growing, body of research on women administrators (conducted almost exclusively by female scholars) has accumulated. Much of this research focuses on the issues surrounding women in the public school superintendency—aspirations, experiences in the role, exits from the profession. The majority of this female superintendency research has openly attempted to depart from traditional, male-centered paradigms and traditional research practices. For example, several researchers have used feminist poststructural or critical feminist approaches (e.g., Brunner, 1994, 1997b, 1999, 2000; Gardiner, Enomoto, & Grogan, 2000; Grogan, 1996; Skrla, 2000). Thus, recent research about women superintendents, at least on the surface, differs in significant ways from research conducted earlier.[5] Certainly new views of women's experiences that had been submerged, excluded, and merged with men's views in earlier research have emerged in these later studies.

This body of research, however, has remained marginalized by the mainstream discourses of educational administration research and has had little noticeable effect on educational administration practices. To illustrate,

252 *Linda Skrla*

of more that 60 sessions sponsored by Division A (administration) at the 1999 Annual Meeting of the American Educational Research Association (AERA), only two sessions focused on gender issues; this chapter is based on a paper that was prepared for one of those two sessions. Similarly, in the 594-page second edition of the *Handbook of Research on Educational Administration* (Murphy & Louis, 1999), one chapter out of 24 deals with gender. When men continue to advance into the superintendency at over twenty times the rate that women do, it is curious that the profession shows little interest in this issue.

I suggest that understanding both the perpetuation of male dominance in the superintendency and the virtual invisibility of the problem might be furthered through examination of underlying normalizations that structure the discourses and practices of educational administration, including the most recent research on women in the superintendency. These normalizations operate reciprocally at both individual and group (institutional and societal) levels. According to Gutting (1989):

> The choice available (and those not available) to the individual at each point in his life history could be read as due to the structure of the culture in which he lives. Conversely, the development of social structures in one direction rather than another could be read as corresponding to a specification of the sorts of individuals than can (and those that cannot) exist in the culture. (p. 216)

Thus, in a position such as the superintendency, the individuals who work in the culture adopt and adapt to the existing norms (normalizations) for what is possible and what is not possible for them to think, say, act, and be; at the same time the culture of the superintendency is shaped by the thoughts, speech, actions, and existence of the individuals who are the superintendents. This, then, is how the productive effects of power operate through normalization. The rules, expectations, understandings, and discourses that make up the normalizations in the superintendency act to produce the normal situation.

In the case of the public school superintendency, there are multiple normalizations at work (including race, professionalism, expertise, and leadership, among others), but there is, in my view, one particularly powerful normalization that plays a key role in the maintenance of male domination in this role—the normalization of femininity and masculinity. That is, the normalization of socially well-understood gender roles, characteristics, behaviors, ways of being undergirds the entire superintendency culture, including the research literature about it. To elaborate, Bardwick and Douvan (1971) describe the package of norms (in other words, the normalization) for femininity as consisting of "dependence, passivity, fragility, low pain tolerance, nonagression, noncompetitiveness, inner orientation, interpersonal orientation, empathy, sensitivity, nurturance, subjectivity, yieldingness, receptivity, inability to risk, emotional liability, and supportiveness" (p. 147). Masculinity, in contrast, is typically defined in terms opposite of those used to describe femininity. Thus, a parallel and opposite list of terms could be constructed for masculinity, which would include independence, assertiveness, sturdiness, high pain tolerance, aggression, competitiveness, outer orientation, self-sufficiency, stoicism, justice, objectivity, unyieldingess, remoteness, risk taking, and rationality.

Jackie Blount (1998, 1999) identified the historical period in which these hegemonic normalizations of femininity and masculinity took root in school administration—the years following World War II. Blount explained that during this time,

> Psychologists, sexologists, educators, and social critics invested considerable energy in the effort to produce scientifically derived definitions of acceptable White middle-class femininity. . . . Gender divisions became increasingly starkly delineated, and those who defied the conventions suffered the burdens of deviance and ostracism. (Blount, 1998, p. 110)

Blount (1998, 1999) also described the role of homophobia in reifying these gendered normalizations in the ranks of teachers and school administrators. Organized and publicly supported efforts to ferret out in schools and fire men or women even suspected of being gay or lesbian led to strict adherence to gender roles by both men and women. Thus, during this time period women who wanted to keep their jobs adopted sweet, passive, and agreeable demeanors and submitted to the males in leadership positions. Men, on the other hand, tried to live up to highly idealized views of dominant masculinity. As Blount (1999) put it, "Not only had school administration been reaffirmed as a masculine domain, but only a few men—those nearly like Greek gods, approaching the ultimate in manliness, need apply" (p. 10).

At the same time that individual women and men in school administration internalized and exemplified rigid gender roles, the culture of the institutions both produced and reflected these same normalizations. As I have argued elsewhere (Skrla, 2000),

> The package of norms associated with the superintendency in U.S. public schools is, I would suggest, constructed based on the assumption that males will inhabit this role. . . . Society expects that men in the position will have those socialized characteristics

254 *Linda Skrla*

and will behave in those socialized ways; and, thus, the role of the superintendent has been created (socially constructed) by society as masculine. (pp. 296–297)

More specifically, according to Bell (1988), "The expectations . . . of superintendents are likely to be based on a taken-for-granted conception of the superintendent as a middle-aged, conservative, married man" (p. 38). The superintendency, thus, has become defined at the organizational level of schooling as a masculine role. Job descriptions and vacancy notices that emphasized managerial skill, budgeting knowledge, and physical plant expertise reflected this normalization.

Even though these hegemonic normalizations of femininity and masculinity emerged and solidified in educational administration more than 50 years ago, little has changed up to the present day. These normalizations are still alive and well and circulating in the discourses and practices of educational administration—and they are still producing the normal situation in our research literature as well—a point that is the focus of reconsideration in this chapter, which I will illustrate with examples of analytic frames that have been used in recent research on women in the superintendency.

Silence

One interesting phenomenon (which I argue is an effect of the normalization of femininity) that has emerged at the individual level in recent research with female superintendents is the finding of silence among women interviewees—the inability, unwillingness, reluctance, or refusal of female school administrators to discuss gender's role in their work lives. This phenomenon has been described by Brunner (1997a), Chase (1995), Skrla, Reyes, & Scheurich (2000), and Smulyan (2000), among others. The following quote from Smulyan's work illustrates one aspect of this silence.

Each of the women tended to examine her own life and job from an individual perspective that rarely included gender as a theoretical or political lens. . . . Even when [the participants] did see and describe issues of gender in their lives and work, they preferred not to credit gender with much influence and not to generalize from it as a way of explaining their own and others' experience. Acknowledging the role of gender in one's life seemed to undermine a [school executive's] stance as a legitimate leader in the existing structure of schools and suggested an inability to control her own life and work.

Although this self-silencing behavior has only recently been described in the research literature, it can be viewed as a manifestation of women's maintenance of long-standing, appropriately feminine norms. That is, women are expected not to notice discrimination, and if they do notice it, they must not speak up about it (Bell & Chase, 1993; Marshall, 1993; Rizvi, 1993). As one of my dissertation study participants described the role of women in schools, "It's almost like what we used to say about children—not being heard" (Skrla, Reyes, & Scheurich, 2000). Thus, to be feminine is to suffer uncomplainingly in silence. To do otherwise is to risk censure for being labeled as a complainer, someone who expects special treatment, or perhaps the most pejorative term of all— a feminist.

In presenting the finding of silence in research with women superintendents, I, along with other researchers, could be argued not to have "found" something distinct and new when we found that our participants were reluctant to speak about the discrimination they faced or, in fact, that they may not have seen or acknowledged to themselves the discrimination as such. What we found, instead, could be one manifestation among many of the normalization of femininity within the culture of educational administration. To be appropriately female is to be silent.

Ambition

Another strongly present manifestation of the femininity normalization is the predominant view that women do not become superintendents because they do not seek the position. This normalization is displayed at the individual level in the stories women tell about themselves and their career paths (Chase, 1995; Grogan, 1996). When women superintendents and other highly placed administrators are asked about their career paths, they commonly describe being content in whatever role they were in, but being "sought out" for a higher position. Young and McLeod (1998) provided an illustration of this view:

> The actual positions women aspired to reflect to a large degree the gender segregation in administration identified by Shakeshaft (1987). That is, while in their certification programs and/or while seeking a position, most saw themselves as principals of elementary schools. . . . In fact, even those women who obtained superintendent and assistant superintendent positions did not always plan to move into these positions. Most described their career progression in the following way: "it just sort of evolved." (p. 9)

256 *Linda Skrla*

I think of this as the "accidental superintendent" story. It, of course, exemplifies the normalized feminine virtue of modesty. The women themselves have internalized this normalization and articulate it by downplaying their own capabilities and ambitions. It is unclear how many women who adopt this stance or tell this story are consciously aware of the need to downplay ambition and how many truly believe that they do not aspire to leadership positions because such an option has not been in their conceptual field. Another possibility was raised by Shakeshaft (1987)—that women truly are happy in teaching roles and see teaching as a career position.

At the organizational level, the feminine/masculine normalizations about ambition play themselves out in the standard discourses of the profession. These views are articulated by powerful people and are seen as nonproblematic. As Guba (1990) points out about the force of such socially shared understandings, "All social realities are constructed and shared through well-understood processes. It is this socialized sharing that gives these constructions their apparent reality, for if everyone agrees on something, how can one argue that it does not exist?" (p. 89).

I had two vivid experiences with the feminine–masculine normalization of women's ambition for the superintendency early in my research career. When presenting a paper at my very first academic conference, one drawn from my dissertation research, at the 1998 AERA annual meeting in San Diego, I was challenged by a highly influential superintendency scholar who attended my session. He questioned the validity of my claims that women were underrepresented in the superintendency due to sexism and gender stratification of the educational administration profession. Furthermore, this senior scholar told me (and the rest of the 50 or so people assembled) unequivocally that there was no problem with sexism in the superintendency. Even though less than 10 percent of superintendents in his state were women, and even though the majority of the students in his program were women, this fellow researcher assured me that women just don't want to be superintendents; they don't get the credentials; they are happy in those elementary principalships and central-office curriculum roles. My second experience with this particular normalization involved an anonymous review of the same AERA paper that I submitted to a top-tier educational research journal. One reviewer commented with great certainty: "There is excellent evidence that nearly all women who become certified and seek the superintendency achieve their first position earlier and easier than their male counterparts. For whatever reason very few women educators are seeking a credential."

I am not sure to what "excellent evidence" this reviewer referred. I am aware of a great deal of evidence (see Banks, 1995; Brunner, 1994; Grogan, 1996; Hodgkinson & Montenegro, 1999) that suggests just the opposite—women are the majority of students in educational administration programs, they are earning superintendents' credentials in record numbers, and many women do, indeed, seek the superintendency (though they themselves downplay these things as discussed previously). Nonetheless the normalization that women are not ambitious (as is appropriately feminine) remains in the discourses and practices of educational administration.

Therefore, I would suggest that women's ambition (or lack thereof) to be superintendents (whether articulated by the women themselves or reified by power voices in the field) is another area of research findings in the study of women in the superintendency that requires reexamination. What is it that we, the researchers, are finding when we find that women who are superintendents did not seek the role? It could be that we are finding normalized femininity in one of its multifarious guises.

Leadership Style

Another strand of the normalization of femininity/masculinity in educational administration about which much has been written is leadership style. Numerous scholars have asserted that there are essential differences in the ways in which women and men lead (see, for example, Banks, 1995; Eagly, Karau, & Johnson, 1992; Gardiner, Enomoto, & Grogan, 2000; Helgesen, 1990; Shakeshaft, 1987). Women's ways of leadership are most often described as caring, connected, and relational, in contrast to male authoritarian or bureaucratic styles. Banks (1995), drawing from Hollander and Yoder, stated, "Men focus more on achieving success in tasks while women seek interpersonal successes; women put more energy into creating a positive group effort; men focus on displaying recognizable leader behavior" (p. 72). Numerous examples exist in recent research of women articulating their views of leading in a special way because they are women. One of the participants in my own dissertation study, for example said, "My personal [style] is supportive and nurturing;" another said, "I don't have the same take on authority that a lot of men do" (Skrla, Reyes, & Scheurich, 2000).

Ferguson (1984), however, took issue with the notion of a distinctly feminine leadership style as being anything but an attempt to turn normalized feminine behavior to fit in existing organizational cultures. That is, by validating stereotypical feminine behavior as a "leadership style," and thus avoiding stereotypically masculine leadership behaviors, women hope to be able to escape the negatives attached to violating gendered norms for individual behavior. Ferguson saw the whole feminine leadership style theory as a misguided attempt to allow women to be sweetly agreeable (consistent with normalized femininity) and also be leaders, while leaving organizational inequalities unchallenged and undisturbed. Jill Blackmore (1999), likewise, worried over whether or not research that attempts to recoup normalized characteristics of femininity and present them as strengths serves only to further disprivilege women by boxing them into stereotypical gender roles.

Again, the question for reexamination arises here: What do research findings about women's ways of leading in the superintendency really represent? Doubtless, women informants say to researchers that their values and behavior as leaders differ from those of the men surrounding them. And there is little doubt that these differences exist. But in unproblematically presenting such findings without considering the powerful force of normalized femininity shaping such differences, researchers may be contributing the maintenance of the very gender stratification many of us wish to dismantle.

Power

A final example of how the normalization of femininity manifests itself in recent research on women in the superintendency is the way in which women's use of power (using the definition of power as sovereign power as discussed earlier in the chapter) has been described. Cryss Brunner has several published articles and a book that have been drawn from her research studies of the ways in which women superintendents use and define power. In a 1994 piece, she said,

> Women in positions of leadership in a given educational setting define power differently than men in positions of leadership in the same educational setting. Women in circuits of power and women in positions of education leadership in a given setting define power as the ability to get things done through collaboration and consensus building, while men in circuits of power and men in positions of educational leadership in a given setting define power as the ability to influence or lead others by having information and knowledge beyond those around them. Women define power as "power to," that is, as the ability to empower others to make their own decisions collaboratively and to carry them out through a collective, inclusive model. Men, on the other hand, view power as "power over," or the ability of one to convince others to do as he wished through any means possible. (p. 20)

Brunner's findings illustrate yet another way in which normalized feminine behavior has been turned and redefined to fit organizational norms. That is, because norms in school administration associate traditional views of power with masculinity, when women are in leadership roles such as the superintendency, they find themselves in the "double bind" that has been well described by Shakeshaft (1987), Tannen (1994) and others. In an organization that has strictly observed gendered norms, it is impossible to be simultaneously feminine and in charge. Thus, the definitions of power adopted by Brunner's participants represent an attempt to reconcile this double bind. By redefining power as "power to" collaborate and empower others, these women are able to maintain appropriately feminine roles in their organizations while in leadership roles. In research findings such as these, it could be that what has been found is, in fact, that the normalization of femininity has again produced the normal. Women leaders have internalized the powerful expectations of femininity and have rearticulated them as their "unique" view of power.

CONCLUSION

The hegemonic normalizations of femininity and masculinity that solidified in educational administration after World War II continue largely unaltered into the present day. These normalizations are significant forces in the perpetuation of the staggering underrepresentation of women in the public school superintendency. Recent research on women in the superintendency, including my own work, in spite of attempts to use new paradigms and different analytic frames for understanding women's experiences in the role, has produced findings that, in a large measure, reify these gendered normalizations. In other words, it could be that nothing has changed for women in the superintendency because, at deeper levels where these normalizations operate within individuals and organizations, nothing has changed. Individual men and women in educational administration have internalized normalizations of femininity and masculinity into their thoughts, behaviors, and desires, and they discipline themselves accordingly. At the same time, the organizational culture of education administration has structured these gendered normalizations into its rules, rituals, expectations, discourses, and practices. Thus, the "double epistemological/practical activity" (Gordon,1980, p. 254) of shaping both individuals and organizations into normalized form based on rigidly defined femininity and masculinity continues to operate largely undisturbed in the practice of educational administration and in our research as well.

260   *Linda Skrla*

NOTES

An earlier, and substantially different, version of this chapter was presented as a paper at the 1999 annual meeting of the American Educational Research Association.

1. The percentage of superintendents who were women in 1952 was 6.7, according to Glass (1992). Women's representation in the superintendency declined precipitously following World War II and only began to rise within the past decade, as Blount (1998) has documented. Current estimates of the percentages of superintendents vary, due to the fact that superintendent gender data is not collected as part of government-maintained databases such as those available through NCES. Glass found 6.6 percent of superintendents to be women in 1992 and Glass, Brunner, & Björk found close to 14 percent female superintendents in their 2000 study. Hodgkinson and Montenegro's 12 percent figure has been used in the calculations for this illustration because it is based on a large sample (over 9,000 superintendents).

2. There have been several high-profile exceptions to this rule in the recent past as major urban districts have hired superintendents who were private business or military leaders. Seattle and Washington, D.C., are notable examples. Nonetheless, the overwhelming majority of superintendents still rise through the ranks of teachers, campus administrators, and central office staff. Many states require teaching experience as a prerequisite for administrator certification.

3. These ratios between men and women teachers and superintendents are appallingly disproportionate, but they actually represent an improvement over 1992, when Glass's 6.6 figure for women superintendents produced a ratio between women superintendents and women teachers of 1 in 1,667.

4. This is intended to be purely an illustration of the magnitude of women's underrepresentation in the superintendency. Many factors over the course of teachers' careers influence who will ascend to become a superintendent. For example, many teachers exit the profession within their first five years. Other teachers enter the workforce after retiring or leaving other fields. District factors such as size, locale, demographics, and politics; personal factors such as strengths and ambitions; and numerous other unknown and unknowable factors also influence leadership succession.

5. Historical explanations for women's underrepresentation in the superintendency have included sociocultural theories (i.e., sex-role stereotyping, gender bias, discrimination, women's socialization) and structural theories (i.e., informal power structures, protégé systems).

REFERENCES

Banks, C. A. M. (1995). Gender and race as factors in educational leadership and administration. In J. A. Banks & C. A. M. Banks (Eds.), *Handbook of research on multicultural education* (pp. 65–80). New York: Macmillan.

Bardwick, J. M., & Douvan, E. (1971). Ambivalence: The socialization of women. In V. Gornick & B. K. Moran (Eds.), *Woman in sexist society: Studies in power and powerlessness* (pp. 133–146). New York: Basic Book.

Bell, C. S. (1988). Organizational influences on women's experience in the superintendency. *Peabody Journal of Education, 65*(4), 31–59.

Bell, C. S., & Chase, S. (1993). The underrepresentation of women in school leadership. In C. Marshall (Ed.), *The new politics of race and gender: The 1992 yearbook of the Politics of Education Association* (pp. 141–154). Washington, DC: Falmer.

Björk, L. G. (1999). Collaborative research on the superintendency. *AERA Research on the Superintendency SIG Bulletin, 2*(1), 1–4.

Blackmore, J. (1999). *Troubling women: Feminism, leadership and educational change.* Buckingham, UK: Open University Press.

Blount, J. M. (1998). *Destined to rule the schools: Women and the superintendency, 1873–1995.* Albany: State University of New York Press.

Blount, J. M. (1999, April). *WWII and the great gender realignment of school administration.* Paper presented at the annual meeting of the American Educational Research Association, Montreal, Quebec.

Brunner, C. C. (1994). *Emancipatory research: Support for women's access to power.* Paper presented at the Annual Meeting of the American Educational Research Association. (ERIC Document Reproduction Service No. ED 373 440)

Brunner, C. C. (1997a). *Searching the silent smiles of women superintendents: Did you say something?* (ERIC Document Reproduction Service No. ED 412 615)

Brunner, C. C. (1997b). Working through the "riddle of the heart": Perspectives of women superintendents. *Journal of School Leadership, 7*(3), 138–162.

Brunner, C. C. (1999). *Sacred dreams: Women and the superintendency.* Albany: State University of New York Press.

Brunner, C. C. (2000). *Principles of power: Women superintendents and the riddle of the heart.* Albany: State University of New York Press.

Chase, S. (1995). *Ambiguous empowerment: The work narratives of women school superintendents.* Amherst: University of Massachusetts Press.

Eagly, A. H., Karau, S. J., & Johnson, B. T. (1992). Gender and leadership style among school principals: A meta-analysis. *Educational Administration Quarterly, 28*(1), 76–102.

Ferguson, K. E. (1984). *The feminist case against bureaucracy.* Philadelphia: Temple University Press.

Gardiner, M. E., Enomoto, E., & Grogan, M. (2000). *Coloring outside the lines: Mentoring women into school leadership.* Albany: State University of New York Press.

Glass, T. E. (1992). *The 1992 study of the American school superintendency.* Arlington, VA: American Association of School Administrators.

Glass, T. E., Björk, L. G., & Brunner, C. C. (2000). *The 2000 study of the American school superintendency.* Arlington, VA: American Association of School Administrators.

Gordon, C. (1980). Afterword. In C. Gordon (Ed.), *Power/knowledge: Selected interviews and other writings 1972–1977 Michel Foucault* (pp. 229–259). New York: Pantheon Books.

Gore, J. M. (1998). Disciplining bodies: On the continuity of power relations in pedagogy. In T. S. Popkewitz & M. Brennan (Eds.), *Foucault's challenge: Discourse, knowledge, and power in education* (pp. 231–254). New York: Teachers College Press.

Grogan, M. (1996). *Voices of women aspiring to the superintendency.* Albany: State University of New York Press.

Guba, E. G. (1990). Subjectivity and objectivity. In E. Eisner & A. Peshkin (Eds.), *Qualitative inquiry in education: The continuing debate* (pp. 74–91). New York: Teachers College Press.

Gutting, G. (1989). *Michel Foucault's archaeology of scientific reason.* Cambridge, UK: Cambridge University Press.

Helgesen, S. (1990). *The female advantage: Women's ways of leadership.* New York: Doubleday.

Hodgkinson, H. L., & Montenegro, X. P. (1999). *The U.S. school superintendent: The invisible CEO.* Washington, DC: Institute for Educational Leadership. (ERIC Document Reproduction Service No. ED 429 352)

Keller, B. (1999, Nov. 10). Women superintendents: Few and far between. *Education Week, 19*(11), 1.

Marshall, C. (1984). The crisis in excellence and equity. *Educational Horizons, 63,* 24–30.

Marshall, C. (1993). Gender and race issues in administration. In C. Marshall (Ed.), *The new politics of race and gender: The 1992 yearbook of the Politics of Education Association* (pp. 168–174). Washington, DC: Falmer.

Marshall, C. (1997). Dismantling and reconstructing policy analysis. In C. Marshall (Ed.), *Feminist critical policy analysis I: A perspective from primary and secondary schooling* (pp. 1–39). London: Falmer.

Murphy, J., & Louis, K. S. (1999). *Handbook of research on educational administration* (2nd ed.). San Francisco: Jossey-Bass.

National Center for Education Statistics (NCES). (2001). *Digest of education statistics 2001* [On-line]. Available: http://www.nces.ed.gov/pubs2001/digest/list_tables.html

Popkewitz, T. S., & Brennan, M. (1998). Restructuring of social and political theory in education: Foucault and a social epistemology of school practices. In T. S. Popkewitz & M. Brennan (Eds.), *Foucault's challenge: Discourse, knowledge, and power in education* (pp. 3–35). New York: Teachers College Press.

Rizvi, F. (1993). Race, gender, and the cultural assumptions of schooling. In C. Marshall (Ed.), *The new politics of race and gender: The 1992 yearbook of the Politics of Education Association* (pp. 203–217). Washington, DC: Falmer Press.

Scheurich, J. J. (1995). The knowledge base in educational administration: Postpositivist reflections. In R. Donmoyer, M. Imber, & J. J. Scheurich (Eds.), *The knowledge base in educational administration: Multiple perspectives* (pp. 17–31). Albany: State University of New York Press.

Shakeshaft, C. (1987). *Women in educational administration.* Newbury Park, CA: Sage.

Skrla, L. (2000). The social construction of gender in the superintendency. *Journal of Education Policy,* 15(3), 293–316.

Skrla, L., Reyes, P., & Scheurich, J. J. (2000). Sexism, silence, and solutions: Women superintendents speak up and speak out. *Educational Administration Quarterly, 36*(1), 44–75.

Smulyan, L. (2000). Feminist analysis of nonfeminist subjects: Studying women in the principalship. *International Journal of Qualitative Studies in Education, 13*(6).

Tannen, D. (1994). *Talking from 9 to 5: How women's and men's conversational styles affect who gets heard, who gets credit, and what gets done at work.* New York: William Morrow.

Young, M. D., & McLeod, S. (1998, October). *Women aspiring to educational administration.* Paper presented at the annual convention of the University Council for Educational Administration, St. Louis, MO.

Chapter 14

Troubling Policy Discourse: Gender, Constructions, and the Leadership Crisis

Michelle D. Young

"Iowa is facing a leadership crisis in K–12 education! . . . Fewer and fewer educators are choosing to go into school administration" (Tryon, 1996, p. 1). According to members of the Iowa state administrators' organization, fewer educators are seeking certification, fewer individuals are applying for administrative job openings, and large numbers of practicing administrators will be retiring in the near future. Echoing these concerns, the Iowa State Department of Education adopted the following statement: "A shortage of qualified school administrators is affecting Iowa—a shortage that could seriously hinder the state's ability to build on its tradition of excellence and create schools to meet the needs of its citizens in the 21st Century" (School Administrators of Iowa [SAI], 1998).

Iowa is not the only state grappling with this issue. National organizations are also sounding this particular alarm. For example, a study sponsored by the National Association of Elementary School Principals (NAESP) and the National Association of Secondary School Principals (NASSP) reported that there is a steadily growing shortage of school leaders, particularly at the secondary level (Houston, 1998). A group of researchers from the University of Missouri at Columbia has created a multistate research group focused on understanding issues related to the predicted shortage of school administrators (also known as the pipeline). Furthermore, newspapers from the *New York Times* and *Education Week* to the *Orange County Register* and the *Eagle* are covering the predicted shortage of school administrators (Chey, 1998; Ferrell, 2001; Houston, 1998; Rosenberg, 1998).

266 *Michelle D. Young*

Reasons proposed for the administrator shortage in Iowa include but are not limited to: expanded expectations, responsibilities, and stressful conditions for school and school-system leaders; inadequate training; insufficient salaries and fringe benefits; and a lack of general awareness of the positive aspects of administration (SAI, 1997a). Like their counterparts in other states, Iowa reports and policy statements listing these problems have been circulated, discussed, quoted, and treated as fact. Furthermore, the high degree of similarity among the reports has created an illusion of consensus regarding the factors contributing to the shortage that made it possible to move prematurely from investigating the causes of the predicted shortage to working on solutions. Thus, the proposed solutions unproblematically mirror the identified problems.

It is not unusual for policy problems, such as the predicted shortage of school and school-system administrators, to be accepted as "natural." In fact, it is rare to find policy analyses that adequately critique the actual policy problem. Scheurich (1994) likens the typical analysis of policy problems to epidemiology. In epidemiology the existence of a disease is not the subject of inquiry.

> In a critical sense, the emergence of the disease (social problem) is seen as "natural" and "real" (an empirical given), much like the natural emergence of the symptoms of a disease. . . . Policy researchers . . . see nothing unnatural or socially constructed about what comes to be labeled or identified as a social problem. (p. 298)

That many policy problems are accepted, and thus validated as presented, is unfortunate. When problems are not carefully scrutinized and analyzed, the recommendations created to address the "problem" may be ineffective (or counterproductive in some cases) and valuable resources may be wasted. More important, however, the issue or situation identified as a problem is still not well understood or substantively addressed.

Recent feminist policy research in educational administration has goaded researchers to question the development of policy. Marshall (1997), for example suggested that we use strategies that allow us to look beyond the center to explore the margins and areas of silence. She encourages researchers to examine the taboo topics, the nonevents, what is not said, and what is not decided. These suggestions, and others like them, are pushing feminist researchers to reexamine traditional methods, theories, and perspectives and to create and apply alternative methods, theories, and perspectives that expand our understandings.

In this chapter, I use a critical feminist strategy[1] to reexamine the predicted shortage of school and school-system leaders. Specifically, I explore the construction of the proposed shortage of school and school-system administrators at the state level through a reexamination of Iowa task force work, reports and policy documents. Based on this reexamination, I demonstrate that the shortage is framed in three distinct ways. The first two constructions are taken from what is included in the documents. One is a construction of the shortage as a serious crisis that must be addressed to ensure the high quality of education in Iowa. A second construction of the shortage is that of a fairly simple and understandable problem that can be addressed through fairly simple and commonsense solutions. These constructions have dominated the discourse on the leadership shortage in Iowa (and the nation) and have left little room for alternative constructions.

Consequently, a third construction becomes evident only when one examines the areas of silence in the policy discourse and the normalizations that made the emergence of this particular policy problem possible. Borrowing from Scheurich's (1994) policy archeology, I asked what conditions, assumptions, and normalizations made the construction of the leadership crisis possible? Additionally, following the suggestion of Marshall (1997), the documents were examined for nonevents and for what was not included. These explorations indicated that the discourse surrounding the leadership shortage has failed to seriously consider the role that gender plays in the shortage. Thus, the leadership shortage is taken to be a gender-neutral one (i.e., gender is not a factor).

Constructions of the shortage that fail to include gender not only effectively deligitimize gender as a consequential factor in the analysis of the predicted shortage, but such constructions are also counter productive to substantively addressing the projected shortfall. One reason it is counterproductive is that the majority of the teaching force from which administrators are recruited are women (National Center for Education Statistics [NCES], 1992).[2] Second, at least half of the candidates in most educational administration programs are women (Miller, 1986). A third reason is that there are many women who are currently certified but not practicing administrators (SAI, 1998). A fourth, and particularly relevant, reason is that there is ample evidence of discriminatory hiring practices that negatively affect women's opportunities in gaining entry to educational leadership positions (e.g., Blackmore & Kenway, 1997; Blount, 1998; Chase, 1995; Marshall, 1993; Schmuck & Schubert, 1995; Shakeshaft, 1987; Skrla, 2000).

Instead of carefully analyzing the predicted shortage, task force members and educational policy leaders appear to have prematurely pronounced that the conundrum of the administrator shortage has been solved. In addition, they have created a fiction in which institutional and individual beliefs and practices that contribute to the shortage are effectively gender-washed. Without a more complete understanding of the

268 *Michelle D. Young*

contributors to the shortage, however, the solutions proposed and/or implemented will likewise be incomplete and thus ineffective. Moreover, unless policy makers, educational leaders and researchers in the field of educational administration acknowledge and address the leadership crisis as a gendered issue, the theories and solutions that grow out of empirical research and task force work will not only fail to adequately address the predicted shortage but will continue to perpetuate the gendered leadership crisis in educational administration.

THE STUDY

In this chapter, I draw upon the work of several Iowa task forces that focused their efforts on the predicted shortage of school administrators. I placed this data alongside the findings of a study focused on the paths women tend to take into educational administration (Young & McLeod, 2001). Similar to research examining the leadership shortage, data from the paths study focused on factors that affected career choices and movements into administration as well as on ways to facilitate paths into administration. Together these data were examined through a critical feminist lens. Such a lens, I argue, illuminates the incompleteness of the current analysis as well as the influential role gender has played in the impending shortage.

Data Collection

Data from the following three sources were analyzed for this manuscript: the individual interview, participant-observation field notes, and documents concerned with the predicted leadership shortage. A purposive sampling technique was used to identify 20 female administrators and educational administration students and eight individuals involved in the hiring and/or recruitment of school and school-system administrators for intensive, semi-structured, open-ended qualitative interviews. The purposive sampling technique involves identifying "information-rich" cases and informants from whom one can learn about issues that are crucial to the purpose of the research (Patton, 1990, p. 169). In this case, research participants were selected based on their personal experience either gaining entry to educational administration, or working with individuals who have attempted to gain entry to educational administration (e.g., headhunters, university faculty), and hiring and/or recruiting school and school-system administrators. Interviews were conducted with female school administrators, female administrative candidates, district human resources personnel, job-placement consultants, university placement-services staff, and educational administration faculty. These interviews were focused primarily on understanding the factors affecting women's entry into the field of educational administration and the perceptions of the predicted shortage of educational leaders.

Additionally, I acted as a participant observer at state level and university meetings where the leadership shortage was being examined and/or discussed. Observations were focused on the developing discourse with regard to the leadership shortage. Field note records were made of what was being said and by whom as well as the way the discourse developed, the way it was sequenced, and what was repeated. Records were also made of the amount of participation by all individuals in attendance at task force meetings, reactions to comments, and the apparent effects of reactions on an individual speaker's further participation.

Finally, documents concerned with the leadership shortage were collected. The work of Iowa leadership-shortage task forces provided the basis of most of the published reports and policy statements on the shortage in Iowa. Reports and policy statements were available in the form of policy briefs, newsletters, and statements on the Internet, primarily from the Iowa Department of Education and the state administrator organization. National and state newspaper articles regarding the shortage were also examined.

Data Analysis

Data analysis was ongoing, open-ended, and inductive. I used the constant comparative method as is appropriate for qualitative research (Lincoln & Guba, 1986; Patton, 1990). Taped interviews were transcribed as soon after the interview as possible; Web-based survey data were converted to a similar text format; and observations and documents were maintained in their original format. After unitizing the data (i.e., identifying units of information in the documents and interview transcripts), I identified working categories within which I located specific data units. I modified these categories as I worked through each of the documents and transcripts. This process has been described by Lincoln and Guba (1986) as the "saturation of categories" or the "emergence of regularities" (p. 350). Comparative-pattern analysis was used to illuminate recurring patterns in the data. I searched for patterns that converged into categories exhibiting "internal homogeneity" and "external heterogeneity" (Patton, 1990, p. 403). I analyzed data for each individual case (i.e., an educational administrator or document) and across cases to identify continuities and discontinuities.[3]

270 *Michelle D. Young*

Theoretical Framework

This study utilized a critical feminist framework to analyze the verbal and written discourse that developed around the predicted administrator shortage in Iowa. To this end, the version of critical feminist theory operating in this study has three interrelated concerns: understanding the discursive constructions of the shortage, exploring the conditions that made their emergence possible (i.e., the power to define and legitimize what counts as an issue of concern), and understanding the consequences of such constructions, especially with regard to gender.

Policy problems, like all knowledge, are constructed from somewhere. They are developed, transmitted, and maintained by and within social contexts through interaction and discourse, and they are presented as real (Berger & Luckmann, 1967). According to Lewis, Grant, and Rosenbaum (1988), the language and linguistic strategies used in discourse reference a shared version of reality. Consequently, although policy discourse may appear to have the quality of objectivity, it actually creates and legitimizes certain categories and disallows others. In this chapter, task force reports, policy statements, and verbal discourse are analyzed as texts—texts that contain certain types of information, that do not include other information, and that contain certain rhetorical strategies and narrative devices that persuade policy audiences to see the predicted shortage in a certain way (e.g., as a crisis) or that seek to garner support for arguments made.

An understanding of the discursive constructions of the shortage can be further supported by an exploration of the conditions that enabled the construction of the shortage to be produced, circulated, and discussed. Although policy often seems to emerge from nowhere in particular, this is never the case (Dehli, 1996; Scheurich, 1994).

> There are powerful "grids" or networks of regularities . . . that are constitutive of the emergence or social construction of a particular problem as a social problem, regularities that constitute what is labeled as a problem and what is not labeled as a problem. These grids, also, constitute the range of acceptable policy choices. (Scheurich, 1994, p. 301)

For the most part, policy analysts are unaware of these regularities (e.g., White male dominance). Although the regularities restrict how the policy analyst thinks and her or his categories of thought, they typically elude the policy analyst's consciousness. Regardless, it can be helpful to identify the parties involved in the identification and (re)definition of a

Troubling Policy Discourse

problem (Marshall, 1997). According to Scheurich (1994), the role of the policy analyst is to

> count, label and describe problems and problem groups; they are, thus, key in the construction of such problems and groups; and, because of their enterprise, they legitimize these constructions. In addition, their discussions and debates about possible policy solutions are similarly key to constraining the range of possible policy choices. (p. 311)

Identifying those who contributed to the identification and definition of the problem can facilitate an understanding not only of why an issue was defined in a certain way (e.g., narrowly or broadly) but also how certain issues are identified as problems while others are not (Anderson, 1990; Bachrach & Baratz, 1963; Scheurich, 1994).

To address the third concern, the consequences of such constructions, one must first understand that the same conditions that constitute and circumscribe our understanding of the policy problem also limit the range of acceptable policy solutions. Second, we must ask a few questions. For example: What happens when these constructions are legitimated and then used as the basis for creating solutions? Who benefits from these constructions and at whose expense? What is overlooked?

In this study, critical feminist theory enabled an examination of how policy discourse regarding the leadership shortage in Iowa that was presented as neutral was actually creating and legitimizing specific constructions of the leadership shortage while other constructions were essentially prevented from being developed. Furthermore, this theoretical frame facilitated an exploration of the potential consequences (both intended and unintended) of the constructions.

THE FINDINGS

In this section I discuss the findings of the study. I begin by providing a description of several documents concerned with the crisis, their focus, their intent and their creation. I then demonstrate how the texts share several important assumptions about the administrator shortage, assumptions that frame the problem. Subsequently, I focus on the role that gender appears to play in the leadership shortage. At times I make comparisons between the policy discourse and the experiences of the study participants, comparisons that expose the inadequacies of the dominant analysis of the leadership shortage.

272 *Michelle D. Young*

Representations of the Administrator Shortage

In the past few years, a number of task force and policy documents have been created concerning the predicted shortage of school administrators. The four documents I have included in this analysis had a significant impact on the way the Iowa educational community came to understand the predicted shortage of educational leaders. Indeed, one of the documents, *The School Administrator Shortage*, was adopted as a policy statement by the Iowa State Board of Education. Furthermore, the content and the messages of the documents have been conveyed to a larger audience through newspaper articles that have appeared across the state (e.g., Villanueva, 1997).

Each of the four documents was notably influenced by the School Administrators of Iowa (SAI) organization. Indeed, three of the four documents (including the one adopted by the State Department of Education) were published by and placed on the Web site of the SAI. Moreover, the idea of creating a number of state-level task forces to address the predicted leadership crisis was attributed to the leaders of the SAI. Although the Department of Education called the task forces together, SAI leaders thoroughly influenced the selection of task force members and the task force's agenda.

A Crisis in the Making

A report titled *The School Administrator Shortage: A Crisis in the Making* was published by the SAI in November of 1996.[4] According to SAI president Gaylord Tryon, "we are facing a leadership crisis in Iowa because of a shortage of school administrators. Unless we take some immediate and proactive steps to address this situation, Iowa will be shortchanging the future of the next several generations" (Tryon, 1996, p. 1). In the report, Tryon further explained that in response to this crisis situation, the SAI had created several task forces to review the problem and to develop strategies for responding to them.

Based on task force discussions it was concluded that the impending shortage in Iowa was due to the following factors: (1)the increased expectations, complexities and responsibilities of the school administrator's role; (2)the stressful conditions of being a school administrator (challenges of having a balance between work and home); (3) the lack of needed resources and support; (4) the insufficient salaries and fringe benefits (especially the difference between the salaries of classroom teachers and beginning administrators); (5) the longer workdays and extended school years; (6) the required attendance at night and weekend activities; (7) the lack of information available about the positives of school administration; (8) the educational leaders not doing a good job of identifying and recruiting quality people into administration; (9) the state retirement system being a "disincentive" for going into higher paid positions; (10) the "glass ceiling" that exists for women and minorities to get hired as school administrators; (11) the possibility of certification and preparation programs not keeping pace with present-day demands; (12) the lack of awareness about the administrator shortage that exists in Iowa ; and (13) the emphasis on the negative aspects of school administration (especially by school administrators themselves) (Tryon, 1996, pp. 1–2).

After listing the factors contributing to the impending shortage, the report notes that "solving the leadership crisis in Iowa is a task that will encompass several years and one that will require the cooperation and support of several groups" (e.g., the Iowa Association of School Boards, the Iowa State Education Association, the Department of Education, the state legislature, business groups, and the university community) (p. 2). However, the report also suggests that the "SAI needs to be at the forefront and provide the necessary support and encouragement in this endeavor" (p. 2).

Subsequently, the report lists four strategies for responding to the shortage. The first strategy focuses on reviewing and improving administrator certification and preparation. The second strategy involves rethinking the roles of the school administrator. The third strategy is to develop a public relations effort to improve the image of educational leadership and to increase awareness of the shortage. The fourth strategy suggested focuses on increasing efforts to identify and recruit classroom teachers into school administration.

Leadership in Crisis

The second report, *Summary: Leadership in Crisis*, was published on the SAI Web site in November 1997. Like the document described above, this document begins with a depiction of the shortage as a crisis. The document reads:

> Leadership [*sic*] in crisis. Without strong leaders, we can't have strong schools. Iowa's schools have long enjoyed high ranking in the national's [*sic*] educational system. And it is Iowa's school leaders that maintain and develop the strong tradition of educational excellence. Iowa needs a new generation of educational leaders to rise to the challenge and to carry the torch for education. (SAI, 1997b, p. 1)

Following this statement the report provides information on the work of the four task forces: The Committee Studying Licensure, The Committee to Develop a Public Relations Effort, The Committee Studying Identification

274 *Michelle D. Young*

and Recruitment of Future Administrators, and The Committee to Review and Rethink the Position of School Administrator.

The report, which focuses primarily on solutions to the impending crisis, claims that the "strategies within are an attempt to address the issues, move forward to a solution, and hopefully, with much effort, put the crisis behind us" (SAI, 1997b, p. 1). This statement, which is not unlike statements made in other administrator-shortage documents, coaxes the reader not only to buy into the idea that the shortage is a crisis situation but also to see the committee as working diligently to address and solve the problem quickly.

As mentioned earlier, the SAI had a notable impact on the organization and selection of the leadership shortage task forces. Furthermore, the SAI has taken a prominent role in the effort to address the looming Iowa administrator shortage. These factors, then, may explain the principal roles suggested for the SAI organization and its personnel in carrying out solutions for the leadership crisis. For example, the recommendations of the Committee Studying Licensure involve the SAI "tak[ing] on administrator preparation" (p. 1). Two potential courses of action were suggested. The first suggestion is that SAI offer preparatory courses in cooperation with the state's Area Education Agencies (AEA). The document reads: "We see becoming a competitor as perhaps the best way to get the attention of the universities as well as to meet immediate needs and overcome identified barriers such as cost, accessibility, and quality of programs" (p. 1). The second suggestion is that SAI "impact course content and licensure requirements through . . . the political process" (p. 1).

Similarly, The Committee to Review and Rethink the Position of School Administrator suggests that the SAI work with other entities in the state to

> conduct a statewide campaign to increase salaries for school administrators and work with the Governor and state legislature to [*sic*] on several initiatives including a "phase IV" program for school administrators, a three-year final average salary in determining IPERS retirement benefits, and a minimum beginning salary for each administrative level. (p. 3)

SAI is also urged by this committee to work with the Department of Education and AEAs to put more emphasis on leadership development and to provide support to first-year administrators.

The School Administrator Shortage

Policy Statement on the School Administrator Shortage was written and published by the SAI and adopted by the State Board of Education on

March 19, 1998. As the name suggests, the report serves as the State Board of Education's policy on the shortage. It is a fairly short document that begins with a statement on the importance of effective leadership to a school's ability to educate the children in the state. This statement is followed by a construction of the predicted shortage as a crisis.

> Now, a shortage of qualified school administrators is affecting Iowa—a shortage that could seriously hinder the state's ability to build on its tradition of excellence and create schools to meet the needs of its citizens in the 21st Century. (SAI, 1998, p. 1)

After maintaining that "Iowa's school administrator shortage is not a recent phenomenon" and detailing the "plentiful" evidence of the crisis (p. 1), the document acknowledges the steps that various groups and their representatives have taken to address the shortage.

The document concludes by identifying four strategies for reducing administrator shortages and for strengthening school leadership that the State Board of Education supports:

1. Endorses recruitment efforts that identify teachers and students for school administrator programs, including specific strategies to recruit women and minorities for school leadership;
2. Encourages higher-education institutions to collaborate with a broad range of education stakeholders in order to rethink administrative roles, to conduct a comprehensive assessment of administrator preparation programs and to redesign those programs to reflect the leadership requirements of the 21st-century schools;
3. Recommends collaboration among administrator preparation programs, the Board of Educational Examiners, area education agencies, school districts, School Administrators of Iowa, the Department of Education and the state Board of Education in order to redesign administrator preparation to include leadership development and mentorships; and
4. Supports licensure requirements that establish research-based performance standards essential to school leadership. (SAI, 1998, pp. 1–2)

It is worth noting that there are two issues in this list that did not appear in previous documents. Nor do they reemerge in subsequent documents. These are developing "strategies to recruit women and minorities for school leadership" (p. 1) and establishing "research-based performance standards essential to school leadership" (p. 2).

276 *Michelle D. Young*

Shortage of Candidates for Principalships

The fourth document, *Problem: Shortage of Candidates for Principalships,* was distributed at a task force meeting held in January of 1999. The document reviews the identified contributions to the leadership crisis and then delineates some of the responses being made by universities in the state. It concludes with further suggestions for addressing the crisis that are listed as "desirable attributes" (Task Force, 1999, p. 1).

Unlike the original list of factors identified as contributing to the administrative shortage published in 1996, gender does not appear at all in this document. The following issues were highlighted as "reasons for the perceived shortage": (1) two-income families make it difficult to fulfill all the requirements of a principalship, not a family-friendly occupation; (2) districts do not actively recruit applicants; (3) districts face real financial pressure from boards of education if they try to provide potential applicants internships (vice-principal positions, etc.)—few opportunities exist to test the water; (4) tuition costs are high and internships are required; (5) in education, those in management can self-select what positions they want to take more so than in other occupations; (6) starting pay is low; (7) there is a lack of security in position as compared to teaching; (8) meetings are held at night; (9) both the public and teachers evidently see administrators as not performing critical roles; (10) there is pressure to live in district (mobility issue); and (11) current leaders "bad-mouth" the position and the pressures and work involved (shoveling mountains of minutia, etc.) (Task Force, 1999, p. 1).

Significantly, although the previously cited reasons for the shortage attribute the crisis primarily to the perceived negative aspects of the job, the solutions that are discussed have little to do with the job of the school administrator. Rather, institutional responses included improving the selection process for educational-administration students, using cohorts, and improving the content and delivery of educational administration courses. Each of these responses addresses the quality of administrative preparation and administrative candidates rather than the availability of candidates. Furthermore, not one of the four suggestions provided to further address the shortage dealt with the perception of the job. However, unlike the descriptions of institutional responses, several did move beyond the quality issue (e.g., districts providing funds to release teachers for the administrative practicum).

The Legitimized Representations

The documents described have placed into circulation and legitimized certain constructions of the predicted leadership shortage, including the ideas that the impending shortage has presented us with a crisis situation and that educational leaders in the state have objectively and handily examined the situation and are creating means for solving the crisis. According to several research participants, it was the SAI organization that first identified the leadership crisis in Iowa. Whether or not this is actually the case, the publicity SAI provided the issue in Iowa provided the organization and its leadership with a certain amount of credibility in later task force work.

Few on the task forces were aware of the fact that the availability of an adequate number of school leaders historically has been a reoccurring concern for U.S. schools and school districts. One example, Callahan's (1962) book *The Cult of Efficiency*, not only discussed similar issues as those raised by the Iowa task forces but also revealed some of the same concerns from the early 1900s. Moreover, the reasons given for past shortages in Callahan's book are similar if not identical to those given for today's (e.g., the job is too demanding). The task force members were aware that the shortage of school administrators was not limited to Iowa geographically. However, task force members had limited information about the nature of proposed shortages in other states as well as the discussions and initiatives taking place in response to those shortages.[5]

Regardless of their limited information, the Iowa task forces developed stories about the predicted shortage of school leaders that were almost identical to those developed in other states (e.g., Seeley, 1997). It is interesting to speculate how this may have happened, although it is certainly not unusual. Indeed, traditional ways of seeing and understanding direct policy discourse and development processes (Young, 1999). In the case of Iowa's leadership-shortage task force, the dominant perspective shaped the identification and definition of the problem, the questions raised, the topics discussed, and the solutions proposed.

A Serious Crisis

Shortly after this problem was identified in Iowa, the crisis message was circulated. Subsequently, task forces were developed to address the looming crisis. Task forces were composed of educational administration faculty, Iowa Department of Education staff, administrative organization leaders, and administrative practitioners, and their specific areas of concern included: the licensure and preparation of school administrators, the image of public education, the identification and recruitment of future administrators, and the job conditions of the school administrator. Over the years in which the shortage was examined in Iowa, membership of these task forces shifted somewhat. However, emphasis was placed on ensuring participation of all stakeholder groups (i.e., school and district administrators, members of the Board of Educational Examiners and State Department of Education, leaders of the SAI organization, and members of the university

278 *Michelle D. Young*

community). The racial composition of the groups has been overwhelmingly White, and the gender composition remained at approximately one third female and two thirds male.[6]

Within the first three task force reports, as in many of the newspaper articles about the shortage, we are presented with a sense of urgency and crisis. Even the names of two of the documents indicate that discourse on the administrator shortage has moved from a predicted shortage in the near future to an immediate crisis that must be addressed at once. For example, the first document begins with the statement:

> Iowa is facing a leadership crisis in K–12 education! At a time when the demands for improving the nature and quality of educational experiences for Iowa's young people are greater than ever, fewer and fewer educators are choosing to go into school administration. (Tryon, 1996, p. 1)

Statements in the second and third documents echo this concern. For example,

> Leadership in crisis. Without strong leaders, we can't have strong schools. Iowa's schools have long enjoyed high ranking in the nation's educational system. And it is Iowa's school leaders that maintain and develop the strong tradition of educational excellence. Iowa needs a new generation of educational leaders to rise to the challenge and to carry the torch for education. (SAI, 1997b, p. 1)

The latter statement not only reinforces the crisis construction, but it also places Iowa schools within a context of competition with other states to maintain high rankings in the nation's educational system.

A Fairly Simple and Understandable Problem

The second construction of the shortage, as a problem with easily identifiable causes and solutions, is presented through an almost step-by-step rendering of the process through which the task forces analyzed the predicted shortage. Indeed, the documents present the image of a problem-free process through which task forces were created, issues were studied and analyzed and solutions were developed and proposed. We see no dissension and the only hints we are given of the existence of alternative points of view come from issues that were "raised" in one document but never addressed in subsequent discourse. The very fact that certain issues were not repeated and/or explored makes those issues seem less important or less visible than others. Indeed, it was the issues that were discussed in detail, highlighted throughout the discourse, and given focused attention within task force discussions that were, in the end, included among the legitimate reasons for why there was a looming shortage.

What were these legitimate and understandable (i.e., they make perfect sense) causes of the leadership crisis? We were told that people do not want to go into administration because of factors such as inadequate compensation, longer working days and school years, increased job-related stress, the negative image of the profession, and lack of job security make the job more difficult and/or less desirable than teaching. We were also told that people do not want to go into administration because leadership preparation is too costly, time consuming, and difficult to obtain. Furthermore, it was argued that some educators who might want to enter administration simply are not able to obtain adequate preparation for leading in 21st-century schools.

The inclusion of leadership preparation with other contributing factors to the predicted shortage presented an interesting twist within the task force conversations. Once leadership preparation was introduced into the conversation, the shortage was no longer the only antagonist for the task force to address. Factors associated with preparation (e.g., quality, accessibility, cost) were, thereafter, referred to in the shortage discourse to emphasize the importance of having a large and well-qualified pool of administrators ready for service and to assert that there was no such pool. Consequently, the claim that there was no large and well-qualified pool of administrators was used to support the idea that the predicted shortage was a crisis. It is important to note, however, that all of these assertions were made in the absence of empirical data.

The increased focus on improving the preparation of school leaders seemed to have contributed to the re-articulation of the crisis from one primarily concerned with numbers to one concerning quantity and quality. Shortly thereafter Iowa's Board of Educational Examiners (BOEE) became involved in reevaluating the licensure and preparation requirements of school administrators. However, it is difficult to ascertain whether or not this would have taken place if the crisis discourse had not emerged within the state.[7] The BOEE had been, in response to the increasing influence of the National Council for the Accreditation of Teacher Education (NCATE) as well as the encouragement of the head of the State Department of Education, Ted Stillwell, reworking the certification and preparation requirements of teachers for several years. Thus, it is likely that administration was already next on the agenda.

Another related factor that may have contributed to the re-articulation of the leadership shortage to a crisis of both quantity and quality was the overlapping membership among the task force developed to focus on improving leadership preparation and that addressing the leadership shortage. Members of the SAI and the leadership-shortage task forces were

280   *Michelle D. Young*

present during BOEE discussions and many of the same people were participants in both task force efforts.

Whether viewed as a crisis of quantity, quality or both, the discourse surrounding the leadership shortage, specifically the repetitiveness of its messages, effectively created the idea that there was consensus among educational leaders with regard to the causes for and approaches to solving the shortage. Furthermore, that these renderings and the methods used to create them were presented to the educational community (and to some degree the public at large) as objective and/or neutral created a sense of legitimacy or reasonableness with regard to the leadership discourse. As a result, the public was left with the impression that the problem (generally defined as an inadequate supply of qualified administrators) had easily identifiable causes and solutions.[8]

The discourse of the leadership-shortage task forces provides a perfect example of the traditional policy-analysis perspective at work (Young, 1999). Dominant ways of seeing and understanding have shaped the identification and definition of the problem, the questions raised, the topics discussed, and the solutions proposed. "Social problems do not achieve their visibility or recognition or status as social problems in an idiosyncratic or random or 'natural' fashion. . . . There is a grid of social regularities that constitutes what becomes socially visible as a social problem" (Scheurich, 1994, p. 301). It is not that the policy discourse was purposefully misleading or that task force members deliberately prevented the presentation of alternative perspectives. Indeed, as Scheurich (1994) argues, no group intentionally creates regularities. Nonetheless, the task force's version of the shortage was presented as the legitimized and consensus understanding, effectively leaving no room for alternative explanations.

Moreover, just as the leadership crisis discourse was constituted by a grid of regularities, the range of acceptable policy solutions was similarly constituted. Although, as in the case of the policy problem, the construction of the range of possible solutions was not an intentional or conscious activity, "The grid of regularities is like a preconceptual field that constitutes some policy choices as relevant and others as virtually invisible; it privileges some choices over others" (Scheurich, 1994, p. 303). In the case of the predicted shortage of leaders in Iowa, the preconceptual field for the policy analysis of and development of policy solutions for the predicted shortage did not include or consider gender.

A Delegitimized Representation

To this point, I have focused on what the documents and task force discussions contained. In this section, I will explore an issue (i.e., gender) that was inadequately addressed in these texts. I begin by demonstrating how gender was transformed into a nonissue by either an inability or an unwillingness to seriously address it within the shortage discourse. I then share data that effectively demonstrates why gender should be a central factor within the shortage discussion. I end the section with one perspective on why gender was not included as a consequential factor in the predicted leadership shortage in Iowa.

Gender: A Nonissue

Traditional policy analysis attempts to understand and solve problems using objective and value-free methods. However, no perspective is objective or value-free (Young, 1999). Indeed, in educational-policy analysis, the dominant and widely believed objective perspective is based on a Eurocentric and male-derived ideology.

> Traditions and state apparatuses structured around the economic market and patriarchal traditions affect policy agendas, determining whether or not a problem is on the public agenda, part of public discourse and possible state intervention, or whether it's marginal or belonging to the private—the world of the individual or the domestic and emotional. (Marshall, 1997, p. 6)

Given the limited purview of the traditional policy-analysis perspective, it is unlikely to provide an adequate examination of the predicted leadership shortage. This is particularly the case for areas that, from a dominant perspective, are either considered nonissues or invisible.

The question of how issues become defined as educational policy problems has been addressed by a number of scholars (e.g., Marshall, 1997; Scheurich, 1994; Young, 1995). Scholars have also examined how potential problems become nonissues. For example, Anderson (1990) described how some problems in schools are overlooked or are not even considered by school personnel. Anderson refers to this phenomenon as the development of nonissues. Similarly, Scheurich and Young (1997) argue that researchers participate in the creation of non- or invisible issues. They use the term "invisibility factor" to describe how some issues are made invisible by either an inability or unwillingness to address them.

Like the examples provided by Anderson (1990) and Scheurich and Young (1997), gender in the leadership-shortage discourse has been framed as a nonissue. Indeed, gender is only mentioned in two of the four documents, and where it is included, it is presented in a superficial manner and given scant space within the text. More telling, however, is that the gender issues that are raised are never readdressed in subsequent documents.

In the first document, *The School Administrator Shortage: A Crisis in the Making*, gender is placed among 13 other factors contributing to the shortage. Specifically, the document identifies "the 'glass ceiling' that exists for women and minorities to get hired as school administrators" as a contributing factor to the shortage. Although, the term "glass ceiling" has been frequently used in business literature to describe the difficulty women have moving beyond certain ranks in the labor market, what is meant by the glass ceiling in this document is left for the reader to decide. Does it mean women have difficulty getting into administration? Does it mean that women have difficulty moving beyond certain entry-level leadership positions? Does it mean something else? It is unclear because the issue is simply raised and then dropped without discussion.

The lack of discussion of the glass-ceiling issue is glaring when compared to other factors identified in the document. For example, the quality of leadership preparation is well discussed in the first document and then revisited and further discussed in subsequent reports. In contrast, the glass ceiling is mentioned twice and within a single document. Specifically, in the strategies section of the first document, the glass ceiling is included as a factor that needs to be reviewed when the SAI "work[s] with the Iowa Association of School Boards, search consultants, area education agencies, and others to review and rethink the position of school administrator" (Tryon, 1996, p. 2). Thus, a serious discussion of gender was both put off and attached to an issue external to the shortage. Similar patterns emerged in task force meetings.

Similarly, in the third document, *Policy Statement on the School Administrator Shortage*, the following statement is included in a paragraph arguing that evidence of a shortage is plentiful:

> Women and racial/ethnic minorities continue to be underrepresented among the state's school administrators. Compared with other states, Iowa ranks low in the number of women superintendents and in the number of racial/ethnic minorities in all administrative positions. (SAI, 1997b, p. 1)

Low numbers of women in administration are presented here not just as evidence of the shortage but also as a problem. Taken out of context, the statement appears to be a serious acknowledgement of the inequities that exist in Iowa's educational leadership cadre. However, there is no discussion regarding why this is the case nor is there a call for finding out. Rather, the underrepresentation of women and people of color appears to have been attributed primarily to recruitment issues. Within this same document, the only solution the State Board of Education endorses in regard to gender is: "recruitment efforts that identify teachers and students for school administrator programs, including specific strategies to recruit women and minorities for school leadership" (p. 1). What these "specific strategies" might be are not explained either.

Unlike the representations of the shortage as a crisis, as a commonsense problem that resulted from factors such as poor compensation for a demanding job, or even as a quality issue, which were each carefully described, discussed, and addressed in regard to solutions, when gender was included, it was simply mentioned. It was not carefully described or discussed. Also, unlike the legitimized representations of the shortage, there is no clear and unified construction of the gender issue. To illustrate, the image of the shortage as a crisis is unified. The shortage is represented as a crisis in each of the documents, essentially legitimizing this construction through repetition. In contrast, although the glass-ceiling issue is raised in the first document as both a contributor to the shortage and as a factor to be revisited in the review of the position of the school administrator, it is never mentioned again in any of the reports. Even in the second document, in which the Committee to Review and Rethink the Position of School Administrator (the committee assigned to investigate the glass-ceiling issues in the first document) reports its recommendations for addressing and solving the shortage, there is no mention of the glass ceiling. When gender appears again, it does so as a new issue: recruiting. This incoherent expression of gender's role in the shortage leaves the impression that gender was given little attention in the task force analyses of the shortage. Indeed, it appears a mere afterthought.

It is difficult to ascertain[9] whether the gender issue was seriously discussed during any of the task force meetings. However, at the meetings I attended the issue rarely emerged. When the gender issue was raised, it was not dealt with in a thoroughgoing way. For example, at one meeting, a female task force member mentioned that women with secondary administrative certification were finding it difficult to obtain positions while males who had not even finished their certification requirements were being recruited for secondary positions. This comment received several nods indicating acknowledgment; however, it was not treated as an issue of relevance to the discussion. Instead the conversation continued as if the comment had never been made. Similarly, in a meeting during which a list of contributors to the crisis was shared, an attendee asked why no gender issues were included on the list. At first, this person's comment received little more than a few blank looks and an awkward silence. Finally, one gentleman broke the silence, stating "Of course, we cannot talk about the pipeline without talking about gender." A few remarks were then made about the difficulty women have gaining employment as secondary principals and superintendents and about the unwillingness of many women to move for a job. Less than three minutes later, however, the group had moved on to another topic.

As noted before, although the makeup of the task forces in terms of gender was somewhat skewed, it is unlikely that merely balancing the task forces in terms of gender or including more women on them would have effectively shifted the leadership shortage discourse to critically consider the role of gender. Mere numbers of women are unlikely to make much difference if the traditional perspective continues to dominate the policy discourse. As Ball (1990) notes, "we do not speak the discourse. The discourse speaks us" (p.18). When in use, the dominant ideology circumscribes to a large degree what is thought and how it is thought. Thus, unless a different perspective is introduced and used, gender is likely to remain a politically disenfranchised and trivialized issue (Marshall, 1997).

Thus, it was not surprising that just as gender was a nonissue for the task forces, it was a non- or invisible issue for most of the women interviewed for the study. The majority of women interviewees discussed the shortage in terms of inadequate salaries, increased time and responsibilities, and the undesirability of living in rural areas. Several also talked about the shortage in terms of quality administrators and quality preparation. Indeed, only three women even mentioned gender as a possible contributor to the leadership crisis. One of these women, it seemed, mentioned gender solely to demonstrate that it was not an important issue. She stated: "I think a bigger issue than gender is time and the expectations of the role of superintendents and principals of school districts."

Although the gender imbalance in Iowa educational leadership was generally portrayed as a nonissue within the discourse on the leadership crisis, when women did acknowledge gender as an issue, a certain type of discursive strategy was often used: "common-knowledge talk." Common-knowledge talk usually started with "Well, as I'm sure you know," or "I think everyone would agree." The information that followed these depersonalizing prefaces was generally thickly laden with victim-blaming ideology. For example, women were described as "land-locked" (i.e., unwilling or unable to move their families to a new area for a job) or as simply not interested in taking on the additional pressure and stress. In other words, the gender imbalance was really the responsibility of the women themselves. An alternative to victim-blaming ideology was the description of problems in depersonalized and distant ways something akin to folklore. One principal, who had just read that there were only seven female superintendents in Iowa, shared the following: "I heard that it used to be real difficult for women to get a superintendency position." Stories of glass ceilings, sexism, and discrimination were presented as distant and thus unconvincing myths of the female administrative experience.

Gender: A Central Issue

When a critical feminist perspective is applied to the shortage issue, the role that gender plays in the shortage is clear. As noted in the introduction to this chapter, the majority of the teaching force from which administrators are recruited are women (NCES, 1992). However, most school administrators in Iowa and the nation are men (Bell & Chase, 1993; Young & McLeod, 2001). What is more, not only are women overrepresented in teaching and underrepresented in administration, but although women are becoming licensed to lead at higher percentages than men, this rate is not reflected in the number of positions they hold (Grogan, 1999; Shakeshaft, 1999). This information alone suggests that attention should be given to gender. Indeed, given that over 70 percent of the teaching force in Iowa is female, that over half the administrative candidates in Iowa preparation programs are female, and that there are substantial numbers of female educators in Iowa schools who are certified but not practicing administrators, task force members should be carefully evaluating this situation and asking themselves, "Why is there a gendered leadership imbalance in Iowa?" and "How can we bring more women leaders into our schools?"

The qualitative interviews described in the methods section of this chapter were designed to address these questions. Through the interviews, I hoped to understand the factors that contributed to the gender imbalance in educational leadership and how such an understanding might be helpful in bringing more women into educational leadership. Interviewees placed emphasis on two factors.[10] First, educational leaders in Iowa currently do not have a comprehensive understanding of how and why women enter administration. Thus, appropriate strategies are not currently in place to facilitate their paths into administration. Second, educational leaders are not adequately informed of (or paying attention to) the factors that are preventing many qualified women from obtaining leadership positions.

In regard to the first factors, findings indicate that women's choices to enter the field of administration are contingent on their aspirations regarding education (i.e., their career commitments, positional goals, and leadership orientations), their experiences with administrative role models and leadership literature, and their opportunities to garner support for entering administration (Young & McLeod, 2001). Thus, the reasons women initially enter education and the commitments they develop are related to the types of administrative positions they are interested in pursuing, the goals they hope to realize while in such positions, and the leadership styles they prefer and ultimately employ. Furthermore, once in the field of education, at least three factors appear to greatly affect women's paths into administration: the administrative role models they encounter, the type of leadership literature to which they are exposed, and the endorsements and/or support they receive.

The presence of the latter three factors appeared to facilitate women's entry into educational administration programs in Iowa and their interest in pursuing administrative positions. Conversely, the absence of any or all of these factors appeared to serve as an inhibitor. One example of this is the ambivalence expressed by administrative candidates who had not received endorsements from their principals. Another example is the satisfaction or resistance women described having earlier in their careers when their only models of school leadership were "intimidator types" or "autocratic."

That the absence of positive administrative role models, leadership literature, and endorsements and/or support may have an inhibiting effect on women's paths into administration provides helpful insight into understanding the importance of ensuring these factors are in place. For example, if positive role models (i.e., role models that are committed to facilitating and supporting the teaching–learning process) are not available to women, either in the form of literature or role models, women may be less likely to pursue a career in administration. Although pure determination may propel some of these women into administration, the process is much smoother for those who are exposed to the idea that a facilitative style of leadership is appropriate in educational administration. Moreover, whether this exposure is provided through educational literature or role modeling, the impact appears to be even greater if coupled with the encouragement and support of administrators, peers, friends, and family members.

The third leadership-shortage policy document, *Policy Statement on the School Administrator Shortage*, included a statement indicating that the State Board of Education would support efforts to recruit more women teachers into administration. If such recruitment efforts are to be successful, however, attempts must be made by task force members to understand why women enter the field of educational administration and the paths they typically take in getting there. Findings from the qualitative interviews indicate that a generic set of efforts, which do not take into account the experiences and preferences of women, will prove inadequate for recruiting and supporting the entry of talented women into educational leadership. Indeed, if the practices currently used to recruit and train administrators in the state continue to be used, we are likely to see little change in the percentage of women interested in and pursuing a career in educational leadership.

In addition to the factors affecting women's entry into the field of educational administration, interviewees also stressed the need to consider factors that affect women's ability to actually obtain an administrative position. These factors, which can be described broadly as discriminatory hiring practices, however, appear to have attracted little attention among educational leaders in the state. It is not that the state does not support equal employment opportunity. Indeed, Chapter 19B.11 of the Iowa Code states:

> An individual shall not be denied equal access to school district, or area education agency, or merged area school employment opportunities because of race, creed, color, religion, national origin, sex, age, or physical or mental disability. It also is the policy of this state to apply affirmative action measures to correct deficiencies in school district, area education agency, and merged area school employment systems where those remedies are appropriate. This policy shall be construed broadly to effectuate its purposes. (Equity monitoring in school standards, n.d., p. 12)

Furthermore, each school district, AEA, and merged area school is required to "develop affirmative action standards which are based on the population of the community in which it functions, the student population served, or the persons who can be reasonably recruited" (Equity monitoring in school standards, n.d., p. 12). Exactly how this policy is implemented in different districts, however, is unknown.

According to research participants, larger districts in the state are subject to more state-level monitoring than smaller districts (primarily because of the Multicultural Nonsexist curricular requirements of this same statute) and thus are more likely to follow the state requirements. One female administrator from a large district described the process used in her district when hiring a new administrator. She stated:

> We have a real prescribed process. We have to advertise, there was a committee that had parent representatives and staff representatives, and a central-office group that may have principals on it—kind of three levels. The interview typically lasts all day. . . . The questions were generated usually from the Office of Human Resources; someone would make sure they were all legal and make copies of the questions and do the paperwork of it. We typically do some sort of ranking after you have met the candidate. There will be descriptors on what kinds of things you are looking for. Then, you rank them high or low, and try to get a numeric value down. . . . Usually there is a category for whether you would not recommend the person at all, consider, or "I recommend."

288 *Michelle D. Young*

In general, participants felt that larger school districts in the state were doing an adequate job with regard to recruiting and hiring female administrators. It was the "field farmer schools" (i.e., small rural schools), the districts with under 1000 students, where gender inequity was perceived to be a problem, and it was considered to be particularly acute in districts with fewer than 400 students. According to one informant, in field farmer schools they do not even consider women for leadership positions. "It is a traditional thing in smaller communities. School board members don't think women have a business perspective and that is the perspective that is needed." Another participant noted "We might as well be realistic about this. When you get out to rural Iowa, you really hit some prejudices."

Field farmer communities are also less likely to follow a prescribed process when positions need to be filled. According to one district administrator, "a prescribed process keeps us all honest. We know what we are supposed to be looking for. All of our selections and comments have to follow procedure and our comments must be in line with the characteristics we picked out ahead of time." Although many districts will send job descriptions to local and state papers and to the SAI organization, some choose not to formally advertise position openings. Rather, some school boards and district educational leaders prefer to obtain recommendations from trusted colleagues or to hire a search consultant to find the right kind of candidates. Each of these practices (i.e., not have a process, not advertising, relying on recommendations from colleagues) appear to reinforce the gender imbalance in educational administration and to allow circumvention of laws governing equal employment opportunity.

One informant, who used to provide recommendations to friends and colleagues seeking to fill administrative positions, indicated that he no longer gets involved in job placement and rarely writes letters of recommendation because "once you take a bite, you have to eat the whole apple." He explained that such practices inadvertently contribute to the low numbers of women and minority administrators in Iowa. First, people tend to hire those like themselves. "Men may not mean to, but they are likely to be looking for leaders like them—men."[11] Second, after a while most people move from making informal recommendations to providing paid search consultant services. For some,

> it is a money game. It is not an altruistic activity where you are trying to see people placed because they are excellent candidates (even if it starts that way) people are placed or recommended for placement because (1) you want a commission, and (2) you want to be seen as "really good" at placing people.

A related issue is how a search consultant goes about recommending people. "Essentially you recommend candidates you believe the district will find acceptable," explained one search consultant. Acceptability involves not only being qualified for the advertised job, but also having characteristics that the district hiring committee associates with quality leadership. These qualities may or may not be explicitly communicated. At times the search consultant may think that they know what the district wants based on stereotypes (e.g., farm communities are looking for certain things). At other times their referrals may be in direct response to district requests. For example, one search consultant shared that when she was doing research on a position and on potential candidates, she simply asked district representatives if they would be willing to hire a woman. "I ask them to be honest. We don't want to waste anyone's time or effort applying for a job they are not going to get."

In contrast, several informants indicated that hiring discrimination is no longer a problem, that the leadership styles associated with women (e.g., facilitating, collaborating) were actually becoming more common and were often among the desirable qualities listed on job descriptions. Indeed, a review of recently posted administrative positions in Iowa did reveal a few listings seeking candidates with "excellent human relations skills," "the ability to work collaboratively with members of the school community," and "a team-oriented leadership style." Interestingly, one woman felt that being a woman (read: having desirable female leadership characteristics) would actually help her gain a position as an administrator. However, the fact is that women are not finding it easy to obtain leadership positions in Iowa.[12] Many find it quite difficult. Although the leadership characteristics commonly associated with the female gender appear to be becoming more (though not completely) accepted and valued, the actual gender has not been.

Regardless of the compelling reasons for focusing on gender, state task forces and policy makers have chosen instead to create a fiction in which the process of gaining certification and obtaining an administrative position are unproblematic for qualified individuals. This fiction effectively whitewashes policies, ideologies, and discriminatory practices that have contributed to the shortage and obscures the reasons why members of some groups do not obtain administrative positions in the same percentages as White males. Moreover, the fiction switches the focus of the shortage from ideologies, discriminatory practices, and faulty policies to individual abilities, choices, and preferences (e.g., women who hold administrative certification but who are not school administrators are often portrayed as choosing not to work as school administrators). Simply put, gender is a nonissue in discourse focused on the predicted shortage of school and school-system leaders.

290   *Michelle D. Young*

Gender and Ideology

The gender imbalance in educational administration is a serious problem and a factor that should be included in the analysis of the leadership shortage. Yet, the gender imbalance and problems underlying this imbalance are virtually invisible in shortage discourse. Why is this? Why are task force members so quick to focus on a bounded set of contributors that are circumscribed by tradition as the reasons for the shortage of "quality" administrators? Why are task force members so willing to argue that educational leaders throughout the state support their limited group of solutions? Moreover, why are task force members unable to address the role that gender has played in the shortage? One possible reason is that society and the dominant ideology in this society are male-dominated.

As early as 1981, Hansot and Tyack described an educational system shaped by male hegemony. In this system, male dominance has cultivated the construction of current conditions, understandings, and ideology; it has framed the deep structures of knowledge and power in our society. Other authors have described this problem without using the term hegemony. Skrla (1998) illuminates and discusses, for example, the highly prescribed "scripts" that we follow. Chase (1995) refers to these scripts as "meaning systems" (p. 6) and as "Western culture's metanarratives" (p.8). Scheurich (1994) describes them as "powerful 'grids' or networks of regularities . . . that constitute what is labeled as a problem and what is not labeled as a problem. These grids, also, constitute the range of acceptable policy choices" (p. 301).

As women and men grow, learn, and interact in a world dominated by male ideology, their ideas of women and men, gender roles, and gendered attributes and abilities are deeply affected. "Social regularities exist as a kind of 'positivist unconscious . . . a level [within the individual but shared across individuals] that eludes the consciousness of the scientist [policy maker and policy analyst]" (Scheurich, 1994, p. 302). As noted by Gosetti and Rusch (1995) the conceptions provided by male-derived ideology are embedded in all facets of our lives (e.g., theories, practices, rules, norms, and standards). Due to its pervasiveness, most men and women move through life without even noticing the constructed nature of their world or the constituted nature of their categories of thought and ways of thinking.

Although pervasive, social regularities are not deterministic of all categories of thought. Alternative ways of thinking and categories of thought do circulate. Most feminists, for example, hold views of society and the social order that differ from the dominant perspective. However, alternative ways of thinking that are typically produced in communities of difference and marginalization of various sorts (e.g., feminist thought,

Black feminist thought; Chicana epistemologies), do not achieve prominent social visibility (Collins, 1991). They rarely achieve even a modicum of the social credibility that the dominant perspective possesses.

In regard to educational administration, Hansot and Tyack (1981) argued that male hegemony prevents many women from moving into administration as well as from advancing within administration. Their conclusions are based on the understanding that the lessons learned and the existence of certain organizational structures and norms serve to reduce the likelihood that women will become school and school-system leaders. Other scholars have argued that male hegemony has produced an ideological milieu in which some women simply do not see administration as an option and in which women in leadership positions appear out-of-place, different, or trying to be something they are not (Chase, 1995; Shakeshaft; 1987; Young & McLeod, 2001). Although this ideological milieu may not be visible to the average person, our society is so deeply enmeshed within it that individuals act in ways that support and reinforce it on multiple levels (i.e., individual, institutional, and societal).[13] Thus, for many, the gender imbalance may seem natural, and the factors that have contributed to the imbalance may seem unproblematic.

Ideology contributes to our inability to see certain problems and thus to work against them. Consider for a moment the discussion of hiring practices presented. In general, the average person or educator would not consider it problematic if hiring-committee members held personal preferences for male leaders or the leadership characteristics associated with men, unless members of that committee verbalized their preference for men over women leaders (constituting overt discrimination) and then acted on those preferences. Indeed, only when discrimination is overt do most people see it as a problem (Scheurich & Young, 1997). However, discrimination was operating in both examples. Similarly, when members of a task force design and recommend policies that support the status quo and in effect favor men over women, they are engaging in discriminatory behavior. The only differences between these examples are the degree of visibility of the problem and intentionality.

The fact that such discriminatory beliefs and practices have stood firm against both laws and strong efforts to support gender equality (see Shakeshaft [1997] for a discussion of such efforts) is a troublesome one and certainly illuminates the tenacity and strength of the dominant ideology in education and broader society. The fact that gender imbalances is not a key concern for educational and political leaders is further evidence of this. Moreover, the lack of attention and concern given to gender imbalances and other forms of discrimination in educational leadership effectively reinforces and strengthens entrenched beliefs about women and leadership. The dominant ideology must be challenged.

292   *Michelle D. Young*

CONCLUSIONS

Scholars have argued that women have much to offer educational administration (e.g., Blount, 1998; Chase, 1995; Grogan, 1996; Shakeshaft, 1987; Skrla, 1998). Indeed the leadership orientation of many women principals and superintendents, including those who participated in this study, have been compared to the orientations of leaders of effective schools (i.e., leadership that is collaborative, that focuses on developing and maintaining relationships, that is concerned with the teaching and learning processes, and that employs a more democratic and participatory style). However, the sociopolitical climate in Iowa does not look encouraging for women in educational administration. Critical gender issues continue to be overlooked or ignored.

I began the findings section of this chapter with an examination of four reports that shared Iowa task force analyses of the predicted leadership shortage in educational administration. Although the task force members spent ample time conferring with one another over the predicted shortage, its cause, and its solution, little effort or importance was dedicated to a comprehensive analysis or discussion of the shortage. Indeed, the problem was assumed to be "known" and "understood" with little effort (i.e., it was an easily understandable crisis). It was only the solutions to the predicted shortage that required extended discussion. The minimal space in policy commentary that was devoted to a discussion of the nature of predicted shortage and the different contexts within which it developed is almost a signal or code that the function of such commentary had little to do with really addressing the problem (Scheurich, 1994). Rather, an analysis of the reports and verbal discourse indicates that the task force's work merely functioned to reinforce status quo beliefs about gender, the role of school and school-system leaders, the resources available to educational leaders, and their training.

The taskforce uniformly failed to seriously address the issue of gender. Instead taskforce members used a language of crisis to bring attention to issues of quantity and quality. The reasons for doing so are not completely clear; however, the ideological underpinnings of the tendency to treat gender as a nonissue are as clear as crystal. White male ideology continues to provide a foundation for how school leaders are thought about, identified, recruited, trained, and hired. Because gender is treated as a nonissue or an unimportant issue within the shortage discourse, a number of factors are being overlooked. If the task force's work is accepted by policy makers, the steps that are eventually taken to address the impending crisis will fall short. What is more, because the work of the taskforce reproduced status quo ideas about educational leadership and the needs of current and

Troubling Policy Discourse

future educational leaders, its recommendations, if implemented, will effectively keep women in Iowa at a disadvantage.

It is possible that some of the proposed recommendations, particularly as written, will not be implemented.[14] However, the reports have already provided a frame for the educators and citizens of Iowa to discuss the shortage. The crisis talk has appeared in newspaper discussions of the predicted shortage (e.g., Villanueva, 1997, p. 1). Similarly, a number of the qualitative interviewees utilized language from the reports to convey their perception of the shortage. Likewise, it has become increasingly accepted by educational leaders that the shortage is not just about numbers but is also about an issue of quality. Indeed, it appears that the task force constructions of the shortage discourse have already obtained legitimacy.

Given the strength and depth of the problem, the efforts made to confront it must be similarly strong and deep. Not only must general awareness be increased regarding the gender imbalance in administration, but the gender imbalance must be presented as a problem, rather than simply as a neutral fact. If quality women administrators[15] are valued, then researchers and practitioners must make efforts to comprehensively understand why women continue to be underrepresented in educational leadership and how we can support and facilitate their paths into administration. This will require a conscious challenge to the status quo and normative understandings. Furthermore, it will require collaborative efforts by administrator and teacher education programs, administrator organizations, educational practitioners, and political leaders. Indeed, given the deep roots of gender inequality and the status quo nature of male-derived ideology, a conscious and collaborative effort will be necessary to effectively increase the number of women educational leadership.

A critical examination of the predicted shortage of educational leaders and the ways in which leadership positions are typically filled demonstrates the strength and depth of the dominant ideology—an ideology that maintains the predominance of White middle-class men in school administration. Unless the leadership shortage is treated as a gendered issue, the solutions that grow out of task force analyses will not only fail to adequately address the predicted shortage but will continue to perpetuate the gendered leadership crisis in educational administration.

NOTES

1. I refer to this strategy as critical feminist because of the influence of critical, feminist, and feminist poststructural work on both my thinking and the development of this particular strategy for examining policy problems. I do not

294   *Michelle D. Young*

assume to have correctly applied any particular version of critical theory or feminist poststructuralism.

2. According to the 1992 NCES report, women comprise a majority of the nation's public-school teaching force (70% of all elementary, middle school and secondary teachers). However, most school administrators are men. Indeed, just over five percent of the school districts in this country are run by women superintendents (Bell & Chase, 1993; Blackmore & Kenway, 1997; Marshall & Kasten, 1994). Similarly, approximately 12 percent of the nation's secondary school principals and 34 percent of elementary school principals are women. In some states, such as Iowa, the percentages of women in administration are even lower. For example, during the 1997–98 school year, only three percent of Iowa school superintendents were women and only 26 percent of public school principals were women. Further, female principals in Iowa are heavily concentrated at the elementary level.

3. It is important to point out that, although I carefully gathered data from multiple sources and triangulated them, the data were limited to a single state. Thus, my data, findings, and interpretation of those findings will also be limited. Additionally, almost all research participants were White and middle-class. Although research with other populations in other areas is likely to reveal some similarities, further research is warranted.

4. Although this report was first published in the SAI newsletter, the following year it was placed on the organization's Web site (SAI, 1997a).

5. One example is the Metropolitan Council of Educational Administration Programs, an organization that represents 18 institutions in the New York City metropolitan area that prepare most of the area's school administrators (Seeley, 1997). Although this group focused on this issue within an urban environment, it is likely that the Iowa task force could have learned from their experiences and conversations. In addition, the Educational Research Service was recently hired to conduct a study on behalf of the National Association of Elementary School Principals and the National Association of Secondary School Principals on the predicted shortage (Houston, 1998). Thus, national statistics and data were available, as were national and regional news articles on the issue (e.g., the *New York Times, Education Week*) (see, for example, Chey, 1998; Houston, 1998; Rosenberg, 1998).

6. The fact that there was a gender imbalance on the task forces certainly may have impacted the content and character of the leadership shortage discourse. However, as will be discussed in more detail in the following section, merely increasing the number of women at the table during state policy debates would not have necessarily and/or dramatically changed the forms of representation created in the state.

7. It is important to note that during the past few years, increased attention has been given in the state to creating state standards, increasing accountability, and improving the preparation of teachers and administrators. Unlike many other states in the nation, Iowa has not, until recently, been concerned with the development of state and district-level standards and benchmarks. Indeed, many schools in the state currently operate without an official curriculum document. This, however, is changing. It is predicted that within the next few years, districts will be required to have standards and benchmarks and to have a plan for evalu-

ating and revising their standards and benchmarks on a regular basis. Similarly, the state has recently become more concerned with accountability measures. Indeed House Bill 2772 requires that within the next three years schools have at least three forms of accountability measures (i.e., student assessments) in place and that the information from these measures be shared with both the state and the schools' local communties.

8. It should be noted that a caveat is placed on successfully solving the leadership crisis. It is argued that the solutions offered by the task forces will only be successful if they have adequate support and various leaders, educational groups, and leadership programs in the state. Indeed in one of the documents, the following statement is made: "It is the hope of each committee that we, along with SAI members and other educational organizations, can put this crisis to rest and watch Iowa's schools thrive and continue to guide our children toward a successful future" (SAI, 1997b, p. 1).

9. It is my intention to conduct further interviews with individual members of the task force, through which I hope to gain a more thorough understanding of the degree to which gender was included in task force meetings that I was unable to attend as well as how it was included in task force discussions.

10. For a comprehensive delineation and discussion of these findings see Young and McLeod, 2001.

11. Research has also demonstrated the sex-based discrimination that affects many female administrators (Blackmore & Kenway, 1997; Schmuck & Schubert, 1995; Shakeshaft, 1987).

12. In Iowa, the percentages of women in administration is lower than the national average. For example, during the 1997–98 school year, less than three percent of Iowa school superintendents were women and only 27.1 percent of public school principals were women (Iowa Department of Education, 1998). Further, female principals in Iowa are heavily concentrated at the elementary level. Given that close to 70 percent of all teachers both in Iowa (Iowa Department of Education, 1998) and nationwide (NCES, 1992) are women, the number of female administrators is disproportionately low.

13. I use the term "most" because as Apple (1996) notes " in any given historical situation, hegemonic control can be found only as the *partial* exercise of leadership by dominant groups (p. 15, emphasis in original). Indeed not all men and women have accepted the gendered division of roles and resources. Furthermore over the years, a number of women and organizations of women have exercised impressive power in resisting Western patriarchy (Blount, 1998).

14. Indeed, the House Education Committee used the leadership shortage discourse to suggest a different solution. On March 10, 1998, the committee approved HSB 183, a bill that exempts superintendents from licensing requirements. "In effect, it would allow people with a business background and no educational background, experience or training to assume the role of school superintendent" (SAI, 1999, p. 1). This approach is counter to the task force discourse that supports increasing rather than lowering standards for educational leaders. SAI asserted that instead of lowering standards, "the legislature should invest more resources in schools, address administrative salaries and benefits, and look at incentives, which would attract candidates for administrative positions" (SAI, 1999, p. 1).

296 Michelle D. Young

15. "Some women's activists seem to assume that women invariably provide good school leadership while men do not. Obviously, this is not true. Some women provide less than stellar leadership, all other things being equal; conversely, some men offer outstanding, sensitive leadership. To say that women should be school administrators simply because of their sex is just as dangerous as the time-honored practice of insisting that only men be leaders because of their sex" (Blount, 1998, pp. 161–162).

REFERENCES

Anderson, G. (1990). Toward a critical constructivist approach to school administration: Invisibility, legitimation, and the study of non-events. *Educational Administration Quarterly, 26*(1), 38–59.

Apple, M. (1996). *Cultural politics and education.* New York: Teachers College Press.

Bachrach, P., & Baratz, M. (1963). Decisions and non-decisions: An analytical framework. *American Political Science Review, 57*, 632–634.

Ball, S. (1990). *Politics and policy in education.* London: Routledge.

Bell, C., & Chase, S. (1993). The underrepresentation of women in school leadership. In. C. Marshall (Ed.), *The new politics of race and gender* (pp. 141–154). London: Falmer Press.

Berger, P. L., & Luckmann, T. (1967). *The social construction of reality: A treatise in the sociology of knowledge.* New York: Anchor books.

Blackmore, J., & Kenway, J. (1997). *Gender matters in educational administration and policy: A feminist introduction.* London: Falmer Press.

Blount, J. (1998). *Destined to rule the schools.* New York: Teachers College Press.

Callahan, R. (1962). *Education and the cult of efficiency.* Chicago: University of Chicago Press.

Chase, S. (1995). *Ambiguous empowerment: The work narratives of women school superintendents.* Amherst: University of Massachusetts Press.

Chey, E. (1998, August 2). Head of all classes: O. C. faces principal shortage in schools. *Orange County Register,* A16.

Collins, P. (1991). *Black feminist thought: Knowledge, consciousness, and the politics of empowerment.* New York: Routledge.

Dehli, K. (1996). Unfinished business? The dropout goes to work in educational policy reports. In D. Kelly & J. Gaskell (Eds.), *Debating dropouts: Critical policy and research perspectives on school leaving* (pp. 7–29). New York: Teachers College Press.

Equity monitoring in school standards (n.d.). *Iowa Administrative Code* (281) Chapter 12 and Iowa Code Chapter 19B.11.

Ferrell, C. (August, 2001). Study: Superintendents mostly male. *Eagle.* [Available online] http://www.theeagle.com/schools/080401superintendentsmales.htm

Gosetti, P. P., & Rusch, E. (1995). Reexamining educational leadership: Challenging assumptions. In P. A. Schmuck & D. D. Dunlap (Eds.), *Women leading in education* (pp. 11–35). Albany: State University of New York Press.

Grogan, M. (1996). *Voices of women aspiring to the superintendency.* Albany: State University of New York Press.

Grogan, M. (1999). Equity/equality issues of gender, race, and class. *Educational Administration Quarterly, 35*(4), 518–536.

Hansot, E., & Tyack, D. (1981). *The dream deferred: A golden age for women school administrators* (Policy Paper No. 81–C2). Stanford, CA: Stanford University School of Education, Institute for Research on Educational Finance and Governance.

Houston, P. D. (1998). The ABCs of administrative shortages. *Education Week, 32,* 44.

Iowa Department of Education. (1998). *The Annual Condition of Education Report.* Des Moines, IA: Iowa Department of Education.

Lewis, D. A., Grant, J. A., & Rosenbaum, D. P. (1988). *The social construction of reform: Crime prevention and community organizations.* New Brunswick, NJ: Transaction Books.

Lincoln, Y., & Guba, E. (1986). *Naturalistic inquiry.* Newbury Park, CA: Sage.

Marshall, C. (1993). (Ed.). *The new politics of race and gender.* London: Falmer Press.

Marshall, C. (1997). *Feminist Critical Policy Analysis.* London: Falmer Press.

Marshall, C., & Kasten, K. (1994). *The administrative career: A casebook on entry, equity, and endurance.* Thousand Oaks, CA: Sage.

Miller, J. Y. (1986). Lonely at the top. *School & Community, 72,* 9–11.

National Center for Education Statistics (NCES). (1992). *American education at a glance.* Washington DC: U.S. Department of Education.

Patton, M. Q. (1990). *Qualitative evaluation and research methods.* Newbury Park, CA: Sage.

Rosenberg, M. (1998, May 10). The task of filling school jobs. *New York Times,* 24.

Scheurich, J. (1994). Policy archeology: A new policy studies methodology. *Journal of Education Policy, 9*(4), 297–316.

Scheurich, J. J., & Young, M. D. (1997). Coloring epistemologies: Are our research epistemologies racially biased? *Educational Researcher, 26*(4), 4–17.

Schmuck, P. A., & Schubert, J. (1995). Women principals' views on sex equity: Exploring issues of integration and information. In P. A. Schmuck & D. D. Dunlap (Eds.), *Women leading in education* (pp. 274–287). Albany: State University of New York Press.

School Administrators of Iowa. (1997a, October 27). *A crisis in the making.* http://www/sai-iowa.org/short1.html Retrieved January 20, 1999.

School Administrators of Iowa. (1997b, October 27). *Summary: Leadership in crisis.* http://www/sai-iowa.org/short2.html Retrieved January 20, 1999.

School Administrators of Iowa. (1998, May 19). *Policy statement on the school administrator shortage.* http://www/sai-iowa.org/shortDE.html Retrieved January 20, 1999.

School Administrators of Iowa. (1999, March 11). Changes in superintendent licensure. *Legislative Briefs, 10*(3), 4–5.

Seeley, D. (1997). Crew to ed admin programs: Let's cooperate! *MCEAP Update,* 1–2.

Shakeshaft, C. (1987). *Women in educational administration.* Newbury Park, CA: Sage.

Shakeshaft, C. (1999). The struggle to create a more gender-inclusive profession. In J. Murphy & K. S. Louis (Eds.), *Handbook of research on educational administration* (pp. 99–118). San Francisco: Jossey-Bass.

298   *Michelle D. Young*

Skrla, L. (1998). *Women superintendents in politically problematic work situations: The role of gender in structuring conflict.* Paper presented at the annual meeting of the American Educational Research Association, San Diego, CA.

Skrla, L. (2000). The social construction of gender in the superintendency. *Journal of Education Policy, 15*(3), 293–316.

Task Force. (1999). *PROBLEM: Shortage of candidates for principalships, particularly secondary positions.* Unpublished document.

Tryon, G. (1996, November). The school administrator shortage: A crisis in the making. *SAI Report,* 1–3.

Villanueva, E. (1997, June 6). Schools' tough test: Filling top jobs. *The Des Moines Register,* 1A.

Willis, P. (1977). *Learning to labor.* New York: Columbia University Press.

Young, M. D., (1995, October). *A parental involvement paradox: Rhetoric and reality.* The Annual Convention of the University Council on Educational Administration, Salt Lake City, UT.

Young, M. D. (1999). Multifocal educational policy research: Toward a method for enhancing traditional educational policy studies. *American Educational Research Journal, 36*(4), 677–714.

Young, M. D., & McLeod, S. (2001). Flukes, opportunities, and planned interventions: Factors affecting women's decisions to become school administrators. *Educational Administration Quarterly, 37*(4), 462–502.

Author Biographies

Maenette K. P. Benham is an associate professor of Educational Administration at Michigan State University. Her research focuses on indigenous women's school leadership. She is the author of *Let My Spirit Soar! Narratives of Diverse Women in School Leadership* (1998, Corwin Press), *Culture and Educational Policy in Hawai'i: The Silencing of Native Voices* (1998, Lawrence Erlbaum), and *Indigenous Educational Models for Contemporary Practice: In Our Mother's Voice* (2000, Lawrence Erlbaum).

Colleen A. Capper, a professor of Educational Administration at the University of Wisconsin–Madison, teaches courses on Spirituality and Leadership, Organizational Theory, and Student Services and Diversity. Her recent work includes *Meeting the Needs of Students of All Abilities: How Leaders Go Beyond Inclusion* (2000, Corwin Press, cowritten with Elise Frattura and Maureen Keyes), "Homosexualities, Organizations, and Administration: Possibilities for In(queer)y" in *Educational Researcher*, as well as other publications.

Cynthia B. Dillard is an associate professor of Multicultural Education in the School of Teaching and Learning at the Ohio State University. Most recently, she served as Associate Dean for Equity and Diversity in the College of Education, where she developed and implemented model programs for the recruitment and retention of underrepresented faculty, staff, and students. Her major research interests include multicultural education, critical pedagogy, and African/African American feminist studies. More recently, Dr. Dillard's interests have been focused in Ghana, West Africa, where she recently built and opened a preschool in the village of Mpeasem, where she was also installed as a Queen Mother of Development in the village.

300   *Author Biographies*

Margaret Grogan is professor and chair of the department of Educational Leadership and Policy Analysis at the University of Missouri, Columbia. She also codirects the UCEA Center for the Study of Leadership and Ethics. She edits a series on Women in Leadership for State University of New York Press. Her current research focuses on the superintendency, the moral and ethical dimensions of leadership and women in leadership. Among her publications are: *Voices of Women Aspiring to the Superintendency* (1996), "A Feminist Poststructuralist Account of Collaboration" (1999), and "Equity/Equality Issues of Gender, Race and Class" (1999). Additionally, she has coauthored with Cryss Brunner and Lars Björk (2002), "Shifts in the Discourse Defining the Superintendency: Historical and Current Foundations of the Position." Together with Mary Gardiner and Ernestine Enomoto, she wrote, *Coloring Outside the Lines: Mentoring WOmen into Educational Leadership* (2000). Grogan received her bachelor's degree from the University of Queensland, her master's in Curriculum and Instruction from Michigan State University, and her PhD, in Educational Administration, from Washington State University.

Julie C. Laible was an assistant professor of Educational Leadership and Policy Studies at the University of Alabama, Tuscaloosa. Julie's research, teaching, and service focused on antiracist and antisexist school leadership and the provision of equal and high-quality educational opportunities for all children. Her work has appeared in the *International Journal of Qualitative Studies in Education*, the *International Journal of Leadership in Education*, the *Journal of School Leadership*, and *Educational Administration Quarterly*.

Catherine Marshall is a professor of Educational Administration at the University of North Carolina, Chapel Hill. Her research interests include educational careers, politics of education, gender issues in leadership, and qualitative research methodology. Among her publications are numerous journal articles and seven books including *Feminist Critical Policy Analysis* (1997, Falmer Press) and *Designing Qualitative Research* (1999, Sage).

Sylvia E. Méndez-Morse is an assistant professor in the Division of Educational Psychology and Leadership, College of Education at Texas Tech University. She received her PhD in Educational Administration from the University of Texas at Austin. She is a faculty member in the Educational Leadership Program and teaches classes on Communication for School Leaders, School and Community Relations, Organizational Communication, Instructional Supervision, and Gender Issues in Educational Leadership. Sylvia has conducted research in educational leadership and educational reform, focusing on administrators leading educational

Author Biographies 301

change efforts that improve the instructional needs of language minority students. In addition, Dr. Méndez-Morse has conducted research concerning Latina educational administrators.

Jennifer Scott received her PhD in Educational Administration at the University of Texas at Austin, where she was a fellow in the Cooperative Superintendency Program. Her areas of research include organizational theory, women superintendents, and gender and linguistics. Her most recent publication can be found in the book *The New Superintendency* (2001, JAI Press). She is currently an assistant superintendent in Longview, Texas.

Linda Skrla is an associate professor in the Educational Administration and Human Resource Development Department at Texas A&M University. She holds BBA and MEd degrees from Sam Houston State University and a PhD from the University of Texas at Austin, where she was a Cycle XI fellow of the Cooperative Superintendency Program. Prior to joining the Texas A&M faculty in 1997, Dr. Skrla worked for 14 years as a middle school and high school teacher and as a campus and district administrator in Texas public schools. Her research focuses on educational equity issues in school leadership, including accountability, high-success districts, and women superintendents. Her published work has appeared in numerous journals, including *Educational Researcher, Educational Administration Quarterly, Phi Delta Kappan, Journal of School Leadership*, and the *International Journal of Qualitative Studies in Education*.

Michelle D. Young is the executive director of the University Council for Educational Administration and a faculty member in Educational Leadership and Policy Analysis at the University of Missouri, Columbia. Dr. Young received her PhD at the University of Texas at Austin in Educational Policy and Planning. Her scholarship focuses on how school leaders and school policies can ensure equitable and quality experiences for all students and adults who learn and work in schools. Dr. Young is the recipient of the William J. Davis award for the most outstanding article published in a volume of the *Educational Administration Quarterly*. Her work has also been published in the *Review of Educational Research, Educational Researcher*, the *American Educational Research Journal*, the *Journal of School Leadership*, and the *International Journal of Qualitative Studies in Education*, among other publications.

Index

Addelson, K., 188
Alcoff, L., 41, 45, 47, 50, 52, 54, 61–64, 185
ambition, 255–256
American Association of School Administrators (AASA), 12, 13, 16
Anderson, M., 51
Anzaldua, G., 163
Appiah, K. A., 152, 153

Badwound, E., 228
Beekley, C., 106
Behar, R., 66
Bethel, L., 135, 136
bifurcated consciousness, 96
Biklen, S., 18
Blea, I. I., 162, 164, 166
Blount, J., 83, 253
Blumberg, A., 13
Blackmore, J., 2, 104
Borg, M., 181
Brennan, M., 249
Britzman, D., 109–110
Butler, J., 85

Chase, S., 107
Clabaugh, R., 12
Clough, P. T., 68
Collins, P. H., 62–63, 144, 146, 148, 150, 189, 196, 197
Cornell, D., 104
Cornwall, A., 85
Cuban, L., 14

Dehyle, D., 223
Delgado Bernal, D., 162, 167
Deloria, V. Jr, 232, 233
Daly, M., 106, 107
Denzin, N., 41, 42
Derrida, J., 104, 109, 124
discourse, 18–19, 86

Eisner, E., 42
Elasser, N., 51
emotion, 94–96
ethics, 25, 188, 196, 203–204
Espin, O. M., 171

faith, 180, 193, 195
feminist research
    Chicana, 161–165
    critical policy analysis, 215
    culture, 38, 133–134
    endarkened, 142–154
    history in educational leadership, 212–216
    native/indigenous, 224
    problems in cross group
        counterproductivity, 43–45
        power imbalances, 45–47
        representation, 41–43
        writing conventions, 48–50
    responses to critiques
        collaboration, 55–58
        evaluation strategies, 58–60
        reflexivity, 53–55
        speaking with/through, 60–64
        textual strategies, 64

Index

Fine, M., 50, 51–52, 57, 61, 62, 64, 144
Flax, J., 17
Foucault, M., 18, 20, 24, 88, 95, 107

Gal, S., 88
Gaspar de Alba, A., 164
Gebhardt, E., 55
gender
  central issue, 285–289
  identity, 84–85
  ideology, 290–291
  language and power, 87
  nonissue, 281–284
  organizations, 86
genderless discourse, 91–94
Go to the Source model, 225, 230
Gordon, C., 250
Gore, J., 250
Green, R., 38
Gutting, G., 252

Harding, S., 39
Hargreaves, A., 20
Harris, A., 153
Harvard University Urban Superin-
  tendents Program, 16
hooks, b., 38, 52, 142, 184
Huyssen, A., 21

Jesus, 180–181, 193–194
Johnson, S. M., 24

Kelly-Gadol, J., 51
knowledge, 20

Ladner, J., 38
Laible, J. C., 40–41, 56, 179–190,
  193–199, 201–209, 211–212, 216
Lather, P., 41, 53, 104, 107, 108, 124,
  203, 205
leadership
  native model, 230–240
  shortage, 271–291
  style, 257
Lesco, N., 37
Levinas, E., 186
Lightfoot, S. L., 135

Lincoln, Y., 41, 42
Lindisfarne, N., 85
Lourde, A., 52, 143
Lyotard, J., 20

Marland, S., 13
Marshall, C., 247, 249, 266, 281
Matsuda, M., 64–65
McLeod, S., 255
Mead, M., 38
Medina, L., 171
Mishler, E., 107
Mohanty, C., 47, 49
Moraga, C., 168
Morrison, T., 38
mourning
  careers, 117–120
  definition, 104
  research, 121–123
  superintendency, 114–117

narrative, 134–142
National Association of Elementary
  School Principals, 265
National Association of Secondary
  School Principals, 265
National School Boards Association,
  12
Noddings, N., 25

Oakley, A., 55
Ochs, E., 88

Packwood, A., 133
Palmer, P., 145, 194–195
Pardo, M. S., 165, 169, 170
Popkewitz, T., 249
Pounder, D., 27
power, 20, 87, 258–259

Reason, P., 46, 56, 58
Reinharz, S., 37, 57
resistance, 20
Richardson, L., 48, 59, 67, 69

Said, E., 43
Sawicki, J., 37

Index

Scheurich, J. J., 107–108, 111, 134, 184, 266, 267, 270, 271
School Administrators of Iowa (SAI), 272–277, 282
Sears, J., 199
Shakeshaft, C., 14, 15, 18, 229, 247
Sikes, P., 133
silence, 106–107, 254–255
Smith, D., 54
Smith, D. E., 86
Spalding, W., 12
Spivak, G., 39
Standing, K., 48
Stanfield, J., 44, 45, 131, 146
St. Pierre, E., 109
subjectivity, 19–20
superintendency
  feminist perspectives, 17–21, 83, 104
  history, 12–16
  human relations skills, 10
  normalizations, 251–254
  reconception of, 22–25
  standards, 16
Swisher, K., 229

Tandon, R., 47
time, 195, 205
Title IX, 213
Tixier y Vigil, Y., 51
traveling, 189–190, 196, 198–199, 207–208, 217
Trebilcot, J., 43
truth, 189, 196, 197, 204–206
Truth, Sojourner, 35, 189

Van Maanen, J., 48
Visweswaran, K., 109, 207

Wagstaff, L., 183
Walker, M. U., 18
Weedon, C., 19
West, C., 182
Wilson, R., 12, 14
Wolf, D., 46
Wolf, M., 67

Young, M. D., 134, 255

Zinn, M., 38